EXPANDING PORTUGUESE EMPIRE AND THE TAMIL ECONOMY

EXPANDING PORTUGUESE EMPIRE AND THE TAMIL ECONOMY

(Sixteenth-Eighteenth Centuries)

S. JEYASEELA STEPHEN

MANOHAR
2009

First published 2009

ISBN 978-81-7304-802-9

Published by
Ajay Kumar Jain *for*
Manohar Publishers & Distributors
4753/23 Ansari Road, Daryaganj
New Delhi 110 002

Typeset at
Digigrafics
New Delhi 110 049

Printed at
Salasar Imaging Systems
Delhi 110 035

Contents

Illustrations

Maps

Tables

Preface

I should begin by thanking the Comissão Nacional Para as Comemorações dos Descobrimentos Portugueses and the Fundação Calouste Gulbenkian, Lisboã, Portugal, for enabling me to pursue my research work in the various archives of Europe through the award of research grants. I express my sincere gratitude to Prof. Luis Adao da Fonseca, Prof. António Manuel Hespanha, Dr. José Blanco and Dr. Pedro Garcia in this regard. This book has in many ways grown quite naturally out of *The Coromandel Coast and its Hinterland: Economy, Society and Political System, 1500-1600* (1997) and *Portuguese in the Tamil Coast* (1998) my two previous books. Nearly ten years have passed since these books appeared in print and so I have made fresh attempts to bring this new book up-to-date with ongoing debate on the Portuguese presence in India and the major issues of the role of their trade structure, functions, trends and the level of development in the Tamil Seas.

I am grateful to the various archives and libraries (mentioned in the bibliography) that extended to me all the facilities to consult their records. They also gave me access to their rare collections, recent publications and periodicals, which were of immense use to me. Hence I wish to place on record my heartfelt thanks to the officials of all these institutions. I thank Prof. L.F.F.R. Thomaz, Dr. João Manuel de Almedia Teles e Cunha, Dr. Paulo Jorge Corino de Sousa Pinto, Dr. Manuel Lobato and Dr. Martin Krieger for their stimulating discussions and suggestions. I am grateful in a very special way to Prof. Emeritus K.S. Mathew, Department of History, Pondicherry University, who has been a source of inspiration, and Prof G. Subbiah, Visva-Bharati, for sharing their friendship and ideas over a number of years now.

The maps were prepared in the cartographic section at the EFEO, Pondicherry, for which I am most grateful to them. Finally,

I express my sincere thanks to Ramesh Jain and Ajay Kumar Jain, and the Manohar editorial team for publishing the book so well.

Berlin
23 June 2004

S. JEYASEELA STEPHEN

Abbreviations

ARCHIVES AND LIBRARIES

AGS	Archivo General de Simancas, Valladolid
AHU	Arquivo Histórico Ultramarino, Lisbon
ANP	Archives Nationales, Paris
ARSI	Archivum Romanum Societatis Iesu. Rome
BA	Biblioteca da Ajuda, Lisbon
BL	British Library, London
BME	Biblioteca Municipal de Elvas, Elvas
BNL	Biblioteca Nacional de Lisboã, Lisbon
BNM	Bibliotheca Nacional Madrid, Madrid
BNP	Bibliothèque Nationale, Paris
BPADE	Biblioteca Pública e Arquivo Distrital, Évora
BUC	Biblioteca Universidade de Coimbra, Coimbra
HAG	Historical Archives of Goa, Panaji
IANTT	Instituto Arquivo Nacionais/Torre do Tombo, Lisbon
IOLR	India Office Library and Records, London
MPJA	Madurai Province Jesuit Archives, Shembaganur
NA	National Archief, The Hague

RECORDS AND JOURNALS

ACE	Assentos do Conselho do Estado
ACF	Assentos do Conselho da Fazenda
APO-BP	Arquivo Portugues Oriental (ed.) Bragança Pereira
APO-CR	Archivo Portuguez Oriental (ed.) Cunha Rivara
ARE	Annual Report on Epigraphy
BEFEO	Bulletin de École française d'Extrême—Orient
BFUP	Bolteim da Filmoteca Ultramarina Portuguesa
BUB	Bataviaasch Uitgaand Briefboek

CAA	Cartas de Affonso de Albuquerque
CC	Corpo Cronológico
CDI	Caixa da India
COCO	Country Correspondence
CSL	Coleçao São Lourenço
CSV	Coleçao São Vicente
DACB	Diary and Consultation Book
DI	Documenta Indica
DR	Dagh Register
DRI	Documentos Remetidos da India
DUP	Documentação Ultramarina Portuguesa
EFI	English Factories in India
EI	Epigraphia Indica
EX	Epistolae S. Francisci Xaverii alia que eius Scriptura
FL	Folio
FSDC	Fort St. David Consultations
GM	Generale Missivien
IESHR	Indian Economic and Social History Review
IND	Inscriptions in the Nellore District
IPS	Inscriptions of Pudukottai State
JEWR	Journal of East—West Relations
JIH	Journal of Indian History
JSEAH	Journal of South East Asian History
JTS	Journal of Tamil Studies
KK	Kanyakumari Kalvettugal
LRV	Livro de Reis Vizinhos
LS	Livro de Segredo
MDR	Monçoes do Reino
MMCG	Miscelaneas Manuscritos do Convento da Graça
MFC	Madras Public Consultations
NOA	Nouvelle Acquisitions
OBP	Overgekoemen Brievien en papiern
OBPB	Overgekoemen Brievien en papiern uit Batavia
OC	Original Correspondence
OIOC	Oriental and India Office Collection
PC	Public Consultations.
RCI	Registo da Casa da India.

RFG	Records of Fort St. George.
SII	South Indian Inscriptions.
SITI	South Indian Temple Insciptions.
TAS	Travancore Archaeological Series.

1
Introduction

Writings on the history of the Portuguese in India, especially by F.C. Danvers (1894)[1] and R.S. Whiteway (1899)[2] towards the last decade of the nineteenth century were based mainly on the chronicles of the sixteenth-century Portuguese writers like Fernão Lopes da Castanheda, João de Barros, Gaspar Correia and Diogo do Couto.[3] Later J.J. Campos (1919) also used the accounts of the chroniclers but focused attention mainly on the Portuguese in Bengal.[4] As the Portuguese chroniclers gave much importance to the political and military activities of the Portuguese *Estado da India,* the scholars too dealt with the military and naval activities of the Portuguese in India. There were not many other research works following these studies for a long time until the middle of the twentieth century.

Even as late as 1923, W.H. Moreland had lamented over the scarcity of relevant Portuguese source material for writing: It is impossible to speak with precision of the details of the Lisbon trade, because its secrets were jealously guarded and I was not able to find any official statistics of the quantity of goods imported or of their distribution among the various consuming markets.[5]

K.M. Panikkar (1953), who was interested in the study of events leading to Western dominance over Asia, put forward the view that the Portuguese established their domination over the Indian economy through their control of the sea.[6] Since his study was not based on Portuguese archival sources, his views were called into question by C.R. Boxer (1969) who used the primary Portuguese sources. He traced the history of the Portuguese and their empire right from the capture of the Muslim stronghold of Ceuta in Morocco in 1415 up to the independence of Brazil in

1825. The theory that the Portuguese had a great impact on the Indian economy did not find acceptance with C.R. Boxer.[7]

Nilakanta Sastri (1964) the doyen of south Indian history, had this to say about the Portuguese presence in India:[8]

> The Portuguese indeed had built up their short-lived and predatory maritime empire much earlier, from the first half of the Sixteenth Century. . . . We need not spend much time on the short-lived and nightmarish rule of the Portuguese in India.

In the course of the 1970s and 1980s, several scholarly monographs have appeared, at once enriching and extending our understanding of the maritime trading activities of the Portuguese in Asia, with easier access to Portuguese archival data to corroborate the new sources with the accounts of the Portuguese chroniclers. Blair Kling and M.N. Pearson (1980) traced the rise of the Portuguese in Asia.[9] Scholars like Bailey and Diffie (1980) viewed the Portuguese as explorers in Africa, as conquerors in India and as traders in South-East Asia.[10] V.M. Godinho's (1981-83) study attempted to integrate Portugal's economic history with the economic structure and development of the Portuguese empire from 1415 to 1640.[11]

Besides these, a number of Indo-Portuguese historical studies have also appeared in the recent past adding to our understanding of the maritime expansion of the Portuguese in various specific trading regions. M.N. Pearson in his recent book looks from the sea to its shores to study the Indian Ocean's impact on land through the movement of goods, people, ideas and religions across the sea.[12] Among such writings must be included the scholarly works of K.S. Mathew (1983, 1985),[13] Anthony Disney (1984),[14] Pius Malekandathil (2001),[15] Afzal Ahmad (1992),[16] Celsa Pinto (1993),[17] and Philomena Sequeira (2005).[18] All these works give importance to the role of the Portuguese in the Malabar and Gujarat regions. T.R. de Sousa (1979) has made his contribution to the study of the socio-economic history of Medieval Goa.[19] The study of M.N. Pearson is mainly concerned with the reactions of the Gujarati merchants to the Portuguese claims of monopoly and how the Gujarati merchants and rulers faced the Portuguese challenge. He holds the view that it was the Gujaratis and not the Arabs who dominated the trade between the Arabian Sea and South-East Asia. He shows that in the Gujarat coast and in the west coast of India, the Portuguese had established an efficient patrolling system to subdue the sea pirates. His exposition of the Portuguese attempt to enforce their supremacy over the maritime trade of the Arabian Sea by restricting the freedom of others through the issue of sailing permits is by itself a revealing feature. Another work by M.N. Pearson (1987) surveyed the Portuguese in India from the viewpoint of Goa.[20] Thus the historiography of the Portuguese expansion was characterized as one of dominance, conquest and control in the Arabian Sea.

The subject of Portuguese maritime trade in the Indian Ocean in general during 'the age of the sail' has nevertheless received much attention. J.C. Van Leur (1955), the Weberian, mentioned that the pattern of Portuguese commerce in Asia remained essentially the same and the differences, if any, could only be regarding the sailing routes and occasionally the volume of commodities.[21] Neils Steensgard (1972), who studied the pattern of Portuguese trade in the Persian Gulf, supported the view of Van Leur that the Portuguese regime did not introduce a single new element into the commerce of South Asia.[22] Niels Steensgard, however, introduced the new concept of redistribution enterprise and showed that the Portuguese activities were similar to the trade practices prevalent in the Middle Ages, rather than the emergent commercial capitalism represented by the joint-stock companies of the Dutch and the English. The regulation of trade by the Portuguese through concessions, customs duties and passes for sailing within Asia prompted Steensgard to characterize the Portuguese activities in the East as redistribution rather than production oriented.[23] Further, the study of Meilink Roelofsz gave importance to Portuguese trade in low-priced essential commodities in Asia, an aspect which Van Leur had neglected in his study.[24] K.S. Mathew examined the volume and organization of Portuguese trade carried on in the initial stages of their presence at Kochi in India. Anthony Disney traced the declining trend of Portuguese trade when attempts were made to revive the Lisbon-Goa trade by forming a company to give a boost to the pepper trade from Kanara and Malabar in 1628-33. The collapse of the Portuguese East India Company began in 1633 with the signing of a truce with the English East India Company. Thus the historiography of the Portuguese in the East, especially in India, developed unevenly with scholars concentrating more on the Arabian Sea region than the Bay of Bengal region.

It may be said here that Goa belonged to the category of Portuguese possessions claimed by right of conquest while numerous other places in the ray of Bengal region did not fall under this category. The expansion of maritime trade alone cannot be described as a conquest merely on the basis of a chain of warehouses officially owned by the Portuguese Crown. One cannot adequately understand the overall contribution of the Portuguese in the Bay of Bengal region to the economy of the Portuguese 'empire' and also the extent of Portugal's impact on the local population.

The term Portuguese 'empire' (whether seaborne or maritime) has been accepted by many scholars even though the Portuguese were chiefly interested in gaining a share in the lucrative, highly complex network of maritime trade in the Indian Ocean region. The *Casa da Índia* (India House) in Lisbon facilitated monopoly in certain commodities from Lisbon. The *Estado da Índia* (the State of India) came to be one of the twofold empires.[25] The viceroys of India had their own vision, about both seaborne and land-based empires in India. Francisco de Almeida, the first Portuguese viceroy of India had contemplated only the establishment of factories in India and the maintenance of commercial relations and the chief reason for this was the inability of the metropolis to provide sufficient personnel to man territories in the East.[26] The second viceroy Affonso de Albuquerque's vision was completely different. He had a more landed vision of empire. He succeeded in creating an empire based on control and domination of the high seas through the establishment of a network of forts. He established fortresses such as Melaka, Goa, etc. In his view, he required at least 3,000 Portuguese men at any given point of time.[27] When such differing voices came up in the early stages of the evolution of the Portuguese empire, astonishingly the nobility strongly opposed Affonso de Albuquerque's vision of empire.[28] One also finds that there was much continued opposition to a centralized vision of empire during the period of the later viceroys such as Lopo Soares and Martim Affonso de Sousa.[29] The *Casa da Índia* in Lisbon facilitated monopoly in certain commodities from Lisbon. The Portuguese possessions in Asia were known as *Estado da Índia* (the State of India), which lay scattered from Ormuz in West Asia to Maçāo in the Far East. This *Estado da Índia* is therefore best defined not as a state or an 'empire' in the sense of the British 'empire', but rather as an enormous commercial network connecting the various points at which the Portuguese had established factories (*feitorias*) and forts (*fortalezas*). The Portuguese who were present in these localities claimed them as *possessão* (possessions) and each *fortaleza* had a very small force paid by the *Estado da Índia* to protect its properties and goods. Scholars like C.R. Boxer, M.N. Pearson and Meilink Roelofsz have shown that in particular areas, like the Persian Gulf, Gujarat and the Coromandel, and with respect to particular trading groups like the Arabs, Gujaratis and the Chettis, the Portuguese had considerable influence over Asia's maritime trade during their period of expansion in the East.

The commercial rivalry and the religious antagonism of the numerically larger Muslim population forced the Portuguese trading empire in Asia to rely on the naval force of Portugal. The Portuguese armada thus extended its sway over the Arabian Sea and the Melaka Straits, besides some of the major trading routes of the Indian Ocean region, in a very effective manner. Many ships of private traders carried the Portuguese flag in the Eastern Indian Ocean region. Nevertheless, there were not many Portuguese on the east coast as compared to the western coast of India. The Portuguese, who arrived on the west coast of India, were initially preoccupied with establishing their first factories and fortresses there and the founding of the *Estado da India* on the same coast which delayed the exploration of the eastern coast of India during the early years of the sixteenth century. It was only under Affonso de Albuquerque (1508-12), the Portuguese viceroy, that they began to expand their commercial activities very widely in Asia. In order to establish their sway over the Indian Ocean, two Sea Captains (*Capitaomor*) were appointed to exercise their naval jurisdiction from the Guardafui Cape to Cambaya and from Cambaya to Kanyakumari (Cape Comorin), respectively.[30] The Bay of Bengal and the South China Sea were not so well guarded when compared to the Western Indian Ocean. In fact the Chinese marine guards defeated the Portuguese fleet in 1517 and the Portuguese presence in the Eastern Indian Ocean region could not be termed as military in character.[31] The military activities of the Portuguese intensified only after the rival European trading companies appeared on the scene in the seventeenth century. The study of G.V. Scammel underestimated the superiority of the Portuguese ships and artillery as a major support for the Portuguese establishments in Asia. Instead he laid emphasis on the role played by the local forces.[32] The study of Genevieve Bouchon and Denys Lombard, showed that when the Portuguese were involved in the commercial conflict in the Indian Ocean regions, they did not disrupt the ongoing commerce. The Portuguese, for instance, did not have sufficient manpower or warships to control the seaborne trade and traffic.[33] However, the *cafila* (convoy of ships) and the *cartaz* (sailing permits) systems were effectively used to achieve Portuguese quasi-monopoly of trade in the west coast of India.

While this was the situation on the Arabian Sea front, the historical studies of the Bay of Bengal region in the age of Portuguese expansion received the attention of scholars like George Parison Winius,[34] L.F.F.R. Thomaz,[35] Sanjay Subrahmanyam,[36] Chandra Richard De Silva,[37] and Jorge Flores.[38] The two last-mentioned scholars have chiefly examined the role of the Portuguese in the island of Sri Lanka while the others have studied the presence of the Portuguese in the south Indian mainland on the eastern coast.

The Portuguese presence in the entire Bay of Bengal region has been placed by Winius under a separate colonial category which he calls a 'shadow empire'. According to him, it represented neither an official initiative nor an extension of royal power to any degree, but it did represent Portuguese commercial, cultural and religious influence in an informal way. It was a *grande soltura*, or a free trading zone controlled loosely from Goa.[39]

There is also a general opinion that the *Estado da Índia* was more of a 'commercial network' than a spatial (empire) entity and that it was mainly concerned with the circulation of goods than with any other form of economic or fiscal activity. Sanjay Subrahmanyam emphasizes the dynamics of Portuguese-Asian trade in contrast to the views of Niels Steensgaard who treats the Portuguese presence in Asia as a static phenomenon. He criticizes the view of Neils Steensgaard and asserts that the granting of concessional voyages yielded tax revenue to the Crown and considerable profit to private Portuguese traders. His writing cover a wider canvas based on information about Portuguese trade carried on in the ports located far and wide in the Bay of Bengal. But his arguments are substantially the same as those of L.F.F.R. Thomaz to whom he has dedicated his book. The study of the maritime history of India, especially of the Portuguese in the Bay of Bengal progressed rapidly when, in the 1990s, much literature began to be poured into the hands of readers by Sanjay Subrahmanyam. It is necessary to make an assessment of his contribution here because this is a historiographical survey. Thus knowledge on this particular theme can be updated, and new arguments and comments reflecting the new developments added.

Sanjay Subrahmanyam's book *Improvising Empire: Portuguese Trade and Settlements in the Bay of Bengal, 1500-1700* (1990) contains ten essays, very loosely written, covering a long span of two centuries. Here he struggles to interweave the published articles (which he now calls essays) but miserably fails. The author tirelessly attempts to show how the presence of the Portuguese (both official and private) in the Bay of Bengal was significant but carefully omits several ports since he is ignorant of (except for Santhome of Mylapore and Nagapattinam) where the Portuguese had traded and settled down. The various important trading settlements such as Punnaikayal, Tuticorin, Vedalai, Devanampattinam are not completely touched upon[40] while Pipli, Hijli and Bandel are totally neglected.[41] Thus one can now see the very poor documentation presented in the book and the depth of knowledge. Further, much irrelevant material has gone into the making of the book. In Chapter 8 of the book, the author provides the structure of Melaka town in 1620, which is completely out of context in the situation mentioned in the chapter. Melaka is not within the reach of the Bay of Bengal (in fact it is in the Malay archipelago), and this fact clearly shows that the author has not made any prudent selection of the material. This is further substantiated by an essay on Pietro Strozzi mentioned in chapter one. This Florentine merchant's direct participation in trade (he first reached the west coast of India in 1510 and later came to the Coromandel coast), his finances and interest in cargoes are not mentioned and in the absence of such vital information, this essay serves no purpose.[42] Therefore, all that one can firmly say is that Strozzi was one of the adventurers who came to the Coromandel in the age of Portuguese discoveries. Another notable feature is that the expanding coverage on the Portuguese settlements with special reference to the aspects of fortifications, mobilization of funds towards it, the expenditure incurred (besides the establishment of the municipality of Santhome) are completely absent. Sadly this book, with all its flaws, has been translated into Portuguese.

Another book by Sanjay Subrahmanyam, *The Political Economy of Commerce: Southern India, 1500-1650* (1990a), is a revised version of his Ph.D. dissertation submitted in 1986 to the Delhi School of Economics. This book contains vague geographical terms such as the 'Central Coromandel', the 'Northern Coromandel' and the 'Southern Coromandel'. The author has no idea either of the geography in historical space and this is evident from his writings when he mentions Point Godavari as the northern limit of Coromandel.[43] This is highly questionable because the details of historical geography do not prove this. Studies so far conducted by examining all the territorial divisions of the Coromandel clearly mention that the Coromandel is the area lying between the riverine basin of Swarnamukhi in the hinterland and the coast extending up to Durgarajapattinam as the northern limit.[44] Thus the northern limit of Coromandel did not at all reach the Godavari Point in the sixteenth century. This is applicable also to the later periods. Subrahmanyam conveniently uses the data of the European trading companies but fails to understand that the Westerners lacked the precise geographical data of coastal India at that time and this has led him to commit this mistake.[45]

Subrahmanyam ridicules and accuses other scholars like Rene Barendse for confusing the proper names, dates and place names.[46] But he himself indulged in such blunders and set a trend as early as 1990, for others to follow, of writing history with no idea of geography at all. In this regard, one may point to the visit of the Portuguese traders in 1506 to Kunimedu mentioned, wrongly, by him as being located in the vicinity of Nagapattinam.[47] Kunimedu is a different port located in the North, far a way from Nagapattinam.

Subrahamanyam opines that Nagapattinam's Moorish quarter was Nagore.[48] This is also wrong because Nagapattinam and Nagore are two different ports. While Nagapattinam is located at the mouth of the Uppanar, Nagore is situated at the mouth of the Kudavaiyar. The author also fails to provide a satisfactory explanation for the merger of Nagore if at all, with the urbanization of Nagapattinam. Further, a contradiction is noticed when one compares the two works: in *The Political Economy of Commerce* he says that Nagore is situated 8 km to the north of Nagapattinam, and in Improvising he says that Nagore is located 5 km to the north of Nagapattinam.[49]

The original ideas of Prof. L.F.F.R. Thomaz published in *Archipel* are repeated by Subrahmanyam while describing the grant of concession voyages and the system operated by the Portuguese in the 1580s. He fails to note the system of grant of trade privileges to *fidalgos*, which was in practice before the grant of concession voyages to private traders.[50] Thus the works of Subrahmanyam completely suffer from various errors which have not been eliminated in a later reprinted edition (paperback) in 2004. The readers can make their own qualitative assessment of Subrahmanyam's contributions and many points can be clarified only by a comparative study of his two books. Interestingly, much of the information is repeated in the chapters and it was unjustified and unnecessary to bring out two books in the same year, one from India and the other from Europe. Did Subrahmanyam not see the duplication? I am sure that even the Publishers in London and New Delhi were not aware. The reader, who is the best judge, can now decide which book to read and what chapter (details of repetitions given separately)[51] so as to save precious time.

In these two books by Subrahmanyam many documents are cited but not fully and properly utilized. This gives the impression that perhaps the details have been lifted from *sumarios dos documentos* (summaries of the documents) preserved in the archives and he did not actually go through the originals. An examination of some of his citations (given separately)[52] elucidates this point. The Portuguese documents are inadequately studied and analysed by him and this presumably is reflected in his writings and his works suffer from flaws or weaknesses and so his ship does not at all sail well.

According to Subrahmanyam, the port of Kunimedu played a small role.[53] He mentions that Kunimedu was important in Bengal trade.[54] It is to be kept in mind that the Marakkayars played a key role in this port and the Portuguese were inclined to settle in the region. They successfully established a settlement at Devanampattinam with the permission of the *nayak* of Gingee. Subrahmanyam, in both the books, never mentions this Portuguese settlement of Devanampattinam (modern Cuddalore) and its importance.[55] That Pattan Marakkayar, Kunju Ali Marakkayar and Mohammed Ali Marakkayar, the famous merchants of Kunimedu, conducted trade in rice with Malabar shows that Kunimedu was a flourishing centre of trade.[56] The manuscripts reveal the Portuguese had exported iron from Kunimedu to Cochin in 1524.[57] Iron continued to be exported by the Portuguese from here till 1547.[58] The availability of iron in the seventeenth century led the English to establish an iron nail factory at Kunimedu. Therefore, Subrahmanyam should not have underestimated the role of Kunimedu port.

After a gap of three years, Subrahmanyam published a third book, *The Portuguese Empire in Asia: A Political and Economic History*, which is yet another macro study. This work remains superficial with a thin set of materials on *Asia Portuguesa*. At the outset it should be mentioned that Prof. L.F.F.R. Thomaz has developed a team of scholars in the Portuguese maritime historical studies in Portugal who concentrate on the Portuguese presence in India, Sri Lanka, Pegu, Siam, Aceh, Japan and China and their writings are available in the Portuguese language but are not popularly known outside Portugal. Subrahmanyam has used their data extensively while summing up the arguments in this book. After a good assembling he prudently presents and makes it easily available in English. Of course this is not an easy task and he should be given due credit for this 'noble harvest'.

Subrahmanyam uses with or without addition or explanation, L.F.F.R. Thomaz's analysis of the changing character of Portuguese participation in intra-Asian trade in the sixteenth century, the concession system of voyages, etc., which were neglected in English language historiography until the 1980s. Thus there is no original material on the book, most of it is borrowed from Thomaz but differs from the traditional presentation of the motives and ideological currents (replacing the nationalist, Weberian and Marxist views) underlying the Portuguese expansion and presence in the Indian Ocean. Under these circumstances, it is pertinent to ask a fundamental question. Did Sanjay Subrahmanyam break new ground? One thing is clear his works are only macro-level studies, highly incomplete, and do not offer a complete and connected account of the Portuguese trade and empire in the different regions of India and Asia.

Subrahmanyam has recently chosen the safe path of writing introductions to published articles and books (details given separately)[59] and publishing them again rather than writing new and original works. However, Subrahmanyam's works filled a gap in our understanding of Portuguese activities in India and Asia since no major study of the Portuguese has been available (in English) since F.C. Danvers, R.S. Whiteway and M.N. Pearson. The writings of L.F.F.R. Thomaz in Portuguese and French are also known only to a select few, and Sanjay Subrahmanyam's volumes fill this void for the time-being.

Scholars like George Davidson Winius and Chandra Richard De Silva have stated that the Bay of Bengal region was never a part of Portugal's empire because only private settlers conducted trade from here. It is true that collaboration between the native Hindus and the Portuguese transcended the boundaries of domestic and transnational trade. The Tamil-speaking Marakkayars, however, reacted violently to the advent of the Portuguese and the encounters were bloody because the Portuguese also plunged into the offensive. This tussle for trade and the scramble for profit between the Muslim Marakkayars and the Christian Portuguese was another important feature of this period—almost an extension of Iberian antipathy towards Muslim domination.

George Bryan Sousa (1986) wrote on the Portuguese empire in the South China Sea and its contacts with the Coromandel, and focused his attention on the Portuguese private traders. As he has pointed out, the Portuguese empire, despite its obvious weakness, lingered on within the changing structure of trade in the South China Sea region and also on the Tamil Coast till the middle of the eighteenth century.[60]

James C. Boyajian (1993) deals with the Portuguese trade in Asia from the late sixteenth century to the middle of the seventeenth century attesting to the importance of the Bay of Bengal which enabled private Portuguese merchants to expand their frontiers of trade. He highlightes the role of the New Christian bankers (Portuguese Jews) in the development of Portuguese trade in South East Asia.[61]

Thus, after wading through these various strands of thought and processes, the present author came to the conclusion that these studies did not adequately link the role of the Portuguese establishment to the vast number of Private traders on the Tamil coast. It was therefore necessary to examine how the Portuguese resorted to the commercial exploitation of the maritime economy of the Tamil coast.

Soon after reaching Malabar, the Portuguese learnt of the availability of pearls in the Tamil coast and also came to understand the importance of rice which was imported in large quantities from the Tamil coast in exchange for pepper and other spices. Similarly, after reaching Melaka in 1511, they learnt about the varieties of textiles exported and the flourishing cloth trade conducted from the Tamil coast. Therefore, the Portuguese set the broad strategy of trading where possible and fighting where necessary in the Indian Ocean, but its practical application varied to suit the changing scenario in the Bay of Bengal and the Tamil coastal region. The existence of traditional export markets of rice, textiles and pearls served as a push factor which contributed to the formation of a Portuguese diaspora along the Tamil coast. The Portuguese gained from the commercial experience of the Chettis and the Marakkayars in these market operations, which enabled them to collect and distribute the same goods within South Asia and in South-East Asia. The knowledge and enterprising spirit of the native traders was thus available to the Portuguese for the development of their commerce. This attracted a large number of Portuguese to the Tamil coast and eventually led to the foundation of settlements there.

Portuguese documents of the early sixteenth century speak of the *segunda enseada* (Second Ocean) referring to the Bay of Bengal. There existed various maritime zones in the eastern coast of India, such as *Costa da Pescaria* (pearl fishery coast), *Costa da Choromandel* (Coromandel coast), *Costa da Orixa* (Orissa coast) and *Costa da Bengala* (Bengal coast). The explorations so far by the scholars of Bay of Bengal studies have not helped one to understand the exact process of developments that took place in the Tamil coastal region in south India in the age of Portuguese expansion. As this subject has not been adequately covered, there was a need to go deeper into this *terra incognita*. Thus by adding geography to its history, the regional imbalance that had crept into the studies of the Bay of Bengal could be set right.

The entire Tamil coast was looked upon by the Portuguese as forming two trading regions with different patterns of production. The region called *Costa da Pescaria* extended from the area south of Adirampattinam up to Kanyakumari where pearls and chanks were extracted and exported from the chief ports of Kayal and Kilakkarai in the sixteenth century. The other region, known as *Costa da Choromandel*, was the northern Tamil coast extending from the port of Adirampattinam in the south with numerous ports and harbours, up to Durgarajapattinam in the north. This northern Coromandel region, criss-crossed by rivers like the Palar, Pennar, Cauvery and their tributaries was fertile and famous for the cultivation of paddy, and had flourishing weaving centres which produced textiles. The present study attempts to examine the Tamil coastal area, which can be classified as a separate entity for of its flourishing pearl fishing in the sea and the manufacture of textiles and production of paddy on the land.

Spatial and Temporal Aspects of the Work

Writing the history of 'Maritime India' is now set in many different directions. The task began with the writings on different broad coastal regions, such as Cambay, Malabar, Coromandel and the Bay of Bengal. Then there is the literature emerging on the intermingling coastal areas on both the western and eastern coast, particularly covering the linguistic zones such as the

Konkan, Orissa and Andhra, besides, the areas with certain special characteristics or features such as the pearl fishery. These histories have been developed with some regional passion after noticing the unevenness in the works produced earlier, during the last few decades. Inadequate coverage of the different historical periods or chronology had been felt by some maritime scholars and they began to give dynastic labels (trade and commerce under the Cholas, Pandyas and the rulers of Vijayanagara) to economic situations and to examine the pattern of overseas trade prior to the advent of the Europeans in India. In this process it may be said that several micro- and macro-level works emerged. While the former were always well appreciated in academic circles the latter did not owing to some limitations such as the absence of in-depth mirco-level analysis. In any case, area-studies became very significant and scholars began to study again and again, in-depth, and so someone as came to be over-studied, while some other areas remained virgin and much neglected. Thus the historiography also developed unevenly. Still, these studies on maritime history have enriched our understanding of trade and commerce in late-medieval India.

The Tamil coastal region is taken as a micro-historical unit which constituted the fulcrum of the entire maritime commercial system between south India and South-East Asia. Its role in the age of Portuguese expansion is examined by pointing out the differences inherent in the macro-maritime zone of the Bay of Bengal as a whole. The geographical position of the Tamil coast, which helped to extend their trading networks connecting the East and the West towards all the important ports with converging or diverging points of routes also comes within the scope of this enquiry with regard to space.

The fleet of Vasco da Gama, then consisting of four vessels, left Lisbon on 9 July 1497, and encountered an Arabian ship on 1 March 1498, in Melinde on the East African coast, laden with Indian goods. With the help of Ibn Majid, an Indian pilot, Vasco da Gama reached Kappad near Kozhikodu on Sunday, 20 May 1498.[62] He was given a grand reception by the Zamorin of Kozhikodu, the native ruler, on 28 May 1498.[63] The next attempt to establish diplomatic relations with the ruler of Kozhikodu was made in 1500, when Pedro Alvares Cabral landed there on

13 September 1500.[64] Pedro Alvares was led by Gaspar da India to the port of Kochi on 24 December 1500. Even though the raja of Kochi was the enemy of the Zamorin, he allowed the Portuguese to load their ships with the necessary cargo of spices. After taking the commodities they set sail for Portugal on 10 January 1501. Later, in 1503, Affonso de Albuquerque, finding no pepper and spices in Kochi, went to Kollam with his ships. The king of Kollam gave him a grand reception and helped him procure all the commodities he required. The next contact came in 1505 when Francisco de Almeida was appointed as the first Portuguese viceroy, who came to Kochi to establish the head-quarters of the Portuguese in India. The earliest Portuguese attempts to reach the east coast materialized when the Portuguese viceroy, Francisco de Almeida, appointed a team of four persons in 1507 to survey the commercial possibilities and to collect information about the tomb of St. Thomas at Mylapore. Religion and trade thus formed the twin objectives of the Portuguese policy of expansion in the Orient.[65]

The present study of the Portuguese in the Tamil coast begins in the year 1507, although the arrival of the private Portuguese traders on the Tamil coast is noticed in sources as early as 1502. The study extends up to the year 1749, when the official presence of the Portuguese in the Tamil coast ended when the only and last settlement of Santhome of Mylapore was taken over by the English from the Portuguese.

The first phase of this study covers the period up to the defeat of the Vijayanagara rulers in the battle of Talikota in 1565. In the first flush of their arrival, relations between the Portuguese and the Vijayanagara rulers remained cordial. The next phase, coinciding with the rise of the nayaks in the Tamil country, witnessed considerable expansion of Portuguese private trade. In Lisbon, the rule of Dom João and Dom Henrique extended up to 1580, when the king of Spain also became the ruler of Portugal. The third phase covers the period starting with the rule of the Spanish kings from 1580 till the arrival of the Dutch in the East in 1597. Dom Henrique, the king of Portugal died in 1580 and his grandson, Filippe II, the king of Spain, succeeded to the throne. One of the important orders he issued on 15 April 1580, soon after his ascension to the throne, was that neither he nor his successors were to interfere in the administration of the Portuguese colonies in the East. Realizing that this was not realistic, he later issued a further order, on 20 November 1591, that all matters regarding the Portuguese overseas settlements should be decided by a council composed of members of his choosing.

In 1591, John Van Linschoten, the Dutch traveller, published his itinerario, which gave an account of the exploits of the Portuguese in India during this period.[66] It was at this time that Filippe I (1580-98), the king of Portugal, debarred the Dutch from buying pepper, spices and other Eastern commodities from the ports of Portugal. This gave added impetus to the Dutch attempts to reach India. They successfully reached the port of Kozhikodu in 1602 and attempted to settle there. These Dutch merchants were, however, captured by the Portuguese and later taken to Goa where they were put to death. This brutal incident prompted Stevan van der Hagen, the Dutch Chief Official in India, to seek an alliance (in 1604) with the Zamorin of Kozhikodu.[67]

The fourth phase covers the period of the Luso-Dutch rivalry in the Tamil coast from 1602 till the fall of Melaka in 1641 to the Dutch, which had a debilitating impact on Portuguese trade in the Tamil coast. When Venkatapatidevaraya II, the ruler of Vijayanagara, died in 1614, his eldest brother's son Srirangaraya became the ruler. Gobburi Jagga Raja, the father-in-law of Venakata, was averse to his succession to the throne. There was a battle at Toppur in 1616, between the forces of Srirangaraya and Jagga Raja. The *nayaks* of Gingee and Madurai supported Jagga Raja. Raghunatha Nayak of Thanjavur was in favour of Srirangaraya and after the battle, Ramadeva, the youngest son of Srirangaraya, was made king of Vijayanagar. At this time, i.e. on 15 March 1630, to be exact, the king of Portugal himself established a company of commerce, contributing 1,500,000 *cruzados* as share capital through a royal order. There was hardly any response from any other individual to contribute towards the share capital of the company, although some municipalities in Portugal and Spain came forward to patronize it. After three years, however, the company was wound up by a royal decree dated 12 April 1633.

The fifth phase extends from 1641 to 1662, when all the Portuguese settlements in the Tamil coast fell into the hands of the Dutch. Chokkanatha Nayaka (1657-62), the ruler of Madurai, invaded Thanjavur and killed Vijaya Raghunatha Nayaka and his son Mannur Dasa. Thus the nayakdom of Thanjavur was annexed by the nayak of Madurai. Alagiri, the stepbrother of Chokkanatha, was appointed as the ruler of Thanjavur. At this time, Rayasam Venkata approached Ekoji, the commander of Bijapur Sultan. Ekoji drove away Alagiri and installed Chengamaladass, the son of Mannur Dasa, as the ruler of Thanjavur. However, Ekoji (the stepbrother of Shivaji) himself occupied the territory (in 1676) by dethroning Chengamaladass in 1676. Thus Maratha rule extended to Thanjavur in 1677. Later Ekkoji's son Thukkoji ruled Thanjavur from AD 1729 to AD 1735.

The rule of the sultan of Bijapur in the region of Pennar came to an end when the Marathas occupied Gingee in 1670. Similarly, the rule of the sultan of Golconda in the Palar region also ended when the Mughals established their authority in the 1670s. Thus the final phase of this study covers the period of the survival of, Portuguese shipping and trade from 1662 up to 1749 when the English finally took over the only surviving Portuguese settlement of Santhome of Mylapore on the Tamil coast.

Design of the Study

The first chapter provides glimpses of the network of seaborne commerce and overland trade on the Tamil coast and its hinterland after the decline of the medieval Cholas in AD 1280 up to the advent of the Portuguese. With the decline of the Cholas, one glorious phase in the history of the Tamil region came to a close and a different political process was set in motion. But the most dramatic change was the emergence of the Pandyas, Samburvarayas, Kadavarayas and the Vijayanagara empire. The political and economic situation in the Tamil region became unstable following the Muslim invasion of the Tamil country in AD 1329-30 which lasted for many years. But the various rulers of the kingdoms benefited from the new trading ventures with the Arabs and the Chinese. Thus the Tamil ports such as

Nagapattinam, Devipattinam, Virapandyanpattinam, Kayal, Kilakkarrai, Periyapattinam, Devanampattinam, Sadurangapattinam, Nagore, Thirumalairayanpattinam, Thirumullaivasal, Krishnapattinam and Pulicat continued to serve as outlets for domestic and international trade in the Bay of Bengal.

The rise of Arab and Chinese merchants in the *Purva Samudra* (the Eastern Seas as the Bay of Bengal was then known) during the medieval period marked an interesting phase before the arrival of the Portuguese. The role of the Tamil trading community expanded, together with the rise of the new dynasties of the Pandyas, Samburvarayas, Kadavarayas and the Vijayanagara kingdom. The Tamil merchants articulated a sense of solidarity through trade guilds. How these institutional forms of trade functioned before the arrival of the Portuguese is examined in this chapter. Horse trade was carried on by the merchant class under the Pandyas and this led to a process of transformation from an agrarian economy to an agro-mercantile economy in the Tamil country. The revenue derived from customs duties levied by the state became an important component of state income. The collection of revenue from the markets by the rulers of the Tamil country at this time also ushered in the birth of the mercantile or commercial era in the Tamil littoral between 1280 and 1500. Hindu and Muslim traders were encouraged by their own respective kingdoms. The first factor that contributed to the growth of Pandya coastal trade networks was the development of the hinterland, particularly in the Vaigai and Tambraparani riverine basin which in turn helped the ports on the coast to flourish. Secondly, the rise of merchant groups in several pockets channellized the resources from the coastal trade and the expansion of overseas commerce. Trade relations between the Chinese rulers and the Tamil kings were fostered through exchange of embassies. Further, the withdrawal of the Chinese traders from the long-distance trade, was followed by regionalized trade within South Asia at the end of the fifteenth century. Thus, developments in the areas of trade, markets, merchants, trading networks in the medieval period on the Tamil coast are explored so as to present the situation before the arrival and penetration of the Portuguese into the Tamil region.

The maritime explorations of the Portuguese in the pearl fishery coast and their commercial activities are dealt with in the second chapter. The historical background of Portuguese attempts to participate in and control the pearl fishery operations at Kayal and Kilakkarai, and to derive revenue from there during the sixteenth and seventeenth centuries is traced in this chapter. Also undertaken here is a study of Portuguese involvement in the pearl fishery as also the pearl fishing operations in the Portuguese settlements of Vedalai, Punnaikayal and Tuticorin, the three settlements that served as key dynamic centres in the expansionary process. Trade in pearls and their exports to Portugal and trade in chanks within Asia are explored.

While expanding their commercial activities, the Portuguese were forced to make certain diplomatic moves. Hence the focus of this chapter is on the political and commercial networks that underpinned the trading system of the Portuguese. The polycentric character of Portuguese trade, especially in strategic commodities like horses, elephants and gunpowder, generated keen interest among the *nayak* rulers. The significance of the Portuguese trade in these strategic commodities helped them establish linkages with the native rulers on the Tamil coast. The trade in strategic commodities depended on the political developments in the hinterland during the seventeenth century with the expansion of the Dutch trade in the Coromandel. It is suggested that some factors such as economic and political were responsible for the growth of the ports of Tuticorin, Nagapattinam and Devanampattinam, highlighting there trade in horses, elephants and saltpetre. This chapter attempts to explore how the pattern of Portuguese trade in strategic commodities depended on the political developments in the *nayak* doms of Madurai and Thanjavur and how it was designed to meet the requirements of Portugal. The significant role of the missionaries in diplomatic dealings between the king of Portugal and the local rulers, which helped maintain cordial relations in conducting the trade in strategic commodities, is also dealt with here.

The export of bulk cargo over long distances, which was the most important and the traditional system of trade that prevailed in the Coromandel coast is traced in the next chapter. Ports of the Tamil coast, such as Pulicat, Santhome, Kunimedu, Devanampattinam, Nagore and Nagapattinam, were the disembarkation points for bulk goods such as rice and textiles for voyages to South-East Asia. The export trade in these goods in the ports of the Tamil coast attest to the prosperity of the local economy and the vast resources of the hinterland.

Some of the practices associated with private shipping and trade are unravelled in chapter five. The Portuguese *Estado da Índia*, in the meanwhile, slipped into a state of lethargy and their power disappeared in the seventeenth century. Even after the Portuguese had to beat a retreat from the Coromandel Coast, some of the Portuguese private traders engaged as shipowners at Porto Novo, Nagapattinam and Madras played an important role in the Tamil coast. The political consolidation of the Golconda and Bijapur kingdoms in the Tamil country between 1630 and 1662 was an important development during this period. How the private Portuguese traders survived and created an alternative way of survival and found new routes and maintained links with the other European trading companies like the Dutch and the English in the Bay of Bengal during this period becomes evident in this chapter. How the Dutch dealt with these entrepreneurs, and finally how they overthrew the Portuguese dominance, is also touched upon. Trading centres like Madras, Pondicherry, Porto Novo and Tranquebar from which the Portuguese private traders operated after the capture of the Portuguese settlements by the Dutch in 1662 are also examined in this chapter. We shall also see how the export of goods such as iron and cannon balls, coir, leather, butter, salt, oil and meat, besides slaves, began to play a vital role. Direct sailings were revived under the Portuguese, which helped in the import of various commodities including aromatics, astringents, cosmetics and perfumes. Out of these sandalwood, eagle wood, amber, lac, benzoin, camphor, and dye stuffs found entry into the Tamil coast.

The Portuguese imported mainly cloves from Moluccas, Amboina and Makassar, pepper from Aceh, nutmeg from Banten, cinnamon and areca nuts from Sri Lanka, precious stones from

Burma and Sri Lanka into the Tamil coast, as will be seen in chapter six. The spices imported into the Tamil coast were re-exported and they found their way to Portugal, while the bullion, which circulated within the Tamil coast, contributed to the progressive monetization of the region's economy.

The development of port towns and the rise of settlements all along the Tamil coast is dealt with in chapter seven. The *Estado da Índia* did not exercise much control over these Portuguese settlements on the Tamil coast during the sixteenth century and they declined into a scattered confederation of territories with small military establishments. The commercial establishments, *feitorias* (trading factories), were slowly turned into *fortalezas* (fortified settlements) on the Tamil Coast in the seventeenth century, although all of those were not listed as possessions of the Portuguese Crown, except Santhome of Mylapore and Nagapattinam. The rise, growth and decline of these two port towns in the context of overseas trade during the period of Portuguese expansion in the East were important because sea traffic was routed through them and the Portuguese held the responsibility to monitor it. These urban centres were to some extent fortified with walls and the main streets in the town were also carefully laid out with buildings adorned with Portuguese architectural embellishments. The urbanization process of the Portuguese settlement of Devanampattinam had also been dealt in the chapter. The rise of Portuguese private traders in these port settlements was significant and they held important positions by virtue of vast investments of funds in trade. These rich private merchants contributed towards the prosperity of the Portuguese settlements to some extent. There were the municipal councils at Santhome of Mylapore and Nagapattinam represented by the Portuguese and Eurasian population which was an influential force on the *Estado da Índia*. With the dawn of the seventeenth century, commerce in the Bay of Bengal became a bone of contention and the Luso-Dutch rivalry resulted in the decline of Portuguese trade and the disintegration of their settlements.

Based on the chapters certain conclusions are drawn at the end of this work. The impact of spatial and political factors, and economic and other aspects that played a significant role are taken into consideration for formulating a theoretical framework. The ways in which the commercial exchanges took place has been examined to understand the contributions of the economy of the Tamil coast to the emerging world economy in the age of Portuguese expansion.

NOTES

1. F.C. Danvers, *The Portuguese in India*, 2 vols., London, 1894.
2. R.S. Whiteway, *The Rise of Portuguese Power in India*, London, 1899.
3. Fernão Lopes da Castanheda, *Historia do Descobrimentos e Conquista da India Pelos Portugueses*, Porto, 2 vols., 1975; Gaspar Correia, *Lendas da India*, 4 vols., Porto, 1975; Diogo do Couto, *Decadas da Asia*, Lisboa, rpt. 1973; João de Barros, *Decadas da Asia*, Lisboa, 1777-8.
4. J.J. Campos, *History of the Portuguese in Bengal*, Calcutta, 1919.
5. W.H. Moreland, *From Akbar to Aurangazeb*, London, 1923 (New Delhi, rpt. 1972), p. 92. The idea of Portuguese dominance in the Indian Ocean and the main channels of trade controlled by the Portuguese was introduced by W.H. Moreland. See his work, *India at the Death of Akbar*, London, pp. 186-8, 192-210. He admitted that Asian ships were active in some areas of the Indian Ocean.
6. K.M. Panikkar, *Asia and the Western Dominance: A Survey of the Vasco da Gama Epoch of Asian History, 1498-1945*, London, 1953, New York, 1959. Panikkar, writing his book forty years after W.H. Moreland, still spoke of Western dominance of the Indian Ocean.
7. C.R. Boxer, *The Portuguese Seaborne Empire, 1415-1825*, London, 1973, p. 48
8. K.A. Nilakanta Sastri, *Sources of South Indian History with Special Reference to South India* (Heras Memorial Lectures), Bombay, 1964, pp. 35, 79.
9. Blair Kling and M.N. Pearson (eds.), *The Rise of Portuguese Empire in Asia before Dominion*, Honolulu, 1979.
10. Blair Kling and Diffie, *The Foundation of the Portuguese Empire*, Minneapolis, 1980.
11. V.M. Godinho, *Os Descobrimentos e a Economia Mundial*, 4 vols., Lisboa, 1981-3.
12. M.N. Pearson, *The Indian Ocean*, London, 2003; see his earlier work, *Merchants and Rulers of Gujarat: The Response of the Portuguese in the Sixteenth Century*, Delhi, 1980.
13. K.S. Mathew, *Portuguese Trade with India in the Sixteenth Century*,

Delhi, 1983; idem, *Portuguese and the Sultanate of Gujarat, 1500-1573*, Delhi, 1985.

14. Anthony Disney, *Twilight of the Pepper Empire*, Cambridge, 1978.
15. Pius Malekandathil, *Portuguese Cochin and the Maritime Trade of India, 1500-1663*, Delhi, 2001.
16. Afzal Ahmad, *Indo-Portuguese Trade on the Western Coast of India, 1600-1665*, Delhi, 1992.
17. Celsa Pinto, *Trade and Finance in Portuguese India*, Delhi, 1993. See also, Celsa Pinto, *Situating Indo-Portuguese Trade History: A Commercial Resurgence, 1770-1830*, Tellicherry, 2003.
18. Philomena Sequeira, *The Goa-Bahia Intra-Colonial Relations, 1675-1825*, Goa, 2005.
19. T.R. de Sousa, *Medieval Goa: A Socio-Economic History*, Delhi, 1979.
20. M.N. Pearson, *Portuguese in India*, Cambridge, 1987.
21. J.C. Van Leur, *Indonesian Trade and Society*, The Hague, 1955, p.118. W.H. Moreland's and K.M. Panikkar's idea regarding Portuguese domination in the Indian Ocean was challenged by J.C. Van Leur in 1955. He said that Portuguese actually failed to gain control of the vital pepper and spice trade.
22. Niels Steensgard, *Carracks, Caravans and Companies: The Structural Crisis in the European-Asian Trade in the Early 17th Century*, Copenhagen, 1972.
23. Ibid., pp. 81-114.
24. Meilink Roefosz, *Asian Trade and European Influence in the Indonesian Archipelago between 1500 and 1800*, The Hague, 1964.
25. James C. Boyajian, *The Trade of India,* p. 3, see also George Davison Winius, The Portuguese Asia "Decadencia" Revisited', in Alfred Honer and Richard A. Preto-Rodas (eds.), *Empire in Transition: The Portuguese World in the Time of Cameõs*, Gainesville, 1985, p. 110.
26. F.C. Danvers, *The Portuguese in India*, vol. 1, London, 1894, p. xxviii. See the viceroy's letter to the king of Portugal on page xxx.
27. See, F.C. Danvers, *The Portuguese in India*, vol. I, p. xxxii.
28. L.F.F.R. Thomaz, 'Factions, Interests and Messianism: The Politics of Portuguese Expansion in the East, 1500-1521', *IESHR*, vol. 27(1), January-March 1991, pp. 97-109.
29. Sanjay Subrahmanyam, *The Portuguese Empire in Asia, 1500-1700: A Political and Economic History*, London, 1993, pp. 71 and 89.
30. Lelleo e Irmao (ed.), *Fernão Lopes da Castanheda*, Porto, 1979, p. 210.
31. C.R. Boxer, *The Portuguese Seaborne Empire*, p. 49.
32. G.V. Scammel, 'Indigenous Assistance in the Establishment of Portuguese Power in Asia', in *Modern Asian Studies* (hereafter *MAS*), vol. 14, pt. 1, February 1980, pp. 1-11.

33. See the Articles of Genevieve Bouchon and Denys Lombard in Ashin Das Gupta and M.N. Pearson (eds.), *India and the Indian Ocean, 1500-1800*, Calcutta, 1987.
34. George Davison Winius, *The Fatal History of Portuguese Ceylon: Transition to Dutch Rule, 1638-1658*, Harvard, 1971. See also, his 'The Shadow Empire of Goa in the Bay of Bengal', *Itinerario*, vol. 3, 1983, pp. 83-100.
35. LF.F.R. Thomaz, 'Factions, Interests and Messianism: The Politics of Portuguese Expansion in the East, 1500-1521', *IESHR*, vol. 27(1), January-March 1991, pp. 97-109.
36. Sanjay Subramanyam, *Improvising Empire: Portuguese Trade and Settlements in the Bay of Bengal, 1500-1700*, Delhi, 1990.
37. Chandra Richard de Silva, *The Portuguese in Ceylon, 1617-1638*, Colombo, 1972.
38. Jorge Manuel Costa da Silva Flores, *Os Portugueses e O Mar de Ceilao, 1498-1543, Trato Diplomatica e Guerra*, MA thesis, Universidade Nova de Lisboa, Portugal, 1991.
39. George Davison Winius, 'Portugal's Shadow Empire in the Bay of Bengal', *Revista de Cultura*, 1991, pp. 273-87.
40. For details on the commercial and political activities of the Portuguese in Kayal (1508-36), Kilakkarai (1508-31), Vedalai (1520-73), Punnaikayal (1544-79) and Tuticorin (1570-1658) see, S. Jeyaseela Stephen, *Portuguese in the Tamil Coast: Historical Explorations in Commerce and Culture, 1507-1749*, Pondicherry, 1998, pp. 62-5, 65-7, 68-72, 72-6 and 77-80.
41. S. Jeyaseela Stephen, *Trade and Globalization: Europeans, Americans and Indians in the Bay of Bengal, 1511-1819*, Jaipur/Delhi, 2003, pp. 64-7, 174-80.
42. Sanjay Subrahmanyam, *Improvising Empire*, pp. 13-14.
43. Subrahmanyam, *The Political Economy of Commerce: Southern India*, Cambridge, 1990a, p. 93.
44. S. Jeyaseela Stephen, *The Coromandel Coast and its Hinterland: Economy, Society and Political System, 1500-1600*, Delhi, 1997, p. 24.
45. The term 'Central Coromandel' has come into currency and Subrahmanyam mentions in his book that the Central Coromandel had ports such as Armagon, Pulicat and Santhome in his book. See *The Political Economy*, p. 51. This view is different from another writer who mentions the ports of Pondicherry, Cuddalore and Porto Novo located in the Central Coromandel. Bhaskar Jyoti Basu, 'Central Coromandel in the Eighteenth Century', Ph.D. dissertation, Visva-Bharati, 1988.
46. See Sanjay Subrahmanyam, 'Introduction: The Indian Ocean Between Empire and Nation', in *Maritime India*, Delhi, 2004, p. xvi.

47. Subrahmanyam, *The Political Economy*, p. 98.
48. Ibid., p. 196.
49. Subrahmanyam, *Improvising Empire*, p. 70.
50. Stephen, *Portuguese in the Tamil Coast*, Pondicherry, 1998, pp. 126-9. I have discussed this point at length based on the discovery of new documents. It is to be pointed out here that there was no element of concession for voyages at all before 1550.
51. The essay on the Coromandel-Melaka trade (1990b) in Chapter 2 in OUP, is repeated in Chapter 3 of *Political Economy of Commerce* (pp. 98-113). With regard to the other chapters, the fourth essay on Nagapattinam, pp. 68-95, in the *Improvising Empire* is again repeated in the former book, pp. 194-206. The sixth essay, pp.129-36, is an uneven chapter with few details on Masulipatnam between 1570-1600. The details on Masulipatnam once again are repeated in *Political Economy of Commerce*, pp. 147-60.
52. Subrahmanyam (1990b: 28), p. 28, only mentions ANTT, *Nucelo Antigo*, Mss no. 808. He has not used the data and if he had gone through the original he would not have missed or failed to notice the details of cash invested for trade at Kunimedu and Nagapattinam by the Portuguese between 26 July 1526 and 15 January 1527, which is furnished in detail in the document. This needs some explanation. I have even provided the physical description of the manuscript vide page 162, footnote no.15, along with details of blank pages of the mss. For details see, *Portuguese in the Tamil Coast*, pp. 124-5. This makes one wonder whether Subrahmanyam consulted this manuscript at all. Another example may be cited on the use of a manuscript ANTT, *Documents Remetidos da India* in Livro 56, fls. 221-4. This reference is just mentioned in Subrahmanyam's *Improvising Empire*, vide p. 80. It is a significant document that contains twenty items of the regulations issued by the king of Portugal for conducting trade at Nagapattinam when he took control of the port administration immediately after the death of Venkatapatidevaraya, the last ruler of the Vijayanagara empire (for details, see, *Portuguese in the Tamil Coast*, pp. 159-61.) Subrahmanyam did not understand the significance of this record but mentions it in passing as found in the summary of the documents.
53. Subrahmanyam, *Improvising Empire*, p. 9.
54. Ibid., p. 100.
55. Stephen, *Portuguese in the Tamil Coast*, pp. 233-6.
56. Ibid., p. 130.
57. Ibid., p. 153.
58. Stephen, *The Coromandel Coast*, p. 117.
59. See editor's preface and introduction, 'The Portuguese and Early Modern Asia', in Subrahmanyam, *Sinners and Successors of Vasco da*

Gama, Delhi, 1998, pp. 5-13. See also, Sanjay Subrahmanyam, 'Introduction: The Indian Ocean Between Empire and Nation', in *Maritime India*, Delhi, 2004, pp. xi-xvii.

60. George Bryan Sousa, *The Survival of Empire: Portuguese Trade and Society in China and South China, 1630-1754*, Cambridge, 1986.
61. James C. Boyajian, *Portuguese Trade in Asia under the Habsburgs, 1580-1640*, Baltimore, 1993.
62. João de Barros, *Decadas da Asia*, Decada 1, Parte I, Lisboã, 1778, p. 275.
63. Fontura da Costa (ed.), *Roteiro da Viagem de Vasco da Gama, 1497-1499*, Lisboã, 1940, p. 42.
64. Raymundo Antonio de Bulhão Pato (ed.), *Cartas de Alfonso de Albuquerque, Lisboã*, 1903, Tomo III, pp. 85-6.
65. Correia, *Lendas da India*, I, p. 739, II, pp. 722-87, III, pp. 419-24.
66. Linschoten reached Goa on 21 September 1583 and served as secretary to the Archbishop of Goa for five years. After the death of the Archbishop he left India on 20 January 1589 from Kochi.
67. J.K. De Jonge, *De Opkomst Van het Nederlandscheh Gezag in Oost Indie, 1595-1610*, The Hague, 1862-5, vol. 3, p. 150. See also, Heeres, *Corpus Diplomaticum Neerlando-Indicum*, The Hague, pp. 30-1.

2

The Trading World of the Tamils: Before the Advent of the Portuguese

The Bay of Bengal, lying geographically at the mid-point of the vast Indian Ocean, played a very significant role as a transit point and meeting ground in the long-distance maritime trade linking the shores of the Mediterranean and India.[1] The east coast of India in fact became prominent because of the availability of its many products of export value such as pearls, corals and textiles.[2] Ptolemy records the ports of the east coast of India, which included the maritime regions of Coromandel and Bengal, as being very significant owing to the brisk overseas long-distance trade conducted in the early Christian era. A passage recorded in the Hatigumpha inscription of Kharavela shows that the king of Kalinga caused the procurement of pearls, precious stones and jewels from the Pandya king during the second half of the first century BC this shows that inter-regional trade had also flourished in that period.[3] The overseas trade of the Tamil coast declined after the fall of the Roman empire, which was followed by the Kalapirar depredations. Long-distance trade seems to have revived in the subsequent period with the development of Chinese contacts. Various ports on the Tamil coast came up where maritime activities and trade were carried on with Canton in the East-West commercial axis (see Map 1). But nowhere did the Chinese establish their colonies.

Ambassadorial Missions of the Pallavas, Cholas and Pandyas: Development of Overseas Trade with China

The beginning of Hindu Tamil commercial contacts with the Chinese ports may be traced to the Pallava period. Narasimha Varman III (AD 844-66) the Pallava kings, had sent ambassadorial

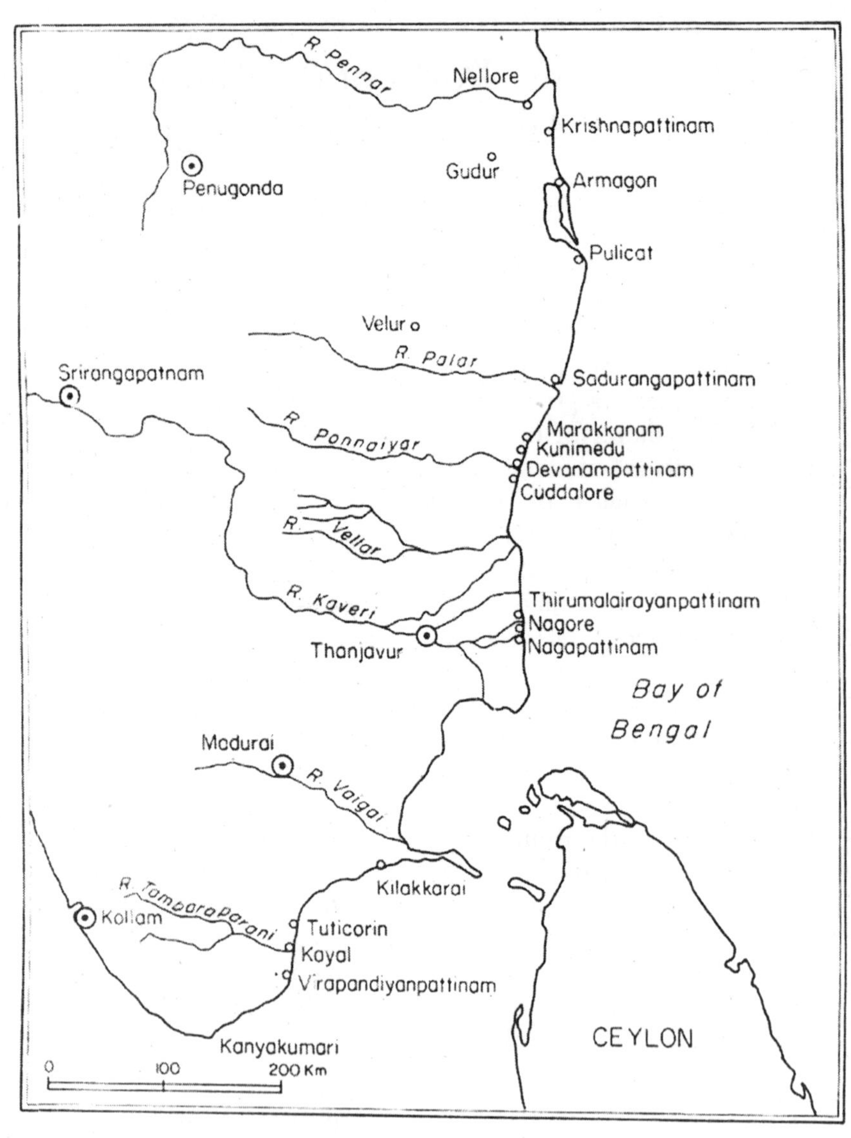

MAP 1: MEDIEVAL PORTS IN THE TAMIL COAST, 1280-1500

missions with gifts of beautiful talking parrots and leopards to the Chinese court.[4] Along with this development the Hindu Tamil merchant guilds emerged during the period, who traded with the ports of South-East Asia and the Far East. In fact the Tamil merchants guild of *manigramattar* had established a colony at Takua-Pa[5] during the reign of Narasimha Varman III. The eastern Indian Ocean, centred in the Bay of Bengal, thus remained the exclusive domain of Tamil merchants trading with South-East Asia. A steady process of agricultural expansion and production of non-agricultural commodities was spurred by the confluence of a number of factors which operated in the political system of the Pallavas during these centuries. The export of rice, spices and textiles was important in this line between the various trading ports of South-East Asia and the Far East which the Tamil Coast had developed during this period. Thus the seaborne trade of the Tamil coast across the Indian Ocean was primarily determined by climate and agriculture and not merely by influences outside the region, which Fernand Braudel calls the long-term (*longue duree*) rhythm of the natural and human presence.[6]

The Tamil coast witnessed a dramatic change with the rise and the consolidation of the powerful empire of the Cholas in the Tamil country in the tenth century. The policies of the Cholas in the field of overseas trade with South-East Asia was an important feature of this time. The port of Nagapattinam situated at the mouth of the Uppanar (10°3′N; 79°5′5S) flourished at that time. The construction of the *cudamani vihara* at Nagapattinam confirms the presence of merchants from South-East Asia. The grants made by king Raja Raja Chola I (AD 985-1014) in AD 1006 to this Buddhist shrine are recorded in the Leiden plates. Further, the Chola ruler Kulottunga's (1070-1120) subsequent confirmation of the endowment to the same shrine is also well known.[7] Rajendra Chola's (1014-44) naval attack on Sangama Vijayattunga Varman, the king of Srivijaya (Java), in 1025 is another piece of evidence that shows the expansion of the Cholas. There was a matrimonial alliance between the Chola ruler and the usurper, Surya Varman I of Java, who was the son of the king of Tambralinga, a Malay kingdom.[8] The Chola kings also raided Kedah (Malaysia) in 1067 as can be gleaned from the Thanjavur inscription.[9]

Nagapattinam (Na-wu-tan-shan) was the premier port of the Cholas as is evident from Chinese records. The discovery of Chinese coins at Vikraman village (Pattukottai taluk) in the hinterland of Nagapattinam in 1942 and 1944 attest to this fact.[10] Spices and aromatics continued to come from Malabar to the ports on the Chola coast to be sent on to China.[11] An eleventh century Rajendra Chola inscription mentions that 87¾ *kalanju* of gold (*cina kanakam*) from China (AD 1018-19) was available at Nagapattinam.[12] The inscription also refers to an endowment for which Chinese gold was gifted. This gift was offered by a merchant who was described as *Kidarattu nayinar* (chief merchant from Kedah) to a temple at the port of Nagapattinam. The name of the merchant is given as Sri Kuruttan Kesavan alias Agralekai.

The *Tisai ayirattu ainurruvar* guild had established a settlement at Laboe Toewa, near Barus and at Pansur in Sumatra in 1088. In the Far East too the Cholas followed a policy of maritime exchange. Chinese sources record four different Chola missions sent from the Tamil coast. King Raja Raja sent one mission in AD 1015. Two other missions were sent during the rule of Rajendra Chola, in AD 1020 and 1033, and one more during the rule of Kulothunga Chola in AD 1077. The fact that the port of Kollam (Quilon) was brought under the control of Kulottunga Chola in AD 1096 shows that spices came very easily to the Chola ports for export to China. This undisputably proves that the limits of the Tamil coast had extended up to Kollam in the medieval period. The spectacular naval attack by the Cholas against the Sri Vijaya kingdom in South-East Asia has to be situated in the broader context of the rise of new powers in the medieval period. The naval expedition of Raja Raja Chola was undertaken to subdue the ruler of Sri Vijaya and to establish full control over the trade network in the Melaka Straits and the Sunda Islands. The politics of plunder conducted by Rajendra Chola from the Tamil coast also finds mention in an inscription of this period.[13]

Trade representatives were sent along with the royal emissaries, mentioned in Chinese as Soli Sanvan (*Chola Thalaivan*?) with gifts. In one instance there included 21,000 *tales* of pearls, 60 pieces of ivory and 60 *kattis* of Gumoli banum (gum?). In another instance, Soli Samudra (*Chola Samudran*), the emissary, presented 6,600 *tales* of pearls, 3300 *kattis* of spices and medicinal herbs.[14] It was at this time that the presence of the Tamil settlements was reported in Guangzhou (Canton) and Quanzhou (Zayton) in China. Further the twelfth-century account *Lingwai-Daida* by Ahou Quefei refers to the Cholas (Zhu-li-yeh) in AD 1178. Zaho Rugua (Chao Jukua) in his *Zhufan-Zhi* (records of the foreigners) also refers to the Cholas (Zhulian) in 1225. The Tamil coast had the capacity to put on the international market huge quantities of relatively inexpensive agricultural products and highly competitive manufactured goods like textiles in exchange for gold.

In Chinese sources during back to AD 1280, the king of Kollam is referred to as Pandya (pi-na-ti). Maravarman Kulasekhara I had in fact annexed the territory of Kollam and its port. It is from this period, that the inscriptions in the Pearl Fishery Coast mention Maravarman Kulasekhara I along with the title of *kollam konda* and *cheranai venra* (one who conquered Kollam or one who won victory over the Cheras). Thus Kollam flourished as a port and became the destination of Chinese voyagers. In the same year, i.e. 1280, the emperor of China sent an envoy to invite the ruler of Pandya to develop maritime trade with his country.[15]

The region of Maravarman Kulasekhara Pandya witnessed considerable commercial contacts with China. The Pandya ruler and the Chinese emperor exchanged several envoys during the short period of eight years between 1283 and 1291. The inscriptions of Maravarman Kulasekhara also testify to the establishment of Pandya hegemony over the Malabar coast including the region of Kollam. An ambassadorial mission which reached China in 1279 with a live elephant and a rhinoceros was highly appreciated by the Chinese ruler. In response to this, an ambassadorial mission sent by the emperor of China reached Kollam in 1280.[16] Later, in 1281, a sculpture of Lord Siva was installed in a temple in Quanzhou (Tsuan-Chou) by one Sambanda Perumal who reached China with the local merchants. A Tamil trading guild was also established in the famous port of Quanzhou. Hara Prasad Ray, who has used the Chinese sources, is of the view that the Sambanda Perumal mentioned in the Tamil inscription hailed probably from the Kumbakonam region. This, however, seems doubtful because the name Perumal generally formed the suffix of Pandya rulers and Cheras but not the Chola kings. Yet another envoy from the Pandya court is reported to have presented precious stones, clothes, etc., to the Chinese emperor in 1284. In return the Chinese emperor sent an envoy in 1285 to the Pandya court to obtain more goods. The third Pandya envoy reached China in 1286 and presented tributes. Again in 1287, the Pandya envoys presented tributes, which reportedly included a strange animal, to the emperor of China.[17] In 1288 another envoy from the Pandya court arrived in China. In the following year 1289, two zebras were presented to the Chinese emperor. In exchange, the emperor sent two high officials as envoys to the Pandya court in 1291. Later, in 1296, the emperor of China sent more envoys to the Pandya court. In 1297, he gifted a tiger-shaped insignia made of two precious stones to the Pandya ruler.[18] Although all of these contacts were primarily diplomatic, they paved the way for establishing trade contacts between the two countries in the early period. The ambassadorial missions generally reached China via Java.[19] Jayanagara, the Javanese king who ascended the throne in AD 1309, assumed the title of Sundara Pandya Devadishvaran which testifies to the political contacts with the contemporary Pandya kingdom in south India. Thus Java was an important terminal point for medieval trade. Prapancha's *Nagarakertagama* written in this period (1365) mentions ships which came unceasingly in large numbers to Java from the Pandya coast.[20]

Chinese sources towards the end of the thirteenth century however, refer to the prohibition of export of the gold, precious metals and bullion from China to the Pandya ports.[21] From the Pandya coast the chief items of export included pearls and spices. Chufan-chih, the Chinese source, mentioned that as a general rule, a pearl was considered very valuable in China of it was perfectly round. The test for its absolute roundness was that it did not stop rolling when put on a plate. Tamil merchants who arrived from the Pandya coast to China were in the habit of concealing pearls in the lining of their clothes and also in the handles of their umbrellas. This type of smuggling was to evade the heavy customs duty levied on pearls in China.[22]

Chinese traders first touched Kayal on the south-eastern coast of India and then left for Kollam on the west coast,[23] as is evident from Chinese sources ascribed to the Yuan (1281-1368) and Ming periods (1368-1500). In the Chinese source, Panhai Zhi Hich, dated in the year 1304, the port of Kayal (Jiayi) is listed as one of the ports trading with Canton. The last ambassadorial mission of China was sent to the Pandya court in 1314. It is said that from the port of Kayal the Pandya ruler had also sent, in return, tribute to the Chinese emperor.[24] Ming sources refer to Kayal under several names such as Jiayi, Jia-yicheng, Jiayicheng and Jiayile.

As the merchants from the *Suvarna bhumi*, which referred to the whole of South-East Asia, brought bricks of gold with them to the Tamil coast, it became very important for the Chinese emperors to participate in this line of trade. They sent envoys with credentials under the imperial seal and also with gold to attract foreign merchants.[25] As a result, huge quantities of gold came from China to the Coromandel coast.

Nagapattinam, an important port, continued to flourish in the thirteenth century; and the Chinese traders called it Na-kia-pot-ta-na.[26] In AD 1267, when the Chinese presence was considerably large at Nagapattinam, a Chinese pagoda was constructed there. Hoards of circular-shaped Chinese copper coins with a square-shaped hole in the centre have been found at various interior sites of coastal Tamilnadu such as Thallikottai and Olayukunnam. All of these attest to the fact that commerce flourished between China and the Tamil coast between AD 713 and AD 1275.[27] Subsequently, with the decline of the Cholas, Chinese traders also stopped visiting this port.

Growth of the Seaborne Trade with Arabia: The Monoposony Policy of the Pandyas

With the rise of Islam in the seventh century, Arab Muslim traders began to arrive to trade and settle on the Tamil coast, and they contracted matrimonial alliances with local Tamil women. Not being landowners themselves, they naturally took to sailing and transoceanic trade. They noted the seasons, sea currents, tides and trade winds along the shores of the Bay of Bengal and undertook sailings from Sri Lanka to Bengal when the south-west monsoon was active from June to September and also sent their ships from peninsular India to Sri Lanka when the north-east monsoon (known as the return monsoon) was active from October to February.

Kayal emerged as an international port in the thirteenth century.[28] It had long-distance trade with West Asia and it flourished under the Pandyas chiefly for the import of horses from Hormuz and Aden. Kayal was by far the most important port where all the ships that came from ports of West Asia such as Hormuz, Kis, Aden, etc., touched before moving on. Towards the end of the thirteenth century, thousands of horses were imported through this port and sent to Madurai. According to Wassaf, a horse was purchased at a price of 500 saggio,[29] equivalent to 220 dinars or red gold. According to another source, as many as 16,000 horses were landed at this port in one season.[30] The demand for horses was always greater than the supply as a large number of horses died during transportation. Yet the importers had to pay the full amount and this money was paid from the Pandya treasury in accordance with the terms of the contract. Several agents, brokers and merchants were engaged in the horse trade and one finds that Chettis were prominent horse merchants who were therefore known as *kudirai* Chettis in the inscriptions.[31] The Pandya rulers imported these horses for their army. This motivated the Pandyas to follow a semi-monoposony policy, allowing Muslims and Hindus to trade in horses at Nagore, Kundranarkovil and[32] Tiruchitrambalam,[33] and supply them only to the Pandya rulers. Several expressions found in the inscriptions of this period, such as *kulichevakarar*[34] (horsemen), *kudirai amman*[35] (horse trooper) and *kudirai andan*[36] (stable man) attest to the fact that import of horses and the animal trade necessitated the employment of various types of skilled persons. Kayal thus developed into a port where the Arab merchants brought their merchandise in their trading vessels. Kayal also had a flourishing pearl trade as pearl fishing developed under the rule of Jatavarman Sundara Pandya I (1251-68) who is mentioned by Wassaf as Sundara Pandi.

The backwaters of Kayal had an opening to the sea and so there was scope for large sailing vessels to anchor there. Fishermen as well as sailors of the Tamil coast and those engaged in pearl fishery operations also preferred to settle in the area since it had so many advantages. Vessels could be easily manoeuvred into anchorage during high tide and small sailing vessels and *kattumarams* could be launched into the sea as tidal waves surfed easily into the waters. These months were dangerous only during heavy monsoon rains. The port of Kayal has been variously referred to as Kahal,[37] Chalia,[38] Chayal,[39] Cael,[40] and Kia-i-le.[41] Commodities such as silk, aromatic roots and pearls were exported from Kayal to Syria, Iraq and Khurasan. This port was so prominent that it figures in the travelogues of Macro Polo (1293) and in the writings of Rasid-al-Din (1300) and Wassaf (1328).[42] Rasid-al-Din records that chinaware was brought by junks to this port where it was exchanged for goods from the Islamic world. The arrival of junks laden with chinaware at this port and its thriving commerce have also been described in the travelogues of Abdul Razzack (1442-4), Nicolo Conti (1420), Chengo-Ho and Ma-huan, the famous travellers of the fifteenth century.[43]

The importance of Bay of Bengal grew when the rise of trade with China and Arabia led to the increased use of gold and copper in the Tamil country. Gold of many different varieties in use, such as kudinaikkal (standard gold),[44] cempon[45] and maripon,[46] is mentioned. A merchant of Arivur is said to have offered a gift of gold weighing 11 *kalanju* and 6 *manjadi* in 1138.[47] When Kulottunga III issued an order levying *pon vari* (tax on gold), the village assembly of Tiruvottiyur is said to have refused to pay the tax. Therefore, he arrested the members of the village assembly, imposed the tax and collected it in 1212.[48] In 1224 fines on criminals were imposed at 3 *kalanju* of gold.[49] Taxes were also levied on gold at places like Kottur, Uthattur and Ilupaikudi.[50] Another merchant hailing from Arivur also made a gift of gold in 1295.[51] Even gold coins such as *pon, kanaku, varahan* and *kasu* were minted by the Pandyas and put into circulation. One *pon* was equal to 52 grains of gold.[52] When the long-distance trade declined in the thirteenth century, merchants conducted interregional trade in the Bay of Bengal.

During the medieval period, hinterland merchants dealing in different commodities lived in different streets in Tirunelveli.[53] These traders were classified into various categories such as retail, wholesale, indigenous and foreign.[54] The cloth merchants were known as *arugai vaniyan*.[55] They sold *pudavai* at many places.[56] Some of the merchants specialized in the pearl trade and one finds mention of pearl merchants of Kaliyamangal.[57] Thus commodity specialization of merchants in trade come into vogue.[58] Some of the merchants engaged in trade at Ilayangudi during the period (1215) must have prospered well as they could purchase lands with the profit they earned from trade.[59] A Pandya inscription from Periyaplayam gives a list of merchants who came from distant places for trade. The names include a Pillai *nadu* and an Eralapuram merchant called Kuthan Kannan, besides others hailing from Turavaalaur, Sundarapandyapuram, Gangaikondacholapuram, Telingakulakalapuram, Vanchi managar (Karur?), Karrupur, Aimpozhil, Kodumbalur and Desiyyakondapattinam.[60] The age and property of a merchant were taken into account for the purpose of tax assessment in Mahabalipuram. It is recorded that those who were above the age of sixteen and did not possess land were to pay half *kalanju* per annum, and landless traders who conducted trade as paid labourers (*kuulikku*) were taxed at the rate of one-eighth of a *pon* annually.[61]

There were inland merchant guilds, i.e. the *vaniya gramattar* which extended its activities to eighteen districts, known as *padinen bhumi* (eighteen areas), located on the banks of the river Kaveri.[62] The merchants of this trade guild lived exclusively in streets called *perunderuvu*.[63] In these places, *ayathu kadavar* collected taxes form the merchant families.[64] The revenue collectors were called *acchu petra peralar*, according to an inscription ascribed to the year AD 1236-7.[65] In some places they were called peralars[66] as evident from an epigraph dated 1303. From every individual Chetti merchant residing in the trading centre of Kudimiyanmalai and its environs within a distance of 24 *kaadam*, a sum of half a *panam* per head per annum was collected.[67] The multiple point and single point taxes collected from the inland Chetti merchants are mentioned as *chetti vanigar* per *kadamai*,[68] and *chetti vari*.[69] The Chettis at Tiruvottiyur paid such taxes.[70] Thus the development of production and exchange in the hinterland contributed towards the growth of the economy of this period.

Rise of the Marakkayars and the Development of Coastal Trade

The economic activity of the Tamil Muslims, known as the Marakkayars, is important in this period. The term '*marakkalarayan*' found in the Barus inscription could perhaps be explained as referring to the indigenized Arabian Muslim traders. Islam had spread on the Tamil Coast and in a few ports Muslim merchants developed trade. This attracted the Delhi sultanates and in fact, Malik Kafur returned to Delhi on 18 October 1311 with 96,000 bars of gold on 312 elephants along with many boxes of pearls and precious stones from Madurai as recorded in the Muslim chronicles.[71] Jalauddin Ahsan was appointed governor of the Pandya region in AD 1329-30 and it became one of the twenty-three provinces of the Tughlaq empire. The maritime trade of the Tamil coast at this time extended from Kollam to Nilawar (Nellore), when the Delhi sultanate ruled from Madurai between 1333 and 1378. The Delhi sultans were only interested in the wealth of the Tamil country and did not have a trade policy.

During the Muslim occupation of the Tamil country (1323-71), Islamic traders settled in the port of Nagore which was strategically situated (10°4′N and 79°50′E) close to the mouth of the Kudavaiyar. Following the decline of Nagapattinam, which flourished under the Cholas, Nagore emerged as an important centre of trade in the fourteenth century. The diary of Vasco da Gama also confirms the importance of Nagore for the Marakkayar community in the late fifteenth century.[72] *Sonaka vari* was a tax collected from the Arabs who traded with the ports of the Tamil coast in the medieval period.[73]

Virapandyanpattinam was another important port that flourished[74] at this time and it was frequented by Arab Muslim merchants as well as Tamil Muslim merchants known as Marakkayars. Qadi Abu Bakar, the Muslim chief of the port, issued an order in 1387, that out of the proceeds from the sale of commodities in this port, a tax of a quarter of one per cent was to be paid for the maintenance of the Jumma Masjid of the place.[75]

Marakkayars had also settled at Kunimedu (11°56) located close to the port of Sadras in the southern direction. This port began to emerge as in noted by Girodamo di Santo Stefano, the Italian traveller who sailed from there. It became the embarkation point on the Coromandel coast and a famous harbour in the fifteenth century.[76] The word Kunimedu is probably derived from the Tamil word *kazhimar* which indicates the mouth of a lagoon. The diary of Vasco da Gama and his account of Tome Pires also mentions this Muslim port as Cunjmeyra.[77]

Inter-Regional Trade under the Telugu Cholas and the Samburvarayas

The emergence of the port of Krishnapattinam (in the present Gudur taluk of Nellore district), alias Kolliturai, as an important trading centre is attributed to the Telugu Cholas. It was an active port patronized by the Telugu Cholas, who ruled the Paka *nadu* region (north Pennar valley) from the twelfth century to the fourteenth century. The Ganda Gopala rulers like Vijaya Ganda Gopala (1250-91) and Raja Ganda Gopala (1291-20) encouraged maritime trade in the region. The port of Krishnapattinam was known as Gandagopalapattinam named as it was after Raja Ganda Gopala, the renowned Telugu Chola ruler. During Vijayanagara period it was known as Rajavibhaadanpattinam.[78] Inscriptions record that a body of merchants in this region had been very powerful. In 1304-05, this merchant body decided on certain rules for conducting trade. One of their members, falsely believed to be a traitor, was murdered. Therefore the trade union while condoning the death openly gave a document to the family of the deceased and his descendants by which they could carry on trade in the future free of duty.[79] The same body of merchants in another case presented a document to another individual on 15 October 1322 as a token of their satisfaction and praise for having murdered two corrupt toll collectors of the region.[80] Various levies were also imposed on different commodities imported into the port of Kolliturai which included, among others, those charged on goods brought by *marakkalam* (ships) *patavu* (boat) and *kalavan* (raft).[81]

Devipattinam, otherwise called Ulagamadevipattinam[82] (in 1242), was an important port in Sevvirukkai *nadu*. Records mention that the pearl trade flourished in Devipattinam in 1216-

41.[83] About a century later, in 1348, it was known as Srivallabhapattinam after King Srivallabha under whose rule the port developed to extend its trade in spices from Malabar and areca nuts from Sri Lanka.[84] Maritime trade was conducted by seagoing vessels of various sizes categorized as big and small. An entry tax of a quarter *panam* was levied on *tonis*. On a *chitturu*, which was larger than a *toni*, a tax of half a *panam* was levied. It is mentioned that the Hindu merchant guild of *nanadesi* was engaged in the organization of overseas trade.[85] The popular *tonis* were used for transporting goods in Devipattinam.[86]

Rajanarayana, the Sambuvaraya ruler (AD 1337-61), desired to develop a port in his kingdom. The port of Sadiravaachanpattinam (Sadras) was renamed Rajanarayananpattinam after him.[87] An inscription dated 5 February 1353 mentions the various tolls and duties levied on articles of merchandise at this port where merchants from many places came to trade.[88] The commodities of maritime trade in this port included pearls, long cloth and other varieties of textiles.[89] With the decline of the Sambuvarayas and the advent of the Vijayanagara rulers in this region we find that Kumara Kampanna, the general of the Vijayanagara army had consolidated the payment of taxes by the *kaikolars* of Thirukazhukundaram who took the cloth to the port of Sadras for sale and export.[90]

Maritime Trade and the Rulers of Vijayanagara

Bukka I, who desired to develop overseas trade, extended the boundary of the Vijayanagara empire in the Tamil country by annexing the territory of the Sambuvarayas in AD 1361-2. The Alampundi plates of Virupaksha, the son of Harihara II of the Vijayanagara empire, mention that he invaded Sri Lanka in AD 1385 and brought in large booty to his father in the shape of precious stones, crystal, semi-precious stones and jewels.[91] *Narayani Vilasam*, a contemporary literary work, mentions that Harihara II erected a pillar of victory in the island of Sri Lanka.[92]

The rulers of Vijayanagara extended their sway not only in south India but also to countries across the seas, which served as a stimuli for overseas trade and commerce. According to Ferishta, the Muslim chronicler so impressive was the rule of the Vijayanagara kings that the ruler of Sri Lanka was impelled to send his envoy to the Vijayanagara court in 1378. Rich presents came from the court of Sri Lanka to the Vijayanagara emperor annually.[93] Fernão Nuniz, the Portuguese traveller, also confirms that the rulers of Sri Lanka paid tributes to Devaraya II. This is corroborated by an inscription found at Nagar in the Chingleput area, where it is recorded that Devaraya II had received a tribute from Sri Lanka.[94]

The port of Pulicat (Pazhaverkadu) (13°29′N and 80°50′E), situated close to the mouth of the river Araniyar, was developed during reign of Devaraya II (1422-46) At that time it was called Anandarayanpattinam.[95] A Telugu inscription found on the southern wall of Adinarayanaswamy temple at Pulicat reveals that the port was also called *pralaya kaveri* since it was often flooded by sea water. Pulicat greatly facilitated sailing vessels seeking shelter during the floods.

The extension of the Vijayanagara rule into Tamil country in the fourteenth century also witnessed further growth of the port of Thirumalairayanpattinam (10°53′N) located close to Nagore that it emerged as the main port of trade during the Vijayanagara period is confirmed by Portuguese sources.[96] It is referred to Portuguese documents as Trimenapatão. Saluva Tirumalaideva Maharaya (1450-86), one of the *Mahamandaleswara* of Vijayanagara kings, who ruled the Kaveri delta region comprising Papanasam, Pattisavaram, Tirukattupalli, Srimushnam, Kudumiyanmalai and Srirangam areas, named this port after himself and called it Tirumalairayanpattinam. This port was situated between two rivers, and he carried out improvements to Thirumalairajanar in the north and Puravudaiyar in the south.[97] The rice-cultivating hinterland was thus connected to the port by waterways to bring paddy and rice for the purpose of export.[98]

Revival of Overseas Trade with China under the Later Pandyas

During Ming dynasty (1369-1644) in China, a strict policy was followed on maritime affairs to deal with foreign kingdoms engaged in maritime trade with China. It was stipulated that all those foreign states wishing to trade with China should pay a tribute to the Ming court. Further, they had to accept the Chinese calendar and investiture, recognizing Chinese overlordship. Maritime trade almost became a state monopoly in China and the Chinese ruler preferred to deal himself with foreign kingdoms. Overseas trade in China in this period was state sponsored while on the Tamil coast it was left to private initiative.

The year 1369 marked the beginning of the Ming dynasty's keen interest in overseas trade with the Tamil coast. Min-tai-tsu, the first emperor, sent envoys regularly to all foreign countries, deputed Liu-shu-mien as the royal messenger to visit the Chola kingdom. With the increase in overseas trade during this period, the emperor is reported to have appointed three superintendents of maritime trade in 1374. They were stationed at Ning-bo, Quanzhou and Guangzhu. The last one was responsible for receiving the trade missions that arrived from Siam, India and Arabia. From then on Chinese ships started arriving at the pearl fishery coast. A study of the Geniza letters written by Jewish merchants shows that Chinese porcelain was taken to Fatimids in Egypt through the ports of the Bay of Bengal as the Chinese merchants embarked from there.[99]

The reigns of Jatilavarman Kulasekhara (1395-1411), Maravarman Srivallabha (1402-44), Jatilavarman Parakirama (1401-34), Maravarman Vikrama Pandya (1404-45) and Maravarman Vira Pandya (1421-46) witnessed the development of overseas trade in the pearl fishery coast. It is learnt that pearls, corals, precious stones, textiles both cotton and silk, animals and aromatic roots were exported from the ports of the Tamil coast to China. It is recorded that on 17 October 1408, Zheng He and others were sent as envoys to the ports of Periyapattinam and Kayal.[100] In return a tributary mission was sent on 5 August 1411 from Kayal by the ruler of the Tamil coast whose, name, however, is not mentioned in the Chinese sources. Again on 18 December 1412, Zheng He and others were sent as envoys to the port of Kayal and a team of Tamil envoys sailed from Kayal on 26 February 1421 to pay tribute to the emperor of China. Once again, on 24 October 1423, the Tamil envoys reached China and paid tribute. Later Zheng He and others were sent again on 29 June 1430 to the port of Kayal. On 14 September 1433 and on 11 August 1436 Tamil envoys were sent from Kayal to pay tribute to the Chinese emperor.[101]

Chinese sources such as the *Xipang Chaogung-Dianlu* (Records of Tributes Received from Countries of the Western Ocean) by Huang Shengoeng, the *Xiyang Fanquozhi* (Records of the Foreign Countries in the Western Ocean) by Ging Zhen, written in 1434, the *Xing Cha Shenglan* (Overall Survey of the Statecraft) by Fe X, written in 1436, Mahuan's *Yiu-Yieh-Lan* or *Yingyai Sheng Alan* (Overall Survey of the Ocean), dated 1451, and Zheng He Sheng's, *Zen Yi Jua* (A Collection References from Zheng He's Voyages to the Western Ocean) throw a flood of light on the overseas commerce conducted between China and the Tamil coast.[102] These sources mention the dates of commencement of such Chinese voyages, dates of returning voyages, dates on which imperial orders were issued along with the dates of visits. It was during this period that Chinese trade with the Tamil coast reached its peak, with as many as seven ambassadorial missions organized and led by the Grand Eunuch Zheng He between 1405 and 1433, as ordered by the Ming emperors of China. Large quantities of Chinese pottery were imported at this time into the Tamil coast.

The port of Periyapattinam, mentioned in an inscription of Maravarman Sundara Pandya, emerged at this time.[103] Marco Polo noted that pearl fishery was done on the coast of Rameshwaram at a depth of not more than ten or twelve fathoms. The boats for pearl fishing used to assemble, first, at a place called Battala (probably Vedalai).[104] Ibn Battuta, the Moroccan traveller had visited the port of Fattan, identified with Periyapattinam, located at about 6 km south of Ramanathapuram in the Gulf of Mannar. Ibn Battuta's ship reached Battala, which was an anchoring point then. The port of Periyapattinam was also called Parakiramapattinam. An inscription from Maramangalam near Tirunelveli mentions merchants going from there to trade with Periyapattinam.[105] These stone records also mention several names of pearl merchants.[106] Further, an epigraph dated AD 1262 in Thirthandathanam mentions various merchants guilds like *anjuvannam*, *manigramattar* and *valarjiyar* of south Sri Lanka which were interested in the pearl trade of the region.[107]

Tomb inscriptions in Periyapattinam tell us that even the Jews had trade contacts with Periyapattinam.[108]

The Chinese source *Dao-Yi-Zhi-lue* (Synoptical Account of Foreign Records) by Wang Dayuan, ascribed to AD 1350, mentions Da Badan, which is identified as Periyapattinam by Noboru Karashima.[109] The discovery of Chinese celadon potsherds found there originating from the longquun kilns of the thirteenth century and the blue and white pottery from the Jingdezhen kilns of the fourteenth century confirm that brisk trade flourished between Periyapattinam and China.

Shifting Contours of Trade from the Bay of Bengal to Malabar

The rise of the ports of Kozhikodu and Kochi accelerated the movement of merchandize and merchants from the Tamil coast in the Bay of Bengal to the Malabar coast in the Arabian Sea region. The capital city of Vijayanagara was located in the interior and far from the coast, which necessitated the development of ports for maritime trade in the fourteenth century. It appears that the Chettis shifted their operations from the Bay of Bengal to the ports on the west coast and further extended their commercial operations with Arabia. Anbarasan, a Chetti merchant from the *Cholamandalam*, on a voyage from the Red Sea via Malabar, had his ship so overloaded with gold that it was in danger of sinking. He therefore left a large treasure chest of gold in the safe custody of Samudri (Zamorin) in a stone cellar dug exclusively for this purpose in Kozhikodu. The merchant on his return in AD 1493 offered the Samudri, one half of the treasure. The latter refused to accept the gift but stated that he had done no more than what was expected of him as ruler. Thus the protection extended to the Bay of Bengal merchants facilitated trade in Malabar prompting the Tamil merchants to move their trading operations there.[110]

The rise of Kilakkarai (90°15′N and 180°15′E) as a port can be traced back to a medieval coastal settlement called Anuthogaimangalam.[111] It was also known as Ninaithathai Muditha Pillayarpattinam after the presiding deity of the temple located in the village.[112] The pearl fishery conducted in here attracted the

Arab traders who eventually settled down towards the south of Arunthogaimangalam calling it Kilakkarai (the settlement by the seashore), which eventually emerged as an important trading centre towards the end of the fifteenth century. The neighbouring port of Periyapattinam went into decline, when the Chinese traders stopped visiting it. In fact, in the fourteenth century the Chinese preferred to conduct trade with the international marts of Kollam and Kozhikodu on the Malabar coast where the agents of Mecca and the merchants of Jeddah assembled. The Muslim traders in the south-eastern coast of India also exported textiles and pearls to these ports at the end of the fifteenth century when operations had reached their peak.

It is possible that the shifting of the overseas trade from the ports of the Tamil oast to the Malabar coast led to the decline of active overseas trade in the ports of the former in the fifteenth century. In fact as many as ten ambassadorial trade missions were sent from China to Kozhikodu between AD 1402 and 1433.[113] The Chinese also visited Kochi from AD 1404 to AD 1433.[114] The fact that pearls and corals found on the south-eastern coast of Tamil Nadu were traded in Kochi confirms the gradual movement of commerce from the eastern Tamil coast to the western Malabar coast of India.[115] Further, the Tamil speaking Chettis, referred to as Zhedi by the Chinese, were merchants by tradition, and monopolized the trade in gems and pearls both in Kochi and in Kozhikodu. This again supports the view of shifting commerce.[116] According to Chinese sources, even textiles from the Tamil coast were received in Malabar for export to China.[117] It is known for certain that Malabar did not produce textiles. Among the varieties of textiles exported to China were *bairami* cloth (*bai-lan-lu*), printed blankets, printed red silk handkerchieves (Xiang-Bu). Cotton handkerchieves painted with human and animal figures such as horses and elephants were produced in the Tamil coast.[118]

It may be said with some certainty that the medieval seaborne trade of the Bay of Bengal, chiefly in horses was conducted through Red Sea ports like Jeddah, Mecca, Mocha and Aden by Arab traders, under the Pandyas too horse trade flourished with Persian Gulf ports such as Basra, Bandar Abbas and Ormuz. Evidence does not support the existence of trade between the Bay of Bengal and ports of the east African coast such as Mombasa, Melindi, Mogadishu, Sofala and Mozambique in this period. The maritime trade of the Bay of Bengal in the East was conducted with the ports of the Malay-Indonesian archipelago and China.

The ports on the Tamil coast emerged as intermediary and intertranshipment centres in the East-West commercial axis of long-distance trade in the Indian Ocean. In the fifteenth century, with the cessation of long-distance trade, commercial activities in the Tamil coast became regionalized. Ports in the Tamil Coast became mere stopping points for ships destined for Kozhikodu, Kochi and Kollam. Spices to China were directly exported from Malabar and not sent through the ports of the Tamil coast. In these circumstances, except for Pulicat and Kayal, the ports in the Tamil country had little opportunity for direct overseas trade transactions. Another feature of this development was the migration and settlement of the Tamil-speaking Chettis and Marakkayars in Malabar from the ports of Tamil coast. The extension of Vijayanagara rule in the Tamil country attracted traders to the island of Sri Lanka to trade in precious stones. The arrival of Arab and Chinese traders propelled the Malabar coastal region into the international web of commerce, gradually displacing the Tamil coast. With the rise of the port of Melaka at the end of the fourteenth century, Chettis began to trade and they were responsible for the expansion of international trade from the Tamil coast. However, during the second half of the fifteenth century, the maritime network of Tamil Nadu acquired a regional character with the decline of long-distance international trade and the growth of regional trade with Sri Lanka and Malabar. The medieval rulers of the country were concerned only with enriching their royal treasury by attracting foreign trade. The Kovilpatti inscription enumerates four *nagarams* on the east coast. Merchants dealing in various goods living in the same region formed their own guilds and these regional guilds were known as Mahanadu Chettis. The Piranmalai inscription in Ramnad mentions sixteen *nagarams* where groups of merchants dealt with specialized commodities. These merchants, dealing in only one type of goods such as cloth, betel leaf or oil, formed themselves into guilds.[119] Thus one finds that many of these hinterland settlements of the trading guilds had become urbanized through overseas trade before the advent of the Europeans.

Ravi Arvind Palat and Immanuel Wallerstein opine that before capitalism there were world empires and world economies. According to them the Indian Ocean is an example of world economy, and they place it around 1500, with the growth of trade and accumulation of riches in the commercialized area of Coromandel (besides Gujarat) and tie this up with rice cultivation.[120] This does not necessarily mean that there was an increasingly singular division of labour as referred to in the concept of a world economy. The situation in the Bay of Bengal was different from Europe: in Europe a capitalist world economy emerged while in India it did not, especially as there was no real subscription of labour to capital which is a crucial part of the development of capitalism, and this is questionable.[121] What happened before AD 1500 in the Bay of Bengal was not touched on by Palat and Wallerstein in their study and this is very significant in the study of world economy.

During the Chola period there emerged worldwide trade—not literally incorporating every single part of the globe then known but at least being carried on throughout Asia—with the establishment of a trade axis which ran all the way from China to West Asia. There was a big leap forward when trade networks expanded and deepened, especially in the respective regions of Raja Raja Chola (AD 985-1014), Rajendra Chola (AD 1014-44) and Kulotunga Chola (AD 1070-1120). These long-distance trade networks only became possible with the rise of the very large Chola empire, and the Cholas had developed communication and transportation to facilitate worldwide trade. Maritime trade became regularized between the Red Sea, the Persian Gulf region and the Bay of Bengal, between South-East Asia and the Bay of Bengal and between China and the Bay of Bengal. Kulotunga Chola abolished customs duties and encouraged trade for which known as he was *sungam thavirtha cholan*.

There was an economic revolution in the Chola period involving agriculture, the textile industry, money and credit, transport and trade, both inland and overseas. The economy became more monetized with a greater volume of money in circulation. This money economy even penetrated the peasant villages. Markets (*nagarams*), according to Kenneth R. Hall, proliferated and became hierarchically organized.[122] This did not provide the basis for the development of capitalism in the region but urbanization, a function of the increasing commercialization, took place in a more striking manner in this period. At this time, Tamil society was economically advanced in the Bay of Bengal region. The rule of the medieval Pandyas allowed the economic trend to continue. However, beginning sometime in the fourteenth century the Tamil region began to decline and stagnate economically and with the decline in trade with China, merchants gradually withdrew from maritime trade. The region became increasingly inward looking, a process which had become fairly complete by the middle of the fifteenth century. The main reason for the economic downturn was the absence of a strong political power in the Tamil country.

With the establishment of Vijayanagara rule in the Tamil country, the economy began to develop once again but in a different way. The city of Vijayanagara became the core area for accumulating precious metals, whereas, the Tamil country became the peripheral area and paid revenues and gave up metals, gems and pearls.[123] The identification of core and peripheral areas is made here only to emphasise the underdevelopment. A significant feature in the Bay of Bengal world system is that the theory of Palat and Wallerstein cannot be imported wholesale into the study because one needs to distinguish between kin-based, tributary and modern capitalist world systems. It is also important to question here whether or not all world systems had core-periphery relations.[124] The trade theories do not seem to be very satisfactory and they are not intended as general explanations of the worldwide emergence of the state but focus on the rise of the state in a specific region. The more recent trade theories emphasizing elite exchange for prestige goods seem even more dubious. If the regional exchange of basic and bulk goods such as rice and textiles in the Bay of Bengal is not to be regarded as vital to state formation, it is even more difficult to see how the exchange of exotic items can be of more than minor significance. Andre Gunder Frank argues that there has been continuously, for some 5000 years, a single world system which now encompasses the whole world.[125]

In south India, merchant capitalism emerged during the medieval period and it could be said to be a primitive accumulation of capital. Merchant capitalism involved only the circulation or exchange of commodities and those who sold them were not their producers. Industrial capitalism for Karl Marx depended on three things: private ownership of the means of production by a social class known as the bourgeoisie, the existence of wage labour as the basis of production, and the profit motive and long-term accumulation of capital as the driving aim of production. These things were very much present in the Tamil coast and hinterland, especially in the textile industry, in some form. Max Weber was like Marx, adamant about the importance of free labour and opined that unfree labour could not make capitalism possible. Although Wallerstein had himself worked in the Marxian tradition, his notion of capitalism is in some respects un-Marxist. He makes no mention of the need for free labour. He rejects Marx's distinction between merchant and industrial capital, and the so-called industrial capital, according to him, was simply a phase in the development of world capitalism. For Wallerstein, capitalism is simply an economic system in which commodities are produced for sale in a market and in which the economic objective is to realize a profit and to accumulate capital over time.

It is to be pointed out here that there are also earlier forms of capitalism which can be called proto-capitalism. For Maurice Dobb, the distinction between merchant and industrial capital is relevant since he is a Marxist.[126] He opines that the beginning of merchant capitalism took place during the fourteenth and fifteenth centuries with the rise of towns within the context of the breakdown of the feudal mode of production. The word *Mudal* in Tamil for capital is used and *Kaikola Mudali* or *Mudaliar* refers to the textile industrial capitalists in the medieval period. There were also the people called *Vellala Mudaliars* who owned lands and in due course of time accumulated wealth through trade in agricultural products.[127] The early bourgeoisies in south India drew wealth primarily from trade rather than production. Traders of various towns, as in Europe, invested in properties. One generally finds the emergence of merchant capitalists who even turned towards control over production in for instance, the textiles trade before the advent of the Europeans in the Bay of Bengal.

Fernand Braudel also prefers an early starting point for the beginnings of capitalism although he does suggest that this was still a form of proto-capitalism rather than capitalism proper.[128] The capitalistic developments of medieval south India did not differ much in a critical way from what began to develop after the advent the Portuguese in the sixteenth century. Merchants focused heavily on trade in staples and not in luxuries or preciosities, and thus they formed the basis for a world economy in the Bay of Bengal. Capitalism emerged as, and continued to expand and evolve as a world system. The Bay of Bengal world economy was politically decentralized and was held together by relations of economic production and exchange. As a world economy, capitalism in the Bay of Bengal contained three major components of zones. The core consisted of Tamil society which had the greatest economic power and which was also the most prosperous zone within the entire Bay of Bengal world economy. Since it concentrated on the superior quality of textile production activities that went on with the system, it also used the most advanced forms of weaving and dyeing technology. The medieval Tamil society also contained the most politically and militarily powerful states such as the Cholas, Pandyas and the Vijayanagra empires within the world system.

The peripheral region was that of the Telugu country invaded by the core, especially by Rajendra Chola. Kultounga Chola also invaded the territory of the Kalinga rulers and exploited the coasts of Andhra and Orissa, the least economically developed area. Production of commodities for sale on the world market, such as diamond mining, took place in south India under the patronage of the Vijayanagara rulers and diamonds were exported to Europe.[129] However, there was a flourishing trade in luxuries which was still outside the system. The peripheral regions of the Andhra and Orissa coasts were politically and economically weak and so it was possible for them to be invaded by the Cholas. The first capitalist state was that of the Cholas, which also happened to be the Indian power to establish numerous merchant settlements colonies in the regions of South-East Asia and East Asia. By 1350 the Tamil world system had substantially disintegrated on the discontinuation of trade with China. Thus one can identify the existence of a world system within which different things went on at different times. The first phase of capitalist world economy in the Tamil coast began approximately in the tenth century and lasted till the thirteenth century. The second phase was marked by the expansion of the world system under the powerful of Vijayanagara empire and it coincided with arrival of the Portuguese, which will be discussed later in this book. As mentioned earlier medieval rulers of the Tamil country were concerned only with enriching their royal treasury by attracting foreign traders. Along with foreign trade, the domestic trade in the Tamil hinterland also flourished.[130] In this context it would be meaningful to examine how the Portuguese ruling class in Europe ventured into commerce in the name of the king initially, and later allowed private traders also to participate in the growing trade in the Tamil region. It would also be interesting to inquire into the Portuguese sway over the seas and the control they could exercise over the merchants, commodities and ports on the Tamil coast. How the Portuguese erupted into the Tamil coast and discovered the Hindus and Muslim traders in commerce, and how they fitted into the then existing commercial web operating on the Tamil coast merits a close examination.

NOTES

1. 'The Guide to Geography' prepared by Claudius Ptolemy in the middle of the second century was perhaps the first text that gave definite information on the ports of the Tamil coast to the Western world. The discovery of a large number of late Roman copper coins found on the Tamil coast belonging to the fourth and fifth centuries AD is ample proof of the continuity of maritime trade. See, K. Karttunen, *India and Early Greek Literature*, Helsinki, 1989.
2. Himanshu Prabha Ray, *The Winds of Change: Buddhism and the Early Maritime Links of South Asia*, Delhi, 1990; see also, *Monastery and Guild: Commerce under the Satavahanas*, Delhi, 1986; R. Champakalakshmi, *Trade, Ideology and Urbanization: South India 300 B.C. to A.D. 1300*, Delhi, 1996, pp. 182-5.
3. D.C. Sircar, *Select Inscriptions Bearing on Indian History and Civilization*, vol. 1, 2nd edn., Calcutta, 1965, p. 217.

4. Hara Prasad Ray, *South India During the 15th Century: Studies in Sino-Indian Relations*, UGC Report, Jawaharlal Nehru University, 1996, p. 19; for the list of missions see p. 18. See also his work, *Trade and Diplomacy Between India and China: A Study of Bengal during the 15th Century*, Delhi, 1993.
5. K.A. Nilakanta Sastri, 'Takuapa and its Tamil Inscription', *Journal of the Malaysian Branch of the Royal Asiatic Society* (*JAMBRAS*), vol. 22, 1949, pp. 25-30.
6. Fernand Braudel, *Capitalism and Civilization: 15th, 18th Century*, Sian Reynolds (tr.), 3 vols., London, 1981-4.
7. *Epigraphia Indica* (hereafter *EI*), vol. 22, pp. 213-16.
8. Lawrence Briggs, *The Ancient Khmer Empire*, Philadelphia, 1951.
9. *South Indian Inscriptions* (hereafter *SII*), vol. 2, pp. 105-9.
10. Bagchi, 'Chinese Coins from Tanjore', *Sino-Indian Studies*, vol. 1, October 1994, pp. 60-3.
11. Hara Prasad Ray, *South India,* pp. 27-8, 31.
12. *Annual Report on Epigraphy* (hereafter *ARE*), 166 of 1965-6.
13. George W. Spencer, *The Politics of Expansion: The Chola Conquest of Sri Lanka and Srivijaya*, Madras, 1983.
14. For a translation of the text, see Hara Prasad Ray, *South India*, pp. 145-6.
15. The date usually given for the foundation of the port of Kollam is AD 825 which is the first year of the Kollam era. See, K.A. Nilakanta Sastri, *Foreign Notices of South India from Megasthenes to Mahuan,* Madras, 1972, p. 150.
16. Hara Prasad Ray, *South India*, p. 61.
17. W.W. Rockhill, 'Note on the Relation and Trade of China with the Eastern Archipelago and the Coast of the Indian Ocean during the Fourteenth Century', in *Toungpao,* vol. 16, 1914, pp. 419-47; vol. 17, 1915, pp. 61-159.
18. Ibid.
19. Tansen, 'Maritime Relations between China and the Chola Kingdom, AD 850-1279', in K.S. Mathew (ed.), *Mariners, Merchants and Oceans: Studies in Maritime History*, Delhi, 1995, pp. 25-42.
20. Prapancha, *Java in the 14th Century*, vol. 3, p. 98, Canto 83, Stanza 4.
21. *ARE*, 292 of 1927-8; *SII*, vol. I, no. 239; Thinakaran, *The Second Pandyan Empire 1190-1312*, Madurai, 1987.
22. F. Hirth and W.W. Rockhill, *Chau-Ju-ka: His Work on the Chinese and Arab Trade in the Twelfth and Thirteenth Centuries Entitled Chu-fan-chi*, St. Petersburg, 1911, p. 95.
23. Ibid., p. 94.
24. Roderich Ptak, 'Yuan and Early Ming Notices on the Kayal Area in South India', *Bulletin de Ecole francaise d' Extreme-Orient*, vol. 80 (1), 1993, pp 137-56.
25. E. Hirth and W.W. Rockhill, *Chan-Ju-Ka,* op. cit., p. 19.

26. K.A. Nilakanta Sastri, *Foreign Notices on South India*, p. 115.
27. The first hoard of coins belongs to the period between AD 713 and 1241, include coins such as those of Kaiyun (AD 713-42) and of Kaihi (AD 1237-41). The second hoard of 1,822 coins belongs to the period up to the reign of Ching Tan (585-1275). The hoard contained 323 coins ranging from the period 142 BC to AD 1252, along with the coins of the Zhan rulers Wei, Tsin and Hu Wei.
28. K.N. Chaudhuri, *Trade and Civilization in the Indian Ocean*, Cambridge, 1985, p. 9.
29. The value of one dinar of gold was equated to two *saggi*.
30. See, Elliot and Dowson, *The History of India as Told by its Own Historians*, vol. 3, London, 1871, p. 32.
31. *ARE*, 556 of 1904.
32. Ibid., 35 of 1914; *IPS*, no. 559.
33. *ARE*, 161 of 1907.
34. *Inscriptions of Pudukottai State* (hereafter *IPS*), ed. K.R. Srinivasa Aiyar, Pudukottai, 1929, *IPS*, no. 172 (1216) (Annavasal).
35. *South Indian Inscriptions* (hereafter *SII*), vol. 16, no. 378, Delhi, 1890-1990.
36. *ARE*, 192 of 1926 (Neduvayil).
37. Rashid-al-Din, see Elliot and Dowson, *The History of India as told by its own Historians*, vol. 3, London, 1871, p. 69.
38. Nicolo Conti. See R.H. Major (ed.), *India in the Fifteenth Century*, Delhi, 1974, p. 7.
39. Ludovico di Varthema, *The Travels of Ludovico di Varthema in Egypt, Syria, Arabia desert and Arabia Felix in Persia, India and Ethiopia AD 1503-1508*, trans. J.W. Jones, ed. G.P. Badger, London, 1928, p. 95.
40. Duarte Barbosa, *The Book of Duarte Barbosa: An Account of the Countries Bordering the Indian Ocean and their Inhabitants* (trans.) M.L. Dames, London, 1918, vol. 1, p. 82.
41. Sastri, *Foreign Notices on South India,* op. cit., p. 115.
42. A.C. Moule and P. Pelliot, *Marco Polo, The Description of the World*, London, 1938, pp. 412-14; Wassaf, see Elliot, *The History of India*, pp. 3 and 69. See also Sharad Shokoohy, 'Architecture of the Muslim Port of Qail on the Coromandal Coast, South India', *South Asian Studies*, vol. 9, 1993, pp. 137-66.
43. R.H. Major, *India in the Fifteenth Century*, pp. 33-49, Sastri, *Foreign Notices on South India*, p. 179.
44. *ARE*, 144 of 1925 (1101).
45. *SII*, vol. 8, no. 151 (1202).
46. *ARE*, 166 of 1956-7.
47. Ibid., 67 of 1986, 464 of 1958-9.
48. *SII*, vol. 8, no. 77 (1247).
49. *ARE*, 202 of 1912.
50. Ibid., 318 of 1923.

51. *IPS*, no. 234.
52. *SII*, vol. 14, no. 238.
53. *Travancore Archaeological Series* (hereafter *TAS*), vol. 12 (1085); *Kanyakumari Mavattla Kalvettugal* (hereafter *KK*), 3 vols., Madras, 1990, see no. 121 of 1968.
54. *SII*, vol. 5, nos. 427 and 447.
55. *ARE*, 7 of 1936-7, 44 of 1936-7, 50 of 1936-7; 284 of 1964-5.
56. TAS, vol. 4, no. 27, pp. 122-3.
57. *ARE*, 490 of 1909.
58. Ibid., 503 of 1958-9.
59. Ibid., 161 of 1907.
60. Ibid., 18 of 1926.
61. M. Ganesan, 'Vaniga Kuzhu Kalvettu', in *Avanam*, vol. 6, July 1995, pp. 36-40.
62. P. Shanmugam, *The Revenue System of the Cholas, 850-1279*, Madras, 1987, pp. 93-4.
63. *ARE*, 337 of 1960-1.
64. Ibid., 125 of 1935-6, 155 of 1935-61, *SII*, VIII, no. 904.
65. Ibid., 276 of 1912.
66. *IPS*, no. 309.
67. Ibid., no. 415.
68. Ibid., no. 285.
69. *SII*, vol. 7, 107
70. *ARE*, 83 of 1941-2.
71. S. Krishnaswamy Ayyengar, *South India and Her Mohammedan Invaders*, Calcutta, 1909, pp. 91-191.
72. Sanjay Subrahmanyam, *The Career and Legend of Vasco da Gama*, Cambridge, 1997; *Diario da Viagem de Vasco da Gama*, Porto, 1945, vol. 2, pp. 250 and 301-3.
73. *SII*, 8, no. 469.
74. *ARE*, 311 of 1964, p. 85. In this inscription the Kollam Year 563 is mentioned and it corresponds to AD 1387.
75. Ibid.
76. R.H. Major (ed.), *India in the Fifteenth Century*, London, 1857, p. 6; Sanjay Subrahmanyam, *Improvising Empire: Portuguese Trade and Settlements in the Bay of Bengal*, Delhi, 1990, p. 9; S. Jeyaseela Stephen, *The Coromandel Coast and its Hinterland: Economy, Society and Political System, 1500-1600*, Delhi, 1997, p. 108.
77. Tome Pires, *The Suma Oriental of Tome Pires and the Book of Rodrigues*, 2 vols., Delhi, 1990, vol. 2, p. 271.
78. Alan Butterworth (ed.), *Copper Plate and Stone Inscriptions*, vol. 1, pp. 411-14. On trade, see also A Collection of the *Inscriptions on Copper Plates and Stones in the Nellore District* (hereafter *IND*), 3 vols., Madras, 1905, vol. 1, G. 39, G. 45, G. 78 and G. 115.
79. *ARE* (CP), 10 of 1918-19.

80. *ARE* (CP), 11 of 1919.
81. *ARE*, 79 (B) of 1963-4. See also, *IND*, pt. I, Gudur, 451, *ARE* 78 (B) of 1963-4.
82. *SII*, vol. 8, no. 404, pp. 214-15.
83. *ARE*, 503 (b) of 1959.
84. *SII*, vol. 8, no. 403, pp. 213-14.
85. *SII*, vol. 8, nos. 403 and 405, pp. 213-15.
86. *SII*, vol. 8, no. 405.
87. *ARE*, 103 of 1933.
88. *South Indian Temple Inscriptions* (hereafter *SITI*), ed. T.N. Subrahmanyam, Madras, 1954-7, Document no. 455-6.
89. *ARE*, 173 of 1932-3.
90. *ARE*, 70 of 1932-3, *SII*, vol. 165.
91. *EI*, 3, p. 228.
92. S. Krishnaswamy Ayyengar, *Sources of Vijayanagara History*, Delhi, 1986, p. 53.
93. Robert Sewell, *A Forgotten Empire*, Delhi, 1962, p. 46.
94. The text of the inscription runs as follows: 'ilam tirai konda' See, *ARE*, 144 of 1916.
95. *SII*, vol. 18, pp. 311-13, lines 23-4.
96. Arquivo Nacional da Torre do Tombo (hereafter *ANTT*), MSS. *Corpo Cronologico* (hereafter CC) t. 2 - 119-103, 2 - 119-104 (1524).
97. T.V. Mahalingam, *Readings in South Indian History*, Madras, 1966 p. 169; *ARE*, 448 of 1922, Papanasam (1453) 524 of 1920 (1450); Pattisvaram, 456 of 1922, Kudumiyanmalai (1458); *SII*, VI, 4, Tirukattupalli (1460); 238 of 1916, Srimushnam (1486).
98. Ibid.
99. S.D. Goitien, 'Letters and Documents on India Trade in Medieval Times', *Islamic Culture,* vol. 37 (3), 1963, pp. 183-205.
100. Ming shi-Lu, Fujiaokanji, Fulu (eds.), *Huang Zhangijan*, Tokyo, 1984. See also Roderich Ptak, 'Yuan and Early Ming Notices', p. 149.
101. Hara Prasad Ray, *Trade and Diplomacy in India-China Relations: A Study of Bengal during the Fifteenth Century*, Delhi, 1991.
102. Yiu-Yieh-lan, (translated by) G. Philip, *Journal of the Royal Asiatic Society of China*, 1951, pp. 523-35.
103. *ARE*, 503 of 1959.
104. *Macro Polo*, *Travels,* vol. 2, pp. 249-50; S. Krishnaswamy Ayyengar, *South India and her Muhamadan Invaders*, p. 64. See also. H.A.R. Gibbs, *Ibn Battuta: Travels in Asia and Africa, 1325-1354,* Delhi, 1986, pp. 261-4. Some scholars have identified the battalar with Kappalar, a creek located in the south-eastern direction. They say that there is a big tank locally called Kappalaru urani, which suggests

that it was once connected with the sea by a channel through which ships must have enterned to anchor. However, this view needs evidence to support it.

105. *ARE*, 157 of 1903.
106. *ARE*, 503 of 1959.
107. *ARE*, 598 of 1926.
108. *ARE*, 35(b) of 1942-3.
109. B.D. Chattopadhyaya, *Coins and Currency Systems in South India,* AD *950-1300*, Delhi, 1977.
110. This episode found in Keraloppathi is summarized by K.V. Krishna Ayyer. *The Zamorins of Calicut from the Earlier Times to* AD *1806*, Calicut, 1938, pp. 85-7. The Tamil Chetti merchants lived in Kozhikodu and in AD 1515 they exported commodities to Aden. See, *CAA*, vol. I, p. 375.
111. *ARE*, 396 of 1907; *SII*, XXIII, no. 396.
112. *ARE*, 398 of 1907; *SII*, XXIII, no. 398.
113. Hara Prasad Ray, *Trade and Diplomacy*. For details, see the list on p. 97.
114. Ibid., p. 108, see also the list on pp. 114-15.
115. Ibid., p. 112.
116. Ibid., p. 113.
117. Ibid., pp. 122-3.
118. Ibid., p. 130.
119. Chillies were introduced and according to sources, by the Portuguese we find Vittala Shenvi, a merchant, specialized in the contract of chillies. See Historical Archives of Goa, Mss. *Moncões do Reino*, vol. 14, fls. 212-13 (AD 1630).
120. Ravi Arvind Palat and Immanuel Wallerstein, 'Of What World System was Pre-1500: India a Part' in Sushil Chaudhuri and Michel Morineau (eds.), *Merchants, Companies and Trade*, Cambridge, 2000.
121. M.N. Pearson, 'The Flows and Effects of Precious Metals in India and China 1500-1700', in *Annales*, 2, 1993, pp. 51-69.
122. Kenneth R. Hall, *Trade and Statecraft in the Age of the Colas*, Delhi, 1987.
123. S. Jeyaseela Stephen, *The Coromandel Coast,* for details on state formation see Chapter one.
124. C. Chase-Dunn, *Global Formations*, Cambridge, 1989, There is a serious danger in applying terms like core and periphery to systems for which they were never originally designed or intended. Janet Abu-Lughod, *Before European Hegemony, The World System* AD *1250-1350*, New York, 1989. Abu-Lughod refers to China as core and Europe as periphery in her study of the thirteenth-and-fourteenth century world systems.

125. Andre Gunder Frank, 'A Theoretical Introduction to 5000 years of World System History', *Review*, 13, pp. 155-248. See also 'A Plea for World System History', *Journal of World History*, 2, pp. 1-28.
126. Maurice Dobb, *Studies in the Development of Capitalism*, New York, 1963.
127. S. Jeyaseela Stephen, *The Coromandel Coast*. See the chapter 'External Trade of Coromandel'. See also, Kanakalatha Mukund, *The Trading World of the Tamil Merchant: Evolution of Merchant Capitalism in the Coromandel*, Hyderabad, 1999.
128. Fernand Braudel, *Capitalism and Civilization*, p. 92.
129. S. Jeyaseela Stephen, 'Diamond Mining Industry, Vijayanagara State Policy and the Regional Economy of Late Medieval South India', *Quarterly Journal of the Mythic Society*, vol. LXXXVI (2), April-June 1995, pp. 81-112.
130. S. Jeyaseela Stephen, 'Medieval Trade of the Tamil Coast and its Hinterland, AD 1280-1500', in *The Indian Historical Review*, vol. 25 (2), January 1999, pp. 1-37.

3

Pearls and Chanks: Portuguese Revenue and Trade

This chapter attempts to explore the struggle of the native rulers to gain control over the pearl fishery region and how the Portuguese also entered the arena in the sixteenth century. It will show how commerce in the ports of Kayal and Kilakkarai and the pearl fishing operations there attracted the Portuguese to the region to establish their settlements in the nearby ports of Punnaikayal and Vedalai from where they could gain entry into the pearl fishery coast during the first half of the sixteenth century (see Map 2). It would also be interesting to examine the events and circumstances that brought the Portuguese to the south-eastern coast of India and from there to other settlements which became flourishing centres of trade under the protection of the Portuguese armada during this period.

THE PORTUGUESE IN KAYAL (1508-1536)

Vasco da Gama mentioned the port of Kayal in his diary and the pearls that were available there in abundance.[1] It is said that the pearls were fished at Kayal which was located fourteen leagues away from the port of Kollam.[2] Dom Manuel (1495-1521), the king of Portugal, therefore evinced keen interest in pearls and ordered Francisco de Almeida (1505-8), the viceroy in India, to acquire both pearls and seed pearls from Kayal and send them to Lisbon. However, Almeida could procure only a small quantity of pearls from Kayal on account of the difficulties, which he explained in his letter to the king dated 20 November 1508.[3]

The port of Kayal slowly developed commercial contacts with the port of Kozhikodu, so much so that the agreement signed

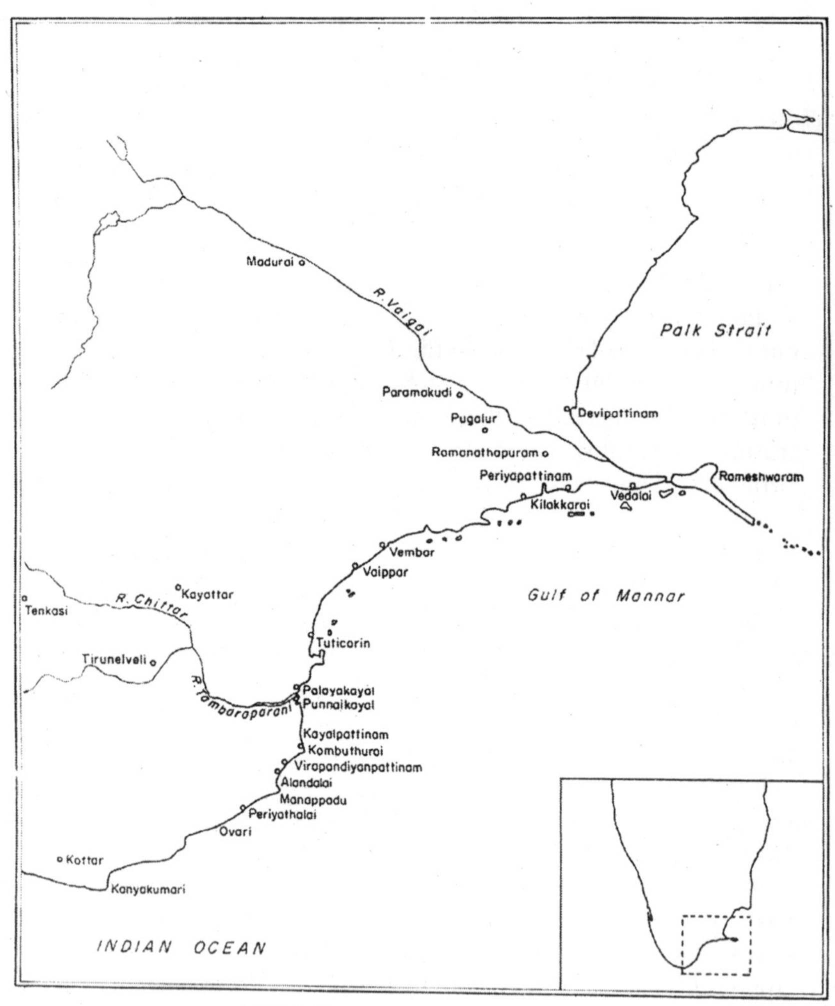

MAP 2: THE PEARL FISHERY COAST

between the Zamorin of Kozhikodu and the Portuguese viceroy in 1513 contained a specific clause to the effect that the Muslim traders sailing from Kayal to Kozhikodu should not be disturbed.[4]

Details regarding pearl fishery were subsequently sent to the king of Portugal by the captain of a Portuguese ship, António de Miranda de Azevedo, who happened to be travelling from Kochi to Sri Lanka via Kayal on the pearl fishery coast in 1519.[5] According to this report, the chieftain of Kayal requested Miranda de Azevedo to sell two ships for the farmer's use at any price he chose to quote. Azevedo, however, did not enter into any agreement with the chieftain but communicated the message to the Portuguese King. He also pointed out that the Portuguese could earn much profit by resorting to pearl fishing in the coast.[6] Although pearl fishing was only seasonal, the revenue derived from the trade was very high according to him. This timely information was immediately taken into consideration and the Portuguese viceroy in India received instructions from Lisbon to send a captain every year with boats and soldiers to help the chieftain of Kayal during the pearl fishing season.[7]

When Portuguese merchants started settling in the pearl fishery coast they found that the local Hindus were under the employ of the Muslims. There were many prosperous Muslims trader there and some of them came forward to help the private Portuguese traders; some even volunteered to serve as sailors on the Portuguese ships. An order issued by the captain of a Portuguese ship from the port of Kayal even mentions the payment to be made to two Muslim pilots who had helped the captain. Some of these Muslims were later employed as sailors by the Portuguese Crown, particularly for crossing the shallow waters with which the Muslim sailors were already very familiar.[8]

In 1520, the Portuguese viceroy appointed João Flores as Captain and Factor in charge of the Coromandel and pearl fishery coasts, to especially look after the trade interests of the Crown. This captain generally resided at Pulicat (Pazhaverkadu) which was at that time strategically more important for their overseas trade with Melaka than any other place on the coast. He, however, came to the fishery coast in the month of February every year to oversee the pearl fishing operations.[9]

When João Flores' term as Captain and Factor of the pearl fishery coast expired in 1522,[10] Bastião Lopez was appointed on 11 May 1522 as the Factor in charge of both the Coromandel and the pearl fishery coast.[11] At that time only two *paraus* (small vessels) were stationed on the Tamil coast, out of which one belonged to the Crown and the other was held by the captain to control and guard the pearl fishery.[12] In 1522, the king of Portugal introduced some reforms to improve the situation in the pearl fishery coast, and for the purpose appointed Bastião Roiz, a *cavaleiro* (knight) as the Factor at Kayal.[13] At the same time Manoel de Frias was appointed Captain of the Coromandel Coast and authorized to claim the sea as the possession of the king of Portugal. Manuel de Frias had successfully negotiated in 1522 the lease of pearl fishery for a fixed sum of 1,500 *cruzados* per annum which was paid as revenue from the pearl fishery to the king of Portugal.[14] João Flores was appointed by the king as Captain Major to stay there with a small force to guard the pearl fishery and enforce revenue payment.[15]

It may be mentioned here that an agreement was arrived at by João Flores with the Muslim chieftain of Kilakkarai (whose name is not mentioned in the records) who was a rival of the chieftain of Kayal. The details of the agreement are not known. However, in 1523, Captain Major Manoel de Frias of the Coromandel coast came to the aid of the chieftain of Kayal.[16] Thus both rival chieftains sought the help of the Portuguese and they were allowed to fish by paying a fixed amount to the Portuguese. It can be clearly seen from a letter written from Goa by António de Fonseca to the king of Portugal on 18 October 1523, that the conflicts between the two local chieftains did not end.[17]

Dom Duarte Menezes, the then Portuguese governor of India (1522-4), extended his support to the Captain of the fishery coast by supplying the necessary victuals and artillery. The resident captain in fact extracted the maximum revenue from the pearl fishery and paid the dues to the *Estado da Índia*. It is said that the revenue amounted to 72,000 *panams*, or about 54,000 *cruzados*, in 1524.[18] Pearl fishey slowly attracted many more Portuguese traders who left the ports of the western coast of India for the south-eastern coast.[19] Other Portuguese traders carried rice, butter, meat, coconuts and firewood to ports like Kombuthurai,

Periyathazhai, etc., near Kanyakumari, besides exporting these items to Sri Lanka as well.[20]

In 1525, Martim Toscano was appointed Captain of the fishery coast. He took up residence at the port of Kayal.[21] Sixteen Portuguese soldiers were then stationed at Kayal, according to an acknowledgment dated 28 October 1525, and provisions such as rice, butter, etc., were supplied to the Captain of the pearl fishery coast by Fernão Barbosa, the captain of the ship *St. Antony*. The total value of cargo supplied was estimated to be 5,860 *reis*.[22] It is evident from several warrants (*mandados*) and receipts (*conhecimentos*) (now preserved at the National Archives of Lisbon, Portugal) issued from Kayal that the supply of provisions towards the maintenance of the Portuguese who were stationed there continued for a long time.[23]

The Zamorin of Kozhikodu on the western coast of India was not content to remain as a silent spectator of the growing influence of the Portuguese on the eastern coast. He, therefore, came forward to help the Muslims who had lost their business at Kayal. In 1528, the Zamorin's fleet attacked the Portuguese at Kayal and Captain João Flores was killed along with twenty other Portuguese in 1528.[24] On hearing this, Martim Affonso de Mello sailed from Kochi with a powerful fleet and subdued and punished the Muslims at Kayal for their alliance with the Zamorin.[25]

João da Cruz, a newly converted Chetti and a horse dealer who lived in the pearl fishery coast was instrumental in preventing the paravas from being exploited by the Muslims while conducting pearl fishing operations. He was also responsible for the large-scale conversion of paravas to Christianity. This mass conversion considerably strengthened the position of the Portuguese in the south-eastern coast of India. This in turn drove the Marakkayars to seek the help of the Zamorin of Kozhikodu who in turn arranged to send many ships under the leadership of merchants like Kunzhali Marakkayar, Pattan Marakkayar and Ibrahim Ali Marakkayar to attack the port of Tuticorin in 1537.[26]

The Portuguese captain of the pearl fishery coast had a team of ten soldiers under him to exercise control over the pearl fishery. However, the Captain alone had the authority to collect the revenue and also to purchase pearls for the Crown. In a report to the king of Portugal regarding the situation in 1530, it was stated that three vessels with ten men controlled the pearl fishery.[27] The struggle between the Muslims and the Portuguese to gain control over the pearl fisheries continued even in 1531 as is evident from contemporary sources.[28] The large-scale conversion of the paravas in 1532 was a turning point and this enabled the Portuguese to gain control over the pearl fishery. The tax at the time of conversion, payable by the paravas to the Portuguese Crown, was fixed at 75,000 *panams*, i.e. the equivalent of 60,000 pardaus.[29] By this time the Muslim traders had also realized that it was no larger desirable to stay at Kayal and therefore, they left and established themselves at a new place calling it Kayalpattinam.[30]

This new settlement of Kayalpattinam, known as *Cale Patão* in Portuguese, was not under the control of the Portuguese but grew up as a rival to the port of Kayal.[31] Fr. Sebastião de Pedro, who lived during this time on this coast, mentions that the Portuguese attacked this Muslim settlement initially in 1536 and once again in 1538.[32] Fr. João de Villa Conde, who visited Kayalpattinam on his way to Sri Lanka on 22 April 1547, calls it as a settlement of Muslims.[33]

Portuguese Contacts with Kilakkarai (1508-1531)

The difficulties faced by the Portuguese in establishing trade contacts at Pazhayakayal drove them to seek other ports of commerce on the fishery coast. They chose to move to the port of Kilakkarai where they were warmly received by the *nayinar* (a petty police official) who held the leasing rights over the pearl fishery there.

The Portuguese called Kilakkarai variously as *Quilcare*,[34] *Calecare*,[35] or *Calocare*.[36] According to Portuguese sources Kilakkarai was famous as a centre of active overseas trade with Sri Lanka. The Malabar region, which was under the control of the Tiruvadi Rajas of Venad, also had active commercial links with Kilakkarai.[37] The entire Tamil country, including the coastal region of Kilakkarai, was under the Vijayanagara ruler. Emperor Krishnadevaraya had appointed various *nayaks* to rule over the several *nayakathanams* of the empire. Kilakkarai was under the control of the *nayak* at Paramakudi where there was a fort.[38] Portuguese documents mention that this *nayak* had control over the coastal areas from Kilakkarai in the north to Rameshwaram in the south. The name of this *nayak* is mentioned as Chembeche Naque, which possibly refers to Tumbichi Nayaka whose inscriptions have been found in this region. He derived revenue from the port of Kilakkarai although according to Portuguese documents pearl fishing was leased out to a rich Muslim who was the *nayinar* of Kilakkarai. The *nayinar* was also responsible for collecting and remitting the revenue to the *nayak* of Paramakudi who retained a small portion of it for himself and remitted the balance to the Vijayanagara treasury every year.

As mentioned earlier, the king of Portugal, Dom Manuel (1495-1521) who desired to exploit the maritime resources of the pearl fishery coast, appointed in 1520 João Flores as the Captain with the responsibility to procure pearls and other commodities from that region for a period of three years.[39]

According to a royal order issued from Lisbon two years later, i.e. on 15 April 1522,[40] Bastião Rodrigues was appointed Captain of Kilakkarai and authorized to issue cartaze (sailing permits) to the Muslims for sailing in the sea at Kilakkarai. This affirms the control by the Portuguese had over the seas. The Portuguese Captain developed very cordial relations with the *nayinar* of Kilakkarai. In a letter written by António Fonseca, a Portuguese resident in Goa, to the king of Portugal on 18 October 1523, it was mentioned that the *nayinar* of Kilakkarai was a very good man with whom the Portuguese had established their first commercial contacts on the eastern coast.[41] The *nayinar* agreed to pay a certain amount to the Portuguese for protection against sea pirates, who were mostly Muslims, and also for permission to scour the deep for pearls during the pearl fishery operations at Kilakkarai. There was intense rivalry and heavy competition among the native lease holders of pearl fishery rights. It was at this time, i.e. in 1523, that the *nayinar* of Kayal sent word to the Portuguese that he himself would give them the same amount as the *nayinar* of Kilakkarai if the latter was not allowed to fish for pearls.[42]

João Flores, the Portuguese Factor and Captain of the pearl

fishery coast successfully held negotiations with the *nayinar* of Kilakkarai on the question of payment of pearl fishery revenue to the Portuguese.[43] As per the second successful contract signed in the year 1527, the *nayinar* of Kilakkarai agreed to pay annually a fixed amount of 3,000 *pardaus* to the Portuguese.[44] Rui Martins, the Portuguese captain stationed at Kilakkarai, paid money and provisions to the soldiers posted there in accordance with an order issued on 24 October 1524 by Lopo de Azevedo, the Captain Major of the pearl fishery coast.[45] Similarly, an acknowledgment gives details of the quantity of rice and butter given to the soldiers as their maintenance allowance.[46] The salary accounts of those employed as soldiers at Kilakkarai were submitted by the Captain of the pearl fishery coast to the *Vedor da Fazenda* (Portuguese Comptroller of Finance) at Kochi for the sanction of payments.[47]

The Captain Major of the *pescaria* is reported to have disbursed 5,860 *reis* in 1525 to the sixteen Portuguese soldiers.[48] The number of soldiers in the regiment stationed at Kilakkarai in 1526 increased to fifty-three. Their salary was disbursed by Martim Toscano who was the Captain Major of the Pearl Fishery Coast at that time.[49]

The king of Portugal was informed in a letter written in 1530 that ten men with a strongly built house and two or three *paraus* (boats) would be sufficient at Kilakkarai.[50] However, in 1531, the Portuguese opted to have six *naos* (ships) with sufficient ammunition indicating the threat perceptions as well as the revenue potential of the Kilakkarai region.[51]

The Portuguese slowly gained control over the waters around the Gulf of Mannar mainly with a view to improving their trade with Sri Lanka owing to its proximity. Their success in this venture was largely dependent upon the control they could exercise over the movement of cargoes traded by the Marakkayars who were their rivals in this region.

The Marakkayars carried rice and textiles to Sri Lanka and exchanged them for cinnamon. However, the king of Kotte in Sri Lanka, pressed by the Muslim merchants, did not always provide the necessary quantity of cinnamon to the Portuguese ships.[52] The Portuguese, who desired to participate in a big way in the commerce of cinnamon with Sri Lanka and pearl fishing in

Kilakkarai, were on the lookout for a more ideal shelter on the eastern coast. They eventually chose Vedalai, a few kilometres north of Kilakkarai for the purpose.

The Portuguese Settlement of Vedalai (1520-1573)

The emergence of Vedalai as a commercial centre, without much opposition from the Marakkayars, began in the year 1520. The earliest traceable source mentions the supply of wheat and other food items to the Portuguese who had settled there.[53] Vedalai, situated on the low sand banks close to the island of Rameshwaram, was selected by the Portuguese because of its strategic location which enabled them to keep a watch over the movement of ships and to ensure that they sailed with *cartazes* to the ports of the Coromandel, Bengal, Pegu, Siam and Sri Lanka. The Portuguese built a small fort at Vedalai with wooden palisades and kept a garrison of some forty men there.[54] Prior permission had to be obtained either from the king of Vijayanagara or his subordinate *nayaka* ruler at Paramakudi to construct such a fort as foreign traders were forbidden to do so. Use of a specific kind of material in building was one of the norms prescribed, according to the then prevailing custom. In 1524, the Portuguese approached the *nayak* of Paramakudi who allowed them to erect only a mud-walled fort with a building of thatched roof at Vedalai, and not a large brick or stone building which might be used later to defy the authority of the Vijayanagara emperors.[55] This was the first Portuguese fort on the Tamil coast. Several straw houses and warehouses for residential and commercial purpose were constructed for the use of Portuguese private residents, merchants and officials at Vedalai. The Portuguese Captain of Kochi, under whose jurisdiction Vedalai fell at that time, paid an official visit in 1525 and inspected the mud fort that existed there.[56]

When the Portuguese started exercising control over the Kilakkarai region from their station at Vedalai, the Marakkayars came into open conflict with them as they began slowly to lose their hold over trade and commerce on the coast. The Marakkayars of Kilakkarai along with the forces of the Zamorin murdered João Flores, the Portuguese Captain in 1528 because he had established cordial relations with the *nayak* of Paramakudi.[57]

Further, these Muslim traders of Kilakkarai sought the help of the Zamorin of Kozhikodu on the western coast. In 1537, the Zamorin sent Kunzhali Marakkayar, his brother Ibrahim Ali Marakkayar and his brother-in-law Ahmad Marakkayar to fight the Portuguese. These Marakkayars caused considerable damage to Portuguese trading vessels and attacked the Vedalai settlement. Martim Affonso de Sousa, the Portuguese Captain Major, fought and won in the naval battle in January 1538.[58] The Zamorin of Kozhikodu took this defeat as a blow to his prestige and sought the help of the king of Sri Lanka for a combined attack against the Portuguese. He dispatched fifty-one vessels carrying eight thousand men and four thousand pieces of artillery to help the king of Sri Lanka.[59] De Sousa captured some of these sailing vessels near Vedalai and a fierce battle was fought on 28 February 1538 in which the forces of the Zamorin were once again defeated.[60]

With the growing influence of the Portuguese in the Kilakkarai region, revenue accruals from pearl fishery in this area to the Vijayanagara treasury almost dried up.[61] Provoked by the growing clout of the Portuguese in the region and the complete stoppage of payment of revenue to the king of Vijayanagara in 1549, the Vijayanagara army with six thousand soldiers attacked the Portuguese settlement of Vedalai in the same year.

These developments are confirmed from the details found in a letter dated 25 October 1549, written by the Bishop of Goa to the king of Portugal.[62] This is further confirmed in another letter written on 3 December 1549 by Fr. Alphonso Cypriani, then residing at Santhome of Mylapore, to the Jesuit Superior General. According to him, when the Vedalai settlement was attacked by the Vijayanagara army, there were only fifteen Portuguese there, all others had fled from the port.[63]

Some years later (1553), the Muslims from Kilakkarai once again attacked the Portuguese settlement of Vedalai to gain control over the pearl fishery, which was still very productive. A fleet from Kochi under the command of Gil Fernandez de Carvalho came to fight the Muslims. An envoy of the *nayaka* ruler from Paramakudi also promised to extend his help to Gil Fernandez to carry out the attack against the Muslims.[64] The Portuguese fleet met the Muslim forces at Kilakkarai on 15 May 1553 and a fierce battle was fought at sea. The Muslims were defeated although they outnumbered the Portuguese forces.[65]

The survival of the Portuguese in the Kilakkarai region depended very much on the support of Tumbichi Nayak of Paramakudi. He had, in fact, even rebelled against the authority of the Vijayanagara emperor of Achyutadevaraya.[66] The Vijayanagara army subsequently marched against him and the territory was taken away and given to another *nayaka*. According to later epigraphs, the coastal region comprising Rameshwaram, Vedalai, Periyapattinam and Kilakkarai was no longer under the Paramakudi *nayakathanam simai* but had come under the jurisdiction of the Pogalur *nayakathanam simai* in 1553 and was then ruled by Ramaraja Chinna Timma. He paid the revenues collected from this region to the king of Vijayanagara promptly.[67]

Later, with the establishment of the *nayakdom* at Madurai, this coastal region also came under the jurisdiction of the Madurai *nayaka*. From 1559 the revenue from pearl fishing was sent to the treasury of the Madurai *nayak* who in turn remitted it to the Vijayanagara emperor.[68]

Portuguese officials kept a strict watch over sailings in the Gulf of Mannar. Although they collected money by issuing *cartazes* to the ships,[69] they also demanded payment from all the small boats taking pilgrims from the mainland to the Ramanathaswami temple located in the northern corner of the Rameshwaram island. Thus they obstructed movement of the large number of pilgrims to the holy temple of Rama.[70]

Because João Fernandez Correia, the Portuguese Captain of the pearl fishery coast, was forcing all pilgrims to pay a fixed amount per head, problems arose between the natives and the Portuguese.[71] The Portuguese Captain further ordered a trench to be dug close to the mudfort at Vedalai to prevent the pilgrims from visiting the temple without paying the pilgrim tax. It is not clear from sources whether this was done with a view to boost revenues or prevent the natives from going to Rameshwaram. As a result the income of Rameshwaram temple dwindled. The temple priests and authorities initially lodged a complaint with the Vijayanagara officials. They also made an appeal to Ramaraya, the king of Vijayanagara to remedy the situation.[72]

The Vijayanagara emperor, who felt stung by the insult offered to God and his devotees, sent an army under the command of Vittala Raya, a cousin of Ramaraya against the Portuguese settlement of Vedalai in 1559. Several Muslims who had earlier lost their fortunes in trade and were driven out of the port of Kilakkarai also availed themselves this golden opportunity to fight against the Portuguese and extended their full support to the Vijayanagara forces. The army attacked the Portuguese settlement of Vedalai. The Captain who could not withstand the attacks escaped, with many others taking asylum in the Vazhaithivu and Anaibar islands off the coast. The mud fort at Vedalai was razed to the ground and the Vijayanagara soldiers filled up the trench dug by the Portuguese.[73] They destroyed the ships anchored in the harbour and killed some Portuguese. An Italian Jesuit missionary, António Criminali, who lived and preached the gospel to the fishermen at Vedalai was also killed. His body was buried the next day in a grave near the beach by António Correia, the cousin of the Portuguese Captain of the fort of Vedalai.[74] Diogo do Couto, the Portuguese chronicler who describes this incident, concludes his account by stating that the Vijayanagara army finally reached Rameshwaram and took a holy bath in the sea considering it as a sacred act. The Portuguese who, had deserted Vedalai reached Mannar and settled there in 1560.[75] They made no further attempts to return to re-occupy Vedalai.

Although the Vijayanagara invasion affected Portuguese trade for some time, they continued to operate from the port of Kilakkarai and organized pearl fishing there.[76] The Portuguese employed three or four catamarans (small boats) generally with about thirty men at a time for security purposes against sea pirates. The expenditure ranged between 12,000 to 20,000 *reis*, as mentioned in the records.[77] The salary of the Captain of the (*pescaria*) pearl fishery coast was fixed at 120,000 *reis*.[78] The writer, stationed at Kilakkarai, was made responsible for the maintenance of the Crown accounts pertaining to the pearl fishery and was paid 40,000 *reis*.[79] The entire expenses were met from the revenues collected from the pearl divers of Kilakkarai and Vedalai. In addition to the fixed revenue paid in cash by the inhabitants of Kilakkarai, four pearls of a specified weight were also to be paid to the Portuguese Crown each year.[80] Similarly, the people of Vedalai also made a contribution of twenty *kuru* (heaps) of chanks from 1564 to 1572 to the Portuguese Crown.[81]

Some years later the yield of pearls from the pearl fishery coast completely dried up and the fishing of pearls moved from place to place. According to the *Orçamento da Estado da Índia*, pearl fishery could no longer be done at Kilakkarai in 1574 but had by then moved to the island of Mannar.[82] Dom Constantino de Bragança, the Viceroy of Goa, therefore, appointed a Portuguese Captain, namely, Jorge de Mello de Castro, in 1582 at Mannar (where a small population of eighty Portuguese lived) to supervise the pearl fishing carried on there.[83] The payment of a fixed tax to the Portuguese, as followed at Kilakkarai, was introduced at Mannar.[84] The amount of the tax was increased in 1595 by Viceroy Mathias de Albuquerque. It consisted of twelve pearls in total of different sizes and forty kurus of chanks.[85] As the pearl fishing operations shifted to the pearl banks of Mannar, the Portuguese also moved over to the Mannar region in Sri Lanka towards the close of the sixteenth century.

Punnaikayal Pearl Fishery (1544-1579)

The Portuguese traders settled on the southern bank of the river Tamraparni in 1544 to conduct their commercial activities in Punnaikayal. This is evident from three letters[86] written from there, dated 14 March 1544, 5 September 1544 and 18 December 1544.[87] Its strategic location, with the sea on one side and the lagoon on the other which could be reached by boat, was an advantage for the Portuguese.[88] A mud fort was constructed here in the same year;[89] it was the second Portuguese mud fort on the Tamil littoral in the eastern coast of peninsular India. The Portuguese Captain and Factor of the pearl fishery coast took up permanent residence here with a garrison of fifty men.[90] According to Portuguese documents, Punnaikayal was almost like an island and was often flooded but the port was eventually saved because one such flood in the Tamraparni river formed a new outlet into the sea.[91]

The parava converts were treated as Portuguese subjects as they paid their taxes and dues directly to the Portuguese Captain stationed at Punnaikayal. Martim Affonso de Sousa, the Portuguese Governor of Goa considered the annual tax paid by the paravas to the Portuguese Crown to be too heavy, so he reduced the amount from 75,000 *panams* to 60,000 by an order issued on 6 January 1543.[92] The order further stated that the tax amount of 60,000 *panams* could be paid in two installments.[93] A sum of 28,000 *panams* was to be remitted during chank fishery conducted in the month of November. The balance amount of 32,000 *panams* was to be paid during the pearl fishery in March every year.[94]

Dom João III (1521-57), the king of Portugal, extended to his parava subjects all possible help for their protection. He sent a letter to the paravas through Miguel Vaz, the Vicar General of Kochi, who was on his way back to India in 1546. The Portuguese governor of Goa was authorized to incur such expenditure as was found necessary for helping the paravas, from the royal revenues if needed.[95] The king's letter further stated that the Portuguese governor should not allow the Portuguese Captain of the fishery coast and his patrol fleet to act tyrannically. This instruction was given only to earn the loyalty of the paravas and thereby increase the profits of the Crown. Further instructions were given to the Vicar General (the ecclesiastical authority next to the Bishop) to point out malpractices or corruption in the Portuguese administration, if any, so that corrective measures could be taken by the king.[96] Thus Lisbon could exercise overall supervision and control over the pearl fishery coast.

Garcia de Sa, the Portuguese governor of Goa (1548-9), issued an order stating that the Captain and his men on the fishery coast should not force the people to pay tax whenever there was no pearl fishery.[97] In fact, Estevão de Gama, the Portuguese governor (1540-2), replaced João Fernandes Correia, the Pescaria Captain, for his misdeeds and bad administration and later imprisoned him at Goa.[98] Martim Affonso de Sousa, the Portuguese governor (1542-5) sent an official, António Roiz da Gamba, to conduct an enquiry into the pearl fishery and put an end to the high-handedness of the Captain.[99] He found the Captain guilty and arrested him. The paravas were naturally impressed by the justice of the Portuguese governors who did not flinch from punishing corrupt officials.

There were frequent conflicts between the Portuguese Captain and the Jesuit missionaries. Sometimes the Factor of the pearl fishery coast kept some pearls for himself. In a particular case in 1546, the pearls possessed by the Captain and Factor were taken away by the viceroy on royal order.[100] The Jesuits complained to the king of Portugal that the parava converts had been oppressed. The Crown therefore inquired of the viceroy in 1546 whether there was any method of collecting revenue from the pearl fishery coast without involving the Portuguese captain.[101] The viceroy was not in favour of any change and he replied to the king. By this time the Jesuits had intensified their missionary activities in this region and in a letter dated 6 December 1547, it was very clearly stated that they had made Punnaikayal their permanent headquarters and were living in the new residence built there.[102]

The king of Vijayanagara used to collect tribute from the *nayak* of Kanyakumari and this native chieftain approached the Portuguese Captain António Moniz for military assistance in a war against the Vijayanagara forces. In return he promised to build a fortress in Kanyakumari at his own expense obliging himself to pay each year 10,000 *panams*.[103] However, the Portuguese Captain of the earl fishery coast refused to extend any military help knowing that their existence in the port settlement of Punnaikayal much depended upon the favour of the Vijayanagara king. The Captain of Punnaikayal seems to have accepted the sovereignty of the Vijayanagara rulers.

However, Vishwanatha Nayak (1559-63), the ruler of Madurai was, annoyed by the activities of the Portuguese because his revenues had been greatly reduced. The paravas regarded themselves as Portuguese subjects and paid taxes and dues directly to the Portuguese Captain at Punnaikayal. Hence the *nayak* planned to attack the Portuguese. When his army invaded Punnaikayal, the Portuguese could not resist and they fled across the estuary. The Portuguese Factor and Captain escaped, and the houses and the boats were set on fire.[104] The paravas agreed in 1551 to pay an annual tribute to the *nayak* of Madurai which consisted of a day's fishing, amounting to 70,000 *pardaus*.[105] However, this payment was not made very regularly to the *nayak* of Madurai in the subsequent years.

Vittala Raya, the Vijayanagara chief attached the Portuguese settlement of Punnaikayal in 1553 because the revenue from there had have been received and the arrears had swelled to huge sums.[106] This time the Portuguese army of 670 men, which came from Kochi, fought back. However, the Portuguese were defeated. Many of them, including missionaries, were taken prisoners. A large sum of 100,000 *panams* was demanded as ransom by Vittala Raya, but the paravas paid only a part of the ransom amount in exchange for the prisoners.[107]

In 1560 the *nayak* of Madurai, again invaded Punnaikayal and demanded two days' fishing of pearls as tribute due to him.[108] A letter written from Goa by Fr. Luís Francisco to members of the Society of Jesus living in the cities of Coimbra and Evora in Portugal noted that during August 1560, the Vijayanagara king came with a force of 20,000 men and attacked Punnaikayal.[109] One section of the army held Fr. Francisco Durão and stripped him naked and tied his hands behind his back. The paravas paid 50 *pardaus* as ransom and got him released from his captors. In the same incident, Fr. João de Misquita received three wounds including a sword thrust. Although the paravas were willing to pay 1,000 *pardaus* for his release, the captors did not agree to release him. Fr. Henriques, however, took shelter at sea along with some parava children and women in many vessels to evade capture.[110] Subsequently, Muslim pirates also attacked the Punnaikayal settlement in 1562. They looted twenty-two boats belonging to the Portuguese and the paravas. These Muslim pirates returned to Malabar with their booty which included three small elephants.[111] A Portuguese detachment of soldiers under the command of Dom Duarte de Menezes fought against these forces and in 1567 Viceroy Dom Constantino ordered the Portuguese Captain of the pearl fishery coast to pay the men who had helped the army at this difficult juncture.[112] Thus Punnaikayal was frequently subjected to threats and plunder.

According to the Portuguese chronicler Diogo do Couto,[113] the fall of the Vijayanagara empire in 1565 was a great blow to Portuguese commerce although the Vijayanagara army, which had plundered and attacked, the Punnaikayal settlement, was never helpful to Portuguese commerce on the pearl fishery coast even much before its defeat at the battle of Talikota.

The frequent attacks on the settlement of Punnaikayal prompted the Portuguese authorities to convert the mud fort into a strong defence made of bricks. A record dated 20 April 1560 now preserved in the British Museum, London, says that Punnaikayal had a fort with a large population of Portuguese residents and some native fishermen.[114] However, this document does not mention the name of the fort even though the Portuguese had a name for it. It is said that forty Portuguese soldiers and a local garrison of troops were stationed there, and in 1562 it had emerged as the chief settlement of the Portuguese on the south-eastern coast of peninsular India.[115]

The pearl banks on the fishery coast had in the meanwhile shifted away from the shores of Punnaikayal towards the island of Mannar thus leading to the decline of Punnaikayal within twenty years, i.e. from 1559 to 1579, thereby marking the end of Punnaikayal's importance as a centre of pearl fishing.

Dom Constantino de Bragança built a fort on the opposite side of Punnaikayal on the island of Mannar. He planned to resettle the paravas to protect them from the incursions of Veerappa Nayaka (1572-96) of Madurai at the end 1580. According to the *regimento de Manar* of 1582, a revenue of 64,000 *panams* was realized out of which a sum of 4,000 was given towards meeting the expenses of the Jesuits.[116] The pearl fishery at Mannar brought an income of about 9,000 *pardaus* towards the end of the sixteenth century.[117] Eventually, however, pearl fishing operations had to be shifted from Punnaikayal to the Mannar region. The parava Christians also moved to new places to escape the tyranny of the *nayak* of Madurai.[118] The Jesuit Provincial also suggested at this time to all the paravas who were living scattered in various places on the coast that they sell all their property and build houses at Virapandyanpattinam to live under a single umbrella instead of living dispersed.[119] Many paravas who did not wish to do so migrated to the Coromandel coast and Mannar in Sri Lanka seeking commercial fortune.

Portuguese Revenues from Pearl Fishery

When the paravas approached the Portuguese in Kochi in 1535 for help, the latter realized the importance of pearl fishery and in order to break the hold of the Marakkayars over the pearl trade in the region, decided to convert the paravas to Christianity as desired by them. A fleet was also sent therefore from Kochi at this time for their protection.[120] The paravas who until then had been exploited by the Marakkayars in the pearl fishing operations, were happy to be converted by Fr. Miguel Vaz and Fr. António do Padrão. These two priests baptized the families of a large number of paravas at seven coastal villages, namely, Kayal, Ovari, Alandalai, Manappadu, Tuticorin, Periyathalai and Kooduthalai in 1536.[121] This mass conversion considerably strengthened the position of the Portuguese in pearl fishing and helped them to earn considerable revenue in the south-eastern coast of India.

Pearl fishery operations were conducted by the Portuguese within the complex of Vedalai-Kilakkarai and Punnaikayal.[122] This is evident from the records of Simão Botelho, the *vedor da fazenda* in Kochi. The receipts and expenditure statements of 1558 show that pearls were received from Pedro Lopez as *dizimo* (thithe) and this was fixed at 5 per cent of 6 ounces of pearls and one-eighth of seed pearls which were sold at the value of 6 *cruzados* each. It was also reported that they received from Punnaikayal one-eighth of seed pearls of 3 ounces at the value of

TABLE 1: REVENUE EARNED BY THE PORTUGUESE FROM THE PEARL FISHERY COAST AD 1525-1605[123]

Year	Amount (in *pardaus* of 300 *reis*)
1525	7,500
1552	3,200
1574	5,000
1581	5,000
1585	9,000
1605	25,000

5 *cruzados*, besides 3 ounces of oysters from João Ferreira and Luíz de Fonseca in 1558.[124] In about approximately twenty year's time, i.e. between 1560 and 1580, we learn from Pedro Texeira, the Portuguese traveller, that pearl fishery operations were then confined to the Kilakkarai-Vedalai complex on the coast[125] where 400 to 600 boats were used. As the legal holder of the pearl fishery rights, the *nayak* of Madurai received one day's proceeds during the season as his share.[126] The actual management of pearl fishery was in the hands of the paravas and supervised mostly by the Jesuits.[127]

PEARL FISHING AT TUTICORIN (1570-1658)

The port of Tuticorin (Thutthukudi), which was shaped like a horse shoe with its opening facing towards the Gulf of Mannar, had emerged as an important place for pearl fishing by 1570. It is referred to as Tytucurim, Tutucurim, Tutocorim and Tucucurij in the Portuguese documents of this period.[128] The tax on pearl fishery was collected by the Pandya ruler at Tuticorin who had cordial relations with the Portuguese. The attacks of the Vijayanagara kings at Punnaikayal in 1560 demanding tax prompted the Portuguese to move their commercial activities to Tuticorin, away from Punnaikayal. Pearl fishing conducted by the Portuguese flourished at Tuticorin as confirmed by a letter written on 6 December 1577 from Tuticorin by Fr. Henrique Henriques to the Jesuit Superior General in Rome.[129] In 1587, the revenue derived from the pearl fishery consisted of 161 quintals of seed pearls and 8 pearls. The pearl harvest was mostly exported from the Tamil coast to Lisbon.[130]

In 1596, the Pandya chieftain of Tirunelveli made a claim for tax even when pearl fishing was not conducted owing to the absence of pearl banks.[131] He continued to demand a tax of 1,000 *panams* from the parava inhabitants of Tuticorin.[132] Angered by the refusal of the paravas to pay the tax, the Pandya chieftain, Alagan Perumal Athivirarama alias Srivallabha II (1564-1606), sacked the port of Tuticorin in 1603 and took the Jesuit Rector prisoner.[133] The paravas then migrated to the neighbouring places and decided not to return to Tuticorin. They were not intimidated by the Pandya ruler since they had accepted the king of Portugal as their sovereign ruler and were therefore under his protection.[134]

Pearl fishery was seasonal as it was very dependent on the environment. The expulsion of the Jesuits from the pearl fishery coast in 1605 for a period of sixteen years, owing to disputes with the Portuguese viceroy in Goa, hampered the smooth operations of pearl fishing. In the meanwhile, Pedro Soares de Brito was appointed Captain of Tuticorin, the chief settlement of the paravas and the Portuguese, to bring the law and order situation under control. Although he was successful in his attempts to restore peace in Tuticorin, disputes between the Jesuits and the Franciscans concerning the control over the parish church of St. Peter in Tuticorin were not resolved.[135] In Portuguese records of 1611 it was reported that pearl fishery had not been conducted for as many as six years continuously on account of the disputes.[136] Jacques de Couttre, the traveller who visited the pearl fishery coast in 1611, confirms that it was so while he was at Tuticorin.[137]

Pearl fishery, which was resumed in 1621, earned a revenue of 12,000 *xerafins*.[138] The paravas and the Portuguese evinced much enthusiasm when pearl fishing resumed in 1621 at Tuticorin owing to the abundant presence of pearl banks.[139] It was only some years later, i.e. 1624, that the Portuguese merchants in Kochi began to buy pearls from Tuticorin. This is evident from a letter written from Goa in January 1624 by the viceroy of India to the king of Portugal.[140] At this time the Dutch in Pulicat were also attempting to settle in Tuticorin. The local people objected to their intrusion and reacted quickly by informing the Portuguese viceroy in Goa to take immediate steps to prevent the Dutch entry into Tuticorin.[141]

The Jesuits who were expelled from the pearl fishery coast in 1605 because of conflicts with the Bishop of Kochi did not return until 1630.[142] Another important reason for their expulsion was that they had also instigated the paravas not to pay taxes and levies to the Portuguese authorities.[143] Fr. Rubino, a Jesuit is reported to have gone to the capital of the *nayak* of Madurai and pleaded for the reduction of annual tax on the paravas from 1,000 *pagodas* to 800. The *nayak* acceded to the request and further reduced the tax to 500 *pagodas*. In 1627, he is reported to have granted complete remission of tax arrears for a period of three years.[144] The paravas were asked by the *nayak* of Madurai in 1631 and made to pay 1,000 *pardaus* as tax. However, the *nayak* granted exemption from payment of tax thereafter when the pearl fishery became unproductive.[145]

Four years later (1634) when pearl fishery was resumed, violence and factional fighting erupted among the paravas and the viceroy had to send a fleet to control the situation.[146] The *nayak* of Madurai, who heard about the pearl fishery operations, appointed one Marakkayar to collect revenue and send it on to him. This official received several gifts including income from fixed pearl divers and was also allowed to use seven large boats for pearl fishing. He was also paid 60 *chakrams* as salary per month by the *nayak* of Madurai.[147] However, he could not do the job entrusted to him by the *nayak* as the paravas continued to pay tribute to the Portuguese.

The tonis of Punnaikayal always went to Tuticorin where pearl fishery was conducted under the protection of the Portuguese Captain. In 1634 and 1637, the Portuguese used armed vessels to protect the coast and prevented the Marakkayar, the officer appointed by the *nayak* of Madurai, from fishing pearls on the pearl fishery coast.[148] The *nayak* of Madurai even sent his soldiers to Tuticorin in 1638 to fight the Portuguese. He demanded that all the pearls fished by all the tonis to be given to him. The Portuguese were not prepared to part with the revenue. As this dispute could not be resolved, pearl fishery operations could not be carried on in the following.[149] António Bocarro, the Portuguese chronicler, says that some time (on the 1640s) the situation in the Kilakakarai-Mannar complex changed on account of the new political developments when the Sethupathis established their control over the region.[150]

Thus pearl fishery remained a major source from which the Portuguese derived their wealth and used it to enhance their power in the pearl fishery coast.

The Trade in *Chanks* and Pearls

Commodities like *chank* were excluded from the scope of the maritime trade of the paravas because such articles were declared by the Portuguese Captain in 1532 as monopoly items.[151] The king of Portugal relaxed the restrictions imposed on the paravas to enable them to establish their own trade contacts. Some paravas who had become rich also built numerous *champanas* (boats) for their trading voyages and evinced interest in commerce.[152] These paravas were therefore able to sell the *chank* for better prices and exported a major portion of their *chank* to Bengal. The *chank* which fetched only 5 *panams*[153] prior to 1536 was now sold at 15 to 20 *panams*, thereby boosting the income of the paravas. While the high quality *chanks* were mainly exported to Bengal for making ornaments, *chanks* of low quality were broken by shell burners called *karaiyalars*, who lived in the region, and lime was produced out of it. This lime was mainly used in the construction of buildings in the region.[154]

Pearls were the main item of trade in the port of Kilakkarai. According to an inscription of 1531, there was a pearl market and its lucrative commerce attracted the merchants from various parts of the country. The *nayaka* ruler of this region received half a *panam* for every hundred pearls that were sold at the local market.[155] The merchants lined up along the market streets with their weighing instruments to buy and sell pearls. Scarlet seeds were used as weights.[156] The pearls reached the city of Vijayanagara, where the capital market of the empire existed. There was an overland trade route from Vijayanagara to Rameshwaram connecting the towns of Chidambaram and Madurai through which the internal trade flourished.[157]

Kayal, which came to be called Pazhayakayal after the conversion of the paravas, had its own pearl market. Travellers like Duarte Barbosa speak very highly of the pearl trade that was carried on by the members of the traditional trading community of Chettis[158] who sorted the pearls according to their weight, shape and quality. The prices were then fixed. John Huyghen Van Linschoten, the traveller (in the 1580s), speaks of two types of pearls, which were known to the Portuguese as *perolas* (pearls) and *aljofar* (seed pearls).[159] The price of *aljofar* was much lower than the price of the former. In the early sixteenth century, pearls weighing about 700 ounces were reported to have been sent to Portugal from India,[160] which, included the pearls from Kayal. The Portuguese ships arriving at Lisbon in 1580s brought huge quantities of pearls, once even to the tune of 1696 *arrobas*.[161]

The Portuguese in Kochi procured seed pearls and pearls from Palayakayal and Kilakkarai.[162]

According to Jacques de Couttre, the traveller who visited the pearl fishery coast in 1611, the port of Tuticorin had a famous pearl market and as many as fifteen varieties of pearls were sold there. The demand was always for the most perfect and the best pearls. A famous pearl merchant called Veera Pandi Chetti lived in Tuticorin.[163]

Various manuscripts preserved in the *Arquivo Historico Ultramarino*, Lisbon, mention that the Portuguese purchased seed pearls called *aljofar* from Kilakkarai and exported them to Portugal. The smallest pieces of the *aljofar* were powdered and used for medicinal purposes.[164]

The growing Portuguese commercial influence, brought about through the conversion of the paravas in Kayal, slowly eroded Muslim influence in the area. The Arab and Tamil Muslims, who found themselves insecure, left Kayal and migrated to Kayalpattinam to seek their fortune. The Portuguese in Punnaikayal thus came to enjoy a monopoly over pearl fishery and extracted revenue from there. It appears that the Portuguese objective in the sixteenth century was to monopolize trade in some products and control and tax those trading in all other products. They were not interested in setting up a long chain of factories and forts on the pearl fishery coast with regular patrolling of the coastal areas to dominate trade as they did on the western coast. They, however, controlled the maritime trade in the Tamil littoral extending from Kilakkarai to Rameshwaram because of the pearls available there. Kayal and Kilakkarai were by far the most dominant ports in the *pescaria* coast. The other coastal settlements of the paravas at Manappadu, Alandalai, Vaippar, Vembar, Ovari and Virapandyanpattinam served the interests of the Portuguese trading settlements of Punnaikayal and Vedalai. Thus the Portuguese exploited the marine resources, especially pearl fishing, in this region during the whole of the sixteenth century. The Marakkayars were relegated to the role of petty merchants, pirates and smugglers particularly trading with Sri Lanka. The Portuguese initially extended their presence in the region of Kilakkarai under the patronage of Tumbichi Nayaka.

Their continued survival in the coast therefore depended on the favour of the *nayaka* ruler. The Portuguese viceroy in Goa exercised only indirect control over the pearl fishery region and he never attempted to develop the settlement of Vedalai after the Vijayanagara invasion in 1559.

Although the Portuguese settlement of Vedalai disturbed the Muslim networks of free trade to a large extent in the sixteenth century, the Muslims did not abandon the port of Kilakkarai or migrate to other ports because Kilakkarai continued to remain significant for pearl fishing. Under the Portuguese, Punnaikayal developed as an important centre and the most important feature was its pearl fishing. These Portuguese trading settlements developed a distinct character with the Portuguese men settling down and constructing houses, marrying local women with a view to living there permanently. The importance of these ports came to rest on their commercial and pearl fishing activities. However, as the pearl fishing operations shifted to the island of Mannar in Sri Lanka, the importance of Punnaikayal and Vedalai dwindled.

Some scholars opine that, the Portuguese did not introduce any element of redistributive enterprise.[165] Others say that the redistributive enterprise of the *Estado da Índia*, or its dependence, was on the forceful collection of taxes rather than the ability to transmit goods and sell them competitively.[166] It has been shown by recent studies that the finances of the *Estado da Índia*, through collection of customs and other taxes, did not really decline till the mid-seventeenth century, for which years documents such as *orcamentos* are available.[167] The *Estado* had continued to show a positive balance till 1634. In other words, the Portuguese empire was developing into a larger collector of revenues through customs rather than profiting through trade and this had happened at many places on the western coast of India. It was also followed by the Portuguese in the pearl fishery coast through the collection of revenues from pearl fishery and taxes.

NOTES

1. *Diario de Viagem de Vasco da Gama*, Porto, Livraria Civilização, 1945, vol. 1, p. 82; vol. 2, p. 233; 'Relação Geografico-comercial dos reinos ao sul de Calecute', in Alvaro Velho, *Roteiro da Primeira Viagem de*

Vasco da Gama, 1497-1499, ed. Fontoura da Costa, Lisbon, 1969, Appendix I, pp. 85-93, see p. 87.

2. Letter of the viceroy to the king of Portugal written from Kochi on 16 December 1505, in *IANTT*, *Gavetas*, 20, Maço 10, doc. 33, fl. 4.
3. Gaspar Correia, *Lendas da India*, ed. M. Lopes de Almeida, 4 vols., Porto, 1975, pp. 908-9; Donald Ferguson, 'The Portuguese in Ceylon in the first half of the Sixteenth Century: Gaspar Correa's Account', *Ceylon Literary Register*, 3rd series, IV, p. 157.
4. António da Silva Rego *As Gavetas do Torre do Tombo*, 9, pp. 140-4; see also Georg Schurhammer, *St. Francis Xavier: His Life, His Times*, Rome, 1977, vol. 2, p. 259.
5. António da Silva Rego, *As Gavetas do Torre do Tombo*, Lisboã, 1964, tomo IV, pp. 142-3. The translation of the original text runs as follows: 'As I came from Cochin, the chief of Cael let me know that if I helped him with two ships he would pay a certain amount to Your Highness. I did not make any agreement with him, as I could do nothing but say that I will communicate with your Highness.'
6. Gaspar Correia, *Lendas da India*, Lisboã, Academia Real das Sciencias de Lisboã, 1858-64, tomo II, pp. 778-9.
7. J.F.J. Biker, *Colleção de Tratados e Concertos de Pazes que o Estado da Índia Paluguesa fez com os reis e Senhores*, Lisbon, 1881, vol. 1, p. 22.
8. Josel Wicki, *Documenta Indica* (hereafter *DI*), (1500-49), vol. 1, Rome, 1948, p. 161.
9. Duarte Barbosa, *The Book of Duarte Barbosa,* op. cit., vol. 2, pp. 122 4; see also *Commentarios do Grande Affonso d'Albuquerque,* Lisboã, 1774, vol. 1, pp. 10-14; Gaspar Correia, *Lendas da India*, Lisboã, 1858-64, tomo I, p. 782.
10. *Cartas de Affonso de Albuquerque*, 7, pp. 172-86; *ANTT*, *Gavetas*, no. 20, Maco 10, doc. 33, fl. 4.
11. *Documentos Sobre os Portugueses em Moçambique e na Africa Central*, 1498-1840, 9 vols., Lisbon, 1962-80, vol. 6, doc. 11, p. 94; see also *IANTT*, *Nucleo Antigo*, no. 873, fl. 82 v.
12. For more details regarding Pulicat and Thirumalairayanpattinam see S. Jeyaseela Stephen, *The Coromandel Coast and its Hinterland: Economy, Society and Political System (1500-1600)*, Delhi, 1997, pp. 141 and 207.
13. Ibid.
14. *IANTT*, *Corpo Cronologico* (hereafter CC) II-114-23, dated 20 March 1524.
15. Ibid., II-7-103. João Flores continued to hold office till his death in 1527, as is evident from a letter dated 16 December 1527 written by his friend Sebastião Pires to the king of Portugal.

16. C.R. de Silva, 'The Portuguese and Pearl Fishing', *South Asia Journal*, vol. 1, 1979, pp. 14-28.
17. *Documentos Sobre Os Portugueses em Moçambique e na Africa Central* (hereafter *Documentos Sobre Os Portugueses*), Lisboã, 1969, vol. 6 (1519-37), p. 207.
18. De Silva, 'The Portuguese and Pearl Fishing', p.18. *Panam* was a silver coin that was in us on the east coast. One *panam* was equivalent to 25 to 30 *reis*.
19. *IANTT*, CC, IIa-117-93.
20. Ibid., II-114-93.
21. Ibid., IIa-129-208.
22. Ibid., IIa-129-74.
23. Ibid., IIa-129-217.
24. António da Silva Rego, *Documentação Para a Historia Das Missoes do Padroado Portugueses do Oriente* (hereafter *Documentação*), Lisboã, 1949, vol. 2, p. 137.
25. João de Barros, *Decadas da Asia*, Decada IV, Livro II, Capitulo VII, Lisboã, 1777-8.
26. Biblioteca da Ajuda (hereafter *BA*), Codice 49-IV-9, fl. 28. Pattangatti was the village overseer. António da Silva Rego, *Documentação Para a Historia das Missoes do Padroado Portugueses do Oriente* (hereafter *Documentação*) Lisboa, 1949-58, vol. 10, pp. 313-14: António Fernandez was Pattangatti of Palayakayal in 1536. Manuel de Lima was Pattangatti of Punnaikayal in 1544.
27. *IANTT*, *Gavetas*, XV-19-11. The translation of the original text runs as follows, 'The fisheries at Cale and Calecare could have some ten men there, in strongly built house with two or three paraos and it would, do without the Coromandel fleet every year.'
28. De Silva, 'The Portuguese and Pearl Fishing', p. 20.
29. Simão Botelho, *Tombo do Estado da India (1546-1554)*, in R.J. de Lima Felner (ed.), *Subsidios Para a História da India Portuguesa*, Lisboã, 1868, p. 244. The Pardaus was equal to half a *varahan*. Duarte Barbosa valued a Pardaus at 320 *reis*.
30. Gaspar Correia, *Lendas da Índia*, III, p. 831; Antonio da Silva Rego, *Documentação*, vol. 2, pp. 336-8.
31. Ibid., pp. 339-42.
32. Correia, *Lendas do Índia*, 3, 831.
33. Elaine Sanceau, *Coleção de São Lourenço*, Lisboã, 1975, vol. 2, pp. 336-8.
34. Joao de Barros, *Decadas da Asia*, Decada I, Livro IX, Capitulo I, Lisboã, 1777-8.
35. *Diario de Viagem de Vasco da Gama*, Porto, 1945, vol. 2, pp. 229 and 301.
36. Dourado's atlas of 1571 mentions the port of Calecare. See Tome

Pires, *The Suma Oriental of Tome Pires and the Book of Francisco Rodrigues,* London, 1944, vol. II, p. 271.

37. Barbosa, *The Book of Duarte Barbosa,* op. cit., pp. 122 and 271.
38. Paramakudi taluk was in Duvvur or Tugavur Kurram in the fifteenth century. For details see *ARE* 511 of 1963. Duvvur Kurram was located in Maymakara valanadu in the eleventh century. For details see *ARE* 34 of 1947.
39. Gaspar Correia, *Lendas da India*, Lisboã, 1858-64, tomo II, pp. 278-9.
40. *IANTT*, Mss. *Nucleo Antigo*, no. 873, fl. 82v. Rodugues was at the pearl fishery coast in May 1522. See *ANTT*, *CC*, III-7-103.
41. *IANTT*, *CC*, I-30-36, fl. 8v-9. The text runs as follows, *Onde Calecare* he Mui bom nomen e vosso servidor e com que se primeiro asemtou o trato o quall he outro de Cale or em vija dyse que davia tamto porque nom pescase *que deria vosa alteza.*
42. Ibid., Letter from António Fonseca to the king of Portugal written from Goa dated 18 October 1523.
43. *Cartas de Affonso de Albuquerque*, Lisboã, 1935, tomo VIII, p. 184.
44. De Barros, *Decadas da Asia*, Decada IV, Livro II, Capitulo VII. This amount was primarily paid by the *nayinar* for providing protection against sea pirates while carrying on pearl fishing. The king of Portugal with a view to controlling the movement of ships in the Pescaria coast appointed a Captain Major with an armada and some soldiers. This fleet provided protection to the Portuguese settlers from attacks by the Muslims.
45. *IANTT*, *CC*, IIa-120-104 (24 October 1524).
46. Ibid, CC, IIa-129-74 (13 October 1525 to 28 October 1525).
47. Ibid, CC, IIa-132-151 (24 December 1525).
48. Ibid, CC, IIa-129-74.
49. Ibid, CC, IIa-132-151. It has also another document in it dated 10 April 1526.
50. *IANTT*, *As Gavetas da Torre do Tombo*, XV-19-11.
51. British Library (hereafter, BL), London, *Additional Manuscripts*, Codice 209021, fl. 65. Pero Vaz Amaral Diogo de Botelho and Manoel de Macedo from Kanya Kumari came to Kilakkarai with an *armada* on 21 April 1531. There was also a Genoese called *Janim* in the fleet. See Maria Herminia Maldonado, *Relação das Naos e Armadas de Índia comos* successors delles que se Poderam saber para noticia e instrucao dos *curiozos e amantes da Historia da India*, Coimbra, 1985, p. 65.
52. De Silva, 'The Portuguese and Pearl fishing', p. 18. It may, however, be recalled that the Portuguese declared cinnamon as the crown monopoly item of trade in 1521.
53. *IANTT*, *Nucleo Antigo*, no. 609, fl. 39 *Receita e Despesa da nau Santa*

Maria de Monte em viagem de Goa para Ormuz e Muscate, 25.1.1520 to 9.1.1521.

54. 'Side lights on South Indian History from the Letters and Records of Contemporary Jesuit Missionaries', *St. Joseph's College Magazine*, Trichnopoly, vol. 18, no. 4, February 1930, p. 202.
55. Samuel Purchas, *His Pilgrims,* Glasgow, vol. 10, 1905, p. 105.
56. Gaspar Correia, *Lenden da India.*, op. cit., tomo IV, capitulo VI, p. 324.
57. Letter of António Miranda de Azevedo from Kochi to King Dom João III dated 8 December 1527, in *As Gavetas da Torre do Tombo*, Lisbon, 1974, vol. 10, pp. 554-8.
58. Correia, *Lenden da Índia.*, tomo III, p. 831.
59. P.E. Pieris, *Ceylon and the Portuguese*, Tellipalai, 1920, p. 48.
60. Letter of João Fernandez Correia to Dom João III written from Goa, dated 10 December 1541 in *IANTT*, *CC*, 1-71-29.
61. Georg Schurhammer, *Orientalia*, Lisboã, 1963, pp. 244-5.
62. Henry Heras, *The Aravidu Dynasty of Vijayanagara*, Madras, 1927, vol. 1, pp. 156-7.
63. *DI*, vol. 1 (1540-9), doc. 86, p. 589. See also letter of Fr. Marcos to Fr. António de Quadros, Provincial of the Society of Jesus in India, written from Punnaikayal dated 24 December 1559 in *DI*, vol. 7, p. 294. See also *Selectae Indicarum Epistolae*, Roma, vol. 21, p. 98.
64. Henry Heras, *The Aravidu Dynasty of Vijayanagara,* Madras, 1927, p. 161.
65. Ibid.
66. A. Krishnaswami, *Tamil Country Under Vijayanagara*, Annamalai Nagar, 1964, p. 239.
67. *ARE*, 1940-3, p. 288. Podatur mentioned in the inscription is identified with Pogalur near Rameshwaram.
68. Heras, *The Aravidu Dynasty,* p.161.
69. For details, see K.S. Mathew, 'Trade in the Indian Ocean and the Portuguese System of Cartazes', in Malyn Newitt (ed.), *The First Portuguese Colonial Empire*, Exeter, 1986, pp. 69-94.
70. A. Krishnaswami, *Tamil Country*, p. 239. Varthema, the traveller, mentions (1508) the importance of Rameshwaram to the Hindus where the impression of the feet of their god Rama could be seen. See Ludovico di Varthema, *The Travels of Ludo Vico di Varthema in Egypt, Syria, Arabia Desert and Arabia Felix in Persia India and Ethiopia,* AD *1503-1508*, J.W. Jones, edited in G.P. Badgar, London, p. 74, Tamil literature also speaks of the importance of this place. See Ahananuru, V. 70: Tevaram, Rameshwaram padigams in III and IV Tirumurai. Duarte Barbosa, the Portuguese writer in the Kannur factory, also speaks of this big Hindu temple at Rameshwaram in the Kilakkarai region as having a large revenue. A portion of this amount was spent

for feeding a large number of Brahmans. The Hindus of the area lived around this historic abode of Siva and they celebrated a great festival once in twelve years. Visiting the temple on this feast day was considered as a sacred act to obtain salvation. The king of Vijayanagara also attended the celebration and he had a holy bath in the various sacred tanks, marked by rituals and music. See Duarte Barbosa, *The Book of Duarte Barbosa,* op. cit., vol. 2, pp. 120-2. Rameshwaram has twenty-two *thirthas* in it. See Kandapurana, canto 43. According to *Padma Purana*, sins like Brahminicide will vanish by a visit to Rameshwaram, see *Padma Purana*, Srishti Kanda, canto 38.

71. João Fernandez Correia was Captain of the Pearl fishery coast in 1540. See Gaspar Correia, *Lenden da Índia,* op. cit., tomo 4, p. 151. João Ferreira de Andrade was Captain of the fishery coast in 1550. Luciano Ribeiro, *Registo da Casa da Índia,* vol. 2, no. 440, fl. 328. Manuel Roiz Coutinho was the Captain of the pearl fishery coast during the years of 1549, 1551, 1555 and 1560. See Armando Cortesao and Luis de Albuquerque (eds.), *Obras Completas de João de Castro*, vol. 3, Coimbra, 1976, pp. 89, 102 and 171.
72. A. Krishnaswami, *Tamil Country*, p. 239.
73. Ibid., p. 240.
74. De Silva, 'The Portuguese and Pearl Fishing', p. 22, see also *Monumenta Xaveriana*, vol. 1, p. 137. *Litterae Indicarum nunc Primum edite*, Florentinae, 1887, XXIV, 15.
75. *BL, Additional Manuscripts*, Codice 2090212, fl. 123. S.G. Pereira, 'The Jesuits in Ceylon in the XVI & XVII Centuries', *The Ceylon Antiquarian*, July 1919, vol. 5, pt. I, pp. 31-41.
76. According to Jorge de Cunha de Sousa, the Captain of Mannar, pearl fishing was conducted at Kilakkarai and also at another place called Karaithivu (Cara diva). He refers to the existence of two pearl banks at two different places. R.J. de Lima Felner, *Subsidios para a Historia da India Portuguesa*, Lisbon, 1868, p. 244. See also *Tombo do Estado da India*, fl. 206. This is corroborated by what is stated in the regimentos (sailing orders). The large pearl fishery was known as Pescaria Grande and the small one was called Pescaria Pequena. See Tikri Abeysinghe, *A Study of the Portuguese Regimentos on Sri Lanka at the Goa Archives*, Colombo, n.d. According to Georg Schurhammer, pearl fishing was conducted in the months of March and September, based on the seasons, which, however, seems implausible as weather conditions in the Gulf of Mannar were not conducive for carrying on pearl fishing twice annually. Marine archaeological excavations conducted in this region during April 1990 show that stone anchors of the 8-inch type were used in pearl fishing. See Natana Kasinathan (ed.), *Seminar on Marine Archaeology*, Madras, 1992, p. 40.
77. Felner, *Subsidies Para a Historia,* p. 244.

78. Ibid.
79. Ibid.
80. *Historical Archives of Goa* (hereafter *HAG*), Codex 1418 (1564-96). See Regimento of Mannar dated 31.1.1582 and 26.2.1597.
81. Ibid. *Coro* in Portuguese is corroborated with the Tamil term Kuru which means a small heap of articles for sale and it is here used in the context of dealing in pearls and jewels.
82. Vitorino Maghales Godinho, *Les Finances de etat Portugais des Indes Orientales (1517-1635)*, Paris, 1982, p. 317.
83. Ibid. See also Pissurlencar, *Regimentos das Fortalezas da India*, Goa, 1951, pp. 358-71.
84. Ibid.
85. Pissurlencar, *Regimentos das Fortalegas des India*, p. 371.
86. Georg Schurhammer, *Epistoale S. Francisci Xaverii alia que eius Scriptura,* Rome, 1944 (hereafter *EX*), vol. I, doc. 22, pp 190-2, doc. 45, pp. 243-7, by Francis Xavier in his letter written from Thazhai on 5 September 1544, says us that Punnaikayal was one of the places attacked by the Telugus. The house and the boat of the Portuguese Captain were set on fire and the Captain had fled.
87. *EX*, vol. I, pp. 222-3. Francis Xavier, in another letter dated 20 August 1544, mentions that the Telugus had left Punnaikayal and he continued to stay at Punnaikayal. See *EX*, vol. I, pp. 220-2.
88. Portuguese sources record this town as Punicale, Ponicale, etc. João de Barros, the Portuguese chronicler refers to Punnaikayal as Chercalle, which means small Kayal, as it was then a new settlement. João de Barros, *Decadas da Asia: Dos Feitos que os Portuguezes Fizeram no Descobrimento e Conquista dos Mares e Terras do Oriente*, Decada I, Livro 9, Capitulo I.
89. R. Caldwell, *A History of Tinnevelly*, Madras, 1881; Delhi, 1982, p. 72.
90. *DI*, vol. 3, doc. 44, p. 252. See also Silva Rego, *Documentação*, vol. 4, pp. 306-7, 310-11; vol. 5, pp. 206-30.
91. Ibid., vol. 10, p. 35.
92. Botelho, *Tombo do Eslada da Índia*, op. cit., p. 244. Botelho opines that the politics of the Jesuits resulted in the reduction of income from pearl fishery to the Portuguese Crown in 1552.
93. Ibid., p. 206.
94. António da Silva Rego, *Historia das Missoes do Padroado Portugues do Oriente (1500-1542),* vol. 2, Lisboã, 1949, pp. 332-1. See also *Documentação,* vol. 2, pp. 103, 132-5.
95. *DI*, vol. 1, no. 110; vol. 2, no. 116.
96. Ibid.
97. Georg Schurhammer, St. Francis Xavier, op. cit., vol. 3, p. 519.
98. Ibid., vol. 2, pp. 209-10.

99. Ibid., vol. 3, p. 342.
100. *IANTT*, *Coleção São Lourenço*, III, 350.
101. Silva Rego, *Documentação*, II, p. 251, IV, pp. 465-7.
102. *DI*, vol. 1, doc. 33, p. 214.
103. Ibid., vol. 5, p. 377; Sanceau, *CSL*, op. cit., vol. 2, pp. 336-8.
104. Georg Schurhammer, St. Francis Xavier, op. cit., vol. 2, p. 74.
105. Diogo do Couto, *Decadas da Asia*, Decada VII, p. 249.
106. Henry Heras, *The Aravidu Dynasty of Vijayanagara*, Madras, 1927, p. 159; *DI*, vol. 3, pp. 252-3; Diogo do Couto, *Decadas da Asia*, Decada 6, Livro 10, Capitulo 98.
107. *DI*, vol. 3, pp. 252-3, 238-9.
108. Ibid., vol. 4, p. 377; vol. 3, pp. 417-19; Diogo do Couto, *Decadas do Asia*, op. cit., 7, 8 II; Silva Rego, *Documentação*, vol. 8, pp. 141, 180-1, 269-70, 303-10, 364-5.
109. Biblioteca Academia das Ciências de Lisboã (hereafter BASCL), *Mss Azul*, no. 12, fl. 142.
110. Ibid.
111. S. Muhammed Husain Nayinar, *Tuhfat-Ul-Mujahiddin*, Madras, 1942, Section 12, p. 84, see also *BA*, Mss Codice 49-IV-50, fls. 278-80.
112. H. De Cunha Rivara, *Archivo Portuguez Oriental* (hereafter *APO-CR*), 6 Fasciculos in 9 vols., 1857-76, vol. V, pp. 397-8.
113. Diogo do Couto, op. cit., Decada VIII, Capitulo XV.
114. *BL*, *Additional Manuscripts*, Codice no. 209021, p. 123.
115. *DI*, vol. 4, pp. 31-2, 267, BASCL, *Mss Azul*, no.12, fls.142-7.
116. Pissurlencar, *Regimentos das Fortalezas da India*, Bastora, 1951, p. 359.
117. J.H. de Cunha Rivara, *Archivo Portuguese-Oriental.*, vol. 3, pt. I(a), Goa, 1857-76, p. 161.
118. *DI*, vol. 1, p. 221.
119. *ARSI*, *Mss Goa*, 53, fl. 15.
120. Gaspar Correia, *Lendas da Índia*, III, p. 823.
121. António da Silva Rego, *Documentação para a Historia das Missoes do Padroado Portugues do Oriente*, Lisboã, vols. 1-12, 1947-58, vol. 2, p. 243, Gaspar Correia, *Landas da Índia* op. cit., vol. 4, pp. 304-5.
122. Simão Botelho, 'O Tombo da Estado da India, 1554', in R.J. Lima Felner (ed.), *Subsidios para a Historia da India Portuguesa*, Lisbon, 1868, pp. 244-6.
123. Sanjay Subrahmanyam, 'Noble Harvest from the Sea', *Institutions and Economic Change in South Asia*, Delhi, 1996, p. 143.
124. IANTT, *Fragmentos*, Caixa 10, Maco 10, no. 12.
125. Pedro Texeira, *The Travels of Pedro Texeira*, tr. W.F. Sinclair, London, 1902.

126. In Sethu Nadu the taxation rate on *valai thoni* per annum was two *panam*, on pearl fishing per *toni* ten chanks and in salt pans per *kudi* a sum of two *panam* was collected during the period of Raghunatha Tirumalai Sethupathi. The document is dated 10 October 1659. S. Raju, *Sethupathi Seppedugal,* Tanjore, 1990, doc. 16, pp. 75-8. It was stated that per *toni* five pearls were given as *magamai* on 20 March 1699. It is mentioned in the Tirupullanai copper plate. See ibid., doc. 43. An agreement was reached on 8 May 1694 between the Dutch and Kilavan Sethupathi. The Brahmins and devotees who wanted to cross the Pampan channel through *toni* could obtain passes and a receipt was issued from the Rameshwaram *karayakathar* and Rameshwaram *pandaram* on 22 January 1610. For details see ibid., copper plate no. 4, p. 13. Mannar pearl fishery came under the jurisdiction of the Sethupathis and the portion belonging to King Dalavay Sethupathi Katha Devar was given as a gift to the Rameshwaram temple on 22 January 1625. Ibid., doc. 5, pp. 19-22.
127. Jose Wicki, 'Duas Relações sobre a Situação da India Portuguesa nos an nos 1568-1569', in *Studia*, vol. 18, 1961, pp. 151-3.
128. Fernão Lopes de Castanheda, *História do Descobrimento e Conquista da India Pelos Portugueses,* 8, Porto, 1975, p. 173, Gaspar Correia, *Lendas da India,* 3 Porto, 1975, p. 823, Jose Wicki, *Documenta Indica*, vols. 1-18, Roma, 1948-88, vol. 13, pp 184-6.
129. Letter of Fr. Henrique Henriques to the Jesuit Superior General, 6 December 1577, Josep Wicki, *DI*, vol. 13, pp. 184-6.
130. *AGS*, *Secretarias Provinciales*, Codice 1551, fl. 204-15.
131. *Archivum Romanum Societatis Jesu* (hereafter *ARSI*), Mss, *Goa Collections,* vol. 33, fl.326, no.14. Tikiri Abeysinghe, *A Study of the Portuguese Regimentos on Sri Lanka at the Goa Archives*, Colombo, n.d., p. 6.
132. *ARSI*, Mss, *Goa*, vol. 47, fl.365, V, no. 33, fl.326.
133. Ibid., no. 66, fl. 3-3v. See also, S. Arunachalam, *The History of the Pearl Fishery of the Tamil Coast*, Annamalai Nagar, 1952.
134. *ARSI*, Mss, *Goa*, vol. 66, fl. 2-7. The Portuguese had erected a mud wall around the port of Tuticorin what was strong enough to withstand attacks from enemies. For details, see *Letters Received by the English East India Company from its Servants in the East*, vol. 1, 1602-13, London, 1896, p. 9. See also, HAG, MDR, Livro 17, fl. 95. The walls of the Tuticorin settlement had been broken and destroyed in a fight between the Captain of Tuticorin and the Jesuits concerning the control of the Church of St. Peter at Tuticorin. According to the list of officials at the various Portuguese settlements in India prepared in 1616, there was no Portuguese Captain appointed at the port of Tuticorin. The post was vacant and the missionaries looked after the

paravas who declared the Crown of Portugal as their ruler. See *Lista de todos as Capitanias e Cargos que ha na India E sua Estimacaoe Rendimento Porcao mais ou menos* (as dated 14 November 1616) in *Revista Portuguesa Colonial e Maritima*, Lisboã, 1900-1, pp. 344-53.

135. *HAG*, Mss, *Monções do Reino* (hereafter *MDR*), Livro 17, fl. 95.
136. Letter of King Filippe to Viceroy Rui Lourenço de Tavora dated 20 February 1610, in Bulhão Pato, *Documentos Remetidos da India*, vol. 1, Lisbon, 1880, p. 342.
137. Couttre et al. (eds.), *Jacques de Couttre*, Madrid, 1990, p. 242.
138. Biblioteca Publica e Arquivo Distrital Evora (hereafter *BPADE*), Mss, CV/ 2-7, fl. 57v; BA, Mss Codice, 51-v-36, fl. 37.
139. Andre Coelho, *Relação de muita importancia que trata das fortalezas prisidiose feitorias que o inimigo Olandes tem nestas da India 1621, BNL*, Mss. *Reservados*, Codex 638, fl. 5.
140. R.A. Deh Bulhao Pato (ed.), *Documentos Remetidos da India ou Livros da Moncoes*, vol. 10, Lisboa, 1972, p. 48.
141. Pissurlencar, *Assentos do Conselho do Estado*, vol. 1, pt. I (1624-7), Goa, 1953, pp. 66-7.
142. Pissurlencar, *Assentos do Conselho do Estado*, 5 vols., Goa, 1953-83, vol. I, p. 361. For conflicts and disorder, see fl. 24 (1610). See also Liv. 5, fls. 75 and 126 (1612).
143. 'Side lights on South Indian History from the Letters and Records of the Contemporary Jesuit Missionaries (1542-1756)' (hereafter, 'Side lights'), *St. Joseph's College Magazine*, Trichnopoly, vol. 18, no. 14, 1929, p. 173.
144. *MPJA, Litterae Annuae*, vol. 3, p. 22, vol. 8, pp. 16, 18, 30. 'Side lights', p. 174.
145. *ARSI*, Mss *Goa*, no. 47, fl. 365v.
146. *HAG*, *MDR*, Livro 19C, fls. 1166-7; ibid., Livro 20, fl. 45v.
147. *ACE*, vol. 1, doc. 18.
148. *HAG*, *MDR*, Livro 19B, 27/2-4; AGS, Mss, *Secretarias Provinciales*, Codice 1490, fl. 194. HAG, MDR, Livro 40, fl. 69; AHU, Mss India, Caixa 6, dated 1 December 1619.
149. *HAG*, *MDR*, Livro 10 D, 44/2/2, fl. 1166.
150. Antonio Bocarro, Decada 13, op. cit., pp. 368-9.
151. The port of Punnaikayal served as an entrepot for sea travel and maritime trade between Sri Lanka and the pearl fishery coast owing to its strategic location. The Portuguese carried rice, butter, meat, guns and ammunition from there to Colombo, Batticaloa and other ports of Sri Lanka. See *IANTT*, *CC*, II-1 14-21, 'Laurence A. Noonan, *John of Empoli and his Relations with Affonso de Albuquerque*, Lisboa, 1989, p. 209. Thus Punnaikayal played a major role in extending the commercial interests of the Portuguese with Sri Lanka.

The Portuguese Captain of the Pescaria coast imported rice into the region and retained the monopoly over rice also. He made rice available at a price which he himself fixed for sale on bith cash and credit. See, Georg Schurhammer, St. Francis Xavies, op. cit., vol. 3, p. 520, vol. 2, p. 450.

152. A single-decked sail-boat as large as a small caravel for twenty-five to thirty persons, used in pearl fishery is called a *champana*. Ibid., vol. 3, p. 377.
153. Ibid., vol. 3, p. 378.
154. Joao de Barros, *Decadas Da Asia*, op. cit., Decada III, Livro IV, Capitulo VI.
155. *ARE* 396 of 1907. The amount collected was allowed to be used towards worship in the local temple. There is a place called Muthupettai which literally means in Tamil 'Market of pearls' and the merchant guild of Naalu pattanattu Pathinen Vishayattar gave their consent for collecting the amount. See *ARE* 398 of 1907. Textiles called *madichilai* were brought by hawkers and taxes were collected on them in 1545-6. The Textile were generally re-exported from here.
156. Castanheda, Historia, op. cit., Livro II, Capitulo XXII, p. 260; Diogo do Couto, Decada da Asia Decada 10, part I, Livro l, Capitulo VII, p. 51.
157. N. Venkataramanayya, *Studies*, p. 297.
158. *ARSI*, Mss *Goa*, no. 53, fl. 15; See also Duarte Barbosa, *The Book of Duarte Barbosa*, op. cit, vol. 2, p. 24.
159. *John Huyghen Van Linschoten*, *The Voyages of John Huyghen Van Linschoten to the East Indies, from the Old Translation of 1598,* ed. R.A. Tiele, London, 1885, vol. 2, p. 733; Garcia de Orta, *Colloquies on the Simple Drugs of India*, Dehradun, 1979, pp. 296-301. The native inscriptions record various kinds of pearls: round pearls (*vattam*), roundish pearls (*anuvattam*), old pearls (*oppumuthu*), small pearls (*kuru muthu*), crude pearls (*karadu*) and flat pearls (*sappattai*). See, *SII*, vol. 2, p. 34, sections 9 and 10.
160. Vitorino Magalhes Godinho, *Os Descobrimentos e a Economia Mundial,* Lisboa, 1965, vol. 2, p. 107.
161. The study of K.S. Mathew has revealed that there is little evidence of pearls in the official Portuguese commercial statistics for the period of 1500-30, when pearl fishery was under the control of the Arab Muslims. K.S. Mathew, *Portuguese Trade With India in the Sixteenth Century*, New Delhi, 1983, p. 134. During the Portuguese period of control over pearl fishery (i.e. after the conversion of the paravas), records attest to the increase in the trade of pearls. They are found in the list of items purchased by the Portuguese. *The Fugger Newsletters*, second series, 1568-1605, edited by Victor Von Klar Wilt, translated by L.S.R. Byrne, London, 1926, p. 45.

162. Duarte Barbosa, *The Book of Duarte Barbosa*, op. cit., vol. 2, p. 124. See also, *Documentos sobre os Portugueses*, vol. 2, p. 9; *AHU*, India, Caixa 3, doc. 168 (1615) 108 Bizalhos; Caixa 5, Document 164, (1618) 71 Bizalhos; Caixa 11, Document 193 (1635) 10 bags of pearls were sent from Goa to Lisbon.
163. Teensma (ed.), *Jacques de Couttre,* Madrid, 1990, p. 243.
164. *AHU*, India Caixa 4, Doc. 25 (1616) 36 sacos of *Aljofar; Assentos do Conselho da Fazenda* (hereafter *ACF*), 1163, pp. 17-17v (1637). Four small bags of pearls were sent from Goa to Lisbon.
165. Om Prakash, *Bullion for Goods: European and Indian Merchants in the Indian Ocean Trade, 1500-1800*, Delhi, 2004.
166. George Davison Winius, 'The Portuguese Asia "Decadencia" Revisited', in Alfred Honer and Richard A. Preto-Rodas (eds.), *Empire in Transition: The Portuguese World in the Time of Cameos*, Gainesville, 1985, p. 108.
167. Details of the Financial statements of the *Estado da India* are available from 1581 to 1634. For details, see Joao Manuel de Almeida Teles e Cunha *Economia de um Imperio: Economia, Politica do Golfo Persico, Elementos Conjuntaraia, 1595, 1635,* Dissertacão Mestrado, Universidade Nova de Lisboa, 1995, p. 322.

4

The Demand for Horses, Elephants and Saltpetre: The State and the Traders

The Tamil country was ruled by many *nayaks* during the sixteenth century.[1] The Portuguese who settled down on the Tamil coast established contacts with the *nayaks* and also the emperors of Vijayanagara. Portuguese documents throw some light on their relations with the *nayaks* of Paramakudi, Gingee, Thanjavur and Madurai in the Tamil country which was then under Vijayanagara rule. After the defeat of the Vijayanagara forces in the Battle of Rakshas Tangadi (Talikota) in January 1565, only some *nayakdoms* such as Madurai, Gingee and Thanjavur emerged as quasi-independent units and survived as centres of local power[2] with their economic activities limited to the region under their respective control. However, these Portuguese sources relating to trade, politics and diplomacy between the *nayaks* and Portuguese have hitherto remained largely inaccessible to scholars.[3]

Historians like Robert Sewell, of course, have drawn much from the Portuguese chronicles to study the relations between Vijayanagara and Portugal.[4] Henry Heras in 1927 used the Portuguese missionary letters, which became an important source about the Jesuit ambassadorial missions to the court of Chandragiri and Vellore, revealing new aspects of Vijayanagara-Portuguese relations, particularly of the political changes that took place in the early seventeenth century.[5] They, however, did not deal with either the economy of the country under the *nayaks* or their involvement in promoting the economy of the region.

Sanjay Subrahmanyam's study has shed some light on Portuguese trade in Mylapore, Nagapattinam and Masulipatnam in the Bay of Bengal region but is not enough about the economy of the region, even though he deals with the overseas trade of the time.[6] None of these studies deal with the *nayak's* role in the development of trade and commerce but highlight the linkages between the commercial activity of the ports on the Tamil coast with the political developments in Tamil Nadu during the *nayak* period in the sixteenth and seventeenth centuries.

While the sixteenth century witnessed the rise of political and economic power centred on exploiting the potentialities of pearl fishery in the south-eastern coast of India, the seventeenth century saw the entry of the Dutch and the English into the arena. Although pearls were the chief item of export from this region, besides chank during the sixteenth century, the growing needs of maritime trade opened up avenues for the Portuguese in various other strategic commodities like horses, elephants and gunpowder. Thus writing the history of the role of ports in pearl fishing during this period makes little sense when pearl fishery was not conducted. Even historians like V. Rangachari[7] and R. Sathiyanatha Aiyar[8] have not dealt with the involvement of native rulers in overseas trade. The reason may be that the Portuguese sources were not adequately tapped and used. Other writers like K. Rajayyan,[9] K. Rajaram[10] and N. Subrahmanyam[11] who have traced the political history of this region and period have not linked the political events that took place in the hinterland with the development of trade in the ports on the south-eastern coast of India. This chapter is designed to help scholars understand the state of affairs before the Dutch firmly established their control in the Bay of Bengal region and how subsequently they posed a new challenge to the Portuguese influence in the region.

The Portuguese established their settlements at Tuticorin, Nagapattinam and Devanampattinam only to secure the profits of trade to the Portuguese Crown. The decline of their trade may be attributed to the ineffective control and the unsatisfactory organization of the *Estado da Índia* in the late sixteenth and early seventeenth centuries. One basic feature of the Portuguese expansion in the south-eastern coast (see map 3) of India was that their activities were confined only to the coastal areas and did not extend very far into the interior.

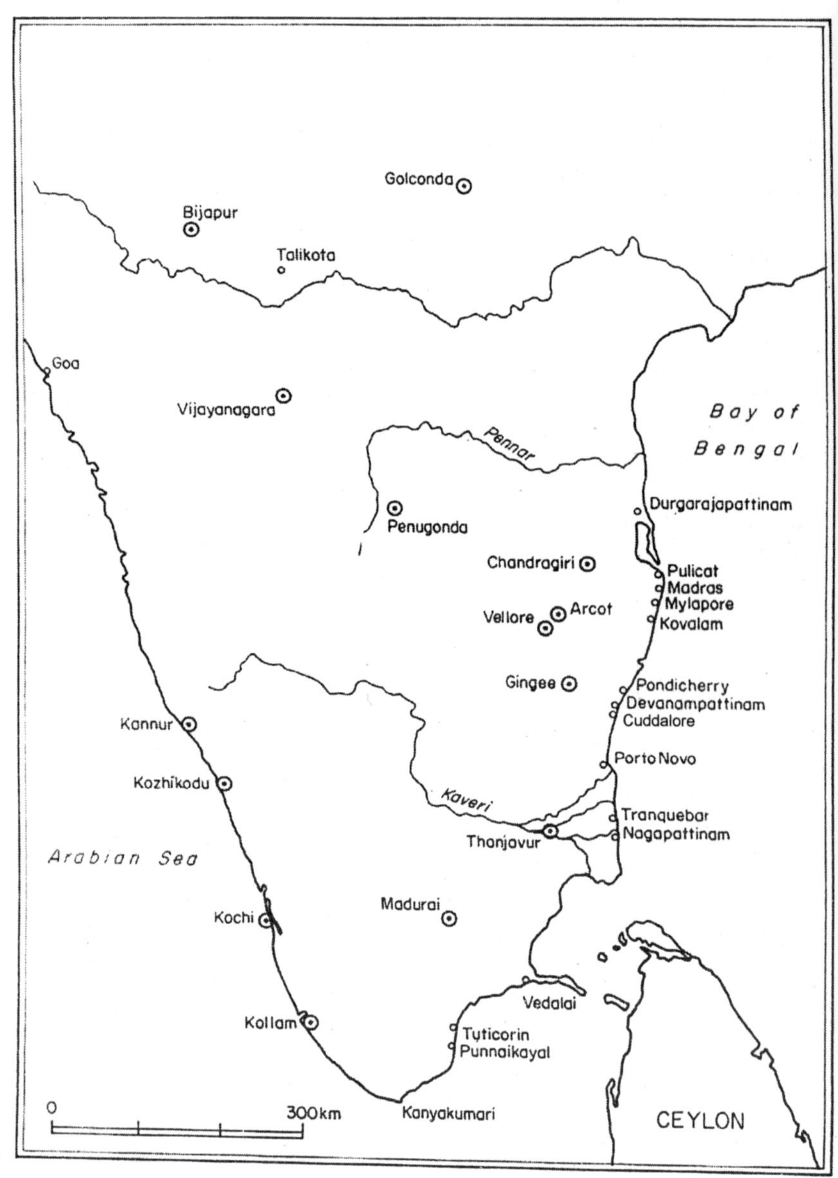

MAP 3: COURT TOWNS AND PORTS IN SOUTH INDIA, 1500-1800

PORTUGUESE TRADE IN HORSES

The medieval horse trade between India and Arabia continued to flourish even after the arrival of the Portuguese. The demand for horses was so great that Martim Affonso de Sousa, the viceroy of Goa (1542-5), had issued instructions to the Portuguese Captain in Ormuz to send forty horses every year to the port of Chaul on the western coast of India and twenty horses to the ports of Bay of Bengal as there was a lucrative trade in animals on the east coast.[12] Dom João de Castro, the Portuguese governor of India (1545-8) had in fact given permission in 1545 to the king of Kannur (Cannanore) to send four ships every year with local merchants to bring horses from Ormuz.[13] Some of the horses imported from Persia and Arabia into Chaul were first sent to the port of Kochi and from there they reached Kanyakumari for resale.[14] Some Portuguese merchants like Pedro Alvarez de Mesquita and Diogo de Lisboã who were stationed at Kanyakumari took the horses in their ships to the east coast ports of Kayal and Punnaikayal. Further, some *casados* (married settlers) in Kochi also used to take horses to the Coromandel coast because of the profit that they could derive from horse trade.[15]

Owing to the great demand for horses, the Portuguese viceroy even encouraged the Portuguese to purchase the horses directly from Arabia. These imported horses were sold to the various *nayaks* stationed close to the various ports of south India although the main sales were at the city of Vijayanagara where the emperor needed the swift moving horses for his army. The rulers still depended on horses to carry on their warfare. The horses brought by the Portuguese to Kochi were purchased by native merchants and then taken to the Tamil country owing to its proximity. According to one record, as many as forty horses were bought at Kochi for resale at Kanyakumari.[16] António Fernandes, a native of the Malabar coast, had his horse-trading establishment at Kanyakumari.[17]

So lucrative was the trade in horses that one Ruy Gonsalves de Caminha, who became the Comptroller of Finance in 1547, was himself a horse dealer before he took up the post.[18] The horses that were brought from West Asia to the ports of the western coast of India were, however, allowed to be taken for resale only after the payment of taxes.[19] Some of the Portuguese merchants who lived in Kanyakumari were constantly on the lookout for information about the arrival of horses from Arabia at Kannur and Chaul so that they could buy them for resale in the Tamil region.[20]

The Portuguese are reported to have sold horses to the *nayak* of Kanyakumari region as early as on 11 October 1512.[21] When they were planning to gain a foothold in the pearl fishery coast, then centred at Kilakkarai, the opportunity to sell horses to the *nayak* of Paramakudi who was in dire need of them for his army was an advantage for the Portuguese.[22] The Portuguese on the pearl fishery coast requested the then viceroy to arrange to supply the horses that came from Ormuz to the ports of Goa, Chaul and Kannur. The viceroy in turn made special efforts to supply the requisite number of horses as per the demands placed by the Captain of the fishery coast so that they could be supplied to Tumbichi Nayaka. Later evidence suggests that some Portuguese private merchants also began to participate in this lucrative trade with the *nayak* of Paramakudi.[23] João da Cruz, a horse trader, in a letter written to Dom João III, the king of Portugal, asked for the exclusive privilege of selling horses in the *nayakdom* of (Chembeche Naque) Thumbichi Nayaka.[24] Some clever Portuguese merchants even, managed to win the patronage of the local ruler who allowed them to carry on their horse trade in the Kilakkarai region.

The king of Portugal had appointed Cosme de Paiva in 1542 as Captain of the fishery coast and he took temporary residence at Tuticorin to protect the paravas against attacks from pirates.[25] He also took an interest in developing the horse trade with Maravarman Sundara Pandya (1531-5), the Pandya ruler of Tirunelveli. During 1544 he sold horses for personal gain and took little care of the paravas.[26] There were several brokers and horse trade agents in Chaul who supplied horses to the Tamil coast.[27] However, the horse trade with the Pandya ruler declined in the second half of the sixteenth century.

Saltpetre from the Coromandel

Saltpetre (potassium nitrate/ KnO_3) was another priority item of the Portuguese trade with India. It was procured in the neighbourhood of Goa,[28] Barcelore,[29] Chaul,[30] Surat,[31] and Cochin.[32] Saltpetre purchased from these places was in turn exported to Portugal[33] and sold to the merchants of Sevilha in Spain.[34] As early as 1524 the Portuguese prohibited the Muslims and the Hindus from enjoying to the in saltpetre trade on the western coast.[35]

The Portuguese who had by 1524 settled at Santhome in Mylapore procured saltpetre from the hinterland and sent it to Kochi for refining and reshipment to Portugal.[36] Some quantity of saltpetre was also sent to Sunda (in Indonesia) by António Dinis, a *casado* from Mylapore who is reported to have sailed in a ship carrying five barrels of saltpetre from the Coromandel coast.[37]

The treaty of 19 September 1547 signed between João de Castro, the viceroy of Goa, with the king of Vijayanagara stipulated that all saltpetre extracted from the various mines in Vijayanagara kingdom was to be sold only to the Portuguese and was not to reach the territory of the sultan of Bijapur. This treaty attests to Portuguese interest in gaining control over the trade in this strategic commodity. The reason was that saltpetre was used in the manufacture of gunpowder and it was scarce in Europe.[38]

Following the defeat of the Vijayanagara forces in the Battle of Talikota, the viceroy of Goa signed a treaty in 1569 with Sultan Adilshah of Bijapur, who agreed to supply saltpetre besides sulphur and iron to the Portuguese. This contract did not, however, go through smoothly owing to the disturbed conditions in the region after 1569.[39] Later, with the founding of the *Companhia Portuguesa das India Orientales* (The Portuguese East India Company) in 1580, the purchase and export of saltpetre to Lisbon became its responsibility.[40]

The development of commerce in the port of Devanampattinam owed a great deal to the rich natural resource of saltpetre which was available in the hinterland. Among all the commodities available in this region, like textiles, indigo, etc., the most prized item was saltpetre owing to its heavy demand by the Portuguese. Saltpetre was necessary for maintaining their military superiority. A passing reference by Fr. Nicholas Pimenta on the availability of saltpetre and its use for production of gunpowder at Gingee[41] lends support to the theory that trade played a complementary role in nurturing the political ambitions of the Portuguese in the Tamil country. The large quantities of saltpetre procured from the hinterland of Devanampattinam were stored in the saltpetre godowns (*casa de salitre*), which figure in the plan of the Portuguese settlement of the period.[42] This important centre of saltpetre trade on the Coromandel coast was, however, granted to the Dutch in 1610 by the *nayak* of Gingee and the Portuguese were driven out from there. Thus procurement of saltpetre in the Devanampattinam region came to a halt.[43] The Portuguese had therefore to move on to other places in the hinterland of the Tamil coast to procure it.

ELEPHANTS FOR THE *NAYAK* OF GINGEE

As Surappa, the *nayak* of Gingee (1550-86) had to pay tribute to the Vijayanagara king, he had to collect the required taxes in the area under his jurisdiction. He was also in need of elephants for his army. Therefore, the *nayak* of Gingee was keen to encourage the Portuguese to settle down in the port of Devanampattinam within his territory and encouraged them to supply elephants. On 13 March 1580, Dom Filippe I, the king of Portugal (1580-98), appointed Damião Paes as Resident Captain at Devanampattinam. This marked the beginning of Portuguese activities in this port and its hinterland.[44] The port gained importance with the advent of the Portuguese. Although the Captain was entitled to hold office for three years, the Portuguese viceroy of Goa allowed him in 1584 to continue for another term of three years, during which period he rebuilt the trading factory with the approval of the *nayak* of Gingee.[45]

There were some natives who were also engaged in overseas trade and they supplied elephants to the *nayak* of Gingee.[46] The name of one Linganna appears as a broker who is said to have once failed in his negotiations with the king of Kandy for the import of elephants to the port of Devanampattinam. On another occasion he is reported to have brought two elephants from Sri Lanka (one big and another small), but without anchoring at the Portuguese port of Devanampattinam, he sailed off to the port of Pulicat because he had had a dispute with a servant of the port official of Devanampattinam when he was in Kandy.[47] The private Portuguese traders who had settled in Devanampattinam did not realize the significance of elephant trade and were also not interested as it was difficult to procure elephants.

A Dutch ship which set sail from Holland in 1607 had to seek anchorage at Devanampattinam on 9 November 1608 owing to adverse winds in the Bay of Bengal. This ship was allowed to anchor at the port by the local port official under the control of the *nayak* of Gingee. Immediately after their arrival in Devanampattinam, Pieter Gerritsz Baugonjte, the Dutch captain along with three other men went to Gingee, the capital of the *nayakdom*. They reached Gingee on 26 November 1608. Muthu Krishnappa Nayak (1597-1624) received them with great joy and offered them a *cowle* (a permit) on 30 November 1608, allowing them to trade at Devanampattinam as the Portuguese had failed to meet the elephant requirements of the *nayak*.[48] According to a letter by a Jesuit, the *nayak* of Gingee received the Dutch very hospitably and requested them to supply elephants, and as quickly as possible, as he was in dire need of them.[49] The Dutch, who learnt that the Portuguese had a powerful presence there and were also friendly with the port official of Muthu Krishnappa Nayaka, attempted to supply the elephants to win favour from the *nayak* of Gingee. They gave rich presents to the *nayak*, and as a result, the Portuguese were driven out of the port of Devanampattinam on 4 November 1609. The Dutch had also sent costly gifts to the king of Kandy to secure elephants from there. According to Dutch sources three elephants were expected to arrive at Thirupathiripuliyur by 1 May 1610. The king of Kandy also sent his envoy to the Dutch with a golden ring studded with blue stones in addition to five sacks of cinnamon. It was further resolved that the Dutch would henceforth make arrangements to supply ten to twelve elephants to meet the requirements of the *nayak* of Gingee.[50]

In the meanwhile, the Portuguese also took, immediate steps to arrange for the supply of elephants to the *nayak* of Gingee in a bid to please the *nayak* and have the Dutch thrown out from Devanampattinam and thereby have the port restored to them. At this time (1616), the king of Ava (in Myanmar) had sent his envoys to Rui Dias Sampaio, the Portuguese Captain of Santhome. An agreement was signed on 29 December 1616 with the king of Ava for the supply of elephants needed by the Portuguese in exchange for Coromandel textiles.[51] Elephants were successfully brought from Siam and Ava to the Coromandel coast. In due course, the Portuguese in Sri Lanka also managed to hinder the import of elephants from Kandy by the Dutch.[52] The friendly relationship that existed between the *nayak* of Gingee and the Dutch did not permit the Portuguese either to sell the elephants or to get back the port of Devanampattinam. The Portuguese, who contacted the king of Kandy and received the elephants, found it easy to sell the animals to the *nayak* of Thanjavur.[53]

SALTPETRE FROM THE MADURAI *NAYAKDOM*

The efforts to procure adequate quantities of saltpetre from the west coast to meet the full requirement of *Casa da Pólvora* (the gunpowder factory) at Goa were not very successful.[54] The Portuguese were thus in need of a regular supply of saltpetre from the eastern coast of India. The king of Portugal had sent repeated instructions since 1588 to Manuel de Sousa Coutinho, the viceroy of Goa (1588-91), to export saltpetre to Portugal.[55] He also requested the viceroy to establish cordial relation with Muthu Veerappa, the *nayak* of Madurai, (1609-27).[56] An annual target of ten or eleven pipas of saltpetre was fixed as the quantity to be exported from India to Portugal according to the royal order of 29 November 1606.[57] In 1630, Domingos Carneiro, a *casado* resident of Barcelore (modern Kundhapur on the west coast), and Fernão Carvalho of Kochi were appointed as brokers of the Portuguese East India Company for the purchase of saltpetre from this region.[58] The services of these brokers were later dispensed with and the *Estado do Índia* itself began to purchase saltpetre directly from the production centres. This step was taken with a view to organize the large-scale procurement of saltpetre in a more efficient and systematic manner.

With the drying up of pearl banks, the Portuguese authorities, who wanted to expand their trading activities in the pearl fishery coast, could not remain idle, especially after having learnt the availability of saltpetre in the territory of the Madurai *nayak*. Pearl fishery was not conducted between 1605 and 1621. The Portuguese therefore encouraged the married settlers of Tuticorin to divert their attention to trade in saltpetre. The *Assentos do Conselho do Estado* (Proceedings of the State Council) at Goa acknowledged that the port of Tuticorin had the most productive hinterland for the procurement of saltpetre.[59] It was also found suitable for carrying on export trade, resulting in the creation of a post of Captain and *Ouvidor* (judge) there.[60] Accordingly, Pedro Soares de Brito, who was living in Kochi, was appointed as the Captain of Tuticorin by Count de Linhares, the Portuguese viceroy of India, primarily to oversee the procurement of saltpetre in this region.[61] The Captain of Tuticorin was thereupon conferred the title of *O Contrador de salitre em toda de Pescaria*, i.e. the contractor of saltpetre for the entire fishery coast.[62]

Saltpetre was also mined in the environs of Madurai. It was reported to have been formed out of decaying nitrogenous matter coming into contact with calcareous earth through a natural process. These salty crusts were extracted from the mines, then mixed with water, thoroughly stirred and then allowed to remain for a few days. The crude saltpetre sediments settled down at the bottom and the water was drained out into shallow pits. This method of extracting saltpetre, which was common during the early seventeenth century, has been described by contemporary European travellers.[63] The crude saltpetre that was extracted from the pit had to be boiled to obtain saltpetre of an inferior quality. A second boiling produced a better quality of saltpetre and the best quality was obtained after a third or fourth boiling. Portuguese documents often mentioned that the saltpetre extracted from the Madurai region was better than that of any other part of India because it required only two boilings for purification,[64] which is why the Portuguese were keen to buy saltpetre from Madurai.

According to the evidence available, the *nayaka* rulers of south India, particularly Vitula Nayak,[65] and others[66] on the western coast and Tirumalai Nayak (1627-59), of Madurai did not allow the Europeans to procure saltpetre until their own requirements had been met. It was one of the main reasons why the Portuguese faced difficulties in purchasing saltpetre in this region. There is no recorded evidence to say that the *nayak* of Madurai was engaged in the manufacture of gunpowder. According to Portuguese sources, two types of saltpetre, *salitre branco* (white saltpetre) and *salitre preto* (black saltpetre), were available.[67] The growing need for gunpowder and ammunition in India and Portugal increased the demand for saltpetre. The outbreak of the Thirty Years War (1618-48) in Europe accelerated the export of saltpetre from India to Portugal.[68]

The price of saltpetre in the market fluctuated between Rs. 1½ and Rs. 6 per *maund* during this period. Moreover, saltpetre brought a profit of over 200 per cent in the Lisbon market.[69] Its high profit in the European market led to fierce competition among the Portuguese, the Dutch and the Danes, all of whom vied with one another to procure saltpetre from the territory of the Madurai *nayak* in the south-eastern coast.

In 1629, Kuttan Sethupathi, the Marava ruler of Ramnad, rebelled against the political authority of the *nayak* of Madurai.[70] Hence Tirumalai Nayak of Madurai was forced to transfer the capital of his kingdom from Tiruchirapalli to Madurai and march against the rebel ruler. He took the Marava country with the help of the Portuguese. A letter written by the Viceroy of Goa to the King of Portugal on 8 November 1630 confirms the fact that Portuguese troops went to the assistance of the *nayak* of Madurai.[71] The Portuguese by rendering this timely help to the *nayak* were able to extract favours from him. The *nayak* agreed to sever his ties with the Dutch. They were not permitted to enter his territories for the purpose of trade and their vessels could not visit the ports of his kingdom.

The Dutch in Pulicat, however, renewed their efforts to improve their relations with Tirumalai Nayak of Madurai, to enable them to procure saltpetre from his kingdom. They also planned to attack the Portuguese settlement at Tuticorin the same year. The *Estado da Índia* in turn requested the inhabitants of Tuticorin to drive the Dutch away.[72]

The Danes, on the other hand, came forward in 1631 to pay a sum of 40,000 *cruzados* to Tirumalai Nayak of Madurai and an annual tax of 3,000 *cruzados* for establishing a warehouse near

Tuticorin to procure saltpetre from the region.[73] All of these developments were discussed at length by the State Council of Portuguese India at Goa on 18 August 1631.[74] Realizing that the *nayak* of Madurai possessed saltpetre, Conde de Linhares, the Portuguese viceroy of India, sent an agent in 1631 to reside at Madurai in order to ensure a stable supply of saltpetre.[75] In these circumstances some court officials who were close to the *nayak* of Madurai came into conflict with the Portuguese agent in Madurai. Further, the missionaries also created problems in the matter of exercising spiritual and temporal powers over the paravas. But the appointment of a Captain and an *Ouvidor* in Tuticorin put a halt to the activities of the Jesuits in Madurai.[76]

The Portuguese agent who resided at Madurai to facilitate the purchase of saltpetre was suddenly arrested at the instance of the Portuguese missionaries.[77] The charges levelled by the missionaries against the agent were found to be untrue and it was shown that he was not a traitor.[78] This turn of events strengthened the hands of the Portuguese officials who were able to establish a better relationship with the *nayak* of Madurai.

The Portuguese, with a view to entering into a contract for the purchase of saltpetre from the *nayak* of Madurai, addressed a letter to him on 3 February 1633.[79] As per the agreement reached thereafter, the *nayak* agreed to sell one *bahar* (local weight) of saltpetre at the rate of 27½ *xerafins* to the Portuguese for each elephant delivered to the port of Tuticorin at the price of 662 *xerafins*. As per the terms of this agreement, the *nayak* could sell saltpetre only to the Portuguese and, in return, the Portuguese could sell the elephants only to the *nayak* of Madurai.[80] The agreement was opposed by Diogo de Mello de Castro, the Portuguese Captain of Sri Lanka, who had to send the elephants. His objection was that the agreement would cause a financial loss to the Portuguese Crown, for the price fixed for saltpetre was found to be too high and that of the elephants too low. Moreover, he contended that better terms could be obtained for saltpetre from the merchants of Bengal.[81] However, a compromise was arrived at finally to send elephants to Madurai in exchange for saltpetre.

The following year (1634), Miguel de Noronha, the viceroy of Goa, concluded another agreement with the *nayak* of Madurai by which the ruler again agreed to exchange Sri Lankan elephants for saltpetre.[83] This agreement was also considered disadvantageous to the Portuguese. This time the Portuguese Captain of Sri Lanka complained in a letter to the king of Portugal in 1634 that the Portuguese had not obtained exclusive rights for the saltpetre as the *nayak* was also selling it to the Dutch.[84] The Portuguese Captain therefore prevented the despatch of elephants to Madurai. He gave a very flimsy reason: that transporting elephants from Sri Lanka to Madurai was risky and difficult because of the famine and drought conditions that prevailed at Tuticorin, Madurai and Sri Lanka.[85]

As per the next agreement, the Portuguese had to supply a consignment of elephants at Tuticorin by November or December 1634, but the elephants could not be delivered even by the end of January 1635. Hence no saltpetre could be purchased from the *nayak* of Madurai.[86] The contract to supply 1,000 quintals of saltpetre in exchange for Sri Lankan elephants was kept in abeyance, without altering the price of each elephant which was fixed at 620 *xerafins* as per the trade agreement.[87] However, as the Portuguese could not supply the elephants the contract was void.

António de Meirelles Andrade, the same Portuguese Captain and *Ouvidor* of Tuticorin who had entered into the previous contract, was very keen, however, on renewing the saltpetre contract with the *nayak* of Madurai.[88] He successfully entered into an agreement on 8 February 1635 with the *nayak* who promised to deliver one *bahar* of saltpetre at the price of 25 *xerafins*. The *nayak* was keen this time to accept in exchange elephants of a minimum height of 3 feet alone. He also fixed the price of each foot at 120 *pardaus*. Further, he wanted the elephants to be delivered to the port of Tuticorin from where he would himself arrange for their transportation to Madurai.[89] It appears from a manuscript, now preserved at the Overseas Historical Archives (*Arquivo Historico Ultramarino*) in Lisbon that the Portuguese once more failed to supply the elephants (see Fig. 1). The *nayak* suggested to the Portuguese that instead of Sri Lankan elephants they supply, piece goods, textiles of silk, Agra velvet with golden base, metals such as sulphur from Siam, gold

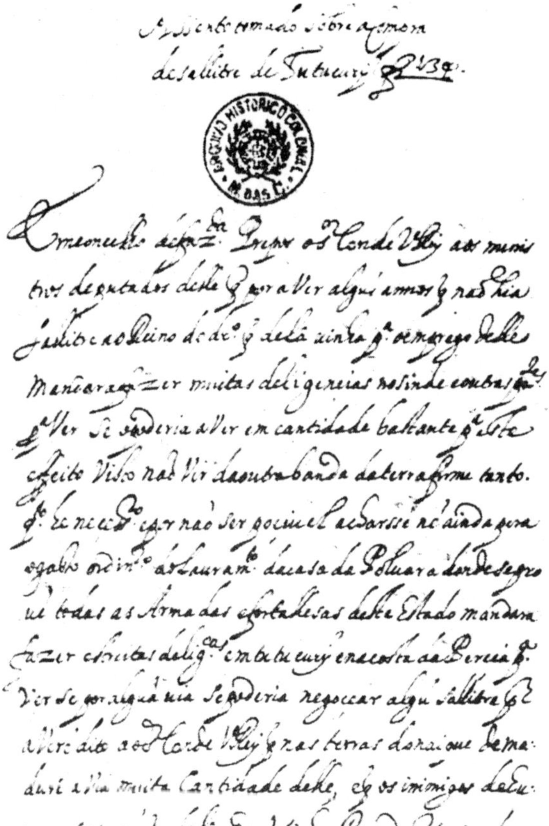

FIG. 1: AN AGREEMENT REACHED BY THE PORTUGUESE TO BUY SALTPETRE FROM THE *NAYAK* OF MADURAI ON 23 FEBRUARY 1635 PRESERVED AT THE OVERSEAS HISTORICAL ARCHIVES, LISBON.

powder from China, lead, jewels of various styles, cloves and ivory. In 1635, Tirumalai Nayak of Madurai received from the Portuguese goods, as listed in Table 2, in exchange for saltpetre at the price shown against each.

The same year (1635), the Portuguese obtained 8,129.5 quintals of saltpetre from the *nayak* of Madurai and exported it from the port of Tuticorin to Goa and thence to Portugal.[90] The next year (1636), they signed a contract with the *nayak* and exported 2,09,800 quintals of saltpetre from Tuticorin.[91] Although the purchase price of saltpetre varied between 7 and

TABLE 2: QUANTITY AND PRICE OF COMMODITIES EXCHANGED FOR SALTPETRE BY THE PORTUGUESE FROM TIRUMALAI NAYAK OF MADURAI IN 1635[92]

Commodity	Quantity Price	(*Xerafins* - *Tangas* - *Reis*)
Cloves	5 quintals	1,184 - 8 - 80
Ivory	2 *bahars*	0,922 - 0 - 40
Lead	60 quintals	1,200 - 0 - 95
Sulphur (Siam)	53 quintals	1,107 - 1 - 00
Grey velvet	21 *covados*	0,094 - 2 - 30
Chita velvet	21.5 *covados*	0,096 - 8 - 45
Agra velvet	41 *covados*	0,102 - 2 - 30
Silk (tabby)	1 piece	0,032 - 0 - 00
Silk (blue & yellow)	1 piece	0,034 - 0 - 00
Silk (white)	11 pieces	0,068 - 0 - 00
Silk (lacquer coated)	11 pieces	0,080 - 0 - 00
Silk (camisole)	1 piece	0,034 - 0 - 00
Silk (damask)	34 *covados*	0,064 - 0 - 00
Silk (cochineal)	180.25 *covados*	1,982 - 3 - 32
Gold necklace	5.2.3. *marc*	1,186 - 2 - 80
Gold necklace	6.3.50 *marc*	1,422 - 9 - 25
Necklace	4.5.1.48 *marc*	1,069 - 3 - 90
Necklace	3.7.24 *marc*	0,944 - 4 - 27
Chain (3 pendulums)	4.1.1.48. *marc*	1,008 - 2 - 23
Necklace	3.1.7.24. *marc*	0,745 - 0 - 35
Necklace	1.1.1.24. *marc*	0,263 - 2 - 40
Cordao	1.4.1.30. *marc*	0,331 - 9 - 90
Necklace	3.4.18. *marc*	0,705 - 1 - 20
Goldpowder (China) (11 packets)	17.4.18. *marc*	4,126 - 8 - 15
Total		18,805 - 2 - 10

10½ *xerafins* per quintal in Madurai during 1638, the Portuguese continued to purchase it.[93] The agreement between the Portuguese and the *nayak* of Madurai seems to have been renewed from year to year. The Portuguese had no other option but to purchase saltpetre at the enhanced price.

Gaspar de Aguilar (1588-1648), a Jesuit, also held negotiations on 22 March 1638, with the *nayak* of Madurai regarding the purchase of saltpetre.[94] Following these negotiations, the Captain of Tuticorin was instructed by Pero da Silva, the Viceroy of Goa, (1635-9) on 11 October 1638, to negotiate the terms of an agreement with the *nayak* of Madurai, who was asked to reduce the exit duty levied on the vessels sailing from Tuticorin to all places so as to encourage the export trade.[95] In 1639, they decided that one would rather have to tusked elephants from Sri Lanka than the elephants with the stipulated minimum height as per the agreement. The Portuguese Captain of Sri Lanka, Diogo Mendez de Brito, was therefore instructed to make all possible arrangements to hunt for the tusked elephants.[96]

On 13 August 1639, Tirumalai Nayak of Madurai sent his representative Ramappa to the Portuguese viceroy in Goa with a proposal which assured the regular supply of saltpetre in return for military assistance in his war against the Marava ruler who had once again revolted.[97] The viceroy, however, refused to help this time fearing that the defeat of the Maravas would embolden the *nayak* to try and conquer Sri Lanka. Although the viceroy could reconcile himself with the changing prospects of trade, he was not willing to allow the conquest of Sri Lanka which would have had a permanent effect on the prospects of Portuguese influence in the area and seriously affect the Portuguese monopoly of trade in cinnamon.[98]

The Madurai *nayak* was even prepared to allow the Portuguese to construct a fortress at Pampan or wherever they desired on the south-eastern coast in exchange for their half. He was also ready to permit them to post a Captain with fifty Portuguese soldiers and one hundred lascars there, in addition to a revenue grant of 3,000 *pardaus* for its maintenance. Further, he promised to build a church at Rameshwaram and seven other churches between Pampan and Tondi, also giving freedom to all those people who might desire to become Christians.[99] Although the terms offered by the *nayak* in return for military assistance were very attractive, the Portuguese declined. The *nayak* was very displeased and decided to impede the saltpetre trade conducted by the Portuguese at Madurai. When the viceroy sent a personal letter enclosed in a golden wrapping, accompanied by gifts, as was customary to the *nayak* for signing a contract to purchase saltpetre in 1640, the *nayak* refused to entertain it.[100] Conde de Aveiras, the Portuguese viceroy, therefore instructed the Captain of Tuticorin to take all other possible steps to procure saltpetre from Madurai.[101] The attempt to procure saltpetre was not successful since the *nayak* forbade its sale to the Portuguese. As a result, saltpetre export from Tuticorin suffered and the survival of the Portuguese was jeopardized, entailing new problems. A fresh attempt was made on 5 March 1643 to enter into a contract, with the *nayak* of Madurai to supply him with elephants in exchange for saltpetre.[102]

Tirumalai Nayak, who felt insulted by the Portuguese response, sent an ambassador to Arnold Heussen, the Dutch governor of Pulicat in 1645, inviting him to trade at the ports of his *nayakdom*.[103] The Dutch visited the court of the *nayak* and successfully concluded an agreement to open a factory at Kayalpattinam, located south of Tuticorin.[104] This gave rise to conflicts between the Dutch and the Portuguese in the pearl fishery coast. The Dutch attacked the Portuguese settlement of Tuticorin on 7 February 1649 with ten ships under the command of J.M. Suycher, the Dutch governor of Sri Lanka.[105] They demanded a onetime payment of 40,000 *pagodas* from the Portuguese within three days. They also forced the paravas and the missionaries to give a written undertaking to this effect.[106]

The Muslim inhabitants of Tuticorin were, however, exempted from this levy. As the amount was not paid within the stipulated days, the Dutch plundered the port of Tuticorin on 12 February 1649.[107] They also carried away the fishing boats of the paravas and left Tuticorin.[108] The Dutch once again made attempts to collect the 30,000 *reis* still left outstanding from the levy imposed on the Portuguese at Tuticorin in 1650. The Portuguese viceroy, in his letter dated 4 March 1653, lamented that the commerce of the Portuguese had entirely ceased and the trade had fallen into the hands of the Dutch, but for which India might have remained the richest jewel in the Portuguese crown![109] Portuguese attempts to save their settlement of Tuticorin failed and the Dutch took possession[110] of the port on 1 February 1658.

Horses and Elephants for the *Nayak* of Thanjavur

The Portuguese, who traded with the ports of Thirumalairayanpattinam and Nagore on the Coromandel coast, had obtained the permission of Sevvappa, the *nayaka* of Thanjavur (1535-63), to settle down at Nagapattinam. In return, they agreed to bring horses to Nagapattinam from the ports of the western coast which received its supply from West Asia. It may be recalled that some Portuguese who specialized in horse trading with the Coromandel had stayed on at Kanyakumari and purchased horses which came from West Asia.[111] Some of the *casados* in Kochi also participated in the export of horses to Nagapattinam.[112] The *nayak* of Thanjavur who was desperately in need of horses used to send his men to purchase horses from the Portuguese at Nagapattinam.[113] Portuguese sources record that some of these horses became sick due to the unfavourable climate even before they could be offered for sale at Nagapattinam.[114]

Although the Marakkayars were the traditional traders in rice and textiles with Sri Lanka, they turned to the import of elephants from Sri Lanka as there was a heavy demand for them in south India. Many elephants were imported by them from Sri Lanka to Nagapattinam.[115] Some of the Marakkayars specialized in the transportation of elephants and there is mention of a merchant, Chilay Marakkayar, who provided his ship for transporting elephants to Goa as requested by the Portuguese viceroy.[116] Sri Lankan elephants were found to be more easily tamed and therefore were greatly esteemed by Achyutappa, the *nayak* of Thanjavur (1563-80), and the other rulers in south India who needed them for their armies. The best and most thoroughly trained elephants were priced between 1,000 and 1,500 *cruzados*.[117] Sometimes the Portuguese also presented these elephants as gifts to south Indian rulers and in one such case one finds that as many as three elephants were presented to the *nayak* of Thanjavur.[118]

During this period the Portuguese in Nagapattinam had control over the seas and therefore insisted that traders obtain sailing permits from the Portuguese Captain.[119] Some merchants, like Khawaja Marakkayar of Nagapattinam, trading with Maçāo in China, collected these *cartazes* from the Portuguese after paying the stipulated amount.[120] There were instances of ships at Nagapattinam being attacked and confiscated by the Portuguese for not observing all the conditions stipulated in the *cartaz* issued by the Portuguese Captain at Nagapattinam. It was insisted that owners of the ships should collect these *cartazes* from Nagapattinam to access its port of call and the same vessel should, on its return journey, pay a stipulated amount for the import of commodities at the Portuguese customs house at Nagapattinam. Although a *cartaz* was issued at a nominal rate of one *tanga* per *cartaz*, Coromandel merchants were prohibited from carrying certain commodities which were declared as items of royal monopoly. Raghunatha (1580-1630), the *nayak* of Thanjavur, was annoyed at the way the Portuguese had acted while issuing *cartazes*. He demanded an explanation from the Portuguese captain as to why a *cartaz* was not given to his ship in December 1624 which was to take merchandise from the port of Nagapattinam. Hence he captured a Portuguese ship at the harbour of Nagapattinam on 27 January 1625.[121]

It is evident from some records that the *nayak* of Thanjavur was more interested in the purchase of elephants than were the *nayaks* of Gingee and Madurai. The reasons this are not explicitly stated in the documents. In 1607, António Vaz Pereira, the Portuguese Captain at Nagapattinam, aware of the *nayak's* requirements, made special arrangements to sell all the elephants that were brought from Sri Lanka to Nagapattinam by the Portuguese to him.[122] In 1614, Jeronimo de Azevedo, the Portuguese viceroy of Goa (1612-17), wrote that the *nayak* of Thanjavur alone enjoyed the exclusive right to buy all the elephants from the Portuguese.[123]

Venkatapatidevaraya II, the titular Vijayanagara emperor (1586-1614), however, was not at all interested in buying elephants. The *nayak* of Thanjavur always wanted the elephants to be delivered at Thanjavur and only then was the payment made. The then ruler of Kandy who did not realize the importance of animal trade, allowed the Portuguese to engage in commerce and elephants were sent from several ports of Sri Lanka for eventual delivery to the *nayak* of Thanjavur. This elephant trade continued up to 1620.[124]

Some of the Coromandel seagoing vessels sailed from Sri Lanka and they carried fourteen to fifteen elephants. These *naus* (cargo ships) were exceedingly strong.[125] The prow of the *naus* were built in such a way as to facilitate their movement in narrow channels and transport elephants safely from Sri Lanka to the Tamil coast. Six elephants were brought to Nagapattinam in 1622 and sold for a total amount of 3,990 *xerafins*.[126] The *nayak* of Thanjavur is reported to have asked for elephants from Sri Lanka on 18 February 1630. This was agreed to by the Portuguese in return for his help in their attempt to capture Pulicat, the chief settlement of the Dutch in the Coromandel.[127]

However, in 1631, when the Portuguese were buying saltpetre in Madurai from Tirumalai Nayak to meet their maximum requirement, they decided to stop exchanging elephants with the *nayak* of Thanjavur. From then onwards ships carrying elephants were diverted to the port of Tuticorin (instead of sailing to Nagapattinam) to be sold to Tirumalai Nayak of Madurai in exchange for saltpetre.[128]

Relations between the *nayaka* rulers of Thanjavur and the Portuguese had been very cordial during this period. The Bishop of Mylapore, in one of his letters in 1610, described the warm help extended by the *nayak* to the Portuguese residents of Santhome when the local officer, taking advantage of the political instability and chaos that prevailed in the region unjustly demanded a large sum of money as tax. The *nayak* came forward willingly to intervene in this matter when approached by the Portuguese although the dispute did not pertain to a matter falling within the territorial jurisdiction of the *nayakdom* of Thanjavur.[129] In appreciation of this timely help given to the residents of Santhome, Filippe II, the king of Portugal (1598-1621), sent a letter on 20 February 1612 to the *nayak* of Thanjavur thanking him for his services.[130] Jeronimo de Azevedo, the Portuguese viceroy of Goa, in his letter to the king of Portugal dated 21 January 1613, replied that the letter sent by the Crown to the *nayak* of Thanjavur had first been sent to the Bishop of Mylapore who would arrange for its onward transmission to the *nayak* of Thanjavur.[131]

It is said that whenever the taxes were not paid by his subjects to the royal treasury, the *nayak* of Thanjavur himself would come in person to Nagapattinam to supervise the collection of taxes. He also collected tax from the Portuguese residents.[132] Once when the *adhikari* of Nagapattinam demanded an unreasonable amount as tax from the Portuguese (in 1632) they sent an embassy to the *nayak*'s court in Thanjavur and the matter was solved amicably in favour of the Portuguese.[133] A considerable part of the tax collected by the *nayak* of Thanjavur was sent as annual tribute to the king of Vijayanagara. Fr. Coutinho who had knowledge about the tribute sent by the *nayak* to the king says in his letter dated 11 October 1608, that the tribute of the *nayak* of Thanjavur consisted of 50,00,000 *cruzados* besides many other things.[134]

In accordance with Hindu tradition, the *nayak* ruler of Thanjavur seems to have been very tolerant towards the other religious groups in his kingdom. His animosities were directed more towards the temporal powers of foreigners and that too only when they infringed upon his own powers. The Portuguese used Nagapattinam port (since 1581) as a naval base to send arms and ammunition for their military operations in Sri Lanka. The *nayak* of Thanjavur, however, came to know about these clandestine activities only much later as these operations were carried out very secretly by the Portuguese. He learnt about them only when Sankili, the ruler of Jaffna, wrote in 1615 about it to Raghunatha Nayak seeking his help.[135] The *nayak* of Thanjavur went to the assistance of the ruler of Jaffna when the Portuguese sent an army from Nagapattinam to fight him. Nagapattinam was attacked by the *nayak* in 1617. Many Portuguese fled to Kochi on 15 March 1617.[136] An army of 1,000 men led by Varunakulathan, the commander-in-chief, was sent by the *nayak* of Thanjavur to assist the king of Jaffna.[137] As the Portuguese *casados* of Nagapattinam had sent a considerable quantity of arms and ammunition to their fellowmen, the ruler of Jaffna was defeated in 1619. He once again appealed to the *nayak* of Thanjavur for military help. An army of 2,000 men sent from

Thanjavur landed at Mannar on 5 December 1620.[138] Finally, the Portuguese were defeated by the *nayak*'s forces when another contingent of soldiers reached Jaffna from Thanjavur on 18 February 1622.[139]

In 1632, the forces of the *nayak* of Thanjavur marched towards Nagapattinam and attempted to destroy the settlement.[140] The main reason for such a sudden attack was that the Portuguese were found to be removing large columns of black stones from one of the temples in Nagapattinam for the construction of their own buildings.[141] After this incident, the *nayak* was glad to invite the English to settle at Nagapattinam. The English ships, which arrived on 9 July 1638, were given a grand reception by the local *adhikari* on the orders of Vijaya Raghunatha (1630-73), the *nayak* of Thanjavur.[142] The State Council of Goa discussed this matter at its meeting and it disapproved of the action of the *nayak*. Later the Portuguese planned to erect fortifications and the *nayak*, who heard about it, approached Nagapattinam in June 1641.[143] The Portuguese residents of Nagapattinam ambushed his forces on the way and carried away several pieces of artillery.[144] Owing to these political developments, the trading activities of the Portuguese passed through many ups and downs during this period.

Portuguese diplomatic relations with the *nayak* of Gingee began after the new development of the Dutch alliance with the *nayak* in 1608. The Portuguese were quick to react and the news reached the court of the king of Portugal who wrote to king Venkata III of Vijayanagara, who then lived in Vellore. The king of Vijayanagara replied to the king of Portugal mentioning that he had ordered the *nayak* of Gingee to evict the Dutch from Devanampattinam.[145]

The Portuguese viceroy of Goa took immediate steps to evict the Dutch from Devanampattinam. The Bishop of Mylapore and the Câmara Municipal of Santhome combined their efforts in 1609 to drive the Dutch away from Devanampattinam. They deputed Fr. Nicholas Levanto, the Rector of the Seminary in Santhome, to go to the royal court in Vellore to plead for the expulsion of the Dutch from Devanampattinam. Fr. Levanto, who undertook the mission, reported in a letter to the Bishop of Mylapore that the king of Vijayanagara had agreed to take away the Portuguese fort in Devanampattinam from the Dutch and had promised to deliver it to the Portuguese.[146] The Portuguese, however, were not successful in dislodging the Dutch from Devanampattinam in spite of the combined diplomacy of the church and the state, both in Portugal and in India.

This chapter has provided a glimpse of the complex nature of the *nayak's* relations with the Portuguese on the one hand and the Dutch on the other, a result of the rivalry between these two European powers to gain control over the ports on the coast and influence at the royal courts in the hinterland. As saltpetre deposits in the Iberian peninsula were meagre, the military had to depend on foreign imports, especially in wartime. The Portuguese attempted to procure saltpetre from the *nayaks* of Gingee and Madurai. Trading in saltpetre became a matter of utmost urgency and the Portuguese took measures to ensure a steady supply from Tuticorin. The military objectives of the *nayaks* and the commercial activities of the Portuguese were determined more by circumstances than by any other long-term objective. Although Tirumalai Nayak of Madurai offered better terms with special privileges albeit for achieving his own goals, the Portuguese viceroy did not accept it as he feared that the Portuguese trade and presence in Sri Lanka might be disturbed and affected. Moreover, during this period the Portuguese were already under great pressure from a powerful commercial rival, the Dutch in the Coromandel. Further, the Luso-Dutch rivalry sparked by battles in the open seas of the Bay of Bengal did not promote peaceful trade in strategic commodities.

The *nayak* of Thanjavur maintained his identity as a ruler zealously protecting his territory against political intrusions. He was very much like the rulers elsewhere in India encountering a new type of aggression, i.e. conquest through maritime trade and proselytization. The Portuguese, although very familiar with the new political strategy, through a new fuel mix of overseas trade and gunpowder diplomacy put into operation for the capture of Goa and Melaka, were not successful in establishing their authority in the ports on the Tamil coast. The *Estado da Índia* also could not exercise control over the private Portuguese settlers scattered over the vast stretch of the Tamil coast.

The Portuguese maintained their separate identity as traders and concentrated on maritime trade from the ports of Tuticorin, Devanampattinam and Nagapattinam. The royal requirement of elephants by the *nayak* of Thanjavur was met by the Portuguese who conducted trade with Sri Lanka, and it flourished chiefly on a mutual understanding. The *nayak* exclusively collected the revenue from the port of Nagapattinam till the death of the last ruler of Vijayanagara in 1642. The following year, the Portuguese established an *alfândega* (customs house) and began to collect revenue, taking advantage of the political changes that had taken place. As the *nayak* of Thanjavur was relieved of the obligation to send his annual tribute to Venkata III, the paramount ruler, he permitted the Portuguese to carry on the port administration by themselves at Nagapattinam.

It may be noted that the trade in strategic commodities such as horses, elephants and saltpetre conducted by the Portuguese passed through different phases. The *nayak* rulers at first followed an open-door policy in trade by inviting the Portuguese merchants to supply them with horses. In the first phase, the nature of trade was one that had been conducted by Portuguese merchants supplying horses for the purpose of profit. In the second phase, the Portuguese having learnt of the availability of saltpetre on the coast changed the pattern of their trade replacing it with an ulterior motive and began to supply elephants to the *nayak* in exchange for saltpetre to be exported to Europe for making gunpowder. This course of trade also added many diplomatic contacts to the courts of the *nayak* rulers. In the third phase, the Portuguese adopted a different trade policy with the arrival of the Dutch in the Coromandel during the early seventeenth century, sending missionaries to negotiate terms with the *nayaks*. However, the Hindu Vijayanagara rulers treated both the Portuguese and the Dutch equally without making any distinction. The good offices of the missionaries, notably the Jesuits, had been used in a larger measure by the Portuguese to succeed and compete with their Dutch rivals in trade who entered the Tamil coast in the early seventeenth century. These Jesuits played an influential role in the courts of the *nayaks* of Gingee, Thanjavur and Madurai. Thus Portuguese administrators in the Tamil coast used their spiritual powers to facilitate trade and diplomacy.

NOTES

1. A. Krishnaswami, *The Tamil Country under Vijayanagara*, Annamalai Nagar, 1964, pp. 181-6; N. Karashima, 'Nayaka Rule in North and South Arcot Districts in South India during the Sixteenth Century', *Acta Asiatica*, vol. XLVIII, 1985, pp. 1-26. See Karashima's, *Towards a New Formation: South Indian Society under Vijayanagara Rule*, Delhi, 1992; S. Jeyaseela Stephen, 'The State, Decentralization and Revenue Farming: Some Aspects of Vijayanagara Rule in the Coromandel Region in the Sixteenth Century', *Journal of the Institute of Asian Studies*, vol. 11, no. 2, September 1993, pp. 1-16.
2. R. Sathiyanatha Aiyar, *History of the Nayaks of Madura*, Oxford, 1924; Vriddhagirisan, *The Nayaks of Tanjore*, Annamalai Nagar, 1942; C.S. Srinivasachari, *A History of Gingee and its Rulers*, Annamalai Nagar, 1943.
3. Arjun Appadurai et al. (eds.), *Gender Genre and Power in South Asian Expressive Traditions*, Philadelphia, 1994, pp. 428-64; Velacheru Narayana Rao et al. (eds.), *Symbols of Substance: Court and State in Nayaka Period Tamilnadu*, Delhi, 1992. Velacheru Narayana Rao and David Shulman focused their attention on the literary sources relating to the Nayak of Thanjavur and they have shown that there is a strong relationship between south Indian folk tales and the courtly literature.
4. Robert Sewell, *A Forgotten Empire*, Delhi, 1962, pp. 280-1.
5. Henry Heras, 'Venkatapatidevaraya I and the Portuguese', *Quarterly Journal of the Mythic Society,* vol. 14, 1923-4, pp. 312-17. See also 'Early Relations between Vijayanagara and Portugal', *Quarterly Journal of Mythic Society*, vol. 26, 1925-6, pp. 63-74. See *The Aravidu Dynasty of Vijayanagara,* Madras, 1927.
6. Sanjay Subrahmanyam, *The Political Economy of Commerce: Southern India, 1500-1700,* Cambridge, 1990a.
7. V. Rangachari, 'The History of the Naik Kingdom of Madur', in *Indian Antiquary*, vol. XLIII, 1914, pp. 1-48.
8. R. Sathiyanatha Aiyar, *History of the Nayaks of Madura*, Oxford, 1924.
9. K. Rajayyan, *Selections from the History of Tamil Nadu, 1565-1965*, Madurai, 1978.
10. K. Rajaram, *History of Tirumalai Nayak*, Madurai, 1982. This work is based on secondary sources. See on the Portuguese relations, pp. 36-7; on trade and commerce, pp. 95-6.
11. N. Subrahmanyam, *History of Tamilnadu (AD 1565-1956)*, Madurai, 1977.
12. Elaine Sanceau, *Coleção de São Lourenço*, Lisboã, 1973-83, vol. 2, p. 120.

13. Armando Cortesão and Luis de Albuquerque, *Obras Completas de Dom João de Castro* (hereafter *Obras*), vol. 3, Coimbra, 1976, pp. 109-10.
14. Ibid., p. 393.
15. Sanceau *Coleção São Lourenço*, vol. 2, pp. 335, 364 and 372.
16. Cartesao and Albuquerque, *Obras*, vol. 3, p. 215.
17. Sanceau, *Coleção São Lourenço*, vol. 2, pp. 300, 335 and 368.
18. Ibid., p. 85.
19. Correia, *Lendas da India*, tomo II, pp. 65-6.
20. Cartesao and Albuquerque, *Obras*, vol. 2, p. 100; vol. 4, p. 50.
21. Letter of Affonso de Albuquerque written from Kannur, *Cartas de Affonso de Albuquerque*, vol. 1, pp. 88-9.
22. Diogo de Lisboã was selling horses in 1524. See *IANTT*, *CC*, IIa-114-4.
23. *IANTT*, *Chancelaria de D. João III, Priveligios*, Livro 1, fl. 97v. Privileges for the sale of horses were given to Andre Luis at Vedalai on 1 February 1538. Orders were also issued from Lisbon in this regard on 2 August 1552.
24. Letter of Joao da Cruz to the king of Portugal dated 20 December 1553. See Georg Schurhammer, 'Iniqitembrane and Bete Perumal: Chera and Pandya kings in South India', *Journal of the Bombay Historical Society*, vol. 3, 1930, pp. 1-40.
25. *IANTT*, *Chancelaria de D. João III*, Livro 21, fl. 39.
26. Letter of Francis Xavier to Mansillhas, 5 September 1544, written from Alandalai. See Hugues Dider, *Correspondance 1535-1552: Lettres et Documents*, Paris, 1987, pp. 132-3; see also Georg Schur hammer, 'Iniqitriberim and Bete Perumal: Chera and Pandya Kings in Southern India, 1544', in *Orientalia*, Rome, p. 263.
27. *BA*, *Livro das Merces que fez Dom João de Castro*, Mss, Codice 51-8-46, fl. 92v.
28. *IANTT*, *CC*, 2a-112-105 (1512); 2a-112-104 (1513); 31-7-84 (1520); 2a-123-83; 2a-123-154; 2a-1124-98; 2a-130-2 (1525); 2a-130-212 (1526).
29. Biblioteca Nacional de Lisboã (*BNL*), Codice 1983, fls. 81-2 (23 November 1625).
30. Sanceau, *Coleção São Lourenço*, vol. 3, Lisboã, 1983, p. 498. Cortesao and Albuquerque, *Obras*, vol. 3, doc. 708, pp. 524-5.
31. *IANTT*, *CC*, I-57-76 (3 August 1536).
32. As early as on 28 July 1525, the residents of Kochi had been prohibited to trade in saltpetre. *IANTT*, Mss *Coleção São Lourenço*, vol. 4, fl.329 (25 January 1547).
33. Anthony Disney, *Twilight of the Pepper Empire*, p. 116.
34. *AHU*, Codice 281, fl. 194.

35. Orders to this effect were issued on 9 October 1524.
36. *AHU, Assentos Conselho da Fazenda* (hereafter *ACF*), 1162, p. 144. India (followed by Caixa, and document number), *CX*, II doc. 44.
37. C.R. Boxer, *Further Selections from the Tragic History of the Sea, 1554- 1565,* Cambridge, 1967, p. 80. (The year is AD 1560.)
38. R.J. de Lima Felner, *Subsidios para a Historia da India Portuguesa,* (*Tombo do Estado da Índia*), Lisboã, 1868, p. 255.
39. H. de Cunha Rivara, *Archivo Portuguez Oriental*, Novo Goa, Fasc.3, fls. 861-2, 896-9, no. 7, p. 74.
40. Disney, *Twilight of the Pepper Empire*, pp. 116-17.
41. Samuel Purchas, *His Pilgrims,* vol. 10, Glasgow, 1905, pp. 217-19.
42. William Methwold, *Relations of Golconda in the Early Seventeenth Century,* London, 1931. See Schorer's account regarding saltpetre, p. 52.
43. Ibid.
44. *IANTT*, *Chancelaria de Dom Filippe I, 1580-1593*, Livro 17, fl. 295v.
45. Archives Mascharaneas no. 453, cited in Achilles Meersman, *The Franciscans in Tamilnad,* Schoneck-Beckenried, 1962. See also *DI*, vol. 12, pp. 729- 30. *Porque Tanto que passar desta vida e ilhe mandei dobrar a* sino e stando nos Antonio caldeiroe Damiao paes e eu porque os mais *senhores erao idos a reparisar hum puncoe tornar logo Scilicet in 1583.*
46. Om Praksh, *Bullion for Goods*, p. 106. The port of Devanampattinam was not under the exclusive domination of foreign traders. A native merchant by the name of Malaya Chetti figures as the richest trader in Devanampattinam.
47. T.I. Poonen, 'Dutch Beginnings in India Proper', *Journal the Madras University*, 1933, p. 37.
48. Poonen, 'Dutch Beginnings', p. 27. The Dutch also paid a sum of 1,500 *pardaus* to the powerful port official of the *nayak* of Gingee for obtaining seven other villages around Thirupathiripuliyur. See also, Om Prakash, *Bullion for Goods*, p. 32.
49. *ARSI, Litterae Annuae: Provinciae Malabarensis 1609*: *Heeres, Corpus Diplomaticum*, vol. I, p. 55; De Jonge, *De Opkomst*, op. cit., vol. 3, p. 280. Tapan Raychaudhuri, *Jan Company in Coromandel*, The Hague, 1962, p. 19. Henry Heras, *The Aravidu Dynasty*, p. 410.
50. Poonen, 'Dutch Beginnings', p. 28.
51. *HAG, MDR*, op. cit., Livro 99/1/3, fls. 301-2, Letter no. 123.
52. *IANTT, DRI*, Livro 6, fl. 5.
53. *IANTT, DRI*, Livro 36, fl. 116.
54. Pissurlencar, Regimentos, vol. 1, pp. 516-17 (7 November 1630).
55. *BL, Additional Manuscripts*, no. 20892, fl. 226a (1617); see also *HAG*, codex 1164, fl. 80v.
56. *HAG, MDR*, Livro 7, 34-36/4/4, fls. 110-15 (7 February 1602).

57. *IANTT, Documentos Remetidos da India* (hereafter *DRI*), Livro 1, fl. 125.
58. Disney, *Twilight of the Pepper Empire*, p. 116.
59. Pissurlencar, Regimentos, vol. 1, pt. 2, doc. 34, p. 66 (13 and 15 October 1625); Sanjay Subrahmanyam, *The Portuguese Empire in Asia.*
60. Pissurtencar, ibid., vol. 1, no. 86, p. 258 (6 February 1630).
61. Ibid., vol. 2, pp. 6-18, 70-1, 84-5; 'Side lights' p. 174. Braganca Perreira, *Arquivo Portuguez Oriental 'Livro das plantas de todas as fortalezas cidades e povações do Estado da Índia Oriental'*, in tomo 4, vol. 2, pt. I, Bastora, Goa, 1935. The Viceroy suspected the Jesuits of collecting taxes and tolls how the paravas and he wanted to put an end to it. This was another reason for appointing a Captain at Tuticorin. See Sanjay Subrahmanyam, *The Portuguese Empire*, p. 265.
62. Biblioteca da Universidade de Coimbra (hereafter *BUC*), Mss, *Carta Geral dos Servidores do Estado da India em 1635*, no. 459, fls. 234-40.
63. F. Pelseart, *Jahangir's India: The Remonstarate of Francisco Pelseart*, Cambridge, 1925, p. 46; Owen C. Kail, *The Dutch in India*, Delhi, 1981, p. 113.
64. *ACF*, Codice 1166, pp. 58 and 65.
65. Ibid., Codice 1161, fl. 166; Codice 1162, fl. 144. The Portuguese contacted Vitulla Nayak for the supply of saltpetre in 1625. Arrangements were made at Basrur and Surat. Oxen carried the saltpetre. See *BNL*, Codice 1983, fls. 80v, 81-2.
66. Ibid., Codice 1162, fl. 212; Codice 1168, fl.119v.
67. *IANTT, CC*, 2a-112-104, 2a-112 105. The English factory records mention three types of saltpetre. See OIOC, *Factory Records of Hugli, Calcutta, Patna, Miscellaneous*, vol. 10, fl. 235. Saltpetre had varied uses in many manufacturing activities. The manufacture of certain types of glass and dyeing of textiles depended on the use of saltpetre to some extent. See Owen C. Kail, *Dutch in India*, Delhi, 1992, p. 113, William Foster, *English Factories in India (1624-29)*, Oxford, 1906-27, pp. 270-355. It was also used for preserving food and for medicinal purposes. See *A'in-i-Akbari*, I, p. 51, II, p. 6 cited in Irfan Habib, 'Akbar and Technology', in *Akbar and His India*, Delhi, 1997, pp. 129-48. Black saltpetre was chiefly used for making gunpowder. It is to be noted that gunpowder is a loose mixture of three substances: sulphur, charcoal and saltpetre. It was not advisable to carry readymade gunpowder in the days before corning of powder was introduced.

    The reason behind it was that when shaken in transit, the sulphur settled at the bottom while the charcoal came up on the top. Therefore the practice carrying the ingredients separately was followed and mixing was done in the field. A Portuguese document described the godowns at the fort of Mannar. It has a reading of (*tres colheres de carregar as pessas*) three ladles for loading the powder. See Tikiri Abeysinghe, *A Study of the Portuguese Regimentos on Sri Lanka at the Goa Archives*, Colombo, n.d.

68. *HAG*, Codex 1419. See also Tapan Raychaudhuri, *Jan Company in Coromandel*, p. 168.
69. William Foster, *English Factories in India: A Calendar of Documents in the India Office, British Museums and Public Relation Office, 1618-1619*, vols. 1-3, Oxford, 1906-67, pp. 208, 215 and 275; Anthony Disney, *Twilight of the Pepper Empire*, p. 117 (the year is AD 1631).
70. Braganca Perreira, *APO-BP*, IV-2-1, pp. 368-9; F.C. Danvers, *Report on Portuguese Records Relating to the East Indies,* 1892, pp. 43-4. The Dutch and the English ordered their Factors at Ahmedabad and Agra to buy saltpetre and transport it to Surat. See William Faster, *The English Factories in India*, pp. 182, and 270-355 (AD 1634-6).
71. Pissurlencar, Assentos, vol. 1, p. 518 (8 November 1630).
72. Ibid., vol. 1, pt. II, pp. 66-7.
73. '*Side lights*', p. 174; *MPJA*, Shembaganur, Mss, *Litterae Annuae*, 1627. Letter to the Superior General of the Jesuits written from Tuticorin on 24 November 1627.
74. Pissurlencar, *Assentos*, vol. 1, doc. 20, p. 357.
75. K.A. Nilakanta Sastri, 'Tirumalai Naik', 'The Portuguese and the Dutch', *Proceedings of the Indian Historical Records Commission*, vol. 14, Calcutta, 1939, pp. 32-40.
76. Pissurlencar, *Assentos*, vol. 3, doc. 8, p. 641 (24 September 1631).
77. Ibid., p. 34.
78. *IANTT*, *DRI*, Livro. 30, fl. 207.
79. *DRI*, Livro 30, fl. 59; ibid., Livro 31, fl. 207.
80. Ibid., Livro 36, fl. 17.
81. *ACF*, Codice 1164, p. 116v.
82. *AHU*, *India, Caixa*, 11, doc. 44.
83. *IANTT*, *DRI*, Livro 36, fls. 415-415v.
84. Ibid., Livro 36, fls. 16-17.
85. Ibid., Livro 36, fl. 7; Livro 31, fl. 227.
86. *BNL*, *Diario de Conde de Linhares Vicerei da India*, fl.260. See C.R. de Silva, *The Portuguese in Ceylon, 1617-38*, Colombo, 1972. See also, Tikiri Abeysinghe, *Portuguese Rule in Ceylon, 1594-1612*, Colombo, 1966. Pissurlencar, *Assentos* (30 August 1635), doc. 9, p. 641.
87. *BUC*, Mss 459, fl. 7.
88. Ibid., fls. 234-40.
89. *IANTT*, *DRI*, Livro. 30, fl. 59, Livro. 31, fl. 207; Livro 32, fl. 156.
90. *AHU*, *India, Caixa,* 11, doc. 44; See also Afzal Ahmad, *Indo-Portuguese Trade in Seventeenth Century 1600-1663*, Delhi, 1993.

91. *ACF*, Codice 1163, p. 16.
92. *AHU, India, Caixa*, 11, doc. 44; See also Afzal Ahmad, *Indo-Portuguese Trade.*
93. *ACF*, Codice 1163, fls. 48v-49v.
94. *IANTT, DRI*, Livro 44, fl. 73; Livro 45, fl. 67.
95. *HAG, Livro de Segredo* (hereafter *LS*), vol. 1, 9/4/5, fl. 21.
96. Abeysinghe, *A Study of Portuguese Regirentos*, p. 79. *HAG*, Codex 1419, fl. 79, Codex 1420, fls. 54v and 183.
97. F.C. Danvers, *The Portuguese in India*, London, 1894, vol. 2, p. 268, See also, J.F.J. Biker *Coleção de Trato e Concertos do Pazes que o Estado da Índia Portuguese fez com os Reis e Senhores em que teve Relações nas Partes da Asia e Africa Oriental desde o Pincipio de Conquista ate ao fim do Seculo XVIII*, vols. 1-14, Lisboã, 1881-7. See also *Tratado de todos os Vice-reis e Governadores da India* (hereafter *Tratados*), Lisboã, 1962, tomo II, p. 103.
98. Braganca Perreira, *Arquiro Portuguese Oriestal*, vol. 4, pp. 368-9.
99. See *Tratados*, tomo II, p. 103.
100. *HAG*, Codex 1420, fls. 54v and 183.
101. J.E. Heeres and F. W. Stapel, *Corpus Diplomaticu Neerlando Indicum*, vol. 1, doc. 70, The Hague, 1907, pp. 445-57.
102. *HAG, MDR*, Livro 52, fl. 172.
103. Pissurlencar, Assentos, vol. 3, p. 135.
104. Ibid.
105. *IANTT, DRI*, Livro 58, fl. 66.
106. Ibid.
107. Ibid.
108. Ibid.
109. K.A. Nilakanta Sastri Tirumalai Naik, The Portuguese, p. 38.
110. F.C. Danvers, *Report to the Secretary of State for India,* Amsterdam, 1966. See also, *Report on Portuguese Records*, pp. 39-40.
111. Armando Cortesao and Luís de Albuquerque, *Obras*, vol. 3, p. 100; vol. 4, p. 50.
112. Letter from António Fernandes to viceroy of Goa, dated 2 August 1546, and the letter of Manoel Lobato to the viceroy, dated 25 August 1547. See *CSL* II, pp. 335 and 364-72.
113. Purchas, *His Pilgrims*, vol. 2, pp. 227-8.
114. *IANTT, CC*, pt IIa-117-156. A Portuguese *casado* of Nagapattinam, by the name of Marcos was appointed by the Portuguese Captain of the Coromandel coast to treat the sick horses. He was paid 4 *pardaus* for rendering this special service.
115. Barbosa, *The Book of Duarte Barbosa*, vol. 2, p. 113.
116. K.S. Mathew, *Indo-Portuguese Trade and the Fuggers of Germany,* Delhi, 1997, p. 211.
117. Barbosa, *The Book of Duarte Barbosa*, vol. 2, p. 117.

118. *HAG*, *Assentos do Conselho da Fazenda,* codex, 116, p. 9. As per this record two elephants were given to the *nayak* of Madurai.
119. *IANTT*, *Colecao Sao Vicente* (hereafter *CSV*), Mss vol. 10, fl.128.
120. Pissurlencar, *Assentos do Conselho do Estado,* vols. 1-4, Goa, 1972. This practice of taking Portuguese *cartazes* for the ships, which began in 1502, continued at Nagapattinam during the early years of the seventeenth century.
121. Pieris, 'The Portuguese in Ceylon', *Journal of the Royal Asiatic Society of Ceylon Branch,* vol. 27, p. 102.
122. Bulhão Pato, *Documentos Remetidos da India,* vols. 1-4, Lisboa, 1880-1935, vol. 3, pp. 55-6.
123. *IANTT*, Mss, *Documentos Remetidos da India* (hereafter *DRI*), Livro 27, fl.116.
124. Tikri Abeysinghe, *A Study of Portuguese Regimentos on Sri Lanka at the Goa Archives,* Colombo, n.d., p. 9.
125. Duarte Barbosa, *The Book Duarte Barbosa*, vol. 2, p. 113.
126. *BNL*, Codice 11410, fls. 95-103v.
127. *HAG*, Mss, *MDR*, Livro 13B, 5-6/3-2, fl. 30v.
128. *AHU*, Caixa da India (hereafter *CDI*) Caixa 11, doc. no. 44.
129. *HAG*, Mss, *Monções do Reino* (hereafter *MDR*), Livro XII, fls. 143-4; A. Silva Rego, op. cit., vol. 7, p. 413.
130. Heras, *The Aravidu Dynasty*, pp. 402-8.
131. Bulhao Pato, *Documentos*, vol. 2, pp. 370-1; Heras, *The Aravidu Dynasty*, pp. 402-8.
132. Antonio Bocarro, 'Livro das Plantas de todas as Fortalezas Cidades e Povacoes do Estado da India Oriental', in A.B. De Braganca Perreira (ed.), *Arquivo Portugues Oriental,* vol. 2, pt. II, Goa, 1937-8, vol. 2, p. 2. The King of Vijayanagara is reported to have increased the tribute to be paid by the *nayak* of Thanjavur from 6 million to 10 million *pardaus* in 1611. See Bertrand, *La Mission du Madure,* Paris, 1848, vol. 2, p. 108.
133. *AHU*, Mss *CDI*, no. 20, doc. no. 4.
134. Heras, *The Aravidu Dynasty*, p. 358.
135. Fernão de Queyroz, *The Temporal and Spiritual Conquests of Ceylon,* S.G. Perreira (tr.), Colombo, 1930, p. 468; C.R. de Silva, *The Portuguese Rule in Ceylon,* Colombo, 1980, pp. 50-1.
136. Bulhao Pato, *Documentos*, vol. 4, p. 73.
137. *HAG*, Mss *MDR*, Livro 15, 9.190,
138. Fernao de Queyroz, *The Temporal and Spiritual Conquests*, pp. 642-5.
139. Silva Rego, *Documentos*, vol. 7, pp. 222, 237, 375-6 and 382.
140. *HAG*, Mss *MDR*, Livro 32, fl. 67; W.Ph. Coolhas (ed.), *Generale Missiven vande Governeurs-Generaalen Raden derVOC*, Deel 1, The Hague, 1960, pp. 338-9.

141. Abdul Rahim, 'Nagapattinam Region and the Portuguese', *Journal of Indian History* (hereafter *JIH*), vol. 53, no. 3, 1975, pp. 483-96.
142. Pissurlencar, Assentos, vol. II, p. 235.
143. *AHU*, Mss *CDI*, no. 14, doc. 116.
144. *AHU*, Mss *CDI*, no. 20, doc. 4, fl. 2.
145. Henry Heras, *The Aravidu Dynasty of Vijayanagara*, Madras, 1927, vol. 1, pp. 445-6.
146. Christovao Soares de Figueira, *Historia y Anual Relacion de las Cosas que hizieron los Padres de la Compandia de Jesus por las Padres de Oriente y outras en la Propagation del Santo Evangelico los anos Passades de 607 y 608*, Madrid, 1614; rpt. 1913, pp. 113-14. Fernao Guerreiro, *Relacao Annual das coisa que fizeram os Padres da Compahnia de Jesus nas suas Missoes*, Coimbra, 1931, tomo 3, p. 76. Henry Heras, 'Jesuit Influence in the Court of Vijayanagara', *Quarterly Journal of the Mythic Society*, vol. 14, p. 138. See also, 'Three Contemporary Letters on the Vijayanagara King Venkata II of the Aravidu Dynasty', paper presented at the Third Oriental Conference. See also *ARSI*, *Litterae Annuae Mission Madurensis*, AD 1609. See Ferroli, *The Jesuits in Malabar*, vol. 2, Bangalore, 1951, pp. 2-3; Fernao Guerreiro, *Relação Annual das coisa*, pp. 114-15.

5

Hinterland Production and Intra-Asian Trade in Rice and Textiles

The Marakkayars owed their powerful position as seafaring merchants in such ports of the Coromandel as Nagore and Kunimedu to their trade in bulk goods such as rice, textiles, etc., within Asia. Their overseas trade was, however, threatened by the Portuguese who began to take an interest in bulk goods and founded new port settlements as they had discovered a new region of great commercial importance. Some important Portuguese settlements on the Coromandel coast such as Santhome of Mylapore, Nagapattinam and Devanampattinam served as land-based bastions for the Portuguese who held sway over the sea in the Bay of Bengal. This chapter examines how the same ports emerged as trade outlets for bulk commodities and functioned as the emporia of the Portuguese following their penetration into the Coromandel, and later how they had to face a new threat from the Dutch who arrived towards the beginning of the seventeenth century.

The capital of the Portuguese *Estado da Índia* in the East, initially established at Kochi in 1505, moved to Goa towards the north in 1530. The Portuguese *Estado da Índia* was not limited to India but was made up of a few forts, fleets and centres of trade what stretched from East Africa to Japan.[1] A large number of adventurous Portuguese sailors, soldiers and officials who saw the trade potentialities of the Coromandel coast struggled to the trading settlements on the eastern coast of peninsular India. In 1520, a Portuguese Captain was appointed as the Crown's representative in this region.[2] Even while he was preoccupied with finding ways to participate in the trading activities of the Tamil coast he was being driven by a desire to seek his own personal enrichment. Although the Portuguese were keen to gain control over the Asian maritime trade in pepper, they found that trading in other commodities such as rice and textiles was also lucrative, as pepper was exchanged for these goods brought from the Coromandel. The Portuguese Captain and Factor stationed initially (in 1520) at the port of Pulicat was given charge of the Coromandel coast. Ships were permitted to sail only after obtaining a *cartaz* (sailing permit) from the Portuguese Captain.[3] He is reported to have issued such cartazes[4] duly signed by him. An amount of 5 *pardaus* per *cartaz* was charged from the owners of seagoing vessels.[5] The Factor at Pulicat maintained some soldiers to assist him in this task.

It was not always easy to make a distinction between the trading interests of the Crown and those of the Factor of the Coromandel. The position held by the Captain facilitated the process of self-aggrandisement. Hence there were many who addressed petitions to the king of Portugal seeking appointment as Captain of the Coromandel Coast.[6] However, many Portuguese Captains, such as Miguel Ferreira, Cristovao Doria, Braz de Gois and Luis de Mello, who were stationed in the Coromandel were found involved in illegal business transactions such as encouraging their own agents to sail illegally from the ports of Coromandel very frequently to conduct trade with the other Asian ports.[7] So vast and so fast was the expansion of Portuguese private trade that the royal representatives in India could not exercise much control over the activities of these private Portuguese traders.

Gaspar Correia, the contemporary chronicler, has mentioned that Manuel de Frias was the first to be appointed Captain of the Coromandel coast in 1522.[8] However, some unpublished documents preserved in the National Archives of Portugal go to show that one Bastião Lopez was the first Factor and Captain of the Coromandel coast appointed by the Crown. It was the practice to appoint the Factor-cum-Captain for a period of three years only. Sometimes his term was extended for another three years. Generally only fidalgos were appointed as Captains and Factors. The royal appointment orders specified the terms of the post and contained details of the appointee's past achievements along with the declaration that the said post was conferred as an award for past services and spelt out the functions to be performed by him such as administer the affairs of the Portuguese people, preside as the officer-in-charge of *provedor dos defuntos* (purveyor of the estates of the deceased) issue *cartazes*, etc.

In 1520 the Factor and Captain of the Coromandel coast resided at Pulicat. Later, in 1530, when Santhome of Mylapore emerged as a prominent settlement of the Portuguese, Miguel Ferreira, the Captain of the Coromandel coast, is known to have taken up residence at Santhome. However, when other similar Portuguese trading settlements came up at Nagapattinam and Devanampattinam, separate Resident Captains came to be appointed at each of these ports instead of one Factor and Captain for the entire Coromandel coast.[9]

The (*feitoria*) trading factory was under the charge of a Resident Factor who was also called *Capitiio e Feitor* (Captain and Factor). He was the administrator of the Portuguese living on the coast.[10] This Factor had at his service some clerks or writers[11] in Santhome of Mylapore, Nagapattinam and Devanampattinam, the three most famous trading centres of the Portuguese on the Coromandel coast,[12] besides other persons and interpreters necessary to assist him in the conduct of maritime trade. He had to submit a detailed report of his trade dealings in the factory at the end of his term and get a certificate (*carta de quitacao*) of acquittance. The account book of the factory was to be entrusted to the chief of the ship that left India, and it was handed over to the Factor of the *Casa da India* in Lisbon on its arrival in Portugal.[13] All the Portuguese Captains were directed to maintain the accounts of the respective factories on the Tamil coast. A letter written by the inhabitants of the settlement of Santhome of Mylapore to the king of Portugal, dated 27 December 1535, mentions that the register containing the receipts and expenditure statements was being maintained there.[14] The accounts book of Manuel da Gama, the Portuguese Factor and Captain of the Coromandel Coast for the year 1526, alone, however, could be traced in the National Archives of Portugal.[15]

An examination of this account book is noteworthy. In the first place, it supplies some very useful data not available in the native inscriptional sources for the study of sixteenth-century coastal Tamil Nadu. In the second place, it furnishes plenty of details useful for the study of the economics, especially the port economy, of the Coromandel coast.

A ship which arrived from Bengal was captured by the Portuguese Captain of the Coromandel coast near the port of Kayal since the vessel did not have a Portuguese sailing permit. The men in the ship were captured, the cargo seized and sold. The information gleaned from this famous account book is furnished in Table 3.

Further, the accounts book contains details (Table 4) of the

TABLE 3: STATEMENT SHOWING SALE OF VARIOUS COMMODITIES BY MANUEL DA GAMA, CAPTAIN AND FACTOR OF THE COROMANDEL COAST, 6 MARCH 1526-8 MARCH 1526

Sl. No.	Name of the commodity	Total quantity	Selling price per unit (in *panams*)	Total amount realised (in *panams*)
A. Dated 6 March 1526				
1.	Safflower	166 faracola	2½	415
2.	Long pepper	19 faracola	13	247
3.	Black pepper	18 faracola	21	378
4.	Horsegram	6 faracola	7	42
5.	Arecanut	8 marks	30	240
B. Dated 7 March 1526				
1.	Rice	255 kottai	10	2,550
2.	Aval	136 kottai	6	816
3.	Jaggery	15 jars	7	105
C. Dated 8 March 1526				
1.	Pepper	37 faracola	13	481

TABLE 4: PORTUGUESE TRADE INVESTMENT AT THE PORTS OF KUNIMEDU AND NAGAPATTINAM, 20 JULY 1526-15 JANUARY 1527

Name of the Port	Period	Total amount (in *reis*)
Kunimedu	20 July 1526 to 15 January 1527	1,19,130
Nagapattinam	30 September 1526	1,802
	2 October 1526	2,64,930

amount of money used for the purpose of trade in the various ports of the Coromandel coast, such as Kunimedu and Nagapattinam, by the Portuguese Captain of the Coromandel.

The Portuguese Captain also collected money through, the sale of contraband seized from merchants in the Coromandel. According to the *Regimento para a reparticao das presas* (Rules for sharing the booty) of the year 1505, 20 per cent of the value of the goods seized went to the king, 53 per cent to the shipowner and the remaining 27 per cent was distributed among the crew. The viceroy was entitled to choose one precious jewel from the seized goods.

Manuel da Gama's accounts book throws considerable light on units of weights and measures in use, commodities sold and their prices. Trade transactions were recorded in the presence of writers. There was, therefore, no scope for misappropriation of funds or for manipulation of accounts. The document contains information about all the amounts realized through sale besides details of money (capital) and goods received. These bits of information things light on how the Portuguese generated the funds required for conducting overseas trade from the Coromandel coast. They also took possession of all the money left unclaimed by the persons who had died while at sea. This was yet another means adopted by them to accumulate the capital required for trade.

As the Portuguese were interested in conducting trade through the port of Pulicat, they entered into partnership with the Tamil merchants in the Coromandel coast in the early sixteenth century. Some native merchants like Nayinar Chetti (Naina Chatu) owned large vessels which were hired by the Portuguese Crown to carry the goods from the Coromandel coast to the port of Melaka in South-East Asia.[16] It may be useful to quote the views expressed by the Portuguese about this Tamil merchant.

Nayinar Chetti is a man firm in his friendship with the Portuguese . . . he works as hard as he can for this. . . . In the service of Your Highness and in matters regarding security he is trustworthy, dependable and without deceit. However he is a merchant and he has made himself very rich. He has the shrewdness of a merchant and he has made himself very rich. He does well in his trade. He sends junks everywhere. He works for his own profit. When foreigners come he gives presents. He is a clever merchant, a man of good and sensible advice.[17]

It must be kept in mind that the Portuguese trade was a Crown monopoly during this period with little or no role for private Portuguese merchants. In the beginning, i.e. 1513, the Portuguese Crown had used only a single type of vessel called *nau de Choromandel* to ferry their rice and textiles from Pulicat to Melaka.[18] The Crown therefore used the ships owned by the Tamil merchants as they did not have enough naus with them. From 1515 onward, *naus* from the western coast came to be used in the Bay of Bengal, and they were known as *nau de rei* (Crown ship). These ships, as per the records, brought gold from Melaka.[19] In 1537, the number of Portuguese *naus* regularly sailing between Pulicat and Melaka was said to be three.[20] From the middle of the sixteenth century, *naus* which were constructed in Goa were sent to Melaka via Pulicat. Later, when Nagapattinam emerged as the main port under the Portuguese, several *naus* were used for undertaking voyages to China via Melaka.[21] The Jesuit missionary, Francisco Xavier, in his letter dated 10 May 1546 described his voyage from Santhome of Mylapore to Amboina via Melaka in a *nau* of 400 tons.[22] It is gleaned from records that the *naus* that sailed from Kochi to Melaka always went around the island of Sri Lanka since there were many shallows in the Palk Strait.

Around this time the Captains were becoming more interested in trade and began dealing in it privately. Cristovao Alvarez, the Captain of the Crown ship sailing from the Coromandel to Melaka and vice versa, brought little revenue to the king in 1548 but enhanced his own private income. [23]

It appears that this system of crown voyages (of royal monopoly) was replaced by a new system of granting the privilege of trade voyages for a fee. This privilege for undertaking trade voyages was given only to *fidalgos* in the beginning. Later, from 1580 onward, the Portuguese Crown introduced another system of granting concessional voyages. This was given to private Portuguese traders. Thus the system of maritime voyages of the *Estado da Índia* depended on policies decided in Lisbon.

Examined below is how the privileges given to the *fidalgos* for undertaking these voyages in the Coromandel deferred from the concessions given to private traders.

Affonso de Albuquerque, the viceroy of Goa (1509-15), followed a policy of centralized control and state mercantilism in Portuguese Asia. Lopo Soares de Albergarsia the next viceroy (1515-18), sought to promote private trade. Thus the Portuguese trade in India got polarized around two different policies.

According to Sanjay Subrahmanyam, the system of granting concessional voyages becomes visible in the 1550s and reached its heyday sometime around 1570.

> In one set of ports the concessionary was not given the exclusive right to make the voyage. But instead given the position of Captain-Major of fleet from the specific port of departure to that of destination. . . . He enjoyed the privilege of buying and selling. loading and unloading before anyone else. . . . In another set of ports, the so-called reserved ports (*portas coutadas*), the concessionary had the exclusive right to trade over a particular concessional route specified with respect both to port of departure and that of destination. . . . It was in this category that trade from Coromandel to Melaka as well as that from Coromandel to Pegu fell in the last quarter of the Sixteenth Century. Thus with the system of concessions, we see for the first time the effective introduction into the Bay of Bengal a system of monopoly over commercial routes claimed by the Portuguese Crown.[24]

With the evolving policy of the *Estado da Índia*, the maritime routes directly operated were stopped in the 1540s. A system of granting trade privileges for voyage was introduced which enabled the Portuguese rulers to retain their monopolist hold over these privileges. This also turned out to be beneficial to the Captain-Major. In the beginning, those privileges were given only to members of the higher nobility. Later they were granted mostly to the aristocratic elite of the *Estado da Índia,* comprised the middle and lower nobility, respectively, of Captain-Majors and their second sons (*filhos segundos*) who were emerging as prominent traders.

Those who were granted these privileges had to prepare and equip the ships at their own cost, receiving initially a subsidy of three thousand *cruzados* from the royal treasury. The next one consisted of granting the privilege for a specified amount of money. Neither these systems was successful as they were opposed by the nobility such as the Captain-Major and were also disliked by the missionaries and the newly emerging class of merchants.[25] This new class of enterprising traders also started challenging the position of the lower-class nobles who were themselves trying to go still further up in the ladder through acquisition of more wealth.

The Jesuits as well as the *fidalgos* opposed the attempts by the *Estado da Índia* to privatize trade routes for different reasons. In the first place, the up-and-coming trading community had been looking for an opportunity to increase its wealth and social status. The Captain-Majors, apart from the income they derived from their own trade, also took approximately 24,000 *reis* per annum from the royal treasury which corresponded to 9 per cent of the income of the *Estado da Índia*.[26] In the second place, the Jesuits' opposition may be attributed to their anti-monopolistic policy since they were one of the financiers of Portuguese trade in the *Estado da Índia*.[27] In 1567, the ecclesiastical authorities in Goa had condemned the orders issued by the royalty granting the sailing privileges exclusively to the Captains who belonged to the lowcr nobility.[28]

Subrahmanyam calls the grant of trade privileges 'voyage concessions'. There was, however, no element of concession at all in these awards. Indeed, it was some kind of a privilege. Privileges given to individuals or institutions in the decade l550-60 later came to be confused with the sailing concessions offered in the 1560s and 1510s. Sanjay Subrahmanyam's view may have to be reconsidered in the light of information discovered in a manuscript entitled *Cazos Diversos e varios que Correm pelas partes da India com suas resollucoes pelo padre Francisco Rodrigues da Companhia de Jesus, Goa,* 1571 (Different and various instances found in India with regard to voyages and solutions suggested by Fr. Francisco Rodrigues of the Society of Jesus), now preserved in the National Archives of Portugal.[29]

Based on this manuscript, it may be said that by AD 1560, the privileges given to individuals were extended to voyages. This goes against the notion of Subrahmanyam who suggested it for

1570. The *Estado da Índia* granted yet another type of privilege which, however, has probably not come to the notice of Sanjay Subrahmanyam.

The manuscript mentioned above also furnishes the details of yet another system of voyages under which the privilege granted entailed the obligation to carry some commodities on behalf of the Crown. This condition was stipulated because the Captain-Major enjoyed the right to select the commodities and fix their price. The Captain-Major received payment for escorting ships during the voyages. Padre Francisco Rodrigues, the Jesuit, condemned this system as, according to him, it was against Canon Law. He said that the Captain-Majors were selling their own souls in exchange for money.[30]

Resentment towards the system gave rise to new trade routes from the Coromandel to Aceh, Martaban, Perak, Kedah and Tavoy. This greatly reduced the earnings of the *Estado da Índia*.[31] Hence, in the 1580s, the *Estado da Índia* wanted to exercise greater control over the trade operated by private merchants. The sailing concessions therefore encouraged, the Portuguese traders who had earlier avoided sailings to escape the numerous obligations imposed on them, particularly with regard to the payment of customs and high freight charges to the Captain-Majors.[32]

Export of Rice to Malabar, Sri Lanka and South-East Asia

Sixteenth-century travellers like Duarte Barbosa and Tome Pires mention that rice was available in plenty on the Coromandel coast.[33] According to early Portuguese sources, many Muslims and Hindus of Malabar owned ships and they sailed to the Coromandel to purchase paddy and rice.[34] Duarte Pacheco Ferreira, the Portuguese Captain of Kollam, attests to the arrival of ships at Kollam laden with rice from the Coromandel.[35] The merchants of Kannur also traded in rice with the Coromandel.[36] The staple food of the people in Malabar was rice but not enough of it was produced locally. The region from Tanur in the north to Kollam in the south received abundant quantities of rice.[37] The rice from the Coromandel was four times cheaper than the rice from the Canara region.[38] The export of rice to Kozhikodu, the chief Muslim settlement on the Malabar Coast, was regular and the town depended heavily on its supply from the Coromandel between 1502 and 1518.[39]

It was customary for the merchants of Malabar in 1501 to visit the Coromandel coast to procure rice in exchange for pepper. Portuguese traders like Duarte Pacheco and Manuel Pessanha, also from Kochi, were reported to have travelled to the Coromandel to procure rice in exchange for pepper. It is further learnt that they sailed from the Coromandel with escorts in 1505 fearing attack by the Marakkayars.[40] This proves that the Marakkayars were feared by these Portuguese seafaring merchants who were engaged in the exchange of rice and pepper between the Malabar and Coromandel coasts.

In 1505 Portuguese introduced very strict control over the movement of native ships in the Bay of Bengal and the Arabian Sea. The natives were forced to obtain *cartazes* from the Portuguese before undertaking such voyages.[41] The Malabar merchants who came by sea route to purchase rice stopped visiting the Coromandel ports from 1508 onwards and instead attempted to reach there via the land routes often on pack animals and bullock carts crossing the Ghats to unload in the Malabar region. The long, distance trade of the Marakkayars was, however, hampered later with the appointment of Manuel de Frias as the Portuguese Captain. He was asked to organize the supply of rice from the Coromandel coast in 1522.[42] The Muslims were prohibited to carry on trade in all high profit-yielding goods and were left to deal in commodities in which the Portuguese had little interest. They were also forbidden to sail freely to places of their own choice for commercial purposes.

Kunimedu on the Coromandel coast was also an important centre of the rice trade. Some merchants like Pattan Marakkayar (Pate Marecar) who hailed from Kunimedu in the Coromandel took up residence at Kochi to participate in the growing rice barter trade.[43] Both Pattan Marakkayar and Kunzhali Marakkayar (Cunhale Marecar) continued to procure rice from Kunimedu where their brothers and other relatives helped organize the collection and storage of the rice. Gaspar Correia, the Portuguese chronicler of this period, records that the rice trade was carried on by the Marakkayars all of whom had partnerships with their friends. Although Kunzhali Marakkayar died at Kunimedu in 1534, his family continued to carry on the rice trade till 1540.[44] Similarly, another merchant called Mohammed Ali Marakkayar (Mamale Marecar) held the monopoly over the export of rice from the Coromandel to Malabar. [45]

The Marakkayars, already familiar with the overland trade routes, shifted their attention to overland trade in rice in order to compensate for their loss in the maritime trade. The Portuguese attacks at sea paved the way for the emergence of the Marakkayars as inland traders. They became distributors of rice on retail and wholesale in Malabar. They went to the interior Ghat villages, sold rice and collected pepper. There was also an agreement with the ruler of Porakkad that no one none other than Mohammed Ali Marakkayar and his brother Shereen Marakkayar (Cherin Marecar) should be permitted to sell rice on the Malabar Coast.[46]

As paddy was the chief crop of cultivation in the Coromandel, rice was available in plenty providing scope for its export to Kochi. There is a reference in 1527 about rice to the tune of 124 *gantas* being exported from the Coromandel to Kochi where it was in great demand because the Portuguese soldiers there were paid their salary partly in rice.[47] The writings of the *Almoxarife* (officer-in-charge of civil supplies) of Kochi emphasized the importance of the Coromandel rice for military payments.[48] Similarly, another letter written by the Portuguese viceroy to the king of Portugal mentions rice, being brought in *champanas* (boats) from the Coromandel coast to Goa by the Portuguese under the Crown account towards payment of soldiers.[49]

Since the Portuguese had introduced restrictions on the movement of sailing vessels carrying rice in the Bay of Bengal region in 1505, the Marakkayars of the Coromandel coast had to pay as much as 100 *pardaus* to get a sailing permit. Hindu merchants, on the other hand, paid only 50 *pardaus* for the purchase of a *cartaz* to trade in rice.[50] The Marakkayars sometimes had to pay whatever amount the Portuguese fixed towards issue of a *cartaz*, to prevent their business voyages from being totally disrupted.

It is further learnt that some private Portuguese traders began to trade in rice in the Coromandel, leading to competition be-

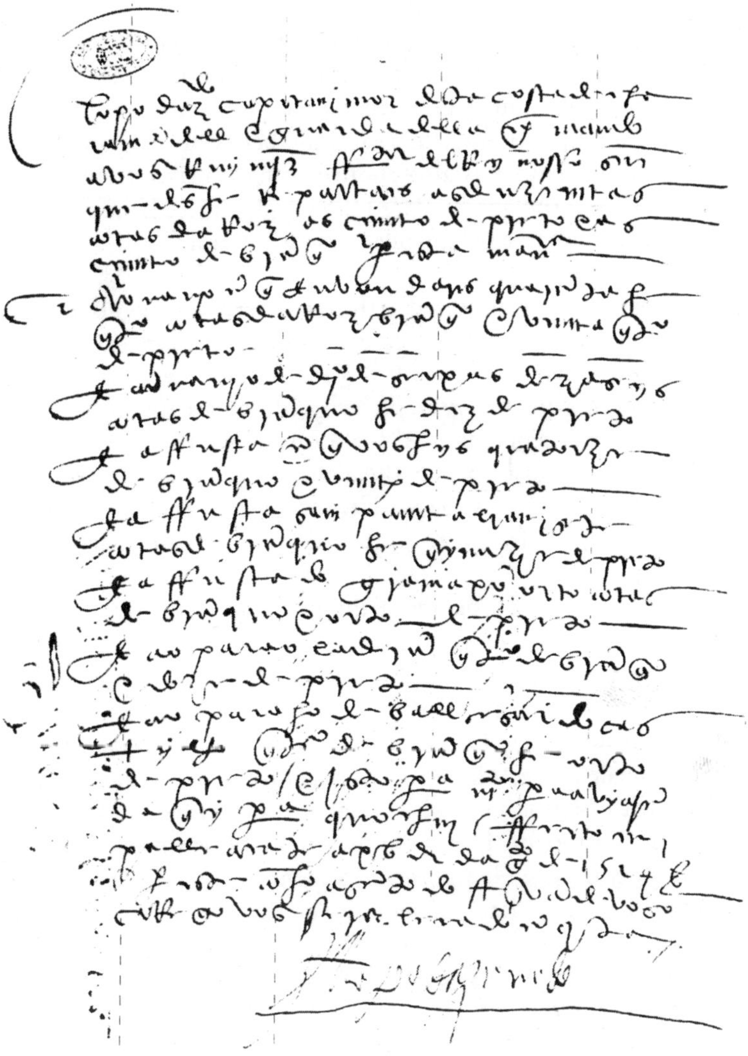

FIG. 2: AN ORDER ISSUED ON 15 AUGUST 1524 BY THE PORTUGUESE CAPTAIN OF THE COROMANDEL TO PURCHASE 200 *KOTTAI* OF RICE AT PULICAT AND TO SUPPLY THE SAME TO KOCHI PRESERVED AT THE NATIONAL ARCHIVES OF PORTUGAL, LISBON.

tween these Portuguese traders and the Marakkayars. The Portuguese armada on the Coromandel coast, which was supposed to guard the Coromandel ships, also oppressed the Portuguese merchants and caused annoyance to them.[51] That there was fierce competition in the rice trade between the Portuguese and the Marakkayars is also confirmed by other contemporary records. These conflicts hindered the supply of rice from the port of Nagapattinam to Kochi, Kollam and Kannur during the middle of the sixteenth century.[52]

Catamarans were also used in the trade between Nagapattinam and Jaffna as the quantity of rice and cinnamon exchanged between these ports was small.[53] Various native vessels such as *fragata, fusta, sampan, catur, paravu* and *toni* are mentioned in a series of records as being used for transporting the rice.[54] Many unpublished manuscripts in the series of *Corpo Cronologico* contain orders issued by the Resident Captain of the Coromandel to the Portuguese Factor to purchase and deliver rice from the Coromandel.[55]

There are also records about the migration of several Portuguese traders from the west coast of India to the east coast seeking commercial fortunes. One Francisco Maneiro employed in the Portuguese factory at Kochi is reported to have left his service to trade in rice in the Coromandel.[56] Similarly, Tristao de Paiva and Cosme de Paiva, who were the *casados* of Goa, began trading in rice with Santhome. Subsequently, they settled down there although Tristao de Paiva continued to be mentioned as an honoured citizen of Goa in the documents.[57]

In the Kaveri delta, particularly in the area lying between Karaikal and Thirumalairayanpattinam, paddy that was cultivated in the Kudavaiyar and Arasalar riverine basin found its way to Nagapattinam from where it was exported.[58] The part of Thirumalairayanpattinam held a prominent place in the rice trade with Sri Lanka and Malabar until the third decade of the sixteenth century. Some unpublished manuscripts preserved in the National Archives of Lisbon contain orders issued by the Resident Portuguese Captain of the Coromandel coast to the Factor of the Coromandel to purchase rice at Thirumalairayanpattinam. The despatch-orders were signed by the Portuguese

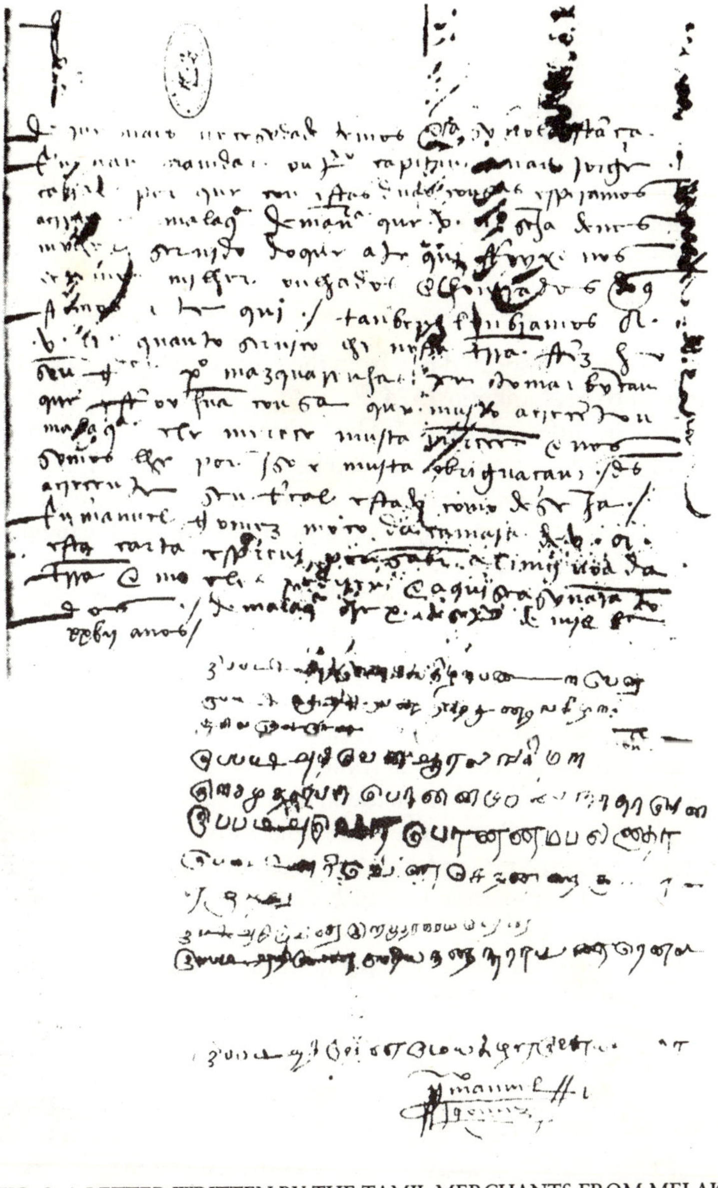

FIG. 3: A LETTER WRITTEN BY THE TAMIL MERCHANTS FROM MELAKA TO THE KING OF PORTUGAL UNDER THEIR SIGNATURES DATED 10 SEPTEMBER 1527 PRESERVED AT THE NATIONAL ARCHIVES OF PORTUGAL.

TABLE 5: PORTUGUESE EXPORT OF RICE FROM THIRUMALAIRAYANPATTINAM AS ON 25 SEPTEMBER 1524[59]

Portuguese owners of sailing vessels	Rice export (in *kottai*)
Lopo de Azevedo	56
Diogo de Seyhas	45
Lopo de Azevedo	35
Fernao Pachequo	40
Antonio Gramaxyo	26
Joao de Sequeira	18
Total	220

officials who transported rice from the port of Thirumalairayanpattinam to Sri Lanka in 1524.[60]

It can be inferred from Table 5 that rice was exported in exchange for cinnamon and arecanuts from Sri Lanka. Later the port of Thirumalairayanpattinam declined because export of rice was diverted to the port of Nagapattinam where the Portuguese had by then settled down.

The Portuguese who first settled in Nagapattinam in 1525 to trade in rice were taken into custody by the Marakkayars. A native man from Pulicat was therefore sent by the Portuguese Captain to deliver a letter to the chief of the Marakkayars. The messenger was given some money as remuneration for the services rendered. After some time, on the intervention of the Portuguese Captain of Coromandel, the captives were released.[61] In due course the Portuguese were able to procure rice besides butter, textiles, salt and oil for their armada from Nagapattinam.[62] They exported of 26 *kottais* of rice to Melaka from Nagapattinam in 1525.[63] Thus, while the Portuguese slowly extended their influence in Nagapattinam, the Marakkayars confined themselves to Nagore.

The natives in the Coromandel did not require much cinnamon but they needed areca nuts for betel-chewing. Therefore the Hindu traders were keen to sell their surplus rice and engaged themselves in overseas trade with Sri Lanka to obtain mainly areca nuts. The Portuguese were also attracted to the rice trade since rice was exchanged for cinnamon, which was in great demand for export to Lisbon. Repeated requests were made in

1525 and 1527 to the king of Portugal to block the Marakkayars from transporting rice from the Coromandel coast to Sri Lanka in exchange for cinnamon.[64] The Portuguese Captain of Colombo, Fernão Gomes de Lemos, had also made similar requests to the Crown. It was difficult for the Portuguese in Sri Lanka to procure cinnamon there, as they had no control over the rice trade in the Coromandel coast in the first half of the sixteenth century.[65] They therefore persuaded the king of Sri Lanka to issue an order expelling the Marakkayars from his kingdom, so that they could purchase cinnamon there.[66] Private traders and corrupt officials among the Portuguese found the cinnamon trade of Sri Lanka very lucrative.

Portuguese ships could thus sail very regularly from the Coromandel to collect cinnamon from Sri Lanka as is evident from Table 6. In 1547, however, many vessels were found to be trading in cinnamon, sailing illegally between the Coromandel and Sri Lanka without *cartazes*.[67]

When famines broke out in the Coromandel and paddy cultivation was affected in the third decade of the sixteenth century, the people of Sri Lanka too suffered due to a decline in the supply of rice from the Coromandel. Even the Portuguese were so severely affected that their Captain pleaded for rice supply from the Coromandel to Sri Lanka.[68] Taking note of the situation there, in 1569 the Archbishop of Goa described the Coromandel as the throat of Sri Lanka, from where rice and other food provisions came.[69] Thus rice trade fluctuated according to the exigencies of the period.

TABLE 6: RECORDED PORTUGUESE SHIPPING FROM THE COROMANDEL TO SRI LANKA, 1519-47[70]

Period	Number of ships
1519	2
1523	1
1524	1
1527	1
1530	2
1545	2
1547	1

Early-sixteenth-century records reveal that the port of Pasai in Sumatra had trade contacts with the Coromandel. Rice from the Kaveri delta region and the surplus available at the port of Nagore greatly facilitated the export of rice to Pasai during this period. Nagore was also a famous trading centre for raw silk brought by Chinese ships in the sixteenth century.[71] The Marakayyar merchants, besides supplying rice to Sri Lanka, also exported it to Pasai since food provisions were scarce there.[72] Rice was exchanged for raw silk which was in great demand for textile manufacture among the weavers in the hinterland of the Coromandel coast.

Giovanni de Empoli, an Italian who visited the port of Pasai, has estimated in his account that seven hundred *velas* of rice from Nagore reached Pasai. The Muslim merchants of Pulicat also exported rice to the tune of 10,0000 *gantas* to the port of Pasai in 1511.[73] A letter written in Arabic by the sultan of Pasai in the year 1512 to the king of Portugal states that the Marakkayars dominated the rice trade with the port of Pasai. The sultan declared that 14 *bahars* of silk could be supplied annually to the Portuguese, if necessary.[74]

Rice was exported from Pulicat to Melaka and it was recorded that between 26 March 1512 and 25 February 1514 a total quantity of 10,946.429 *gantas* of rice had been exported. Table 7 shows the quantity of rice exported during 1524-5 at various intervals through different ships which sailed from Pulicat.

The Rice exported to Melaka was chiefly exchanged for spices. Private Portuguese traders carried on their rice trade from Pulicat

TABLE 7: PORTUGUESE EXPORTS OF RICE FROM PULICAT TO MELAKA, 1524-5[75]

Date	Ship	Captain	Quantity (in *gantas*)
06 Aug.1524	*Navio Santiago*	João Rodrigues	3,240.00
10 Aug.1524	*Navio Conceição*	–	14,160.00
10 Aug.1524	*Nau Rui Marcos*	João Correia	3,100.00
15 Aug.1524	*Fusta Sta. Catarina*	Domingos Fernandes	2,880.00
08 Apr. 1525	*Navio Conceição*	João Paes	1,575.00
10 July 1525	*Navio Trinidade*	João Fernandes	2,000.00
15 July 1525	*Navio . . .*	Luis Affonso	15,280.00

for the purpose of private profit. The Portuguese officials also supported the rice trade to increase the customs revenue in Melaka.

The Portuguese settlement of Santhome of Mylapore had no natural harbour. According to some contemporary sources, ships could reach Santhome only by sailing close to the coast by taking advantage of the wind. During the hot summer months of May and June, ships could sail into the open sea as close as possible to the wind and make way southwards. The first course was more promising even though wind movements could not always be predicted with complete accuracy.[76] Further, sailings from Goa to Pegu via Santhome, peaked every year from 15 April to 20 April before the first monsoon and between 8 August and 24 August before the second monsoon. Similarly, from Pegu, ships left between 15 January and 25 January to arrive at Santhome first and then sailed to Goa between 25 March and up to the beginning of April.[77] There was an *adhikari* (officer) stationed at Mylapore to collect revenue from the port, which sent the king of Vijayanagara.[78] The Portuguese in Mylapore also participated in the rice trade. We find the Portuguese Captain of Santhome complaining to the Viceroy at Goa in 1581 that the flourishing rice trade of Masulipatnam with Melaka had affected the Portuguese rice trade of Mylapore.[79] Although the Bishop of Mylapore (in 1610) tried to ensure supply of rice in a bid to revive the rice trade of Santhome with Melaka, his efforts were not very successful. The very next year, i.e. in 1611, however, the resident Captain of Melaka reported that rice from Nagapattinam was received and it was chiefly through the efforts of the Bishop of Mylapore. Moreover, rice was cheap at Nagapattinam.[80] When cultivation of paddy was affected in the hinterland of the port of Devanampattinam, the Bishop of Mylapore arranged for 300 *gantas* of rice to be supplied from Nagapattinam to Devanampattinam.[81] The native merchants also brought enough consignments of rice to the port of Santhome the following year (1612). Many vessels carrying rice to Melaka were seized by the Dutch in Pulicat owing to commercial rivalry. In these circumstances the Portuguese in Santhome could not carry on their rice trade successfully.[82]

Export of Textiles from Pulicat and Santhome

Pulicat, which had a natural harbour and a rich hinterland with many weaving villages, posed no difficulty for the Portuguese in the pursuit of their overseas trade in textiles (see Map 4). This was one of the factors that enabled the development of trade. Although a team of Portuguese explorers came to Santhome of Mylapore in 1507, sent by Francisco de Almeida, the first Portuguese viceroy of India, they were probably not aware of the prominent role being played by the Chetti merchants in the textile trade till about the time the Portuguese first settled in Melaka in 1511. It was here that the Portuguese just learnt of the Chettis and their flourishing cloth trade. The Hindu merchants in the Coromandel coast were not only encouraged but also requested to continue their trade with Melaka. It is gleaned from the report of the Portuguese Captain of Melaka that ships from Pulicat which reached Melaka brought rich cargo. The trade with Pulicat brought good revenue to the Portuguese factory at Melaka. Between 1511 and 1528, twelve ships left Pulicat for Melaka and ten ships arrived from Melaka as shown in Table 8: The textile cargo value during the period is given in Table 9.

The supply of textiles from Pulicat to Melaka was substantial enough to warrant the appointment of a *shahbhandar* (port officer) at Melaka exclusively to look after the welfare of the

TABLE 8: RECORDED PORTUGUESE SHIPPING FROM/TO PULICAT, 1511-28[83]

Period	Departures from Pulicat to Melaka	Arrival at Pulicat from Melaka
1511	–	1
1512	1	–
1513	2	1
1514	2	2
1516	–	4
1518	–	–
1520	–	–
1524	2	–
1525	3	–
1527	2	1
1528	–	1

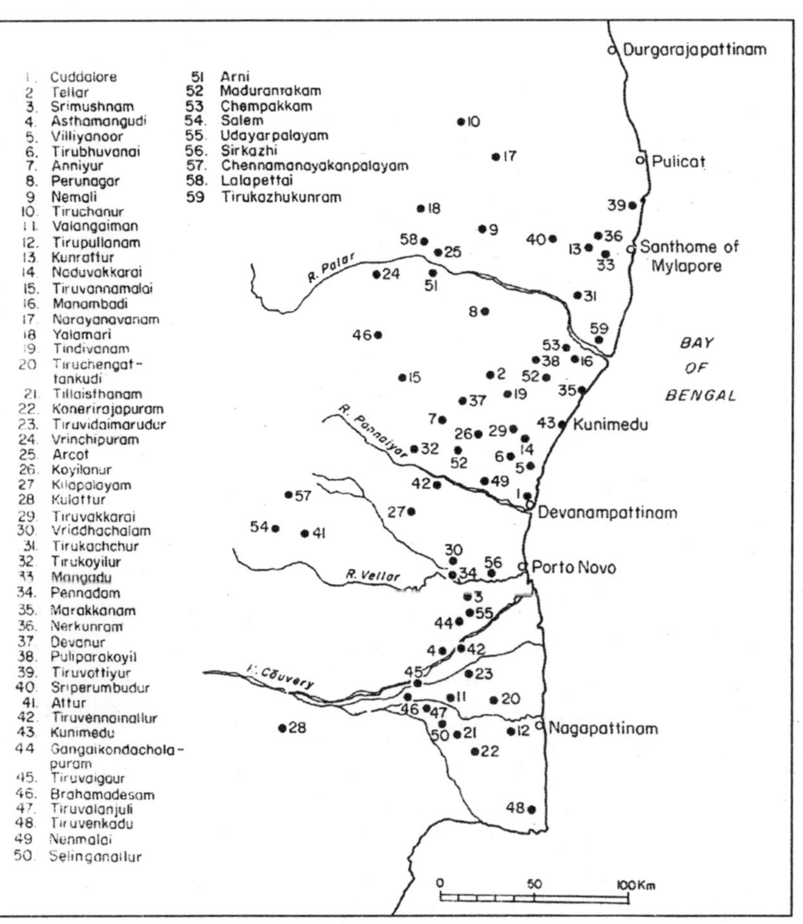

MAP 4: IMPORTANT WEAVING CENTRES ON THE COROMONDEL COAST

TABLE 9: PORTUGUESE EXPORTS OF TEXTILES FROM THE COROMANDEL TO MELAKA, 1511-22[84]

Period	Value (in *cruzados*)
1511	9,000
1512	15,000
1515	12,000
1522	90,000

Tamil merchants arriving there.[85] The textile trade between Pulicat and Melaka was so lucrative that the sultan of Melaka, although he had lost his kingdom to the Portuguese in 1511, continued to trade with the port of Pulicat. In a letter addressed to the king of Portugal it is mentioned that the sultan owned a junk which was captured by the Portuguese near the port of Pulicat.[86]

Textiles formed the most important commodity of maritime trade at Pulicat and the Chetti merchants dominated the trade. They, however, had to face very tough competition from Gujarati traders who brought cloth from Cambay and Chaul.[87] As the Chettis had assisted the Portuguese in capturing Melaka from the Sultan by providing them will information and ships, they preferred to come under the protection of the Portuguese, which helped them to face the challenge posed by the Gujarati traders. Nayinar Chetti, the famous trader who assisted the Portuguese, was appointed *shahbhandar* in Melaka and *bendhara* (officer-in-charge of civil and criminal matters) for services rendered to the Portuguese Crown.[88]

The Chetti merchants were allowed by the Portuguese Captain of Melaka to pay customs duty at a concessional rate of 6 per cent while all other traders were asked to pay 10 per cent. Further, Jorge de Albuquerque, the Portuguese Factor of Melaka, declared that more privileges would be granted to the Chettis who hailed from the ports of the Coromandel coast if they settled down at Melaka.[89] In order to develop commercial activities, Manuel de Frias, the Portuguese Captain of the Coromandel, initially resided at Pulicat and looked after the collection of textiles for export to Melaka. From this it may be inferred that the Chetti merchants dominated the textile trade with Melaka and the Portuguese played only a secondary role in the early decades of the sixteenth century.

Droughts and famines, which continuously ravaged the Coromandel region during 1531, 1532, 1535 and 1540, affected textile production. This resulted in the decline of textile trade with Melaka to the tune of 4,000 *cruzados,* and these years witnessed a gradual withdrawal of Coromandel merchants from the cloth trade as is evident from a letter written in the year 1540.[90] The letter further mentions that the export of textiles at this time consisted of black cloth alone. Only one ship sailed in 1540 from Pulicat to Melaka.[91] The earlier periods had witnessed an annual average revenue of 1,00,000 *cruzados* from the commerce between Pulicat to Melaka. But this flourishing trade had come to a halt.

Two letters written in October and November of 1545 suggest that trade with Melaka declined with the fall in the supply of textiles from the Coromandel.[92] The *Vedor da Fazenda* (Comptroller of Revenue) at Kochi reported that only about half the number of ships were then plying in the Bay of Bengal compared to the previous period and they had obtained Portuguese *cartazes.*[93]

The introduction, in 1548 of the system of granting trade privileges 1548 was a turning point, marking the revival of the Portuguese textile trade between the Coromandel ports and Melaka. Portuguese ships sailing for Melaka left Pulicat at the end of August or the beginning of September. The voyage usually

TABLE 10: RECORDED PORTUGUESE SHIPPING FROM PULICAT TO MELAKA, 1537-64[94]

Period	Pulicat
1537	4
1538	1
1539	1
1540	1
1546	3
1548	1
1559	1
1562	2
1564	1

lasted a month and the return voyage from Melaka was generally made in the month of January.[95] In 1548, the captaincy of the cargo ships was given, as a rule, to a *fidalgo* (noble) as a reward for services rendered in the past to the Portuguese Crown. The captain of the ship was also given many privileges. He was allowed to load his own cargo on his ship before the cargoes of all other merchants. He could take one hundred and fifty bales of textiles free of duty or transport those of other merchants who had to pay him the freight and duties payable on them. This brought him a straight profit of 3,000 *cruzados*.[96] He was paid a year's salary in advance and he could take four merchants with him along, with their cargoes, who paid freight to him on his onward journey to Melaka. Another special privilege he was entitled to was that the Captain of Melaka was to allow whichever merchant wished to, to sail back with the captain of the ship on the return voyage to the Coromandel.[97] Thus a system of a regular official Portuguese textile trade came into existence.

Procurement of textiles from the various places on the Coromandel coast was an important activity. An agreement signed between the king of Vijayanagara and the Portuguese viceroy on 19 September 1547 greatly facilitated the organization of the textile trade at this time.[98] There was a provision in the agreement which specifically stated that all textiles in the kingdom of Vijayanagara, particularly from the Coromandel region under the rule of several subordinates, should be sold only to the Portuguese. This agreement certainly helped the Portuguese to a great extent. They transported textiles in the navios of Santhome to Melaka and the *naus* of the Moluccas, besides the Crown ship leaving annually from Pulicat.[99] Thus, till the 1560s Pulicat continued to be a dominant port on the Coromandel coast trading with Melaka.

A letter written from Kochi by Simao Botelho, the *Vedor da Fazenda*, dated 30 January 1552, mentions that the trade carried on from the port of Pulicat to Melaka brought less profit and it was very expensive when compared to the earlier periods. Hence he suggests that many more Portuguese merchants should be allowed to buy ships and to carry freight. As they would pay the duties in Melaka, the Crown's revenue would increase and the merchants would gain.[100]

According to some scholars,[101] the decline of Pulicat and its international trade was the result of the fall of Vijayanagara empire in the Battle of Talikota. This is not a very tenable reason because by this time the Portuguese had already started trading with Melaka directly from Santhome. Further, the Melaka trade from Pulicat was linked with Goa and this reduced the role of indigenous merchants in the Melaka trade, being operated directly from Pulicat. To suit their own convenience, the Portuguese diverted all shipping to Goa and the port of Pulicat became only a transit point in the onward voyage to Melaka. Even the return voyages from Melaka to Pulicat were not favourable to indigenous merchants because ships did not touch the other Coromandel ports but were destined for Goa directly. Due to these reasons the indigenous merchants in Pulicat had to divert their trade and their commercial establishments from Pulicat to Santhome. The Coromandel merchants trading with Melaka paid the freight in advance and ensured their return voyages in the same ship.[102] Since such facilities were now made available at Santhome in the 1560s, the indigenous merchants preferred to abandon Pulicat and settle at Santhome to participate directly in its growing commerce. This shift in the Portuguese trading activities to Santhome brought about the gradual decline of Pulicat. It was during this period that Santhome became a significant commercial centre for rich merchants on the Coromandel coast.

Weaving Centres and Types of Cloth

Since medieval times, textiles were being manufactured in various places in the hinterland of the port of Pulicat such as Tlruvottiyur, Manali, Kunrattur, Poonamallee, Velacheri, Adambakkam, Kottur, Ezhumbur (Egmore) and Koyambedu (see Map 4).[103] Woven textile fabrics produced in distant places such as Kanchipuram, Manimangalam, Thirukachiyur, Uttiramerur, Acharapakkam and Thirukazhukunram reached the port of Santhome of Mylapore owing to the demand by the Portuguese for export.[104] Painted cloth was produced in the village of Mambalam where many dyers and painters lived. All these varieties of textiles were sent to Santhome for export.[105]

Portuguese sources mention various types of cloth produced through different methods such as *larvado* (figured), *desperdicios* (waste), *estampado* (stamped design) and *tecido* (waterproof) on the Coromandel coast. Sources also indicate the names of various textiles such as *tapis, sarassas* and *morins*. Out of these types, *morin* was produced in many places like Santhome of Mylapore, Kunimedu and Nagapattinam. White cloth produced in Masulipatnam also came to the Coromandel ports for export. Painted cloth was produced in Krishnapattinam and Durgarajapattinam. Blue cloth was called *mouri* or *morin. Taferciras* was known as *tapisarassa*; the coloured pieces were used for skirts by men and women. *Beatilha* was very fine muslin and the length varied between 15 and 25 yards. *Birome* was called *bairami* and in Chinese texts it was known as *bai-lan-lu,* which was white cloth. *Comunivas* were also known as *cotonias,* on cotton cloth in two colours. *Diopogins,* known as *Drongans,* were textiles with two colours, especially red and white, red and green and red and blue. *Sarasa* was patterned (painted) cloth with figures of foliage or birds. *Chila* or *chela* was white or yellow cotton cloth with black chequered stripes and the average size was fifty-five full arms' length. *Guingons* known as *gingham* was plain cotton cloth, somewhat coarse. These *ginghams* carried a chequered pattern.[106]

Portuguese documents record that the Coromandel textiles meant for export were always packed in bundles of a hundred and twenty pieces of cloth. The purchase and sale prices of blue cloth have been well recorded while those of other textiles such as Java and Malay cloth, painted, printed and white cloth, are not available.

The sale price of blue cloth produced in the Kunimedu-Devanampattinam region was very high in Melaka since the

TABLE 11: PRICE DETAILS OF BLUE CLOTH, *c.* 1550[107]

Places of export	Purchase pricein Coromandel (single piece) (amount in *pardaus*)	Sale price in Melaka	Profit margin
Santhome	1.18	12	102%
Nagapattinam	1.20	8	67%
Kunimedu	1.50	15	100%

region was famous for the cultivation of the best variety of indigo which was used to produce the excellent dyers blue cloth. The *morins* of the Santhome region ranked second followed by Nagapattinam which had the lowest sale price in Melaka for blue cloth.

Overseas trade from the port of Santhome with Melaka began to flourish with the introduction of the system of granting sailing privileges to the nobles.

Table 12 shows that regular voyages were undertaken from Santhome to Melaka. Taking advantage of the regular trade, the Portuguese Captain of Melaka selected and seized some of the goods that were brought by the Coromandel merchants.[108] He thus enhanced his personal income while the merchants were deprived of their profit in trade. A letter written on 3 December 1568 by Fr. Lourenço Paes to Leão Henriques confirms that these activities of the Captain of Melaka very much hindered the growth of trade from Santhome.

Following the fall of the Vijayanagara empire in 1565, the Qutub Shahi rulers firmly established their kingdom in Golconda and began to show an interest in developing the Masulipatnam port. The sultan of Golconda sent his envoys to Melaka asking the Portuguese Captain to divert their trade to Masulipatnam. The Captain stopped the *nau* (cargo ship) of Coromandel that was about to set sail for Santhome. He further issued an order immediately permitting the ship of the Muslims to depart for Masulipatnam. The cargo of the impounded ship was unloaded and transferred to the Muslim ship. All the twenty-nine

TABLE 12: RECORDED COROMANDEL-MELAKA VOYAGES, 1560-5[109]

Year	Name of the Captain	No. of voyages undertaken
1560	João Rebello	2
1561	Luis Mendes Vasconcelos	2
1562	Pero Henriques	2
1563	Martim Castilho de Vasconcelos	2
1563	Luis Cristovão Lobo	2
1564	Pedro de Sousa	1
1565	Jorge de Menezes	2

Santhome-based merchants were ordered by the Portuguese Captain of Melaka to travel towards Masulipatnam instead of Santhome in 1567.[110] Further, the Portuguese resident Captain of Melaka deported the rest of the merchants in a decrepit ship owned by him after collecting the expenses of the voyage from them. The merchants were thus forced to incur heavy expenditure towards their return voyage to Coromandel.[111]

In the 1570s, Portuguese private traders were encouraged to undertake voyages from Santhome to Melaka and the number of voyages generally allowed to each individual was restricted to two, on the premise that if the first voyage happened to be a loss, the private trade could at least recap his losses from the second voyage.[112]

Sailing privileges were granted on exclusive routes on which nobody else, including indigenous merchants of the Coromandel, were permitted to operate. This system denied to the native shipowners the right to sail and operate their ships in overseas trade on these routes. This provoked the Tamil traders to rise against the Portuguese resulting in disputes.[113] Ultimately this policy led to the decline of native shipping in the trade between Santhome and Melaka during this period.[114]

Based on the work of L.F.F.R. Thomaz, Sanjay Subrahmanyam and Om Prakash mention that there was an attempt on the part of the king of Portugal to secure fixed profits from the voyages. They have calculated the net average profit per Coromandel-Melaka voyage at 6,000 *cruzados*.[115] In certain cases it has been found that the minimum bid amount was as low as 4,000 *cruzados*.[117] No fixed return could be expected since the bid

TABLE 13: SANTHOME-BASED VOYAGES TO MELAKA, 1577-87[116]

Buyer	1577	1584	1585	1587
Simão Abreu Pereira	2	–	–	–
Andre Teles de Menezes	–	2	–	–
Francisco de Sousa	–	2	–	–
Nuno Pereira de Miranda	–	–	2	–
Affonso Delgado de Brito	–	–	–	2
Jorge de Menezes	–	–	–	2
Total	2	4	2	4

varied from year to year and from person to person. The fall in the bid amount merely indicates a decline in the long-distance trade between the Coromandel coast and Melaka during this period. Moreover, the entry duty was enhanced from 6 to 8 per cent. This enhancement included the levy of additional tax on goods other than spices besides the tax levied for the fortification of Melaka. This resulted in the gradual withdrawal of the Coromandel merchants from the Melaka trade.[118]

The increased 8 per cent tax on commodities other than spices, collected at the Melaka port, led the Javanese merchants to also withdraw from trading in Coromandel textiles at Melaka after 1574. Even those who had been exempted from payment of exit duty earlier were forced now to pay.[119] In due course, the income of the Portuguese customs house at Melaka also declined.[120] The Coromandel merchants could not sell the fabric and the Javanese merchants, could not buy the textiles there owing to the increased taxation.[121] The trade between Santhome and Melaka suffered till 1591. The residents of Melaka, therefore requested the king of Portugal to reduce the suddenly increased customs duty with a view to reviving commerce. Dom Filippe I, the king of Portugal (1580-93), in turn, asked for information from the Portuguese viceroy of India regarding the issue of new directions to remove the tax impositions.[122] He also wanted to know whether such a relaxation of customs duty would affect the royal treasury of Melaka and of the Crown.

Some years later, i.e. in 1590, the difficulties experienced by the Santhome merchants were brought to the notice of the king of Portugal. Following this a royal order was issued in 1591 to the Portuguese viceroy at Goa, that for the merchandise exported from Santhome to Melaka, duties were to be paid only at Santhome and not in Melaka.[123]

TABLE 14: RECORDED SHIPPING FROM SANTHOME TO MELAKA, 1591-3[124]

Period	Number of ships
1591	2
1592	1
1593	1

The king of Portugal, in order to remove the difficulties encountered in the Melaka-Coromandel commerce, in 1596 ordered a further reduction of customs duties on the merchandise going from the Coromandel to Melaka.[125] Based on the royal instructions, the viceroy issued new orders reducing the customs duty from 8 per cent to 6 at Melaka as before.[126] This move, however, did not revive the commerce as expected. A letter written by the clerk of Melaka factory to the king of Portugal mentions that the new regulation introduced in 1598 making it compulsory to obtain prior approval of the officials of the Melaka customs house authorizing voyages from the port of Santhome had dealt a severe blow to the growth of commerce between the Coromandel and Melaka.[127] In April 1598, the viceroy issued orders that voyages between the Coromandel and Melaka could be made without despatch orders from the customs house of Melaka.[128] However, the Coromandel merchants preferred to sail other ports where better conditions prevailed.

The Melaka-Coromandel commerce almost reached its nadir at the end of the sixteenth century. On 15 January 1601, the King of Portugal Filippe II (1598-1621), issued instructions to the Portuguese viceroy of India to find other ways to promote the Melaka-Coromandel trade.[129] The Portuguese Captains of Melaka made use of the services of the Tamil merchants there and borrowed money from them in 1601 and sometimes engaged them as factors.[130] However, the attempts made by the Portuguese viceroy in 1608 to bring about an improvement in the situation were fruitless.[131]

Some private Portuguese traders like Luis Ferreira had been carrying Coromandel textiles to Melaka.[132] Further, there is mention of one Pero Fernandes engaged in the cloth trade particularly with Melaka.[133] Commerce in textiles from Santhome was organized by Francisco Correia de Brito, the Portuguese Captain, who sent these textiles to Banten and the Moluccas.[134] According to records (13 August 1607) the Portuguese obtained cloth from the ports of Pulicat and Santhome. The types of cloth obtained at these places appear to be different. Table 15 shows the consignment of textiles obtained from the port of Pulicat in 1607.

TABLE 15: CONSIGNMENT OF TEXTILES OBTAINED AT PULICAT, 1607

Sl. no.	Type of cloth	Length (in *covados*)	Breadth
1.	Taferciras	10	1 1/3
2.	Pratudas de seda	17	1 1/3
3.	Pacheiras intero	17	1 1/3
4.	Pacheiras seutade	8 1/2	1 1/3
5.	Beatilhas	16	1 1/4
6.	Teados	9	1 1/2
7.	Biromes	16	1 1/4
8.	Counivas	16	1 1/4
9.	Diopogins	4 1/2	1 1/2
10.	Panos de mocas	4 1/2	1 1/2

SOURCES: See note[135]

Further, we find that the Portuguese were able to obtain textiles in Santhome itself in 1607. The types textiles of Santhome are shown in Table 16.

Contemporary English sources indicated that at Santhome *kali gesso* (fabric with glass pieces) was made in addition to linen made of cotton wool. Calico cloth was also manufactured at Santhome.[136] The famine that ravaged the Coromandel in 1630 caused the death of many weavers in the region of Santhome and Pulicat. Thus production of cloth was also affected.[137] Export of textiles by the Portuguese from Santhome to Melaka commenced once again in 1634. As the Dutch were unable to compete with the Portuguese in the textile trade, they sought an opportunity to capture Melaka.[138] Even as late as 1634, the Portuguese who did not have their own collection centres in the hinterland of Coromandel, continued to procure the cloth from the Hindu traders who, in turn. collected it from the weavers in the interior

TABLE 16: CONSIGNMENT OF TEXTILES OBTAINED AT SANTHOME, 1607

Type of cloth	Length (in *covados*)	Breadth
Saracas e pais	5	1 3/4
Portes de chila	8 1/2	1 2/3
Guingons pardos	12	1 1/8

villages.[139] The Bishop of Santhome wrote in 1635 that the city of Santhome, which was one of the most prosperous trading ports in India, had fallen so low that it had but a few residents and had no trading capital.[140] Some years later, the Dutch suddenly moved towards the region of Santhome. They attempted to purchase textiles from persons with whom the Portuguese had been doing business in Ponneri, as they needed more textiles to improve their trade. It is known that in the 1640s the Dutch had entered into regular contract with the weavers and paid advance money for the manufacture of patterned cloth.[141]

Textile Exports from Kunimedu and Nagore

The trade in textiles had also spread to other ports on the Coromandel coast like Kunimedu and Nagore from where cloth was exported to the South-East Asian markets. In fact, the *shahbhandar* of the port of Pasai in Sumatra sent his own ships to make direct purchases of Coromandel textiles, since he knew well the textile manufacturing centres there.[142] The Marakayyars also procured textiles directly from the weaving villages around the port of Kunimedu and transported them in their own ships trading with Pasai. Thus Kunimedu continued its trade with Pasai till 1537.[143] When Pasai came under the domination of Aceh, the Marakayyars preferred to trade with the new emporium of Aceh.

The Marakayyar traders of Nagore are known to have established links with Gujarati Muslim merchants to conduct trade with Aceh in Sumatra. The Portuguese learnt about the textile trade of the Marakkayars from a merchant whose ship was captured by them in 1527. He further reported that the Gujarati merchants had obtained the required *cartazes* from the Portuguese to make purchases at the port of Kollam situated towards the extreme south of the western coast. They had made arrangements to reach the Coromandel coast to trade with Aceh.[144] This merchant further revealed that Nagore was an intermediary port from where the Coromandel Muslim traders established stable commerce with Aceh.[145] During this period, it is known that three ships set sail annually from the port of Nagore to Aceh. The Marakayyars traded in textiles of various varieties collected from the hinterland. Therefore, in 1527, the

Portuguese Captain Lopo Vaz de Sampayo was asked by the Portuguese viceroy to specially attack and capture the Marakkayars's ships[146] as their operations were hampering the growth of Portuguese commerce at Melaka as well as the Portuguese cloth trade which had began to be operated from the nearby port of Nagapattinam. However, not many details of export of the textiles from Nagapattinam by the Portuguese are available in records till 1584.[147]

Export of Textiles from Nagapattinam, Porto Novo and Devanampattinam

Artur Gallejo de Castelo Branco, the Portuguese Captain of Nagapattinam, made some serious efforts to collect textiles from the weaving villages in the hinterland of Nagapattinam in 1584 to boost the trade with Aceh.[148] He made contact with the textile suppliers with great success. He was able to purchase several varieties of textiles such as *morins* (blue cloth), *pintados* (painted cloth) and *pachaveloes* (gold-brocade cloth) from the hinterland of Nagapattinam port.[149] The cloth that was meant to be taken from here to Sri Lanka had to be officially cleared for which a *renda da chapa,* i.e. a stamp duty, was charged thus bringing some income to the Portuguese.[150]

The ruler of Gingee, Muthu Krishnappa Nayaka (1594-1614), evinced a desire to develop another port of trade in his kingdom since Devanampattinam happened to be the only port from where the the Portuguese conducted overseas trade in textiles. His ancestors, particularly his grandfather Tupaki Krishnappa Nayaka (1567-78), and his father Kondama Nayaka (1580-93) had earlier permitted the Portuguese to settle at Devanampattinam and carry on trade from there. The earliest commercial interest of the Portuguese in Porto Novo may be traced back to the year 1597, when the court of Muthu Krishnappa Nayaka in Gingee was visited by Fr. Nicholas Pimenta. The port was developed at the mouth of the river Vellar.[151] He invited the Portuguese to settle down at the port of Krishnapattinam (11°30′N) which was named after him. The name Porto Novo was apparently given by the Portuguese as they started trading from this new port.[152] Today the place is known in the vernacular as

Parangipettai. The village of Agaram in the environs of Porto Novo was inhabited by Hindus and the Portuguese settlement sprang up near the seashore. There was no factory as such in Porto Novo since no Captain was exclusively appointed. Private traders conducted the textile trade without any control being exercised by Portuguese officials. The prosperity of this port induced the Dutch to also seek permission to settle there but they were refused by the *nayak*. This is mentioned in the letter written by the Portuguese viceroy of Goa, dated 28 November 1604 to the king of Portugal. Along with the Portuguese the Chetti merchants also traded in cloth, particularly contributing to the growth of the textile trade at Porto Novo (to the 1630s).[153] The domination of Chettis at Porto Novo continued for many years with Seshadri Chetti acting as the head of the merchants at there.

Further, there is evidence that in 1640 textiles such as *enrolladas* of white, *saracas,* and *taferias* were also taken from the port of Porto Novo to Nagapattinam.[154] Since cotton was grown extensively in the hinterland of Porto Novo,[155] long cloth was chiefly manufactured there.[156] Besides long cloth, such other varieties as *morins* (blue cloth) and *beatilhas* (veil cloth) were also produced in Porto Novo.[157] The hamlets of Manampathi, Agaram and Ariyaghosti, located in the neighbourhood of Porto Novo, emerged as important weaving, dyeing and bleaching centres. Cloth bleaching was undertaken on a large scale at Bhuvanagiri as it was situated on the banks of a river where good and sufficient water was available.[158] Textiles also came from far away places like Udayarpalayam and Salem for export from Porto Novo. Customs duty and toll were collected on the textiles that were brought to Porto Novo.[159] Textiles of various sorts, both printed and woven besides blue cloth and *guineas,* were brought to Devanampattinam from the hinterland villages for export. Thus, all of these Coromandel ports developed as important outlets for the textiles that were produced in the immediate hinterland.[160]

Portuguese Textile Merchants

The increase in the production of the textiles owing to the demand from European trading companies and the big margin of profit in the cloth trade were incentives for the Portuguese merchants to engage in it. João Alvares, a rich and famous *casado* of Nagapattinam, was trading in textiles with Aceh in 1620. It was he who had informed the king of Portugal in 1621 of the sultan of Aceh's attempt to capture Melaka and of his effort to seek the help of the sultan of Johore in the proposed siege of the Portuguese port settlement.[161] Gonçalves Perreira, a *fidalgo*, conducted private trade in textiles in 1624 from Nagapattinam with Tennaserim and Mergui.[162] Domingos de Seixas was a leading merchant trading in textiles in 1632. He also imported sugar to Nagapattinam.[163] Martym Costa Falçao, the son of Estêvão Rebello, was a private trader based in Nagapattinam and in 1637 was trading in textiles with Trang.[164] António de Mendonça de Britto, a resident of Nagapattinam, purchased a ship in 1639 and sent it laden mostly, with textiles to Melaka.[165] Pedro Vaz a *casado* of Nagapattinam trading in textiles with Maçāo settled permanently in Maçāo. His name is found in the register of the permanent residents of Maçāo under the date line 3 October 1640.[166]

Several ships of the Portuguese merchants of Nagapattinam carried huge quantities of textiles and so they were attacked by the Dutch. However, the Portuguese *Estado da Índia* could not provide protection to its ships. Bartholomeu a textile merchant, sailed from Nagapattinam to Melaka in 1641. His ship, which carried textiles and yarn valued at 3,808 *florins*, was seized by the Dutch.[167] The ship of Thomas Paulo, another resident of Nagapattinam trading with Banten in textiles, was captured by the Dutch in July 1644. The Dutch declared that Paulo's ship and crew would be released only if a ransom of 1,687 *reals* was paid immediately to them. Further, they also demanded that a bill of exchange be issued for 5,500 *reals*.[168] The ships of Amaral Castel Branco and Jacome Cardoso Barreto, which sailed from Nagapattinam to Melaka carrying rich cargo in 1645, were also captured by the Dutch.[169] The merchandise seized by the Dutch consisted of 214 bales of cloth amounting in value to 3,000 *reals*.[170] Pinto was a rich, famous Portuguese textile trader who helped the English in Madras.[171] Francisco Vieira de Figureido was wealthy and prominent casado of Nagapattinam. He was trading in textiles in 1650 with Makassar and Sunda. Green Hill, the English agent in Madras, approached da Figureido to help them in their trade.[172] The English and the Dutch companies invited several Portuguese merchants to help them promote their trade.

There is evidence to show that some of the Chettis continued to send their ships with textiles to Melaka as late as 1630. Two leading merchant ships of the Chettis came with letters from Melaka.[173] Malayya Chetti, alias Astrappa Chetti, was a leading textile traders who owned vessels trading with the Moluccas and who had entered into a contract with the Dutch in the year 1634 to procure textiles for them from the Coromandel for export to South-East Asia and Europe,[174] for which purpose Malayya Chetti had invested huge capital in the hinterland weaving villages.[175] This deprived the Portuguese of textiles in the Coromandel coast.

The brother of Malayya Chetti, known as Chinnana, and his cousin Kesava Chetti were partners in this textile trade. Malayya Chetti had such contacts that he even procured textiles made in the *nayakdom* of Gingee. Understandably the Portuguese in Nagapattinam could not procure textiles.[176] The death of the *nayak* of Gingee at this time came as a further setback for the Portuguese as they could not enter into any treaty with the new ruler for the monopoly supply of textiles from his territory.[177]

The Dutch East India Company slowly ousted the Portuguese from the lucrative Intra-Asian textile trade. The export of textiles and raw silk by the Dutch went up from 16 per cent in 1619-21 to 55 per cent towards the end of the seventeenth century. On the other hand, the Dutch trade in spices, which was about 74 per cent in 1619-21, rose to 84 per cent in 1648-50 and then declined to 23 per cent during 1698-1700.[178]

After the conquest of Melaka from the Portuguese on 14 January 1641, the Dutch learnt from the Coromandel traders that profits on Coromandel textiles were as high as 50 per cent.[179] However, their profits had declined to 20 per cent by 1678.[180] The export of Coromandel cloth by the Dutch East India Company (VOC) to Batavia (Jakarta) also declined steadily from 873 pieces a year in 1723-5 worth 5 million Dutch *guilders* to 166 pieces worth 815,000 Dutch *guilders* (in 1780-1) later.[181] Some stray eighteenth-century references indicate that the

Portuguese in Santhome could carry on their textile trade even up to the middle of the eighteenth century. Thirty bales of cloth such as *ginghams* and *morins* were kept under the care of the Bishop of Mylapore in 1749 who had agreed to take care of its export.[182]

Development of Portuguese Port Administration

The port of Nagapattinam, which had a natural harbour, developed as a major trading centre in rice and textiles under the Portuguese after 1562, mainly due to the system of granting sailing privileges which helped the growth of overseas commerce. However, it led to much rivalry between the resident Captain who was in charge of Nagapattinam port and the local casado community. The Portuguese Captain was given the privilege to undertake two voyages from Nagapattinam to Ujang Selang and Bangeri in Thailand. This privilege to sail was obtained by Antonio Ferreira da Camara, a *fidalgo,* for 6,050 *xerafins.*[183] The Portuguese settlers on the east coast were also willing to offer incentives to the Hindus in Nagapattinam to beat the challenge posed by the Marakkayars of Nagore.[184]

The *nayak* of Thanjavur had stationed an *adhikari* (officer) to collect *renda da praia* (entry duty) and to run the port administration.[185] The Portuguese Captain at Nagapattinam was given certain concessions by the *nayak* in respect of customs payment to the tune of 200 *xerafins* a year.[186] It is evident from records (1640) that the *adhikari* appointed by the *nayak* of Thanjavur collected 3.5 per cent customs duty on exports, while there was no import duty except a charge of 5 *panams* on every vessel that entered the port of Nagapattinam.[187] A couple of years later (1645), the king of Portugal framed the regulations of the Nagapattinam customs house.[188] The regulations were accepted by the Portuguese settlers and the traders of Nagapattinam on 31 January 1645. They were reconfirmed and notified for the purpose of information to the public by the municipality of Nagapattinam on 20 August 1645.[189] The new order of the customs house of Nagapattinam prohibited private traders with the English, the Dutch and the Danes after 15 November 1646.[190]

The regulations issued by the king of Portugal for conducting trade in bulk goods in the port of Nagapattinam were declared as follows:[191]

1. Tax, as ordered, was to be paid on all types of goods coming from several places in the hinterland to the port of Nagapattinam, failing which the commodities would be confiscated and taken into the royal account of the king of Portugal.
2. An entry duty of 5 per cent was to be levied on such items as cereals, vegetables, provisions and food stuffs coming into Nagapattinam for sale or export from the surrounding countryside.
3. A tax of 2 *panams* was to be paid on every *maund* of areca nuts coming into Nagapattinam.
4. Those who desired to conduct trade in cinnamon at Nagapattinam would have to obtain a licence of royal approval. No customs duty was to be collected from those who were engaged in the cinnamon trade.
5. Five per cent of tax was payable for the coir brought for sale to the port of Nagapattinam. Merchants of Santhome who sold coir and other goods at Nagapattinam were also to pay such a tax to the king of Portugal.
6. All ships and seagoing vessels coming from Sri Lanka, Tuticorin, Mannar, Jaffnapatnam, Porto Novo and other Portuguese ports were exempted from paying taxes on the sale of goods but would have to pay an exit duty.
7. No exemption from the payment of customs duty was given to the newly built ships at Nagapattinam.
8. The duty on goods and commodities coming from the ports of the Danes, the English and the Dutch was fixed at 7 per cent.
9. All resident merchants of Nagapattinam fort and town irrespective of the category they belonged to, such as the Portuguese, Hindus, Muslims and others, were to pay export duty at 7 per cent of the value of goods towards the royal revenue. This included 1 per cent towards the cost of fortification of the settlement of Nagapattinam.
10. The portion of duties collected from the customs to be paid

to the *nayak* of Thanjavur was to be properly calculated and paid to him by the *Juiz de Alfandega* (Customs Appraiser). He had to obtain a receipt for the portion of the revenue paid to the *nayak*.

11. Separate registers were to maintained for the receipts and expenditure of the customs house.
12. The accounts of the customs house prepared were to be checked once every three months.
13. The transactions of the customs house were to be recorded in a book separately for each merchant so that there were no mistakes in respect of royal revenues.
14. The *kanaku pillais* had to maintain the customs house records and were to be paid 2 *xerafins* per month as salary for writing the accounts.
15. A salary of 20 *pagodas* was to be paid to the *Alcaide mor* (commander of a fortress) and 7 *xerafins* to the *Juiz de Alfandega* per annum.
16. The supervising officers working in the customs house were to be paid a salary which was to be met from the customs revenue.
17. All customs revenue collected from the port was to be kept in a safety vault in the customs house.
18. The *porteiro* (doorkeeper or security guard) of the customs house had to know both the Tamil and Portuguese.
19. There were to be two sets of keys of which one was to remain with the *Juiz de Alfandega* and the other with the *porteiro*.
20. The *Alcaide-mor* was to be the principal police officer in the customs house.

Many inferences can be drawn from the above said regulations. The cinnamon trade was encouraged by the king of Portugal through the exemption of tax, since the Portuguese had difficutly in procuring sufficient quantities of cinnamon owing to the political conditions in Sri Lanka. Trade in areca nuts between Sri Lanka and Nagapattinam was also encouraged because of its demand (by the Tamils) for betel-chewing. Ships that were newly built at Nagapattinam did not receive any concession from tax. Thus Portuguese commerce in bulk goods at Nagapattinam developed well because of the absence of a nearby Dutch settlement, unlike, in Pulicat from where the Dutch hampered the growth of commerce in Santhome.

According to available records pertaining to the period between 1624 and 1650, an average of six ships left the port of Nagapattinam annually.[192] Syrian Christians from the Malabar coast also sent their ships to Syriam situated on the coast of Myanmar (Burma) through Nagapattinam.[193] The flourishing trade in bulk goods conducted by the Portuguese attracted the attention of Dutch who attacked on 20 July 1658. The port of Nagapattinam, finally fell into the hands of the Dutch on 23 July 1658. The Portuguese were allowed to leave for Goa after the Dutch occupied Nagapattinam.

Rice and textile products of the Coromandel were in great demand in all South Asian and South-East Asian markets. Details of goods mentioned in Portuguese records throw considerable light on the bulk cargo that formed a substantial part of the goods involved in the long-distance trade. The Portuguese began to trade in rice and textiles because the hinterland of the Coromandel coast had abundant supplyies. These commodities were initially required for the exchange of spices in Malabar. The Portuguese began to export rice and textiles to South-East Asia when they needed to buy spices from there. The trade in bulk goods was more in the hands of private Portuguese merchants than with the Crown. This trade in bulk goods continued during the sixteenth and seventeenth centuries. The *Estado da Índia* was not very successful in its venture to organize the supply of bulk commodities from the Coromandel coast compared to the Dutch East India Company in the seventeenth century. The trade in rice and textiles attracted a large number of Portuguese private traders who traded it successfully from the Tamil coast. Hence it may be said that J.C. Van Leuis characterization of the intra-Asian trade[194] as being chiefly in luxury goods needs connection. The official Portuguese trade in rice and textiles suffered because of the lack of funds for investment and the officials appointed for the development of trade were chiefly interested in building up their own fortunes than in the profit of the Crown. Native participation and involvement in the Portuguese enterprise was large and diverse. Nayinar Chetti and many other Tamil merchants gave cooperated with the Portuguese. Similarly Khwaja Marakkayar and other Muslim Tamil traders also extended their cooperation land helped to expand Portuguese trade. Thus it is clear that the Portuguese sought native assistance and were forced to develop and communicate a practical approach as merchants to deal with Tamil merchants in order to make profits.

NOTES

1. L.F.F.R. Thomaz, 'Les Portugais dans les mers de archipel au XVI Siecle', *Archipel*, vol. 18, 1979, pp. 105-25.
2. Correia, Lendas, vol. 2, pt. 2, chap. 9, p. 721.
3. Ibid., tomo I, p. 298.
4. Cunha Rivara, *APO*, fasc. V, pt. I, pp. 30-1.
5. K.S. Mathew, *Portuguese Trade with India in the Sixteenth Century*, Delhi, 1983, pp. 80-1.
6. Elaine Sanceau, *Cartas de D. João de Castro*, Lisboa, 1954, p. 293.
7. Ibid.
8. Correia, op. cit., pt. 2, chap. 9, p. 721.
9. King Filippe I appointed Damiao Pacheco as Captain of Devanampattinam. See, *IANTT*, *Chancelaria de D. Filippe I*, Livro 17, fl. 295v.
10. *IANTT*, *Chancelaria de Dom João III*, Liv. 25, fl. 39.
11. *IANTT*, *Chancelaria de Dom Sebastião e Henrique*, Liv 45, fl. 250; see also, Liv. 2, fl. 478; Liv. 22, fl. 146; Liv. 6, fl. 7.
12. Ibid., Liv. 22, fl. 54; Liv. 22, fl. 275v; *Chancelaria de D. João III*, Liv. 67, fl. 52.
13. See, *Cartas de Affonso de Albuquerque*, Lisboã, 1884-1935, tomo II, p. 305.
14. Antonio da Silva Rego, *As Gavetas da Torre do Tombo*, vol. 2, Lisboa, 1947, pp. 712-18.
15. *IANTT*, *Nucleo Antigo*, Mss. no. 808, 'O Livro da Receita e despesa do Feitor do Choromandel'. The account book comprises 58 folios in all, numbered serially. Some of the folios such as 1, 1v, 5, 6, 7, 8, 9, 26, 27, 28, 29, 30, 31, 32, 33, 34, 35 and 36 are blank without any writing in ink. Hence it is not the original and seems to be only a copy. This rare document was probably made by archivists after salvaging the original records from the 1776 earthquake of Portugal. Its authenticity can be vouched for as one finds no writings on the missing pages of the account book.
16. *IANTT*, *CC*, Ia-13-74, fl.14.

17. Letter of Brito to Affonso de Albuquerque, 6 January 1514, in Artur Basilio de Sa, *Documentação*, vol. I, pp. 45-6.
18. *IANTT*, *CC*, II-53-93, f1.319v.
19. Ibid., 1-16-106.
20. Ibid., 1-60-17, fl. 8. For details of 1537-40, CC, 1-60-17. The text runs as follows. '*Dues tres naos que cad ana de Paleacate a Malaqua com Roupae mantimentos*'.
21. For details, see S. Jeyaseela Stephen, *The Coromandel Coast and its Hinterland in South India: Economy, Society and Political System, 1500-1600,* New Delhi, 1997.
22. Georg Schurhammer, *St. Francis Xavier: His Life, His Times,* Rome, 1977. See vol. 2 for details.
23. *CSL*, vol. 2, p. 436.
24. Sanjay Subrahmanyam, *Improvising Empire*, pp. 36-7.
25. Letter of Governor Francisco Barreto to the king of Portugal written from Bassein dated 6 January 1557, in *As Gavetas do Torre do Tombo,* vol. 4, pp. 233-45.
26. Receipts of the revenues of the Portuguese State of India in Samuel Purchas, *His Pilgrims,* Glasgow, 1950, vol. 9, chap. 10, p. 165.
27. *IANTT*, Mss Livraria, no. 805, Cap. 3, fls. 166 and 168.
28. Ibid., no. 805, fl. 167.
29. Ibid., no. 805.
30. Ibid., no. 805, fl. 100. The text runs as follows: 'If the Portuguese were sincere Christians and believed with Christ that it was easier for a camel to pass through the eye of a needle than for a rich man to enter the kingdom of heaven.' It suggests that the chief concern of the Portuguese in India seemed to amass wealth.
31. Sanjay Subrahmanyam, *The Political Economy*, pp. 147-56.
32. Pyrad da Laval, *The Voyage of Pyrad da Laval to the East Indies, the Maldives, the Moluccas and Brazil, 1607-1610,* ed. Albert Grey, London, 1887-9, vol. 2, pp. 131-2.
33. Duarte Barbosa, *The Book of Duarte Barbosa*, vol. 1, p. 81; Tome Pires, *The Suma Oriental*, vol. I, pp. 76-7.
34. J.F.J. Biker, *Colleção de Tratados e Concertos de Pazes despazes de Estado da India Portuguesa Fez com os Reis e Senhores*, Lisboa, tomo I, pp. 21-3; Barbosa, *The Book of Duarte Barbosa*, vol. 2, p. 97.
35. Fernao Lopes de Castanheda, *Historia do Descobrimento e Conquista da India Pelos Portugueses,* vol. 2, Porto, 1975, p. 97.
36. Barbosa, *The Book of Duarte Barbosa*, vol. 1, p. 81.
37. Pires, *The Suma Oriental*, vol. I, pp. 76-7.
38. João de Barros, *Decadas da Asia*, vol. II/1-4 Lisboa, 1973; Fernão Lopes da Castanheda, Livro VI, Capitulo 91.
39. Gaspar Correia, *Lendas da India, Porto,* 1975, tomo I, pt. II, Capitulo VIII, p. 559.

40. Ibid., tomo. I, pt. I, pp. 428-30; J.F.J. Biker, Colleção de Tratados p. 22.
41. For details see K.S. Mathew, 'Trade in the Indian Ocean and the Portuguese System of Cartazes', in Malyn Newitt (ed.), *The First Portuguese Colonial Empire,* Exter, 1986, pp. 69-84.
42. Silva Rego, *Historia das Missães do Padroado Portugueses do Oriente,* vol. 1, Lisboa, 1949, p. 417.
43. Correia, Lendas, tomo 3, p. 820.
44. Ibid., tomo I, p. 610; tomo 3, pp. 553-7.
45. Ibid., tomo I, pp. 428-32 and 481; Fernão Lopes da Castanheda, Historia, op. cit., Livro I, p. 121.
46. Ibid., tomo I, p. 430. They had also traded in spices particularly in cloves. See *IANTT, CC,* I-13-113.
47. *IANTI, CC,* I-38-50.
48. Ibid., *CC,* IIa-30-196 (February 1512).
49. Ibid., *CC,* I-7-62, fl. 1v.
50. Ibid., *CC,* I-30-36 (October 1523).
51. Ibid.
52. Ibid., *CC,* I-77-26, fl. 1v (November 1545).
53. Letter of Nuno Alvares to Giverne dated 13 October 1545, in *CSL,* III, 335.
54. Catamarans and *tonis* were used for shipping rice from Nagapattinam to Jaffna. *IANTT, CC,* II-114-21, II-117-22, II-119-103 and II-120-17. *Fustas* and barks were also used for carrying rice to Kochi, *IANTT, CC,* II-41-144.
55. *IANTT, CC,* II-118-32.
56. Ibid., *CC,* I-9-92 (1520).
57. Ibid., *CC,* I-7-62, fl.1v.
58. C.R. Boxer, *Francisco Viera de Figureido: A Portuguese Merchant Adventurer in South East Asia, 1624-1667,* The Hague, 1967, p. 2.
59. Ibid., *CC,* II-118-32; II-119-103 (1524).
60. Ibid., *CC,* IIa-119-103; IIa-109-104 (1524).
61. *IANTT,* CC, IIa-115-95 (25 May 1524).
62. *IANTT, CC,* IIa-119-103 ; *IANTT, CC,* IIa-119-104 (25 September 1524); *IANTT, CC,* IIa-121-44 (15 November 1524).
63. *IANTT,* CC, IIa-119-109.
64. *IANTT, CC,* I-25-68 (1 October 1519). Letter of Joao de Silveria to King Dom Manuel of Portugal, in Genevieve Bouchon, *Mamale de Cananor,* Paris, 1975. See the document in the appendix p. 187.
65. *IANTT, Cartas dos Vice-reis da India,* no. 15. Letter of Cristovao Lourenco to King Dom Manuel, dated 13 January 1522.
66. Chandra Richard De Silva, 'Portuguese Policy towards the Muslims in Ceylon', *The Ceylon Historical and Social Studies,* vol. 9, 1966, p. 114.

67. See the letter of Fr. Nicolau, S.J. to the Portuguese governor in Goa, *IANTT, Coleção Jesuitica,* Mss 1047, fls. 1-8.
68. *CSL*, III, p. 335.
69. Jose Wicki, Duas Relações Sobre a Situação da India Portuguesa nos Annos 1568 e 1569, *Studia,* vol. 8, 1961, p. 213.
70. Bouchon, *Mamale de Cananor,* op. cit., pp. 186-8; *As Gavetas do Torre do Tombo,* 4, pp. 140-44 (1519); *Documentos Sabre os Portugueses em Mocambique e na Africa Central,* vol. 4, p. 204; *IANTT*, *CC*, II-114-21 (1523); *CC*, I-38-1, fl.6 (1530); Schurhammer, St. Francis Xavier, op. cit., vol. 3, pp. 317 and 324 (1527); *Coleção São Lourenço,* 3, 326 and 335 (1545); Armando Cortesão, *Obras Completas*, vol. 3, pp. 88-9.
71. Bulhão Pato, *Cartas de Affonso de Albuquerque com Algumas Documentas que as Elucidam,* 7 vols, Lisboa, 1884-1935, vol. 8, p. 95.
72. *IANTT*, *Chancelaria de D. João III,* Liv. 18, fl. 108v; *CC*, IIa-117-154; IIa-117-194; IIa-117-195; IIa-118-31; IIa-125-2; IIa-126-87; IIa-126-102.
73. Schurhammer, St. Francis Xavier, op. cit., vol. 2, p. 550.
74. *AHU*, Codice no. 281, fl. 281b.
75. *BNL*, Codice 1976, fls. 7-11; Couto, Decade, op. cit., X, pt. 130 Liv. 1, Cap. III, pp. 14-16 (1581); *HAG*, *MDR*, Liv. 3B, Cod. 52-55, fl. 2.
76. Lotika Varadarajan, *India in the Seventeenth Century: Memoirs of François Martin,* Delhi, 1980 (hereafter *Memoirs*), p. 227.
77. R.J. de Lima Felner, *Subsidios Para*, vol. 1, Lisboa, 1930, pp. 74-5.
78. See S. Jeyaseela Stephen, *The Coromandel Coast and its Hinterland*, p. 163.
79. *BNL*, Codice, no. 1975, fls. 310-311. See the letter of the viceroy to Conde de Vidigueira, 1609-10. Rice and foodstuffs were sent owing to the calamity and famines that prevailed in Devanampattinam during 1609-10.
80. *DRI*, tomo II, pp. 76-7. II, pp. 78-112; *IANTT*, *DRI*, Livro 4, fl. 56. See for the year 1612, Livro 5, fl. 47.
81. Lotika Varadarajan, *Memoirs*, p. 1593.
82. Ibid., pp. 325 and 338.
83. S. Jeyaseela Stephen, 'Pulicat Based Shipping and Trade, 1500-1530', *Purabhilak Puratava,* 1991, pp. 1-15.
84. *IANTT*, *CC*, I-77-18.fl.2v; *CC*, Ia-II-50; II-53-93. fl.319v; II-46-98; I-16-106; I-60-17, fl.8v; I-68-86; Elaine Sanceau, *Cartas de D. João de Castro,* Lisboã, 1954, p. 213; Biblioteca Municipal de Elvas, Mss. no. 5/381.
85. Letter of Rui de Brito Patalim to the king of Portugal dated 6 January 1514, in *IANTT*, *CC*, I-14-49; *CAA*, vol. 3, p. 94. Pires, *The Suma Oriental*, vol. 2, pp. 273-4.

86. Letter of Albuquerque to the king of Portugal dated 1 April 1512, in *IANTT, CC*, I-22-80.
87. Correia, Lendas, op. cit., Capitulo XXI, tomo. 2, pt. I, p. 162; Capitulo XXVI, pt. I, p. 216.
88. Artur Basilio de Sa, *Documentação*, vol. 1, pp. 66-74; L.F.F.R. Thomaz, 'Nina Chatu e o Commercio Portugues em Malaca', in *Memorias do Centro de Estudos de Marinharia*, vol. 5, Lisboa, 1976, pp. 3-27. See the text of the Royal letter.
89. Simao Botelho, 'Tombo do Estado da India', in *Subsidios para a Historia da India Portuguesa*, Lisboa, 1848, pp. 104-8; Diogo do Couto, *Decadas da Asia*, Lisboa, 1777-8, decada 5, pt. II, p. 138; letter of Garcia Chainho, Factor of Melaka to the king of Portugal dated 31 August 1521, in *ANTT, CC*, III-7-115.
90. Correia, Lendas, op. cit., 4, pp. 131-2, *IANTT*, CC, I-68-86.
91. *IANTT*, CC, I-68-88.
92. Sanceau, *Coleção São Lourenço*, vol. 3, p. 250.
93. *IANTT*, CC, I-76-102, fl. 3v, CC, I-77-18, fl. 2v.
94. *IANTT*, CC, I-60-17, fl. 8v; 1-7-62, fl. 1; I-68-86; *BA*, Codice, 52-VII-63, no. 33. Schurhammer, *St. Francis Xavier*, vol, 2, p. 100; *IANTT*, *Chancelaria de D. João III*, Liv. 64, fl. 39v.
95. Codice Cadaval, Mss 972; Arquivo da Casa Cadaval, fls. 1v-2, 26v-28v. See also Texeira da Mota, *Un Manuscrito Nautico Seis Cartista Re Encontrado Centro do Estudos de Cartografia Antiga*, Lisboa, 1975, p. 11.
96. Elaine Sanceau, *CSL*, op. cit., p. 235.
97. Antonio Baiao, *Historia Quinhista in Edito do Segundo Cerco do Dio Ilustrado a Correspondencia Original Tambem in edita de D. João de Castro D. João de Mascarenhas e outras*, Coimbra, 1925, p. 308.
98. Felner, *Subsidios para*. See, Black textiles, *IANTT*, CC, 1-68-86(1540); Silk cloth CC, 1-60-17, fl.8v. (1537).
99. Elaine Sanceau, *CSL*, vol. 2, 493. See also Armando Cortesão and Luis de Albuquerque, *Obras Completas de D. João de Castro*, Coimbra, 1976, p. 394.
100. *IANTT*, *Gavetas*, XV-19-37.
101. Sanjay Subrahmanyam, *Improvising Empire*, p. 40.
102. Ibid., pp. 241-4.
103. *ARE*, 1 of 1933; 221 of 1929-30; 197 of 1912.
104. *SII*, vol. 2, pt. II, no. 73; *SII*, vol. 8, no. 4; *ARE*, 300 of 1909; 195 of 1922-23; *SII*, vol. 7, no. 448; 170 of 1933.
105. Love, *Vestiges of Old Madras*, vol. 1, London, 1913, p. 77.
106. *BNL*, Codice, 2702, fls. 648-648v; Municipal Library of Elvas, Codice no. 5/381, fls. 3-3v.
107. Municipal Library of Elvas, Codex, 5/381, fls. 3-3v.

108. Subrahmanyam, *Improvising Empire*, p. 40.
109. Cunha Rivara, *APO*, fasc. 5, no. 370, p. 472; no. 625, p. 657; and no. 542, p. 592; *RCI*, vol. I, p. 133; *IANTT*, *Chancelaria de D. Sebastião*, Liv. 15, fl. 29, Liv. 15, fl. 11; Liv. 19, fl. 226v.
110. Letter of Fr. Lourenço Paes to Leão Henriques, written from Melaka dated 3 December 1568, see also the letter of 15 November 1567, in Jose Wicki, *DI*, vol. 7, doc. 87, p. 355.
111. Subrahmanyam, *Improvising Empire*, pp. 341-4.
112. E.P. Mendes da Luz, 'Livro da Cidades e Fortalezas que o Coroa de Portugal tem nas Partes da India, e das Capitanias e mais Cargos que nelas ha, e da Importancia deles', *Studia*, no. 6, July 1960, fls. 78, 84; L.F.F.R. Thomaz, 'Les Portugais dans les mers de l'Archipel au XVIe Siecle, *Archipel*, 18, 1979, pp. 105-205.
113. *IANTT*, *CC*, I-77-26; L.F.F.R. Thomaz, *Os Portugueses em Malacca 15111580*, vol. 2, Baccalaureate thesis, University of Lisbon, 1964, pp. 267-70.
114. *AHU*, India, Caixa, I, doc. 22 (June 1598).
115. Subrahmanyam, *Improvising Empire*, pp. 39 and 74. See Om Prakash, 'Long Distance Maritime Trade in Asia: Decline and Revival', in K.S. Mathew (ed.), *Studies in Maritime History*, Pondicherry, 1991, pp. 29-37.
116. *IANTT*, *Chancelaria de D. Sebastião: Doações*, Liv. 40, fl. 228; *APO-CR*, fasc. 5, doc. 452; *RCI*, vol. 1, pp. 141, 287; vol. 1, no. 1156, p. 272.
117. *BNL*, Codice 1540, fls. 89-91v; Three Voyages of Malacca given to Simão Texeira were at the price of 12,010 *cruzados* during 1598-9.
118. *APO-CR*, fasc. III, pt. IIa, doc. 2004, pp. 568-83.
119. Artur Teodoro de Matos, *O Estado da India Nos anos de 1581-88 Estructura, Administrativa, e Economia, Alguns Elementos, para O seu Estudo*, Ponta Delagada, 1982, p. 37.
120. *AHU*, Caixa, India, XI, doc. 15 (1592); *APO-CR*, fasc. III, pt. Ia, doc. 94, pp. 328-9.
121. *APO-CR*, fasc. V, pt. 3a, doc. 1002, pp. 1364-7.
122. Royal letter of the king of Portugal to the viceroy, dated 25 January 1598, in *APO-CR*, I, doc. 75, p. 122, and another letter dated 10 February 1598, *APO-CR*, III, doc. 313, p. 828.
123. Letter of King Filippe I to Mathias de Albuquerque written from Lisbon, dated 1 March 1594, *Boletim da Filmoteca Ultramarina Portuguesa* (hereafter *BFUP*), vol. 2, doc. 75, p. 207.
124. *HAG*, *Privileges Alvares e Regimentos*, Liv. 2, fl. 260v; *Chancelaria de D. Sebastiã*, Liv. 19, fl. 226v; Liv. 71, fl. 18; *Chancelaria de D. João III*, Liv. 15, fl.23; *APO-CR*, fasc. 5, doc. 542. pp. 592-3;

Chancelaria de D. Sebastião, Liv. 71, fl. 29vo; Liv. 15, fl. 11; Liv. 71, fl.29. *BPADE*, Mss. *Reservados*, 752, fl. 24v; *APO-CR*, V, no. 633, p. 689; *AHU*, Mss. *Caixa da India* (hereafter *CDI*) Caixa XI, doc. 15; *APO-CR*, fasc. III, pt. IIa, doc. 25, pp. 801-4; *HAG*, *MDR*, no. 313. Codice 12-25/4/1.

125. *AHU*, Codice, 281, fl. 346v; letter of the king of Portugal to the viceroy D. Francisco da Gama, Lisboa, 2 January 1596, *BFUP*, 3, doc. 25, pp. 431-5.
126. Order of the viceroy of Goa, dated 14 April 1595, in Pissurlencar, *Regimentos das Fortalezas da India*, Bastora, Goa, 1951, pp. 245-6. At Malacca 3 per cent was levied for the town as well as 6 per cent for the exchequer. The export duties went to 4.5 per cent of which 3 per cent was for the Crown and 1.5 per cent for the fortification of the town. See, *DRI*, *Apontamentos sobre a alfandega e Malacca 1610*, vol. 1, p. 321; *NA*, *OBP*, VOC 1642, III, fl. 436. See also, C.R. Boxer, *Portuguese Conquest and Commerce in Southern Asia, 1500-1750*, Variorum, London, 1990.
127. *APO-CR*, III, pt. 2a, doc. 325, pp. 801-4.
128. *APO-CR*, III, pt. 2a, doc. 351, p. 900.
129. *AHU*, ACF Codice, no. 282, fl. 22v.
130. *BFUP*, vol. 3, p. 527. See the royal letters dated 2 January and 24 January 1601, in ibid., p. 529.
131. *DI*, vol. I, doc. 19, p. 168 (2 January 1608) pp 318-19. See also the royal letter dated 13 March 1587 in *BFUP*, vol. 2, p. 268.
132. *HAG*, *MDR*, Liv 19, fl. 195v.
133. See *Studia*, vols. 13-14, 1964, p. 82.
134. *BL*, Additional Manuscripts, no. 28432, fl. 10v.
135. *BNL*, Codice 2702, fls. 648-648v. (13 August 1607)
136. *Letters Received by the English East India Company from its Servants in the East (1602-1617)*, 6 vols, London, 1896-1902, vol. I, p. 70.
137. William Foster, *English Factories in India: A Calendar of Documents in the India Office, British Museum and Public Relations Office, 1618-19* (hereafter *EFI*), vols. 1-13, Oxford, 1906-21, vol. 3, *1630-3*, p. 256.
138. *NA*, *OBP*, VOC 1634, I, fls. 930 and 935.
139. *NA*, *OBP*, VOC 1635, I, fls. 63 (15 August 1634).
140. *IANTT*, *DRI*, vol. 32, fl. 57 (24 February 1635) *HAG*, *MDR*, Livro. 45, fl. 269 (30 November 1638).
141. *NA*, *OBP*, VOC 1047, fl. 423, 724v (15 June 1647)
142. *IANTT*, Nucleo Antigo, 808, fls. 3-3v.
143. *IANTT*, *CC*, 1-59-58; Artur Basilio de Sa, op. cit., *Documentação*, vol. 2, p. 250 (1537); see also Anthony Reid, 'Sixteenth Century

Turkish Influence in Western Indonesia', *Journal of South East Asian History* (hereafter *JSEAH*), vol. 10, no. 3, 1969, pp. 400-1.
144. *IANTT*, *CC*, I-22-80 (5 September 1527).
145. Ibid.
146. Ibid.
147. *BL*, *Additional Manuscripts*, no 9853, fls. 52v-53v. There is evidence to show that the private Portuguese settlers also sometimes stole several bales of textiles from the ships of the Marakkayars on the shores in Nagapattinam. However, they were asked to replace the textiles before the voyage whenever they were found guilty.
148. *IANTT*, *Chancelaria de D. Filippe II*, Liv. 7, fls. 304v-5.
149. Biblioteca Municipal de Elvas (hereafter BME), Mss 5/381, fls. 3-3v.
150. P.E. Pieris, *The Kingdom of Jaffnapatnam*, Colombo, 1944, p. 7.
151. A. Krishnaswami, *Tamil Country Under Vijayanagara*, Annamalai Nagar, 1964, pp. 280-3.
152. Samuel Purchas, *His Pilgrims*, vol. 10, London, 1908, p. 208.
153. Vijaya Ramasamy, *Textiles and Weavers in Medieval South India*, Delhi, 1984, p. 146.
154. Antonio Bocarro, 'Livro das Plantas de Toda as Fortalezas, Cidades, e Povacoes do Estado da India Oriental', in *APO-BP*, Goa, 1937-8, pt. II, pp. 361-2.
155. Lotika Varadarajan, *Memoirs*, vol. 1, pt. I, p. 310 (17 January 1674).
156. *Records of Fort St. George* (hereafter *RFG*), *Diary and Consultation Book* (hereafter *DACB*), 1681, Madras 1913, p. 32.
157. *RFG*, *Letters to Fort St. George*, 1685; Madras, 1929, p. 181.
158. Lotika Varadarajan, *Memoirs*, vol. 1, pt. I, p. 312.
159. *RFG*, *Public Department*, 1735, Madras, 1927, doc. 248, p. 81.
160. T.I. Poonen, 'Dutch Beginnings in India Proper', *Journal of the Madras University*, 1933, pp. 1-70. See p. 15. For textile varieties of Devanampattinam, see *NA*, *OBP*, VOC 1066, fls. 113-17. See, Om Prakash, *The Dutch Factories in India*, Delhi, 1980, p. 28.
161. *LRV*, Livro 1, 47/1, fl. 114.
162. *IANTT*, *DRI*, Livro 62, fl. 15.
163. *IANTT*, *Fragmentos*, Caixa 3, Maco 3, doc. 17.
164. *IANTT*, *DRI*, Livro 62, fl. 18; *IANTT*, *DRI*, Livro 62, fl. 19v.
165. Tikiri Abyasinghe, *A Study of Portuguese Regimentos*, p. 74.
166. C.R. Boxer, *Asia Sinica e Japonica*, Macao, 1988, vol. I, p. 242.
167. *DR*, 1641, see the entry dated 1 March 1641; *NA*, *OBP*, VOC 1136, fl.286, 17 November 1641; *NA*, *OBP*, VOC 1136, fls. 227r-227v.
168. *DR*, 1644-46, p. 94.
169. *NA*, *OBP*, VOC 1158, fl. 642r. (28 November 1645).
170. *DR*, 1643-4, p. 252; *GM*, vol. II, p. 190 (13 January 1643).
171. *BNL*, Mss, Codice 8358, fl. 45.
172. *RFG*, *DACB*, 1686, p. 55.

173. C.R. Boxer, *Portuguese Conquest and Commerce in Southern Asia, 1500-1750,* London, 1990, p. 117.
174. J.E. Heeres, et al. (eds.), *Dagh-Register Gehouden in 't Casteel Batavia, Van het Passerende doer leer plasetse als over geheel Neder landts Indie, 1624-1682* (hereafter *DR*), 31 vols, The Hague and Batavia, 1887-1931. See 18 March 1626, p. 261.
175. *HAG, MDR*, Livro 19D, 2-4/4-2.
176. Ibid.
177. S. Arasaratnam mentions that Malayya Chetti died in 1636. See his work, *Merchants, Companies and Commerce on the Coromandel Coast, 1650-1740,* Delhi, 1986, p. 223.
178. J. Bruijn, F.S. Gaastra, and I. Schoffer, *Dutch Asiatic Shipping in the 17th and 18th Centuries,* vol. 1, The Hague, 1987, vol. 1, p. 192. See Table 41.
179. Letter of Van Twist to the directors dated 17 December 1642, in Bouwstoffen, *Voor de Geschiedenis der Nederlanders in den Malaiischen Archipel,* vol. 3, The Hague, 1886-1955, p. 97.
180. W. Ph. Coolhas (ed.), *Generale Missiven Van Governeurs-Generaal en Raaden Aan Heren XV11 Der Verenigde Oost-Indische Compagnie, 1610-1725* (hereafter *GM*), 7 vols, The Hague, 1960-79, See, vol. 5, p. 248 (21 December 1678); OIOC, *Factory Records Java,* G/21/4 (27 January 1675-6).
181. Rurdge Larhova, 'The Power of Cloth: The Textile Trade of the Dutch East India Company (VOC), 1600-1780', Ph.D. dissertation, Australian National University, 1994, p. 96.
182. H. Dodwell, *A Calendar of the Madras Despatches, 1744-1755,* Madras, 1920, p. 398.
183. *BNL*, Fundo Geral, Codice 1540, fls. 89-91, *Relação dos Cargos do Estado da India que Estao Vendidos por Ordem de sua Magestade para as Despensas do Estado.*
184. Biblioteca Apostolica Vaticana (hereafter BAV), Vatican City, Mss 7746, Cap. LXVIII.
185. Bulhão Pato, *Documentos Remetidos da India ou Livros dos Monções,* vols. 1-4, 1880-1935, Lisboa, vol. 3, p. 413.
186. K.A. Nilakanta Sastri, 'Two Negapatam Grants from the Batavia Museum', in *South India and South East Asia: Studies in their History and Culture,* Mysore, 1978, pp. 200-2.
187. *IANTT*, Mss *DRI*, 'Regimento de Alfandega de Negapatão', in Livro 56, fls. 221-4 (31 January 1645).
188. Ibid., fl. 221. The residents of Nagapattinam mentioned that the payments of customs duties brought no revenue for the king of Portugal and were collected by the *nayak* alone in 1619. See, *AHU, India Caixa,* no. 6, doc. 47 (20 February 1619).
189. *HAG, MDR*, Livro 56, fl. 225.

190. *HAG*, *MDR*, Livro 57, fl. 109.
191. *IANTT*, Mss *DRI*, Livro 56, fl. 221-4.
192. Sanjay Subrahmanyam, *Improvising Empire*, see Table 1, p. 223.
193. *HAG*, *MDR*, Livro 12, fl. 8.
194. J.C. Van Leur, *Indonesian Trade and Society*, The Hague, 1955, p. 118.

6

Private and Official Trade in Diverse Commodities: Its Scope and Scale

The Portuguese traded chiefly in textiles and rice in exchange for spices and bullion, but according to many references they also exported iron, cannonballs, butter, salt, oil, meat, coir and slaves, which they needed for their own, use as well as for the purpose of trade and profit. This included both the coastal and long-distance trades which helped them to continue for centuries in spite of the various problems that cropped up in the seventeenth and eighteenth centuries with the arrival of the rival European trading companies. This chapter shall examine the features of realignments undertaken by private Portuguese leaders in the wake of difficulties and how they successfully continued their trade in both the export and the import of diverse commodities.

As early as 1513, Affonso de Albuquerque, the Portuguese viceroy in Goa, noted that the Portuguese travelled freely all over India by land and sea and all of them were engaged in the sale and purchase of commodities (see Map 5).[1] Within India, the Tamil coast in the Bay of Bengal region was favoured for private trade by the Portuguese as they were in close contact with local merchants particularly the Mudaliars, Chettis and, to some extent, the Marakkayars who were found to be very useful as agents, brokers and even transporters. Many of these Portuguese traders found the local conditions very conducive and that they, like the Marakkayars, married native women and settled down. Thus the *casados* emerged as influential traders maintaining intimate relations with the native merchants. These *casados* could also easily borrow money from the Coromandel Chettis. For instance, Diogo Nuniz, a trader, borrowed 1,000 and 700 *cruzados* from two Chetti merchants.[2] This practice of taking

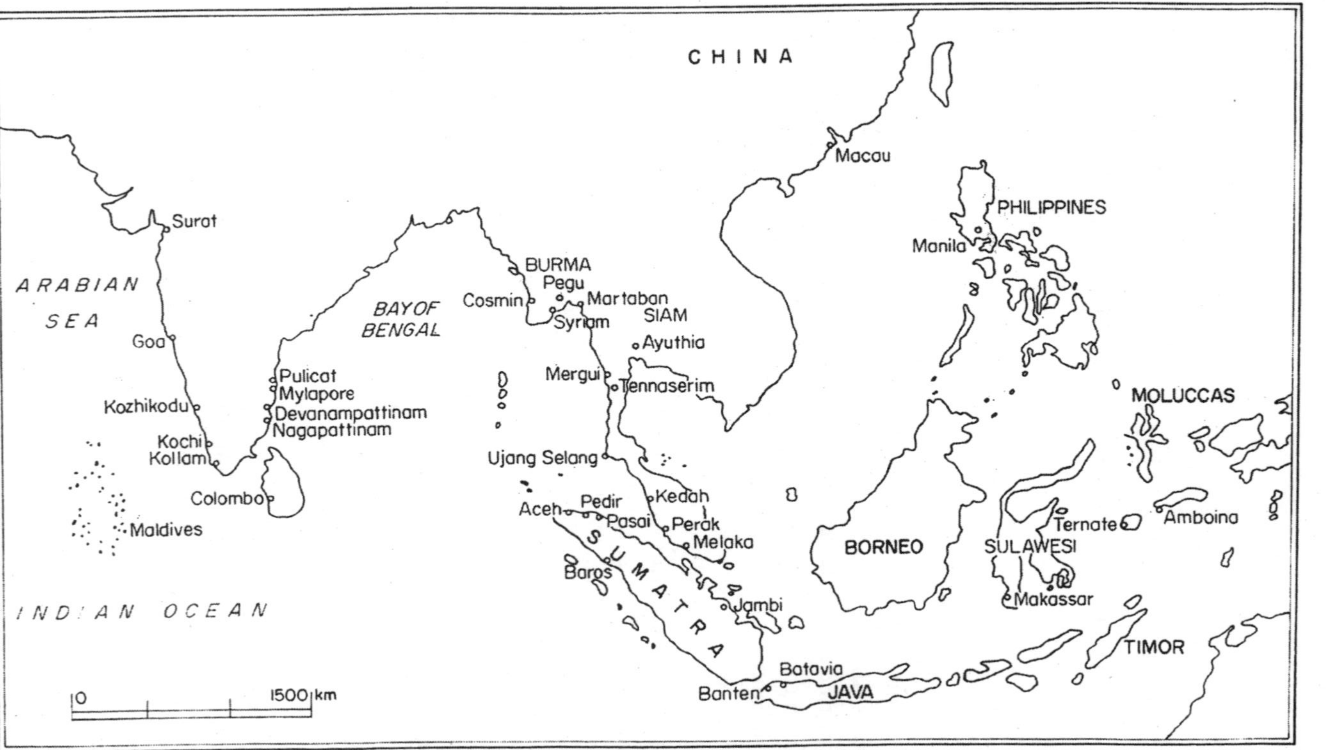

MAP 5: PORTUGUESE COMMERCIAL NETWORK IN ASIA

loans from native merchants slowly disappeared when the Portuguese themselves became rich enough to own ships and small seagoing vessels.[3] The Portuguese private traders' commerce could flourish because of the good relations they had with the Coromandel merchants.

The trading activities of these casados did not, however, bring much profit to the royal treasury.[4] According to one report, private traders such as Gaspar Preto, Pedro Alvares de Mezquito, João Gomez, Alvaro de Castanheda, Lopo Correia, Matheus de Cunha, Symão de Cunha, Tristão Rodriguez and Pedro Alvarez de Setubal did not contribute much towards the Crown income.[5] Many of the Portuguese traders who had settled down in the Coromandel coast did not seem to have been concerned about the king of Portugal. They were more keen to join hands with the native merchants to promote their own interests. Attempts were therefore made to bring these private Portuguese traders under the control of the *Estado da Índia* for which Captains were posted at various ports in the Coromandel. In 1537, some of these private Portuguese traders addressed a petition to the king of Portugal, requesting him to appoint someone among them as Captain on a permanent basis, who, they said, would be more suitable to look after their interests. The king refused it on the grounds that it would directly affect the Crown trade.[6]

Export of Iron and Cannonballs

Portuguese officials were interested in procuring metals, such as iron, available at the ports of Pulicat and Kunimedu. They purchased it for export to Kochi as shown in Table 17.[7] This iron

TABLE 17: PORTUGUESE EXPORT OF IRON FROM THE COROMANDEL TO KOCHI, 1524-47[8]

Date	Ship	Volume
17 May 1524	*Navio Santiago*	–
20 August 1524	*Navio Maria Anuniciada*	2 pipas & 15 arcos
04 September 1524	*Navio Santiago*	3 pipas
. . . January 1547	*Navio* . . .	1 arobba, 3 arratels and 6 arcos

TABLE 18: EXPORT OF CANNONBALLS FROM PULICAT TO KOCHI AS ON 16 AUGUST 1524[9]

Name of the vessel	Captain's name	Quantity in numbers
Parau Santhome	Balthasar de Castlo	50
Parau St. Antonio	João de Sequeira	50
Navio Santiago	Simão Goncalves	150
Total		200

was used for making cannonballs.[10] Further they also procured cannonballs which were manufactured at Pulicat and exported them to Kochi as shown in Table 18.

Export of Coir

Coir was exported by the Portuguese from the ports of Coromandel to Kochi to be made into rigging for their vessels. (Table 19).

Export of Butter, Salt, Oil and Meat

As butter was scarce in Melaka, Portuguese officials in the beginning carried it from Pulicat to Melaka. It was also exported from the ports of Thirumalairayanpattinam and Pulicat to Goa and Kochi in 1524. It was generally carried in hollow bamboo poles. Salt, oil and meat were other items of export to areas where there was a demand for them. The details of such exports from Pulicat (Tables 20-4) show that there was no regular trade.

TABLE 19: EXPORT OF COIR, 8 AUGUST-24 AUGUST 1524[11]

Date	Name of the vessel	Quantity in *marru*
8 August 1524	*Navio Santiago*	2
17 August 1524	*Parau Santhome*	1
17 August 1524	*Fusta pantaliao*	1
18 August 1524	*Navio St. Antonio*	2
24 August 1524	*Navio Anunciada*	2

TABLE 20: PORTUGUESE EXPORT OF BUTTER FROM PULICAT TO MELAKA, 1512-18[12]

Period	Quantity in *marakkals*
26 March 1512 to 25 February 1514	1209.00
1 November 1515 to 31 May 1518	300.10

TABLE 21: BUTTER EXPORTED FROM THE PORTS OF THE COROMANDEL TO GOA AND KOCHI, SEPTEMBER-OCTOBER 1524[13]

Date	From	To	Name of the vessel	Quantity (*marakkals*)
4 September 1524	Pulicat	Kochi	*Navio Santiago*	25
25 September 1524	TR Pattinam	Goa	*Parau St. Antonio*	12
8 October 1524	TR Pattinam	Goa	*Parau Santhome*	14

TABLE 22: EXPORT OF SALT, AUGUST-SEPTEMBER 1524[14]

Date	Name of the Ship	Quantity in *kottai*
20 August 1524	*Nau St. Maria Anunciada*	8
4 September 1524	*Navio Santiago*	6
27 September 1524	*Nau St. Maria Anunciada*	1

TABLE 23: EXPORT OF OIL, AUGUST- NOVEMBER 1524[15]

Date	Name of the ship	Quantity
20 August 1524	*Nau St. Maria Anunciada*	1 jar
4 September 1524	*Navio Santiago*	16 fardos
27 September 1524	*Nau Maria Anunciada*	2 jars
13 November 1524	*Nau St. Maria Anunciada*	2 jars

TABLE 24: EXPORT OF PORK FROM THE COROMANDEL TO GOA AND KOCHI, MARCH-SEPTEMBER 1524[16]

Date	Name of the vessel	Quantity
26 March 1524	*Navio Santiago*	3 jars
17 August 1524	*Fusta Pantaliao*	3 jars
4 September 1524	*Nau. St. Maria Anunciada*	10 jars
4 September 1524	*Nau. Santiago*	6 jars

Leather Exports

Some bulk goods like leather were exported by the Portuguese for the purpose of profit. Export of leather from Santhome of Mylapore to Japan has been reported in the years 1635 and 1636 as there was a heavy demand for it. The variety of leather articles made in Japan facilitated its export to that country. Some quantity of leather was also exported from Mylapore to Maçāo and Siam.[17] In 1643, Portuguese in Santhome in fact arranged for the export of a large quantity of leather and hide, some 30,000 to 40,000 pieces, to Japan.[18] Goatskin was also exported from Nagapattinam and Porto Novo to Goa.[19]

The Slave Trade

Slave labour has been described as one of the buttresses of the Portuguese empire in Asia. Slaves were brought mostly from Africa (Moçambique and Mombasa) Arabia, Persia and Gujarat to the ports of Goa, Chaul, Kochi and Kannur.[20] The Portuguese themselves needed a large number of slaves to work as sailors in the galleys, as labourers in the shipyards and in their workshops.[21] Muslim merchants and Portuguese private traders from the west coast carried shiploads of famine-stricken people who had sold themselves as slaves from the Coromandel ports.[22] The slaves thus brought by the Malabar merchants from the Coromandel coast were bought by the Portuguese in Goa and sold to the *Mestições* in the northern ports of Bhatkal and Dabul.[23] In a letter written to Ignatius Loyola, the founder of the Society of Jesus, from Kollam on 5 December 1550, Fr. Nicolo Lancilliot complained that the casados bought ten to twelve slaves every time. In one instance, twenty-four slaves were bought by a single man.[24] The Portuguese settlement of Melaka also received many slaves from India.[25] In South-East Asia, Makassar was the base for many of the slave traders as it was an important market for male and female slaves.[26] It was also the major transhipment point for slaves in the region. Private Portuguese traders who purchased these slaves employed them in their ships carrying pepper to Jambi.[27] Slaves from Panarukan in Java were also reported to have been sent to Melaka.[28] Thus, slaves trading was a part of the commercial activities in which the west coast of India and South-East Asia played an active role. The Portuguese who had settled on the east coast owned slaves who were employed in their homes.[29] There is no evidence to suggest that the Portuguese in the Tamil coast traded in slaves. It may be said that slave trade as such did not exist on the Tamil coast in the sixteenth century, although the lot of the poor outcasts there may have appeared to the Portuguese as nothing better than that of slaves.

Slaves became popular as a commodity of trade on the Coromandel coast in the seventeenth century only with the advent of the Dutch. Aceh received slave labour to expand its pepper plantations and also to work in its tin mines. Jan Pietersz Coen, the Dutch official, observed that slave trade was even more important than the trade in textiles on the Coromandel coast.[30] The famines of 1618 and 1620 in the Coromandel led many of its victims into the clutches of slavery. It was easy to obtain slaves from the Coromandel coast as people there were willing to sell themselves or their children into bondage to overcome the rigours of famine. Slavery for them better than death. It was estimated that within two years as many as 15,000 to 20,000 victims of famine were taken to Aceh as slaves.[31] In December 1622 itself as many as, 1000 such victims, mostly women and children, were exported from the Coromandel to Batavia. Another batch of 700 famine victims were sent to Batavia. Yet another Dutch ship carried 200 a few weeks later to Batavia.[32] During the next two years (1623 and 1624), 1123 and 928 natives, respectively, were exported to Batavia.[33] The supply of slaves dried up when natural conditions improved and so Dutch trade in slaves also declined. This forced the Dutch later (in 1626) to send four of their ships to Arakan (Mrauk-u) to fetch 250 slaves from them for re-export to Batavia and Aceh.[34] Considerable profit was derived from the sale of these slaves at Aceh.[35]

The Dutch thus actively participated in the export of slaves while the Portuguese did not do so as the missionaries were against it. Sometimes people were even kidnapped only to be sold as slaves. Augustin de Beaulieu, a traveller of the seventeenth century, reported that he met a few Coromandel slaves in Aceh who had been brought from Nagapattinam. These slaves requested him on 2 March 1621 to rescue them by paying their owners what they had paid for the salves. He, however, could rescue only four Christian slaves who were former residents of Nagapattinam. The *Santa Casa da Misericordia* (The Holy House of Mercy) of Nagapattinam paid him 400 reals towards expenses incurred by him on this account. Augustin de Beaulieu carried out his rescue mission successfully with the help of Kunzhali Marakkayar on 23 March 1621.[36]

The Portuguese on the Tamil coast also banned the sale of slaves in Tuticorin and Nagapattinam on humanitarian grounds. The entry of people to be sold as slaves in Tuticorin and Nagapattinam was prohibited on 28 June 1632. The prohibition was enforced with the help of the missionaries.[37]

In 1645 one of the regulations of the customs house in Nagapattinam was that the Marakkayars had to pay as much as 10 *pardaus* for each shipment of slaves they exported from Nagapattinam.[38] The port eventually emerged as a big centre of the slave trade under the Dutch. It is recorded that after the fall of the Portuguese settlement of Nagapattinam into the hands of the Dutch on 23 July 1658, up to June 1660 a total of 3,695 slaves had been purchased by the Dutch and shipped to Batavia via Jaffna.[39]

Padre Antonio Luis of Santhome of Mylapore reported baptizing a slave who belonged to Nunes Valentine, then living in the English settlement of Madras. The missionary was asked to leave the place and the slave boy was confined for eighteen days by the Governor and the Council of Madras forced him to confess the name of the priest who had baptized him.[40] The reason for his detention was that the slave had embraced Catholicism and not Protestantism. Further, the slave convert could not be exported as he had become a Christian. It may be added here that Madras by that time had emerged as a leading, centre for the export of slaves.[41] The Portuguese living in Santhome and Madras were not slave dealers but they were employed as clerks in the *choultry* in Madras by the English East India Company. A handsome amount of 2 *panams* was paid to the Portuguese clerk for writing a single sale deed. For writing a letter to procure the return of a runaway slave he received 2 *panams*.[42]

Shivaji had issued a *cowle* in March 1678 and had strictly prohibited the European trading companies on the Coromandel coast from engaging in slave trade.[43] The text of the charter runs as follows: 'Under the Muslim government it had become lawful for the Europeans to buy men, women and children from here without hindrance. But now so long as I (Shivaji) am master of these lands, you (Europeans) should not buy or transport any women, men and children.'

It may be said that the Portuguese on the Tamil coast did not trade in slaves although they were interested in availing themselves of the services of slaves. Some of them made efforts to free the slaves with the help of the Portuguese missionaries at Tuticorin and Nagapattinam. It appears that in the seventeenth century the Dutch and the English were responsible for promoting the slave trade on the Coromandel coast when it was under the Golconda rulers.

Import of Diverse Goods to the Coromandel

The Portuguese imported a variety of goods from various ports of Asia to the Coromandel. Some of the imports were needed by the nobility in the *nayaka* courts of Tamil Nadu while many others were in demand by the public. At the beginning of the sixteenth century, the marakayyars who visited the port of Pasai in Sumatra always sold rice and textiles and purchased luxury goods such as silk and china ware.[44] The Portuguese who arrived in 1513 also attempted to continue and develop the trade in silk and china ware. As they were not welcomed by the Chinese, they attacked the port of Canton in 1517. Thus relations between the Chinese and the Portuguese were initially strained. Later the Portuguese succeeded in establishing cordial relations with the Chinese through diplomatic contacts and in 1519 Lourenço de Mello was appointed Captain of the China Sea.[45] Although he attempted to develop trade, he was successful as some Portuguese were taken as captives by the Chinese in 1524. This incident seriously affected Portuguese trade contacts with China.[46]

It is learnt through a letter written by Diogo Ferreira in 1539 that Chinese traders for the first time visited the port of Nagapattinam in their junk. They brought some luxury cargo from China and left Nagapattinam carrying textiles.[47] After this the Portuguese made contact to develop trade with China and Leonel de Sousa successfully executed an agreement with the

Cantonese in 1554 after which the Portuguese were officially permitted to trade with the ports on the southern China coast.[48] Private Portuguese traders also arrived at an agreement with the local population which made it clear that the Portuguese would trade with China only as merchants and not as smugglers.[49] Following this agreement, some private Portuguese traders and Coromandel native merchants began to trade with Macao via Melaka.

Silk and Porcelain from China

According to Portuguese sources a ship owned by Khwaja Marakkayyar was used by the Portuguese on the Tamil coast to conduct regular voyages from Nagapattinam to Maçāo.[50] Other Portuguese ships from Goa and Kochi also traded with Maçāo via Nagapattinam where there was a great demand for Chinese goods. These departures were always delayed at Melaka on the pretext of unfavourable winds as the traders preferred to arrive in Nagapattinam only. The onset of the monsoon on the west coast began by this time and they easily avoided reaching Cochin and Goa. This facilitated the sale of Chinese goods, particularly silk brocade and porcelain, at Nagapattinam where there was a ready market for them.[51] The crew members colluded with the Coromandel merchants and the Captain of Nagapattinam to carry on this illegal trade for a very long time. Contemporary Portuguese records refer to many such instances. In one case, silk worth 14,000 *pardaus* brought from Maçāo was sold at Nagapattinam.[52] So in order to prevent the dumping of Chinese merchandise at Nagapattinam, avoiding to reach Cochin and Goa the Captain of Melaka was authorized to scrutinize the cargo of the Coromandel merchants destined for the port of Nagapattinam and to see that the ships departed on time.[53]

The trade in Chinese goods at Nagapattinam flourishing in 1580 due chiefly to arrival of the Chinese junks, which gave rise to piracy in the open seas near the Coromandel coast.[54] The Marakkayars resorted to piracy because they were deprived of the opportunity to trade across the seas.

In 1582, the viceroy of Goa sent an armada under Captain António de Sousa Godinho to protect the Portuguese navios and

Chinese junks from attacks by pirates.[55] Even this armada could not prevent pirate's attacks. The Portuguese traders at Nagapattinam then appealed to the king of Portugal to provide the necessary security against such attacks. The king gave his approval in 1587 for maintaining another armada exclusively for the protection of the Chinese junks that sailed to and from the port of Nagapattinam.[56] Two years later, it was ordered that additional protection should be provided to ships sailing between Nagapattinam and Mação by the armada of Bengal. The State Council of India decided to give additional protection to the merchants trading between China and the Coromandel. An armada of six galleons was engaged in this task in the month of August every year.[57] Direct commercial contacts between the Coromandel and Chinese ports revived with the entry of the Portuguese in the trade of luxury commodities. Traders like Ambrosio Borges sailed in 1597 from Santhome of Mylapore and established trade links with China.[58] Nagapattinam had regular trade with China hill as late as 1618.[59]

Owing to the great demand for Chinese merchandise such as silk and china ware in Nagapattinam, many ships sailed to Tennaserim as well, where these items were available. The goods were brought from China via Cambodia and Laos through the overland trade routes. Instead of conducting long-distance trade from the Coromandel to Mação via the port of Melaka, Chinese goods were purchased by the Portuguese at Tennaserim. These voyages to Tennaserim also brought good revenue to the Portuguese in the Coromandel.[60]

Import of Luxuries, Aromatics and Cosmetics from South-East Asia and Sri Lanka

Other imports included some aromatics, astringents, cosmetics and perfumes. Sandalwood paste, famous for its cooling effect on the human body was imported from Aceh.[61] Roberto Nobili, the Jesuit missionary, mentions three different varieties of sandalwood: white, red and yellow. The red variety was grown in Tamil Nadu while the other varieties came from Timor and Java. The yellow variety was considered to be the best of all. The sandalwood that was brought to the Coromandel from Timor in exchange for textiles was called *Timuran paccai* by the Tamils.[62]

According to Fernão Guerreiro, a Jesuit visitor, Portuguese merchants from the Coromandel, on their return journey, brought luxury items such as aloe wood or eagle wood (a kind of fragrant wood) the smoke of which was used for perfuming dresses. Amber was another import to the Coromandel. This famous perfume called by the trade name of *ambergis* was extracted from the large intestine of the whales that came from Thailand.[63] Merchants also imported a large volume of musk from Arakan.[64]

The two-way trade between the Coromandel coast and the various ports of Asia also turned out to be beneficial for the textile manufacturers as it enabled the merchants to bring lac from Pegu, used for the dyeing of textiles.[65] Lac was also imported from Martaban as described by Duarte Barbosa. The root of the Chang plant which yielded a fine red dye was much in demand. Sapan wood and Brazil wood were also used in dyeing in Chandragiri and Santhome areas.[66] Dye roots collected in Mannar in Sri Lanka from a wild shrub called *chaya ver* by the Portuguese after the Tamil word meaning colour, were also exported to the Coromandel. It is reported, that in 1582 seven *bahars* of dye roots were sent to the Coromandel.[67] Further, scarlet dye was imported from West Asia to Pulicat to be used in the dyeing of textiles.[68] The port of Santhome received much of its sealing wax from Siam, which was also used in the textile industry.

The Portuguese imported benzoin which was used in medicine as an antiseptic as there was a heavy demand for it. Camphor was one of the main items of import sought by the Hindu merchants from Barus in Sumatra.[69] This camphor was brought to Pulicat in cylinders made of bamboo reeds and was widely used for the preparation of confectionery.

Areca nuts from Batticaloa and Thirikonamalai also reached Nagapattinam. These nuts, which were in great demand for betel-chewing, found their way to the royal capital of the *nayak* ruler at Thanjavur where there was an established market for ready sale.[70] From the port of Nagapattinam areca nuts were transported via Thiruvarur to Thanjavur, the main overland trade route.[71]

Luso-Dutch Rivalry and the Misdeeds of the Portuguese Captains in Mylapore

The commercial rivalry between the Portuguese and the Dutch on the Tamil coast in the seventeenth century was more acrimonious than it had been between the Portuguese and the Muslim traders in the sixteenth century. The Luso-Dutch struggle affected the official and private commerce of both parties in the region and ultimately paved the way for the decline of the Portuguese. However, Portuguese private traders managed to survive on the Tamil coast almost up to the middle of the eighteenth century. This section will examine how the Portuguese carried on their private trade in the changing environment.

The Dutch arrived in Masulipatnam in February 1605, and they secured the right to trade at the port from the sultan of Golconda. On 26 April 1606, they came to Pulicat and attempted to obtain permission from Jagga-raja, the local ruler, to establish their trading settlement. The negotiations failed and the Dutch suspected of a secret deal between the Portuguese and the native ruler. Angered by the setback, the Dutch burnt two Portuguese ships in Santhome. Later, they established a factory at Nizampatnam located at the mouth of the river Krishna.

In 1610 the Dutch once again attempted to settle down at Pulicat and this time they succeeded in obtaining permission from Venkata II, the Vijayanagra ruler.[72]

In order to oust the Dutch from Pulicat, in 1606 the Archbishop of Goa sent an envoy with the gift of a horse to King Venkata II.[73] The king of Portugal, in his letter dated 10 December 1607, addressed to the viceroy in Goa, also urged him to maintain the best of relations with the ruler of Vijayanagara, and thereby ensure the expulsion of the Dutch from Pulicat.[74] Rui Lourenço de Tavora, the viceroy of Goa (1609-2), sent Captain Manuel de Frias in 1610 to attack the Dutch settlement of Pulicat as they had begun to hamper the textile trade conducted by the Portuguese.[75] The commercial rivalry between the two became so very intense that, on 9 June 1612, the Portuguese in Santhome decided to attack Pulicat.[76] One ship from Kochi was sent to Mylapore by the Portuguese viceroy to help in the attack, on the

Dutch.[77] Ships from Nagapattinam and Santhome were also provided by the Portuguese to attack the Dutch in the open seas.[78] On 12 June 1612, the combined forces of the Portuguese on the west and the east coasts attacked and sacked the Dutch factory and destroyed it, killing three of its employees. Others were made prisoners along with the Dutch Factor. They were brought to Santhome. Some of the Dutch company's merchandise also found its way to Santhome.

However, from the correspondence between Santhome and Lisbon, it is evident that the activities of the Captain in Santhome were not very beneficial to the Portuguese. In one of the letters in 1612, the king of Portugal wrote to the viceroy of Goa that the Captain in Mylapore had disobeyed the royal orders and was acting like a rebel. On the orders of the viceroy in 1612, the Bishop of Mylapore took charge of the post of Captain and an enquiry was ordered against the former Captain of Santhome.[79] *Cafilas* (convoys of ships) were also sent in 1613 to Kanyakumari from the west coast to provide security for the trading vessels on the Tamil coast.[80] The Portuguese viceroy appointed a Captain for 'Meliapore' in 1610, who replaced the recalcitrant Captain of Santhome, to deal with the Dutch in Pulicat. He was also allowed to maintain a troop of soldiers. The Portuguese settlers in the town of Santhome, however, were so frustrated by the state of affairs that they preferred Manuel de Frias to be chosen and he was made the Captain of the town. About 1,500 to 2,000 soldiers were stationed at Santhome to meet the threat of Dutch attacks at Nagapattinam and Santhome.[81]

The Dutch also realized the need to have a fort at Pulicat to ensure the security of their trading activities. In a bid to obtain favour and support, they gave costly presents to the Vijayanagara ruler in Vellore and obtained a new grant on 12 December 1612 to erect a fort at Pulicat. The Dutch began to construct the fort and called it Casteel Geldria. Having strengthened the fortifications in Pulicat, they then laid siege to Mylapore in 1613 in retaliation for the destruction of their factory by the Portuguese. The *nayak* of Thanjavur came to the assistance of the Portuguese when the Dutch attacked Santhome.[82] After plundering Santhome the Dutch left for Pulicat.

In 1616, William Methwold, the English traveller, observed

that the Dutch in Pulicat were like a bad neighbour to the Portuguese settlement in Santhome.[83] On 27 January 1616, the Dutch once again laid siege to Santhome but returned to Pulicat without success.[84] The Portuguese attacked the Dutch in Pulicat in 1617 and this time they burnt two Marakkayar ships which were helping the Dutch to carry on trade from Pulicat.[85] The king of Portugal wanted to halt the expansion of Dutch commercial activity in the Coromandel and for this purpose organized an armada with funds drawn from Crown revenues.[86] Thus the Dutch-Portuguese rivalries around Pulicat continued till 1619.

The viceroy of Goa, in the meanwhile (July 1616), had appointed Rui Dias de Sampaio as Captain to deal with the situation in Santhome. The Captain carried out extensive raids on the coast and the natives were taken by surprise. In due course of time he is also reported to have disobeyed the royal orders even despatching his own ships to Pegu on 20 February 1619, when voyages were prohibited owing to the war between the kings of Pegu and Ava.[87] Even when the merchants of Santhome complained about the Dutch who disturbed their voyages to Melaka, the Captain did not act. He was interested in keeping Portuguese ships sailing to Pegu because such traffic helped boost his own private income.[88] He even undertook voyages (on 26 February 1624) himself to Pegu without obtaining the permission of the viceroy of Goa.[89] Records further reveal that Rui Dias de Sampaio also carried on illegal trade with Pegu and many other ports in Asia till his death in 1629.[90]

The viceroy of Goa later opted for António Manuel and he was appointed as the Portuguese Captain of Mylapore in 1621. As Manuel was corrupt, Dom Luís de Britto, the Bishop of Mylapore, wrote to the king of Portugal on 2 January 1622, saying that 'Your Majesty is poorly served in this Estado even if little and not at all in matters of war.'[91] António Manuel was himself doing a lot of mischief in Santhome resulting in considerable loss of revenue to the king of Portugal. He was also found to be dealing privately in the spice trade, making huge profits.[92]

It has been mentioned that António Manuel, the Captain of Mylapore, was a bad administrator. Although ships and soldiers were sent from Goa to Mylapore to fight against the Dutch, he did not take any active steps. On the other hand he bought a ship at an undervalued price resulting in gain to himself and loss to the royal treasury. He obtained from the Portuguese governor a permit to undertake a voyage to Melaka where he made a profit of 7,000 *cruzados*. He exported textiles valued at 4,000 *cruzados* of which goods worth 2,000 *cruzados* were in the name of the bishop. All of these underhand dealings of the Captain increased the debt of the royal treasury. He later purchased two ships although he was not supposed to enter into such deals. Nevertheless he managed to purchase each ship for 90 *xerafins* and had the writer of the port issue proper certificates. At the same time, he reported to the authorities in Goa when he went there that everything was fine in Mylapore. There was much tension in Mylapore because of the Dutch presence there and trade was severely disturbed. His deeds became so intolerable that the Bishop of Mylapore was prompted to address a letter calling for an enquiry against him.[93]

The Bishop of Mylapore was therefore requested to depose António Manuel and himself take charge as the Captain of Mylapore in January 1624.[94] Before the expiry of his term, António Manuel decided to leave Santhome. However, in August 1623, in his attempt to escape, he was killed when his ship exploded.[95] Legal proceedings were initiated against him the next year.[96] The members of his family, in the meanwhile, cleverly transferred and invested their funds with the Dutch in Pulicat.[97] After the death of António Manuel, his sons and daughters were taken into custody on 16 February 1625, but the ill-gotten wealth could not be appropriated to the *Estado da Índia*.[98] This is indicative of the growing rivalry between the monarchy and the nobility, or perhaps the new class of rich trading families.

António Coelho, a *fidalgo*, was appointed Captain in 1621 in Santhome and was vested with the responsibility of ousting the Dutch from Pulicat. This is evident from a letter dated 24 February 1621, requesting the support of a big armada to counter the growing Dutch influence in the Coromandel. In the letter he explained how aggressive the Dutch were and further lamented that they were indulging in intrigues in order to sow the seeds of suspicion in the minds of local rulers against the Portuguese, as well as among Muslims and Hindu traders.[99] The Dutch in the meanwhile attacked Santhome in August 1623.[100] Some Portuguese soldiers were sent from Kochi to join the ships of the Coromandel to fight the Dutch.[101] The Dutch, however, captured Santhome in August 1623, and this was possible because there was no proper administration in the settlement where virtual anarchy reigned. The Portuguese felt the need to appoint a *fidalgo* to enforce law and order among the Portuguese residents.[102] The Dutch occupied Santhome only for a short period as the settlement was recaptured by the Portuguese on 23 September 1623.[103]

Diogo de Mello de Castro was appointed Captain of Santhome in 1625. In order to attack the Dutch in Pulicat in 1627 he mobilized a contingent of 200 men and a few ships in Mylapore.[104] The money required for the purpose was remitted on 4 April 1627 to India from Portugal for equipping an armada in the Coromandel.[105]

The forces mobilized were not found adequate to face the Dutch. In a letter written to Filippe III, the king of Portugal (1621-40), by the viceroy of Goa in 1628 it is mentained that an armada was sent to Santhome of Mylapore to fight the Dutch. The viceroy further stated that he had spent 20,000 *pagodas* (equal to 60,000 *xerafins*) to take the Dutch settlement of Pulicat. By way of further assistance he sought sanction for an additional 12,000 *pagodas* from the king.[106] Further, payment of the salaries of the Portuguese army and additional expenses incurred in the Coromandel was also passed by the Revenue Council of India in Goa on 9 March 1629.[107] Accordingly, on 20 March 1629, 12,000 *pagodas* were given to Diogo de Melle de Castro, the Captain of Santhome, towards the expenditure to be incurred in connection with the attack on the Dutch fort of Pulicat by the Portuguese.[108]

The annual letter of the Jesuits in 1630 mentions that the Dutch relentlessly continued their attacks against the Portuguese in Santhome. They attacked and sank a ship in Santhome.[109] They also continued to impede commerce in the Portuguese settlement.[110] The State Council of India in Goa therefore decided to send four galleons to Mylapore as per the decision taken at its meeting on 11 August 1630.[111]

Domingos de Camara succeeded Diogo de Mello de Castro as

Captain of Santhome on 11 February 1632.[112] Although various Captains were appointed from time to time they were not successful in dislodging the Dutch from Pulicat as the latter's commerce was growing well.[113] In the meanwhile, on 23 June and 29 July 1634, the Bishop of Mylapore wrote two letters to the viceroy giving an appraisal of the Dutch affairs in the fort of Pulicat and also about the Portuguese.[114]

As the Portuguese were desperately in need of the support of the king of Vijayanagara to drive the Dutch away from Pulicat, they approached Venkata III the ruler of Vijayanagara (1630-41), in 1633 through Fr. Alexio Mexia, the Jesuit in Santhome. He pleaded with the king of Vijayanagara on behalf of the Portuguese Captain of Santhome to return the Dutch fort in Pulicat to the Portuguese.[115] On hearing from Fr. Alexio Mexia that the king favoured the Portuguese, the Captain of Santhome sent rich presents to him.[116]

In order to drive away the Dutch an agreement was signed between Conde de Linhares, the Portuguese Viceroy (1629-35), and Venkata III, the king of Vijayanagara. The king agued to assist the Portuguese by mobilizing his forces and attacking the Dutch settlement of Pulicat from the land while the Portuguese were to launch an attack from the sea. The Portuguese in return promised to pay the king 30,000 *xerafins*, twelve horses and six elephants for his assistance.[117] A fleet of twelve ships was sent by the Portuguese to attack the Dutch settlement at Pulicat. Ammunition, horses and elephants were agreed to be given and they were also received at Santhome. It was also decided to attack the Dutch on 17 March 1635.[118] The aldermen of Nagapattinam were ordered by the Portuguese viceroy on 17 March 1635 to join the armada to attack Pulicat.[119] The king of Vijayanagara, however, failed to act according to the agreement.[120]

The Dutch had easy access to Santhome since their merchants were trading there, who kept them informed of what was happening there.[121] Therefore, the viceroy, Dom Filippe Mascarenhas (1641-51), in a letter addressed to António Amaral de Meneses, the Captain of Santhome, ordered that all the Dutch merchants who had been permitted to trade in Santhome should be driven out. However, the Dutch put to good use the knowledge they already had about the Portuguese settlement. They attacked Santhome in 1641 in retaliation for the Portuguese disturbing their commercial operations in the port of Pulicat. The Portuguese Captain of Santhome, however, joined hands with the Dutch and this caused the Portuguese viceroy to write that year that *he (the Captain of Mylapore) seems more a factor of the Dutch than an officer of Your Majesty.*[122] Thus the Portuguese settlement of Santhome had to struggle on its own for its survival against the Dutch.

João de Sousa Pereira, the next Captain of Santhome, in his letter dated 4 December 1642 to the viceroy of Goa, requested that a garrison be kept at Santhome as a precautionary measure to face the attacks by the Dutch who planned to capture the town in the near future.[123] The Portuguese, who had been trading on the Coromandel coast hated the Dutch who had cornered a substantial portion of their profits from trade. The Dutch hostility towards the Portuguese, in the course of time, was not confined to only Santhome but spread to all other Portuguese settlements on the coast.[124]

The Luso-Dutch rivalry in Nagapattinam was intense even when the Dutch were actively participating in politics and trade in Sri Lanka in the 1640s. A Dutch fleet from Sri Lanka was sent out to raid the Portuguese settlement of Nagapattinam and it arrived there on 12 April 1642. As the Dutch attacked the port, the villagers fled to other places for safety. Following an agreement on 13 April 1642, the Portuguese attempted to the settlement of Nagapattinam. The Dutch left the place only after the Portuguese paid a ransom of 10,000 *pagodas*. Thirty-two hostages were kept by the Dutch who demanded payment of an additional 40,000 *pagodas* from the residents of Nagapattinam for their return.[125]

Some days later, on 22 April 1642, the *nayak* of Thanjavur who had heard about the Dutch capture of Nagapattinam, attacked them. A sum of 11,000 *pagodas* was given by the Portuguese in Nagapattinam to the *nayak's* commander who drove the Dutch out and saved the town.[126] The Portuguese residents in the meanwhile addressed a letter to the Portuguese viceroy on 22 May 1642 asking for ammunition and soldiers to help the *nayak* in the war against the Dutch.[127] The Portuguese settlers in Nagapattinam at that time had no proper organization to unite them. They therefore felt the need to have someone at the helm to provide the leadership to direct the war against the Dutch and take charge of the administration of the settlement of Nagapattinam. As the post of the Portuguese Captain of Nagapattinam remained vacant for some time,[128] the Rector of the Jesuit College at Santhome, who was previously at Nagapattinam exhorted many of his friends there to apply to the king of Portugal, João IV (1640-56), for the position.[129] António de Amaral de Meneses was eventually appointed Captain by the viceroy on 27 January 1643. A sum of 30,000 *xerafins* was also sent on 3 August 1643 to Nagapattinam to meet its military expenditure.[130]

The conduct of the Portuguese officials in Nagapattinam, however, did not change for the better. About a decade later, the aldermen of Nagapattinam wrote to the Portuguese viceroy regarding the irregularities committed by some of the officials at Nagapattinam. In fact, João de Moraes Pinto, the *ouvidor* of Nagapattinam in 1662, was accused with sufficient proof of irregularities committed and so the aldermen requested the viceroy on 1 November 1643 to take immediate action against him.[131] João Pinheiro de Gamboa (1652-5), was another Captain against whom many complaints were lodged on 4 July 1653 by the people of Nagapattinam.[132] Finally, when he was removed from the post, he made attempts to get reinstated in the post of Captain of Nagapattinam. The members of the municipality of Nagapattinam wrote to the viceroy in Goa confirming that the privileges earlier enjoyed by João Pinheiro de Gamboa had been totally withdrawn.[133]

It was reported in the Jesuit annual letter as early as 1648 that the sea (Bay of Bengal) was swarming with Dutch ships and navigation was dangerous as the Dutch attacked the Portuguese ships.[134] The behaviour of the Portuguese officials made the task of the Dutch in Nagapattinam that much easier. On 20 July 1658, a Dutch fleet appeared at Nagapattinam and easily took control of the Portuguese settlement and from 23 July 1658 began to rule here. The Portuguese residents were allowed to leave for Goa with all their movable properties.

Violence, Disorder and Anarchy in the Portuguese Settlements

According to an unpublished manuscript in the National Archives of Lisbon, the king of Portugal, Dom Filipe I (1580-98), appointed Francisco de Sa as *ouvidor* for the first time with civil and criminal jurisdiction of the entire Tamil coast. He resided at Punnaikayal as this settlement had a large Portuguese and native Christian population.[135] The entire judicial system in Portuguese India at that time was built on the pattern that was in practice in Portugal, with the Relaçao (High Court) at Goa in 1544. The *Ouvidor Geral* (the Chief Judge) and the Desembargadores (the Superior Judges of College) held positions in this court as Crown representatives. The Portuguese judge of Punnaikayal, appointed by the Crown of Portugal was subordinate to the High Court in Goa. He was the representative of the king of Portugal in the region. Thus the administration of Punnaikayal was brought under the Crown. The Portuguese did this without the approval of the local *nayaks* because their administration was not based on territorial but social control.

It is to be noted that there was a rise in violence and disorder in the Portuguese settlements after the arrival of the Dutch. Crimes increased when the post of Captain fell vacant. A mestiço who was a relative of Francisco de Freitas, living in Santhome stabbed a compatriot, Symão de Brito. He was immediately confined in a church. Later, when the injured man died, an enquiry was held in Santhome. The enquiry report revealed that the *mestiço* was guilty and he was punished. Similarly, Lopo Alvares de Moura, a rich merchant who had kidnapped the wife of another settler in 1594, was also found guilty and he too was punished.[136] Thus administration of justice was reasonably effective.

There were several factions among the Portuguese in Santhome and this led to conflicts, violence and disorder. On 18 February 1595, an order was passed by the Captain of Santhome to put an end to factional fights among the residents of Mylapore.[137] Preventive steps were ordered to be taken on 6 January 1602 through the arrest of criminals to curb the violence arising from factional fights.[138] Instances of rioting in Santhome continued for a long time and it is clear from a letter dated 3 September

1606, written by Fr. M. Roiz residing at Santhome to the Jesuit Superior General in Rome, that the Portuguese had been quarrelling and fighting among themselves for more than two or three years.[139] Another letter mentions that there were many factional fights among the Portuguese settlers of Santhome. The internal fights were often so intense that at times they took on the dimensions of a civil war. However, no solution could be found for these fights as neither the judge nor the Portuguese Captain in Santhome was provided with a security force to arrest and punish those engaged in it. On all Fridays during the season of Lent, the priests in their sermons fervently trenched against violence and hatred and exhorted their followers to be peaceful.[140]

As there were always complaints about the lack of justice (*falta justica*) in the *Estado da Índia*, and in order to remedy the situation and to punish criminals, the king of Portugal appointed separate *ouvidors* at Tuticorin,[141] Santhome[142] and Nagapattinam.[143] It was the duty of the judges to dispense justice in all civil and criminal matters. The post of *ouvidor* was also very lucrative. From the text of a letter written from Goa (October 1596), we find that the post of *ouvidor* was very powerful.[144] It said: 'If Simon had a law degree, I think it would be a good thing for him to ask for an appointment here as a judge or a Crown attorney since he is your son they are unlikely to refuse him and these men are kings here.'

The appointment of a bishop for Santhome of Mylapore was expected to bring about a change for the better in the social environment there. However, the situation did not improve very much.[145] In 1613, Dom Jeronymo de Azevedo, the viceroy of Goa (1612-17), wrote to the king of Portugal that there was lack of discipline among the Portuguese scrambling for profits of trade and Santhome was inhabited by such people who were accustomed to living without restraints. Morality, truth and justice had no meaning and the Portuguese continued to live there in a manner unbecoming for Christians.[146] The viceroy lamented that disorder and division among the *fidalgos* and the residents in Santhome was responsible for the rise of Dutch influence in Pulicat.[147]

In 1615 the missionaries in Santhome felt that it would be useful to post a Captain there immediately with authority and also place a garrison to help him put an end to the abuse of law indulged in by the resident subjects. This would also provide protection against the Dutch who came to the Coromandel coast often.[148] Hence, with a view to establishing a fortified military prison in Santhome, the Revenue Council of India in Goa, in 1616, decided to meet the expenditure and appoint an officer only to establish a fortified military prison in Santhome. There was, however, to be a contingent of soldiers and the salary was sanctioned by the Revenue Council of India in Goa. This council also gave its assent to the appointment Francisco de Oliveira as the commander on a salary of 10,000 *reis* along with all admissible perquisites and allowances.[149]

The Portuguese residents of Nagapattinam had a relatively more peaceful life with less factional fights and disturbances throughout the sixteenth century.[150] However, from 1601 the disorderly activities intensified and the king of Portugal ordered the culprits to be punished.[151] The viceroy of Goa requested the judge to award severe punishments to criminals and to initiate action to enforce law and order in the settlement.[152]

As the king of Portugal received many complaints against the Captains of the Portuguese settlements, particularly Santhome, he sent a detailed questionnaire to the Captain of the fort of Santhome seeking answers.[153] The questionnaire sought details about the trade connected with several articles which were in great demand in Portugal and also about the salaries and private incomes of the officials in order to ascertain the actual position.

In spite of the official Luso-Dutch rivalry, widespread maladministration and violence in the Portuguese settlements, a large number of Portuguese settlers survived as shipowners, financiers, wholesale and retail traders. They were not only influential in the Bay of Bengal region but also turned out to be very helpful to the English, the Dutch and the Danes who were their political opponents and potential trade rivals in the Orient.

The commercial influence that the Portuguese private traders wielded in the Bay of Bengal region has led Sanjay Subrahmanyam to conclude that Portuguese influence was not merely confined to those areas that fell within the territorial jurisdiction of the *Estado da Índia* but also extended to the ports all over Asia.

Portuguese Traders Diaspora

The concept of trade diaspora, at first introduced by Abner Cohen, was subsequently elaborated in the writings of Philip Curtin.[154] Fernand Braudel too had dealt with this aspect in his studies.[155] An exploration of the relatively open mercantile activities of the floating groups of Portuguese may help us to understand the concept of trade diaspora in the Bay of Bengal region and the reason for the decline of the official Portuguese trade during this period. However, K.N. Chaudhuri has cautioned historians about using the concept of trade diaspora as an analytical tool.[156] It may be said that the phenomenon of migration of Portuguese private merchants from one cultural zone to another was an important feature of the quick expansion of Portuguese maritime trade. Moreover, the presence of a Portuguese diaspora was manifested in the growing economic stature of Portugal as a regionally dominant economic power. The Portuguese traders had their own common identity which transcended religion, language and their Western mode of life. Hence the Portuguese fall within the description of a diaspora in the Bay of Bengal trading zone. Let us examine how the Portuguese traders emerged as a diaspora in the early sixteenth century and how they continued to remain so even after the fall of the Portuguese settlements to the Dutch in 1662.

It is evident from early seventeenth-century records that these Portuguese private traders also entered into profitable dealings with the Dutch. An order to imprison some traders like Domingos de Silva, a *casado* of Santhome, was issued by the viceroy of Goa as the former had sailed in a ship from Batavia on 21 July 1642.[157] Similarly, private traders like Damião Martim and João de Levanto traded with Banten in the English ships from Madras. The Portuguese Captain in Santhome took them into custody because he considered them traitors for having served the English Company.[158]

Complaints to this effect have been found in many Portuguese records.[159] Even the Marakkayars borrowed money from the Portuguese at 100 per cent interest. The Marakkayars found that there was no more risk at sea.[160] As the Portuguese East India Company ceased to exist in the year 1642, Dom João IV, the king of Portugal (1640-56), wanted to induce the private Portuguese traders to ship all their merchandise on all routes, including the *Carriera da Índia* (Goa-Lisbon route).[161] A royal order was therefore promulgated on 11 December 1642, which declared that Portuguese subjects could carry on free trade in all directions without any restrictions,[162] except in cinnamon which was still reserved as a royal monopoly item of trade.[163] From 1645 onwards, however, the private traders among the Portuguese living in the Coromandel Coast are known to have established contacts with the English and the Dutch and stopped paying the custom duties at the Portuguese ports.[164] They had established such good relations with the Dutch that there was no need for them to altogether abandon the Coromandel coast even after the capture of all the Portuguese settlements by the Dutch in 1662. In fact, records confirm that many Portuguese merchants established cordial relations with the English and the Dutch.

Commercial Activities between the Portuguese Private Traders and the Dutch and the English

Private Portuguese traders worked in cooperation with both the Dutch and the English although it was not in consonance with the policy of the Portuguese establishment in Goa at the political level. Some Portuguese traders continued to remain in business at Nagapattinam conducting trade with the Dutch even after the fall of the town. A lively trade in textiles was conducted between Nagapattinam and Batavia by Portuguese private traders. The Batavia Council, therefore decided to promote its trade and passed a resolution to encourage the Portuguese without subjecting them to harassment.[165]

The Portuguese Captain of Santhome did not like the English Company engaging in trading activities at Madras. The flourishing trade in Nagapattinam attracted the English in Madras who wanted to trade there as well.[166] The Portuguese private traders who desired to trade with Maçāo used the port of Madras as their base to conduct trade.[167] Some Portuguese also wished to trade with the sultanate of Aceh and sent their ships from Madras.[168] Thus Portuguese traders began to conduct trade regularly from Madras with Banten, Aceh and Macao.[169] In

1686, a Portuguese resident of Santhome freighted a ship and loaded it with 700 *corjas* (packets) of textiles in order to set sail to Banten.[170] António do Amaral, Luís Gonçalves de Fonseca and António Rodrigues da Guerra were some of the famous merchants trading with the Dutch in Batavia.[171] The VOC shipping lists also contain these Portuguese names.[172] As many Portuguese private traders had joined hands with the English East India Company and entered into partnership, the VOC officials began to voice complaints. They mentioned in their reports that the Portuguese ships were flying either English or native flags and also carried Englishmen on board. Jermias Van Vliet, the Dutch governor of Melaka in 1644, mentioned that 'if the Dutch continued to allow this Anglo-Luso trade it would be like cancer which would inwardly eat the Dutch East India Company'.[173]

According to English sources, many Portuguese private traders who lived at the port of Durgarajapattinam, located a little north of Pulicat, settled in Madras. The Portuguese population in the white town in Madras was said to be around two-thirds of the white population in the year 1675. The English traders in Madras therefore could not find accommodation in the white town and as a result were forced to live in the black town. The Portuguese who lived within the white town of Madras did not pay rent to the English Company as desired by the English Council there, while the English had to pay rent like the natives since they lived in the black town of Madras. The English contingent of soldiers in Madras was composed of almost two-thirds Portuguese in 1675. As these Portuguese soldiers always assembled in the thousands every week at a particular place and discussed things of common interest, the English Company became alarmed about allowing them to continue this weekly assemblage. The matter was referred to the council of the English Company in Madras, which met on 29 February in 1675. As there was no other way out, the English Company and the council resolved to maintain the status quo. The reason mentioned was that the Portuguese viceroy had announced exemption of taxes for a period of three years to those who would agree to settle in Santhome. Hence the English feared the migration of many Portuguese which might bring ruin to the English settlement of Madras.[174]

In due course of time, there arose many problems for the Portuguese. These problems were mentioned in a complaint lodged by forty-five Portuguese inhabitants of Madras to the English governor and council on 20 September 1678. They demanded equal justice for both the English and the Portuguese residents of Madras. They stated that although several criminal offences had been committed by the English in Madras no action had been taken against them. They also said that the disposal of the case of Manuel Barriga de Lima had been delayed for no reason. This Portuguese man was accused of killing a fellow Portuguese with a pistol in the middle of a street, and as there was no proof, he was kept in prison for many years. The Portuguese residents therefore requested the English to free him at the earliest.

It is mentioned that the Portuguese had been living in Madras under the protection of the English Company since 1659. After their arrival in Madras, they invited many painters, weavers, workmen and others to join them. Thus the Portuguese had brought prosperity to Madras and also increased its income. In times of war, the Portuguese had readily joined the army of the English as captains, soldiers, etc., when even the English settlers did not do so. Further, the Portuguese had built their houses at their own expense and had paid considerable amount of customs duty which could be found in the customs book of the *choultry*.[175] These Portuguese residents, who should have enjoyed the privileges in the English settlement, were denied them by the English East India Company although the prevailing norms, allowed a foreigner who lived in a place for four years continuously was entitled to.

Portuguese Shipowners in Porto Novo

Following the extension of the kingdom of Bijapur to the Tamil country in the 1640s, the Marakkayar merchants of coastal Tamil Nadu were eager to come to the Portuguese settlement at Porto Novo to trade with the various ports of South East Asia. Even those Marakkayars who had fled to other ports, where the Portuguese had little control, were now attracted to Porto Novo.

Ships belonging to the commander-in-chief of the Bijapur army sailed from Goa on the west coast of India to Porto Novo on the east coast,[176] confirming the re-establishment of good relations between the sultan of Bijapur and the Portuguese viceroy in Goa. The Portuguese were also quick to take advantage of the changed circumstances to modify their trade policy from one of hostility towards the Muslim traders to that of friendly cooperation with them.

Many private Portuguese textile traders preferred to remain at Porto Novo, the chief port of the sultan of Bijapur, since trade and commerce flourished there. According to one account, there were six leading Portuguese textile merchants who were living in Porto Novo as on 21 February 1673.[177] The names of many Portuguese traders who later became shipowners in Porto Novo, such as Manuel Texeira Pinto, João Soares, Manuel Correia, António de Almeida and Manuel Soares de Almeida, figure prominently in the records of the period 1681-6. The ships of these Porto Novo merchants sailed to Pegu, Aceh, Melaka, Goa and Manila.[178]

There were also a few *mestiços* in Porto Novo who were trading with Banten via Madras. They carried textiles and in return brought nutmegs from Banten.

The ships of the Portuguese traders in Porto Novo secured *cartazes* from the English in Madras to send their ships from

TABLE 25: PORTUGUESE SHIPPING FROM PORTO NOVO, 1681-6[179]

Destination	1681	1682	1683	1684	1685
Pegu	2	1	1	1	3
Aceh	3	3	3	2	2
Melaka	1	1	1	1	–
Goa	1	1	1	1	2
Manila	–	–	–	1	–

TABLE 26: *MESTIÇO* SHIPPING FROM PORTO NOVO TO BANTEN, 1675-81[180]

Arrival	Departure
1675 - 2	1676 - 1
1680 - 1	1681 - 1

Porto Novo to the ports of South-East Asia.[181] These ships first left Porto Novo, reached Madras and from there sailed towards the other ports of destination.[182]

Portuguese Shipowners in Madras and their Trade with Manila

The Portuguese traders who later became shipowners appointed only Portuguese sailors in their ships since they were known as great navigators who could ensure the safety of voyages. By 1631, the Portuguese shipowners in the Coromandel started sending their ships to Manila since it was found very profitable.[183] Some of the ships that sailed from Madras to Manila were owned in partnership by the natives and the Portuguese traders. The names of the ships were registered under the place names of Tiruvottiyur and Thondaiyar, located in the environs of Madras, where these ships were built. These names were given to prevent possible attacks by the Dutch against English or Portuguese ships.

In 1680, the English Council in Madras reported that its income from trade and customs duties had increased chiefly because of the Portuguese shipowners.[184] As trade between Madras and Manila flourished, the high-handed activities of the English Company officials began to affect Portuguese private trade. In one case, in 1680, Francisco Carneiro, who came in a ship from Manila, was forced to deliver all his goods including valuable merchandise, such as gold ingots and copper, to Pedda Venkatadri, the chief native merchant of Madras as ordered by Streynsham Master, the English official (1675-80). As the goods also partly belonged to the governor of Manila, Francisco Carneiro lodged a complaint to the governor of Madras and

TABLE 27: MADRAS-BASED PORTUGUESE SHIPPING TO MANILA, 1678-9[185]

Name of the ship	Name of the individual	Date of voyage
Kandiyur	Domingos de Perreira	8 June 1678
St. Michael	João Domingos	13 June 1678
Tiruvottiyur	Francisco Carneiro	4 June 1679
Thondaiyar	Thomaz Peres	12 June 1679

desired that justice be rendered to him and the English official punished. Further, he wanted compensation and asked for a refund at the earliest.[186]

In spite of such incidents, the private Portuguese shipowners in Madras carried on their shipping and trade with the help of Portuguese pilots (Table 28).[187] Out of the thirty-nine voyages from Madras to Manila conducted by the Portuguese between 1674 and 1702, seventeen were undertaken in partnership with the natives and twelve independently by the rich Portuguese private traders of Madras.[188] Of the hundred and fourteen voyages conducted on the Madras-Manila route between 1707 and 1752, one out of every four ships was also owned by Portuguese traders based in Madras. Thus Madras was an English settlement only in name, in reality a majority of the white town population consisted of Portuguese residents.[189]

In Manila, the Spanish governor levied high customs duties for goods brought by ships owned by the native merchants of Coromandel.[190] This hike in the customs duties continued in Manila even during 1726-8.[191] Further, trade with Manila was also prohibited in principle, especially for Protestants. This greatly facilitated the Portuguese and Luso-Indians in their trade

TABLE 28: PORTUGUESE SHIPPING AT THE PORT OF MADRAS, 1719-53[192]

Year	Number of ships	Year	Number of ships
1719	1	1735	1
1720	1	1736	2
1721	1	1737	2
1722	1	1738	2
1723	4	1739	5
1724	2	1740	1
1725	1	1742	2
1726	2	1743	3
1727	2	1744	3
1728	2	1745	4
1729	3	1746	2
1730	1	1750	5
1731	3	1751	3
1732	1	1752	1
1733	1	1753	4

with Manila from Madras.[193] Hence many ships sailed under the Portuguese flag from the Coromandel coast to Manila where they paid customs duty to the Spanish governor.[194] These ships brought back *piasters* from Peru and Mexico which came via Acapulco to Manila since silver was in great demand on the Coromandel coast.[195]

Between 1707 and 1713, many Portuguese private traders also operated shipping from Madras to Batavia (see Table 29) as found in the records of that period.

The ships of these Portuguese traders carried enormous quantities of textiles to Batavia, which brought them huge profits. All Portuguese ships from the Coromandel were well treated by the Dutch authorities in Batavia which encouraged the development of trade.[196] Most of the Portuguese private merchants who lived in Santhome and Porto Novo were encouraged to trade with the Dutch in Batavia. Some Madras-based private Portuguese traders also participated in this lucrative textile trade, as shown in Table 30.

TABLE 29: DEPARTURE OF SHIPS FROM BATAVIA TO MADRAS, 1707-13[197]

Year	Number of ships
1707	1
1708	1
1710	2
1712	1
1713	1

TABLE 30: BATAVIA-BASED PORTUGUESE SHIPPING TO COROMANDEL PORTS, 1726-33[198]

Destination	Year	Number of ships
Madras	1726	1
Santhome	1726	1
Madras	1727	1
Porto Novo	1730	1
Madras	1732	1
Porto Novo	1733	1

REVIVAL OF TRADE AND NATIVE MERCHANTS IN SANTHOME

On 21 January 1712, Mullah Pir Zudia was appointed *faujdar* in Santhome. He had an annual income of 9,000 *pagodas* from the *jagir* in and around Santhome. The Mughals were also interested in reviving trade in Mylapore. The resident Mughal *subedar* of Porto Novo arrived at Mylapore around this time to arrange for more ships to undertake voyages, besides the two French ships he had planned to send to trade with China. The merchants of Mylapore also agreed to permit all ships under the Mughal banner to sail from Santhome to China.[199]

The caste conflicts between the Idangai (left-hand) and Valangai (right-hand) groups in the English settlement of Madras in 1707 were another important development of this period. These conflicts led to migration of several merchants of the left-hand castes to Santhome. The leading *komatti* Chettis left the troubled town of Madras for Santhome to conduct their trade more peacefully.[200] Further, in the year 1717, when members of the right-hand and left-hand castes clashed because of certain ceremonies conducted before the public, the Chetti merchants of the left-hand caste deserted the English settlement of Madras and went over to Santhome. Several Chetti merchants' names are mentioned in the Portuguese records, such as Callaba Chatim, Bal Chatim, Mar Chatim and Narapa Chatim, who continued to carry on their banking and trading activities in Santhome.[201] The Chettis who migrated to Santhome were mostly wealthy merchants and so they contributed towards the growth of the trade in Santhome during this period.[202]

Although the English promised the Chettis that they could use the English flag, those merchants of the left-hand caste who had migrated to Santhome could not be induced to return to the English settlement of Madras. They settled in Santhome and had developed trade contacts with many Gujarati merchants with whom they exchanged everything needed for trade. Dayala Das was one such rich Gujarati *sarraf* in Santhome.[203] The migration of the Chetti merchants from Madras led to the closure of several shops and the mint also stopped functioning.[204] This made the English furious, and on 27 June 1743, they punished the Madras-based Chetti merchants who traded with Santhome and also those who traded with the merchants of Santhome.[205]

During this period (in the 1740s), the Muslims were encouraged by the Mughal rulers to pursue overseas trade. According to records, the shipowning merchants of Santhome included a large group described by the English as pathans. *Mohammed Baksh* was a ship from Santhome which regularly traded with Pegu. *Nabi Baksh* was another ship which traded with Tennaserim.[206] The ships of the Muslim traders who lived in Santhome during this period left only from the port of Madras and not from Santhome for the fear of attacks by the Marathas.[207] Since the Santhome-based overseas trade flourished during this period, Mamrez Khan from Kovalam (near Mahabalipuram) came to reside permanently in Mylapore in August 1746 to carry on trade with Tennaserim.[208] Trade transactions between Tennaserim and the port of Santhome continued. The ships also carried letters and in one case, the Muslims in Tennaserim sent letters to the chief of Mylapore. Guntur Balu Chetti, a native merchant of Pondicherry, also had letter communication with Thailand.[209]

Private Portuguese trade on from the Tamil coast in the sixteenth and seventeenth centuries had also been very prosperous and formed a substantial part of the inter-port trade of Asia, even though the eighteenth century was a period of decline in Portuguese influence and power. The trade was almost invariably conducted in some form of partnership with indigenous merchants. In the seventeenth century even concession voyages had reached their twilight years and the Portuguese found it more lucrative to engage in trade outside the system.

Some scholars have pointed out that the Portuguese commercial enterprise cannot be called a royal mercantalist empire in which the state only participated in trading for itself. The private presence, through corrupt officials, had worked well outside the system and it was an integral component of the Portuguese presence in the Tamil coast. The king of Portugal had parcelled out the growing tributary income which included the royal customs, revenues and monopoly of trade of its empire in certain pockets in Asia to *fidalgos* and nobility.[210] This large private involvement undermined the position of the crown trade in terms of not only siphoning off the Crown's capital but also resulting in the misuse of other resources, human or otherwise.

The Captains appointed by the king soon began to appropriate some of the Crown's receipts for themselves.

Moving away from this interpretation of the Portuguese presence as a purely royal mercantalist concern, some scholars like V.M. Godinho have argued for a decline of the Portuguese in Asia during the seventeenth century only in the face of actual defeats.[211] Sanjay Subrahmanyam accepts what Godinho and other historians have said on the structural break that occured in the mid-sixteenth century, but he differs slightly. This simplistic interpretation of this phase as a reorientation of the enterprise is untenable because in a continual contestation between various factions and interests such commercial reorientations were not at all easily possible and says that the private trade of the Portuguese has brought essentially a widening of commercial network possibility rather than decline.[212] The question of survival of the Portuguese shippers and sailors arose with the Dutch and the English gaining domination over the trade with Asia. Portuguese private trade contributed towards the growth of Dutch and English had as the Luso-Indian traders were able to continue trading in spite of the decline of Portuguese official commerce. This provided continuity for Portuguese trade and their settlements on the Tamil coast till the first half the eighteenth century. The decline of the Portuguese should be seen more as a political setback as it cannot be attributed to their inability to cope with the competition against the English or the Dutch.

NOTES

1. Raymundo Antonio de Bulhão Pato (ed.), *Cartas de Affonso de Albuquerque*, 7 vols., Lisboa, 1884-1935 (hereafter *CAA*,), vol. I, pp. 138-9.
2. *IANTT*, *CC*, I-68-88. The document records that the Chettis demand money from Diogo Nuneiz who had taken loan from them. He had no money to return because his business was at a loss.
3. Miguel Ferreira owned four ships. See Elaine Sanceau, *Cartas de D. João de Castro*, Lisboã, 1954, p. 293.
4. *IANTT*, CC, I-9-92.
5. *IANTT*, CC, II-49-24.
6. *IANTT*, CC, I-59-58 (1 September 1537); Silva Rego, *Documentação*, vol. 2, pp. 249-55.

7. Correia, Lendas II, 567-8, III, 578; see also Schurhammer, St. Francis Xavier, vol. 2, p. 571.
8. *IANTT, CC*, IIa-115-67, IIa-118-69, IIa-118-172 (1524); Sanceau, (*Cartas de D. João de Castro*, XLIII, fl.329 (1549).
9. *IANTT, CC*, IIa-118-38; IIa-118-40; IIa-118-41.
10. *IANTT, CC*, pt. II-118-38, II-128-40, II-128-41.
11. *IANTT, CC*, IIa-117-170; IIa-118-45; IIa-118-48; IIa-118-52; IIa-120-103.
12. *IANTT, Chancelaria de D. João III*, Liv. 18, fl. 108v; Liv. 4, fl.72.
13. *IANTT, CC*, IIa-118-69; IIa-119-104; IIa-120-25. See also S. Jeyaseela Stephen, 'Transactions of Trade at the Port of Thirumalairayanpattinam in the Cauvery Delta and the Portuguese', *Proceedings of the Indian History Congress*, 57th Session, Calcutta, 1996, pp. 245-52.
14. *IANTT, CC*, IIa-118-69; IIa-118-172; IIa-119-112.
15. *IANTT, CC*, IIa-118-69; IIa- 118-172; IIa-119-112; IIa-121-41.
16. *IANTT, CC*, IIa-114-41; IIa-118-49; IIa-118-69; IIa-118-172.
17. *NA, BUB*, VOC 856, fl. 486 (13 August 1635); VOC 857, fl. 81 (13 February 1636); VOC 861, fl. 118 (28 February 1639).
18. *NA, BUB*, VOC 866, fl. 132 (1 April 1643); VOC 867, fl. 136 (17 April 1644).
19. Antonio Bocarro, *Decade 13*. See the description of the settlement of Nagapattinam.
20. The slaves from Persia and Arabia were delivered in Kochi on 9 May 1524. See *IANTT, CC*, II-101-44, II-102-19; further, Kochi also received six slaves from another ship which also arrived on 9 May 1524. See *IANTT, CC*, IIa-115-40. We find the names and ages of the slaves who happened to be in the age group ranging from eleven to twenty-two. Slaves from Africa and the Persian Gulf region came to the ports of the western coast of India on 13 April 1522. See *IANTT, CC*, I-100-122. The Portuguese had purchased sixty-two slaves on 1 April 1526 and sixty-seven slaves on 9 March 1526 in Goa where there was a slave market. See, *IANTT, CC*, 2a-132-109, *CC*, IIa-132-8. At Kannur the Portuguese had bought 108 slaves on 12 March 1526. See, *IANTT, CC*, IIa-132-19, IIa-132-20.
21. On 23 August 1522, Arab slaves in Chaul were employed in the galleys. See *IANTT, CC*, II-103-74. On 17 September 1527, four Gujarati slaves were employed in sailing. See *IANTT, CC*, II-103-150.
22. Barbosa, *The Book of Duarte Barbosa*, vol. 2, p. 125: See also Janette Pinto, *Slavery in Portuguese India, 1510-1842*, Bombay, 1992.
23. 'Apontamentos de Miguel Vaz para Dom Joao III and written from Evora during November 1545, published in Georg Schurhammer and E.A. Voretzsch, *Ceylon Zurr Zeit Jess Konigss Bhuvaneka Bahu und Franz Xaviers*, 1539-52, 2 vols, Leipzig, 1928, vol. 1, p. 48.
24. *DI*, vol. 2, pp. 123-31. See Silva Rego, *Documentação*, vol. 7, doc. no. 13, p. 32.

25. *IANTT*, *Chancelaria de Dom João III*, fl. 108v. Melaka received as many as 343 slaves, both male and females, between 26 March 1512 and 25 February 1514.
26. Issac Comelein (ed.), *Begin ende Voortangh vande Verenigde Nederlandsche Geoctroyerde Oost-Indische Compagnie, Vervat tende de Voor naesmste Reysen, hi} de in Woonderen der Selve Provincien Derwaerts Gedaen,* 2 vols, Amsterdam, 1646 (hereafter *Begin ende Voortangh*), vol. 1, p. 34 (1603).
27. H.T. Colenbrander and W. Ph. Coolhas (eds.), Jan Piertsz, Coen, *Beschedien Omtrent Zijn Bedriif in Indie,* 8 vols, S. Gravengahe, 1919-1953 (hereafter Coen, *Beschedien)*, 7, p. 306 (5 December 1617).
28. *Begin ende Voortangh*, vol. 1, p. 59.
29. *DI*, vol. 5, doc. 97, p. 665.
30. *Coen*, *Beschdien*, III, 209. See the letter of Coen to Van Uffelen in Coromandel dated 22 July 1622.
31. Lotika Varadarajan, *Memoirs*, p. 1070.
32. *GM*, vol. 1, pp. 121 and 131.
33. *Coen*, *Beschiedin*, III, 281-2; see *DR*, 1624-9, 33 (2 March 1624) and 99 (20 November 1624).
34. S. Arasaratnam, 'Slave Trade in the Indian Ocean in the Seventeenth Century', in K.S. Mathew (ed.), *Mariners, Merchants and Oceans*, Delhi, 1995, pp. 195-208, especially see p. 201.
35. *RFG*, DACB, 1687, pp. 6-7; Lotika Varadarajan, *Memoirs*, p. 1070.
36. Denys Lombard, *Memoires d' un Voyage aus Indes Orientales: Un Marchand Normand a Sumatra,* Paris, 1996, pp. 129-30.
37. *HAG*, *MDR*, Livro 19c, 67-70/5-2, fls. 95-6.
38. *IANTT*, *DRI*, Livro 56, fl. 221.
39. *GM*, III, pp. 335-55. See also *GM*, II, p. 791.
40. *RFG*, *DACB*, 1678, p. 136. In September 1687, 665 slaves were registered for export from Madras. An export duty of 1 *pagoda* on each slave was levied. See Love, *Vestiges* vol. 1, pp. 545-6. A considerable amount of profit was derived from the sale of slaves at Aceh. See, *RFG*, *DACB*, 1687, pp. 6-7; see also Lotika Varadarajan, *Memoirs*, p. 1070.
41. According to the books of account, a sum of 32 *pagodas*, 29 *panams* was collected for registering slaves in Madras. See *DACB*, 1678, p. 156.
42. *RFG*, *DACB*, 1678, pp. 61-2.
43. K.A. Nilakanta Sastri, 'Shivaji's Charter to the Dutch on the Coromandel Coast', *Proceedings of the Indian History Congress*, Calcutta, 1939, pp. 1156-65.
44. João de Barros, *Da Asia*, decada III, pt. I, ch. I, Cap. IX.
45. *RCI*, no. 115 & 97.

46. Biblioteca Academia das Ciencias de Lisboã (BASCL) Mss *Cartas do Japão*, vol. 1, fl. 249-255, 22v-27.
47. Schurhammer, St. Francis Xavier, vol. II, p. 549.
48. Letter of Leonel de Sousa to Infante Dom Luis dated 16 January 1556, in *IANTT*, *Gavetas*, pt. IIa, Maço 10, no. 15. See Silva Rego, *As Gavetas do Torre do Tombo*, vol. 1, pp. 910-15, Lisboã, 1966; BA, Mss *Jesuitas na Asia*, 49-1V-50, fl.460.
49. BPADE, Evora, Codice, CXV/2-1, Livro 18, fl.155; Manuel Texeira, *The Portuguese Missons in Malacca and Singapore, 1511-1598*, vol. 1, Lisboã, 1967, p. 348. See in BASCL, *Enformação de alguma Coisas de... Reyno da China, Cartas do Japão*, vol. 1, fls. 249-55.
50. *IANTT*, *Coleção São Vicente*, vol. 10, fl. 128.
51. *APO-CR*, fasc. I, pt. 2a, doc. 5, pp. 61-74.
52. *IANTT*, *Coleção São Vicente*, vol. 10, fl. 128.
53. Letter of Viceroy Dom Duarte de Menezes dated 28 January 1588, *APO-CR*, vol. 3, pt. 1a, p. 123, 3 August 1591; *APO-CR*, vol. 3, pt. 1a, pp. 328-9.
54. *APO-CR*, fac. I, pt. 2a, doc. 5, pp. 64 and 69; *HAG*, *MDR* (AD 1585-89), Livro 3A, Codice 13-15, fl. 1; *IANTT*, *Coleção São Vicente*, vol. 10, fl.128; Diogo do Couto, *Decada*, 10, 1, 425; and 10, 11, 116; *APO-CR*, fasc. I, pt. IIa, doc. 5, pp 61-74: see also Hay, *Derebus Iaponicus et Pervanis*, Antwerp, 1615, p. 835. *IANTT*, Mss *Convento da Graça* (AD.1598) tomo CX3, 7. L, pp. 1-4; AGS, *Secretarias Provinciales*, Mss no. 1550, fl. 670-689v.
55. *APO-CR*, fasc. III-I, doc. 33, p. 116.
56. *APO-CR*, fasc. III, 24, X, 140; *HAG*, *MDR*, no. 3a, 56-58, fl. 5.
57. *IANTT*, Mss *Convento da Graça*, tomo CX 3, VI-L, pp. 1-4. AGS, *Secretarias Provinciales*, Codice 1479, fl. 258v.
58. The Chinese mention Mylapore as Mai-la-pu. George Philip, 'The Seaports of India and Ceylon', *Journal of the China Branch of the Royal Asiatic Society*, vol. 19, pt. 1, 1884, pt. I, p. 222.
59. BNL, *Relação de Algumas cousas deste Estado da Índia Pelo Capitania de Meliapore*, Mss, Fundo Geral, 7150, doc. 14.
60. AGS, Codice 1551, fl. 121; BFUP, XIV, doc. 149, p. 575.
61. Duarte Barbosa, *The Book of Duarte Barbosa*, op. cit., pp. 196 and 207; Tome Pires, *The Suma Oriental*, vol. 1, pp. 161 and 227; João de Barros, *Da Asia*, op. cit., decada I, pt. II, p. 174.
62. Danvers and Foster, *Letters Received by the English*, vol. 2, p. 337.
63. *IANTT*, *Manuscritos da Livraria*, Mss 1104, fls. 97-8.
64. Pires, *The Suma Oriental*, vol. 1, p. 98; Barbosa, *The Book of Duarte Barbosa*, II, p. 152; Marcelo de Ribandeneira, *Historia de las islas del archipelgo y reyno dela grand China tartaria Cochin-China, Malaca, Siam, Camboxa y Iappon*, Barcelona, 1601, II, p. 171.

65. Barbosa, *The Book of Duarte Barbosa*, 2, p. 153.
66. R.H. Major, *India is the 15th Century*. See *The Travels of Nicolo Conti*, p. 78.
67. Fernão Queyroz, *The Temporal and Spiritual Conquest of Ceylon*, translated by S.G. Pereira, Colombo, 1930, p. 1194.
68. Duarte Barbosa, *The Book of Duarte Barbosa*, vol. 2, pp. 77-8, 132, 162.
69. Pires, *The Suma Oriental*, vol. 2, p. 272.
70. S. Arasaratnam, *The Dutch Power in Ceylon*, Amsterdam, 1958, p. 448.
71. Manuel Barradas, *Descrição da Cidade de Colombo*, Lisboã, n.d., p. 290. Adelino de Almeida Caldão, *Livro que trata das India edo Japao'*, p. 39; Tikri Abyesinghe, p. 9; Tome Pires, *The Suma Oriental*, vol. 1, p. 83.
72. Heeres and Stajul, *Corpus*, vol. 1, pp. 83-5.
73. *ARSI*, *Litterae Annuae Provinciae Malabarensis*, letter of Fr. B. Coutinho to Fr. Acqua Viva, dated 4 November 1606 written from Santhome.
74. *ARSI*, *Litterae Annuae Provinciae Malabarensis*, letter of Fr. Albert Laerzio to Fr. Alvarez, dated 20 November 1608, written from Kochi.
75. Silva Rego, *Documentação Para a Historia*, vol. 9, p. 237.
76. *IANTT*, Mss. *DRI*, 1612, doc. 326, p. 424.
77. *HAG*, Mss. *Livro de Segredo* (hereafter *LS*), Livro 1, 1/5, fl. 2.
78. *HAG*, *MDR*, Livro 12, 15/3/4.
79. Bulhão Pato, *DRI*, vol. II, p. 226.
80. *HAG*, *Registo de Cartas de D.João de Azevedo Para el Rei*, letter no. 16, in *MDR*, Livro 12, 54-56/6-2, fls. 169-72.
81. Ranvers and Falter *Letters Received by the English East India Company from its Servants in the East*, vol. 5, p. 39.
82. *IANTT*, Mss *DRI*, 1613, doc. 342 (dated 7 March 1613).
83. William Methwold, *Relations of Golconda in the Early Seventeenth Century*, London, 1931, p. 3.
84. *IANTT*, Mss *DRI*, Livro 9, fl. 5.
85. *NA*, *OBP*, VOC 1066, fls. 170-1 (dated 8 May 1617).
86. *HAG*, *MDR*, letter no. 109 (dated 4 January 1616) in Livro 12, 54-56/6/2, fls. 217-18.
87. Bulhão Pato, *Documentos Remetidos*, vol. 5, doc. 1114, p. 190; *IANTT*, *DRI*, Livro 11, fls. 576-80.
88. Ibid., vol. 3, doc. 502, pp. 189-91; *IANTT*, *DRI*, Livro 8, fl. 233.
89. *BNL*, Mss Codice 1816, fl. 162.
90. Bulhão Pato, *Documentos Remetidos*, vol. 4, doc. 937, p. 265; vol. 3, doc. 574, p. 288; vol. 4, p. 254.
91. Ibid., vol. 10, pp. 303-4, 320-3.
92. *HAG*, *MDR*, Livro 18, fl. 134.

93. *BNL*, Mss Codice 1975, fls. 351-351v (3 January 1622).
94. *HAG*, *MDR*, Livro 19, fl. 9v.
95. Silva Rego, *DRI*, vol. 10, pp. 134-5.
96. *HAG*, *MDR*, Livro 18, fl. 133.
97. *HAG*, *MDR*, Livro 19, fl. 56v.
98. *HAG*, *MDR*, Livro 21, fl. 33.
99. Bibliotheca Nacional de Madrid, Spain (hereafter *BNM*), Mss Codice no. 2352, fl. 417.
100. *NA*, *OBP*, VOC 1070, fls. 288-9 (27 November 1619).
101. *HAG*, *MDR*, Livro 17, fl. 48v.
102. *HAG*, *MDR*, Livro 12, 14/1/3, fls. 29-30.
103. *HAG*, *MDR*, Livro 18, fl. 134.
104. *BPADE*, Mss, Codice CV/2-7, fls. 70-1v.
105. *HAG*, *MDR*, Livro 24, fl. 347.
106. *BNL*, Mss Codice 1975, fls. 108v-109. See, *ACE*, vol. 1, p. 190. In order to overcome the mounting expenditure of the *Estado da Índia*, it was ordered on 8 February 1624 by the viceroy of Goa that all persons engaged in business would not be paid salaries on government account.
107. *HAG*, *MDR*, Livro 26, fl. 394.
108. *HAG*, *MDR*, Livro 26, fl. 162.
109. *MPJA*, *Litterae Annuae*, 1630.
110. *HAG*, *MDR*, Livro 27, fl. 34.
111. *HAG*, *MDR*, Livro 29, fl. 80.
112. See, *ACE*, vol. 1, doc. 128, p. 401.
113. *ACE*, vol. 14, doc. 17, p. 47.
114. *ACE*, vol. 2, doc. 8, pp. 504 and 514.
115. *BNL*, Mss *Fundo Geral*, 7640, fls. 60-62v; see *ACE*, vol. 2, p. 508 (13 July 1634).
116. *BNL*, Mss. *Fundo Geral*, 7640, Decada 4; *BPADE*, Codice CV/2-7, doc. 20, fl. 60.
117. *IANTT*, *DRI*, Livro 32, fl. 9.
118. *LS*, Livro 1, 2/2, fl. 2v.
119. *LS*, Livro 1, 2/2, fl. 3.
120. *HAG*, *MDR*, Livro 13-B, 5-6/3-2.
121. *ACE*, vol. 3, doc. 12, p. 480 (26 May 1646).
122. *HAG*, *Regimentos e Instruções*, 1640-6, no. 4, fl. 166v. C.R. Boxer, *Portuguese India in the Mid-Seventeenth Century*, Bombay, 1980, p. 40.
123. *ACE*, vol. 2, doc. 138, p. 381.
124. *LRV*, Livro 1, 22/3/4, fls. 54-54v. In 1619, Andre Coelho, the Portuguese Captain of Nagapattinam, was even felicitated by Fernao de Albuquerque, the Portuguese Governor (1619-22), for capturing a Dutch ship that had sailed near Nagapattinam.

125. *IANTT*, Mss *DRI*, Livro 51, fl. 118 (22 May 1642); *DRI*, 48, fl.118 (20 December 1643).
126. *MPJA*, *Litterae Annuae*, 1642.
127. *HAG*, *MDR*, Livro 51, fl. 118. See also *IANTT*, *DRI*, Livro 51, fl. 12 (20 December 1642).
128. *ACE*, doc. 142, p. 393.
129. *MPJA*, *Litterae Annuae*, 1642
130. *ACE*, doc. 166, p. 440.
131. *IANTT*, *DRI*, Livro 56, fl. 128.
132. *ACE*, vol. 2, doc. 140, p. 255.
133. *IANTT*, *DRI*, Livro 55, fl. 532.
134. *MPJA*, *Litterae Annuae*, 1648.
135. *IANTT*, *Chancelaria de Dom Filippe I*, Livro 15, fls. 434-434v.
136. Letter of Miguel Ferreira to D. João de Castro, dated 26 June 1546, written from Santhome of Mylapore in Sanjay Subrahmanyam, *Improvising Empire*, pp. 245-6; see also the Annual Letter of Francisco Cabral written from Goa on 17 December 1594, in *DI*, vol. 16, pp. 750-1.
137. *HAG*, *MDR*, Livro 3B, 52-55/2.
138. *HAG*, *MDR*, Livro 8, 15-17/3/2.
139. *ARSI*, *Litterae Annuae Provinciae Malabarensis*, Letter of Fr. M. Roiz to Fr. Alvarez, dated 1 November 1606, written from Santhome of Mylapore.
140. *ARSI*, *Litterae Annuae Provinciae Malabarensis*, 1606-7.
141. *IANTT*, *Chancelaria de D. Filippe I*, Livro 25, fl. 130.
142. *IANTT*, *Chancelaria de D. Filippe II*, Livro 20, fls. 177v-178. Gaspar Dias Cordoso was appointed as *ouvidor* of Santhome for a period of six years. See, *Chancelaria de D. Filippe II*, Livro 16, fl. 113v. We find that Duarte Figureido Pinto was appointed *ouvidor* of Santhome city for a period of six months vide an order issued from Goa dated 16 May 1718. See *HAG*, *LRV*, no. 8, fl. 72.
143. *HAG*, *MDR*, Livro 8, Codice 15/12/3.
144. C.R. Boxer, *Portuguese India in the Mid-Seventeenth Century*, Bombay, 1980, p. 13.
145. Letter of Dom Jeronymo de Azevedo, the viceroy of India, to the king of Portugal, written from Goa in December 1613, in Bulhão Pato, *Documentos Remetidos*, vol. 3, p. 284.
146. Henry Heras, *The Aravidu Dynasty of Vijayanagara*, Madras, 1927, vol. 1, p. 577.
147. *HAG*, *MDR*, Livro 12, fl. 72.
148. *HAG*, *MDR*, Livro 12, 14/1/3.
149. *ACF*, vol. I, doc. 52, fls. 59v-60 (14 May 1616).
150. *BL*, London, *Additional Manuscripts*, no. 28432, fl.10 (18 December 1599).

151. *HAG*, *MDR*, Livro 8, 48/1/5.
152. Ibid.
153. *APO-CR*, pp. 228-36 (25 March 1589).
154. Abner Cohen, 'Cultural Strategies in the Organisation of Trade Diasporas', in C. Meillassux (ed.), *The Development of Indigenous Trade and Markets in West Africa*, London, 1971. He describes the concept of trade diaspora as interrelated commercial networks of a nation socially interdependent but spatially dispersed communities. See also Philip D. Curtin, *Cross-Cultural Trade in World History*, Cambridge, 1984. He has examined Jakhanke's commercial activities in the Senegambia region.
155. Fernand Braudel, *Capitalism and Civilization, 15th-18th Centuries: Perspectives of the World,* Sian Reynolds (trs.), 3 vols., London, 1981-4, pp. 22, 24-5.
156. K.N. Chaudhuri, *Trade and Civilization in the Indian Ocean*, Cambridge, 1985, p. 224.
157. *HAG*, *LS*, Livro 1, 21/4; fl. 52v.
158. *Letters Received by the English East India Company from its Servants in the East*, vol. 3, p. 264.
159. *IANTT*, Mss *DRI*, Livro 30, fl. 39v (1635).
160. *NA*, *OBP*, VOC 1066, ff. 113-17. See the report of the Captain of Santhome, dated 5 June 1617, regarding trade with the Dutch.
161. *IANTT*, *DRI*, Livro 35, fl. 105.
162. *IANTT*, *DRI*, Livro 48, fls. 109 and 338.
163. *IANTT*, *DRI*, Livro 54, fl. 208.
164. *IANTT*, *DRI*, Livro 56, fls. 125 and 138.
165. *NA*, VOC, no. 671.
166. *HAG*, *ACE*, vol. 2, doc. 9, p. 13 (1644).
167. Nicolao Manucci, *Storria do Mogur*, vol. 3, p. 206; *RFG*, *DACB*, 1686, p. 55.
168. *RFG*, *DACB*, 1668, p. 14; Lotika Varadarajan, *India in the Seventeenth Century: Mémoirs of François Martin*, Delhi, 1984, p. 235.
169. *RFG*, *DACB*, 1686, p. 55; Lotika Varadarajan, *Memoirs*, p. 235.
170. *DR*, see the entry dated 28 December 1679.
171. *NA*, *OBP*, VOC, no. 1163, ff. 205r.
172. Frank Lequin, *Het Personnel Van de Vereneigde Oost Indische Compagnie in Azie in de Achtiende Euw Meer in Het Bijzonder in Bengalen*, 2 vols., Leiden, 1982.
173. *DR*, 1643, p. 127.
174. *RFG*, *Public Consultations,* entry dated 29 February 1675-6; see Talboys Wheeler, *Madras in Olden Times: A History of Presidency,* Madras, 1861, p. 674. See Appendix 1.
175. *RFG*, *DACB*, 1678-9, pp. 165-6; see, Talboys Wheeler, *Early Records of British India*, London, 1878, pp. 50 and 57.

176. Lotika Varadarajan, *Memoirs,* vol. 1, pt. I, p. 360.
177. Ibid., p. 158.
178. *IANTT, CC,* 11-49-24 (1514); *IANTT, Cartas Orientais,* no. 59, summary is available in Portuguese; Sanjay Subrahmanyam, *Improvising, Empire,* p. 233.
179. *OIOC,* G/14, *Cuddalore and Porto Novo 1681-1687;* Sanjay Subrahmanyam, *Improvising Empire,* p. 203.
180. George Bryan Sousa, *The Survival of Empire: Portuguese Trade and Society in China and South China Sea, 1630-1754,* Cambridge, 1986. See Table 5.6, p. 121; see also, *RFG, DACB,* 1675-81.
181. Lotika Varadarajan, *Memoirs,* p. 374.
182. *DACB,* 1687, p. 44.
183. James C. Boyajian, *Portuguese Trade in Asia Under the Habsburgs, 1580-1640,* Baltimore, 1993, pp. 225-6, 241-2.
184. Love, *Vestiges of Old Madras,* vol. 1, p. 35.
185. *RFG, DACB,* 1678-9, pp. 116-17.
186. *RFG, DACB,* 1681, pp. 56-7.
187. Quiason, *English Country Trade with the Philippines, 1664-1765,* Quezon City, 1966, pp. 36-7. See for details on the survival of the Portuguese trade on the west coast in Celsa Pinto, *Trade and Finance in Portuguese India: A Study of the Portuguese Country Trade, 1770-1840,* Delhi, 1994.
188. *OIOC,* G/19, *Fort. St. George, 1655-1750;* Quiason, *English Country Trade,* pp. 42-4.
189. Quaison, *English Country Trade,* pp. 68-70, 79.
190. Alfred Martineau, *Memoirs de Francois Martin,* vol. 3, Paris, 1932-4, p. 385.
191. *Correspondance du Conseil Superieur de Pondichery et de la Compagnie, 1726-1730,* ed. A. Martineau, Pondicherry, 1920, tomo I, p. 15.
192. *RFG, DACB,* 1719-54. See also Sousa, *The Survival of Empire,* Table 6.14.
193. Alfred Martineau, *Memoirs de Francois Martin,* vol. 3, p. 343.
194. Bibliotheque Nationale de Paris, Mss. *Nouvelle Acquisitions* (hereafter *NOA*), no. 9354, *Compagnie des Indes—Memoire au Sujite du Commerce General des Indes Orientates par Guillaume Fevrier, 1738.*
195. BNP, *NOA,* Mss. 9354, Martineau, *Memoirs de Francois Martin,* p. 354.
196. *NA,* VOC 666 (2 July 1643); *NA, BUB,* VOC 867, fl. 493.
197. RFG, *DACB,* 1707-13. See also Sousa, *The Survival of Empire,* Table 6.2.
198. *RFG, DACB,* 1715-33. See also Sousa, *The Survival of Empire,* Table 6.5.

199. *HAG*, *LVR*, no. 5, fl. 84v.
200. *RFG*, *Public Consultations* (hereafter *PC*), 20 August 1707.
201. *HAG*, *LVR*, no. 8, fl. 93v (17 January 1720).
202. *RFG*, *Despatches to England*, 1714-18, 3-7 January 1717, para 30, p. 106; see, 17 August 1717, para 45, p. 115. See also *Despatches from England*, 1715-18, 8 January 1718, para 47, p. 108.
203. *PC*, vol. 74, pp. 109-13 (8 March 1744).
204. *RFG*, *Country Correspondence* (hereafter *COCO*), vol. 1, pp. 46-7.
205. *OIOC*, *Madras Public Consultations* (hereafter *MPC*), vol. 73, pp. 172-6.
206. H. Dodwell, *A Calendar of the Madras Records, 1740-1744*, Madras, 1917, pp. 126-7; H. Dodwell, *Calendar of the Madras Despataches, 1744-1755*, Madras, 1920, pp. 204 and 378.
207. *OIOC*, *Public Despatches to England*, vol. 13, pp. 3-70.
208. *BPADE*, Mss codice CXVI/1-37, ff. 1-34; Frederick Price, and K. Rangachari, H. Dowwell, *The Private Diary of Ananda Ranga Pillai, 1736-1761* (hereafter *ARP Diary*), 12 vols. (rpt.), Delhi, 1985, vol. 2, p. 214. See also S. Jeyaseela Stephen, 'Maritime Trade between Tamil Coast in South India and Thailand: An Analysis of New Archival data in Europe and India (AD 1624-1760), in *Proceedings of the Sixth International Conference on Thai Studies*, vol. 7, Chiang Mai, 1996, pp. 209-18.
209. *ARP Diary*, vol. 6, pp. 347-8.
210. James C. Boyajin, *Portuguese Trade in Asia Under the Habsburgs, 1580-1640*, Baltimore, 1993, p. 7.
211. Vitonm Maghalcs Godinho, *Les Finances de etat Portugais des Indes Orientales (1517-1635)*, Paris, 1982.
212. Sanjay Subrahmanyam, *The Portuguese Empire in Asia: A Political and Economic History*, London, 1993.

7

Spices, Metals, Precious Stones and Bullion Imports: The Changing Shape of the Tamil Economy

In the medieval period, merchants from the Tamil coast developed overseas trade contacts with South-East Asia then known as Suvarna Bhumi. According to South-East Asian sources, the Chetti merchants from the Tamil coast are known to have discovered the gold mining areas in South-East Asia which resulted in the import of gold in abundance. Pepper, cloves, nutmeg and mace produced in the Moluccas, Banten, Amboina, Ternate, Tidore, Makian, Motir and Bacan were brought to the port of Melaka by Malay and Javanese merchants who exchanged them for textiles from the Tamil coast. It is reported that as many as thirty varieties of textiles were sold by the Chettis, the Arabs and Tamil Muslims in various South-East Asian markets in return for spices.[1] Thus, along with bullion, spices also found their way to the Tamil coast during the medieval period. Trade in other luxury items was also carried on through contacts with China before the arrival of the Portuguese. It is to be seen whether the same pattern of overseas trade continued after the arrival of the Portuguese and how actively they were involved in the import trade during the sixteenth and seventeenth centuries.

Cloves from the Moluccas, Amboina and Makassar

Clove (*lavangum* in Tamil), the flower of the plant *caryophyllum aromaticum,* grew naturally in the Moluccas. The earliest evidence of Portuguese interest in cloves may be traced to 2 March 1514. Affonso de Albuquerque, the Portuguese viceroy of India, ordered Rui de Araujo, the Factor in Melaka to send 50 quintals of cloves to Kochi every year so that a sufficient quantity of the spice could be exported to meet the demand in Lisbon.[2] Nayinar Suriya Deva, one of the principal Tamil merchants of Melaka, was therefore granted *cartazes* by the Portuguese Captain of Melaka to sail to the Moluccas to procure the required quantity of cloves. The cloves thus collected from Moluccas were exported from Melaka via Pulicat to Kochi and finally to Lisbon. Ships of the Hindu merchants were hired by the Crown to bring bulk quantities of spices and silk on their return voyages from Melaka.[3] Crown voyages from the Coromandel to Moluccas via Melaka between 1545 and 1550 was also highly profitable.[4] Many Portuguese aspired to the post of Captain so that they could become actively involved in the Coromandel-Melaka-Moluccas Crown voyages since they were so lucrative. Individuals like Gabriel de Ataide, Manuel de Vasconcelos, Maria Pinheiro, João Ferreira, Vicente de Lagos and Isabel de Pina petitioned their king to be allowed to undertake commercial voyages citing reasons of poverty, death in battle, marriage expenses of their sons and daughters, etc. The king of Portugal, therefore, found it convenient to issue orders for regulating these voyages so that they could serve as a source of revenue to the exchequer.[5]

The Dutch also secured the help of some Portuguese traders, like Pero de Ataíde, to promote their trade in Java. Ataíde assisted the Dutch to purchase spices without the knowledge of Javanese merchants to avoid any opposition.[6] As the finer varieties of cloth from the Coromandel coast were in great demand all over South-East Asia, the Portuguese were eager to monopolize the trade. Hence they took every step to prevent the Dutch from making inroads into their own sphere of influence.[7] The difficulties encountered by the Dutch and the English in the Coromandel coast were so overwhelming that in 1611 they were forced to obtain cloth from the Surat region. The textiles of Gujarat were found suitable only for bulk trade.[8] On 28 February 1612 the Portuguese being ordered the capture Hindu merchants and their ships in South-East Asia engaged in supplying cloves to the Dutch.[9] Further, the Dutch soon realized that the Portuguese had a monopolistic hold over the cloth trade in the Coromandel region. The Portuguese *naus* continued to impede the Dutch from gaining a foothold in the textile trade in Pulicat.[10] It was only in 1616 that the Dutch understood the significance of the Portuguese Coromandel textile trade with South-East Asia. The Portuguese carried on their textile trade by diverting their capital meant for the acquisition of precious stones in Coromandel.[11] The approval of the *conselho da fazenda* (Revenue Council) in Goa was obtained for diverting the capital.

The Portuguese planned to make the Dutch presence in Moluccas untenable by preventing them from making purchases of textiles from the Coromandel coast.[12] Further, the Tamil merchants were in turn warned that their ships would be burnt if they helped the Dutch in clove trade.[13]

The cloves imported into the Coromandel were also sent to the interior places of India for resale at a very high margin of profit.[14] So much so that Francisco Pelsaert, a traveller of the early seventeenth century (1627) mentions that the price of cloves in the Coromandel ports was only 1.80 *florins* per pound whereas it sold at 3.84 *florins* in Agra.

Trade between the Coromandel and the Moluccas was so interdependent that in 1612 Henrick Brouwer, the Dutch official in Japan, described the Coromandel coast as the left arm of the Moluccas. This was because the Dutch realized that without the textiles of the Coromandel, there could be no business with the Moluccas.[15]

The Dutch were also interested in the clove trade and since 1612 had also followed the Portuguese practice of entering into contracts with suppliers. Even the prices at which textiles were to be exchanged for cloves were mentioned in these contracts.[16] However, according to Van der Hagen, the Dutch Factor in Java, the conditions imposed upon the natives by the Dutch in the clove contracts in the seventeenth century were four times more severe than those laid down by the Portuguese in the sixteenth century.[17] Therefore there was severe competition between the Portuguese and the Dutch to obtain cloves from the Moluccas.

Amboina, another chief centre for the supply of cloves, also received textiles from the Coromandel coast. Trade with Amboina was conducted via Melaka which was the redistribution centre for Coromandel textiles. Portuguese commercial contacts with Amboina received a boost following the appointment of

António Pais as Captain in Amboina in 1562.[18] A letter from Dom Sebastião (1557-78), the king of Portugal, written in March 1565 to Dom António de Noronha, the viceroy, stressed the importance of Amboina and proposed the construction of a factory there. He was also requested to procure cloves in Ternate, which would increase the profit from the trade in cloves.[19] However, the assassination of Sultan Hairun of Ternate at the instigation of the Portuguese Captain Diogo Lopes de Mesquita triggered a native revolt against the Portuguese in 1575. The Portuguese had to restrict their trading activities in Amboina to cloves.

In due course of time the export of textiles from the Coromandel to Amboina continued and increased with the construction of a fortress in 1591 by the Portuguese at Amboina.[20] Textiles, particularly from Santhome, continued to be exported in exchange for cloves.[21] However, the arrival of the Dutch in India in 1595 to explore the possibility of procuring Coromandel textiles from the Pulicat region hastened the decline of the Portuguese clove trade as the Dutch, began to corner the textile products of the Coromandel.

According to Portuguese sources, sixty *corjas* (packets) of *beatilhas* (fine plain textiles) were purchased from Pulicat at the rate of 15 *xerafins* per *corja* from the local agents for export to Amboina. Similarly, the value of thc export cargo in 1598 was estimated at 3,192 *xerafins*.[22] However, with the fall of the Portuguese forts in Amboina and Tidore in 1605, the Portuguese clove trade virtually collapsed.

There were also reports of sailings from Makassar in the island of Sulawesi to Nagapattinam by the Portuguese in 1625 to fetch cloves from there. Cloves were brought in large quantities to Makassar till about 1632.[23] The merchants from Makassar paid 100 *reals* per *bahar* of cloves at Ceram in the region surrounding Makassar.[24] In 1635, the price of cloves in the Coromandel was only 1.50 *florins* per pound and this was much cheaper than in the previous year (1627) when it was sold for 1.75 *florins* per pound.[25] The reason was that many of the ships that had sailed from Nagapattinam had brought huge quantities of cloth to Makassar. This trade in cloves continued even in 1637. It is reported that two ships were engaged in the Makassar trade in cloves based at Nagapattinam. Table 31 shows that ships sailed

TABLE 31: RECORDED SHIPPING FROM NAGAPATTINAM TO MAKASSAR, 1644-52[26]

Year	Arrival	Departure
1644	–	1
1645	1	–
1646	1	2
1647	1	–
1649	2	–
1651	1	1
1652	1	2

regularly from Nagapattinam between 1644 and 1652 and brought cloves from Makassar for export to Portugal.

Thus the clove trade between Makassar and Nagapattinam continued till 1651-2. Thereafter, the trade was conducted on a smaller scale until the Portuguese were expelled from Makassar in 1669.[27]

Pepper from Aceh

Pepper was another commodity produced extensively in the Indonesian archipelago. The island of Sumatra too had many extensive pepper groves. Jambi was one of the main centres where pepper was traded. Pepper was treated as an item of royal monopoly and sailings for procuring pepper were in Crown ships and the private ships of the Portuguese. According to the *Novo regimento para o trato de pimenta e de outras especiarias* (New sailing orders issued towards signing pepper contracts and other spices)[28] issued from Evora city on 1 March 1570, the king of Portugal started granting permits for such voyages from the Coromandel in order to encourage Portuguese trade in spices and also to help them to compete effectively with the Arabs. The ships of the Coromandel and Portuguese merchants, which sailed from Nagore and Nagapattinam to Aceh to procure pepper and other spices, were therefore readily given permits by the Portuguese Captain of Nagapattinam because the Crown was interested in procuring it at Nagapattinam itself rather than undertaking voyages.

It would be appropriate to Let us examine how the new liberalized regulations helped the Portuguese consolidate their pepper trade. Although the Portuguese discovered the Cape route they did not succeed initially in impeding the trade carried on by the Arabs in the Red Sea region before the first half of the sixteenth century. The bulk of the pepper was obtained in Malabar.[29] A Portuguese ambassadorial mission arrived at the court of the sultan of Aceh in 1593 with a view to secure a foothold there for their pepper trade. However, it was not successful since the sultan was not in favour of the Portuguese purchasing pepper in Aceh.

The king of Portugal ordered the viceroy in Goa on 24 March 1605 limit the contracts for the export of textiles from the, Coromandel to the exchange of pepper and cloves in South-East Asia.[30] The contracts thus executed under the above said orders indicated the price at which the textiles were to be exchanged for pepper.[31] Following the decline of Melaka as an important trading port towards the end of the seventeenth century, Portuguese merchants diverted their commercial contacts to Aceh.[32] It may be recalled that Sumatra, ruled by the Muslim sultan, was famous for the special variety of its long pepper.[33] The Portuguese policy during this period was aimed at capturing the trade in pepper and spices from the hands of the Muslim traders chiefly based at Aceh. Voyages from Nagapattinam to Kedah were given a meagre sum of 1,000 *cruzados*.[34] Private Portuguese traders based at Nagapattinam were also encouraged to trade with all the ports of South-East Asia when the commerce of Melaka declined. This was done by granting concessional permits for voyages from the Coromandel to Kedah.[35] Nevertheless, Portuguese efforts to capture the pepper trade from the Muslims in Aceh did not succeed, primarily because the Portuguese at that time had no customs house at Kedah which could exercise some control over the trading activities of private Portuguese merchants there.[36] Another reason was that Kedah, besides being a Muslim sultanate, was located far away from Aceh on the opposite side of the Melaka coast, rendering it difficult for the Portuguese to exercise effective control over Aceh.

Having learnt that the Muslim traders were actively engaged in a flourishing pepper trade with Mecca, the king of Portugal issued an order in 1585 to the viceroy at Goa, asking him to impede the overland commerce in pepper and other spices carried on by the Arab traders with West Asia.[37] Instructions were also issued to attack the ships engaged in the pepper trade between Aceh and the Coromandel.[38] The sultan of Aceh, however, granted special privileges in 1586 to Muslim traders engaged in the pepper trade between Aceh and the Coromandel.[39] Thus the pepper trade of the Arabs flourished up to 1598. It has been estimated that the volume of pepper reaching Jeddah from South-East Asia at the end of the sixteenth century was more than the quantity of pepper exported by the Portuguese to Lisbon.[40]

It is evident from Portuguese records of 1603 that textiles continued to be exported from Santhome in exchange for pepper from South-East Asia.[41] According to another record dated 10 October 1615, the Marakkayars of Kunimedu and Nagore sailed in two ships carrying white cloth and *pintados* (painted cloth) from the Coromandel to Aceh to exchange for pepper.[42] On 24 November 1615 more ships from Kunimedu and Nagapattinam arrived at Aceh to buy pepper.[43]

Tension between the Portuguese and the Danes was also building up since the arrival of the latter (20 November 1620) at Tranquebar (Tharangambadi) very close to the Portuguese port of Nagapattinam.[44] The Danes too were interested in the lucrative pepper trade. The Bishop of Mylapore, in a letter dated 2 September 1624, stated that the Danes had sent two *naus* to the port of Tennaserim to procure pepper which came from Aceh.[45] In 1629, however, the Portuguese were able to drive away the Acehnese forces that besieged Melaka. The Portuguese were thus able to consolidate their position in Melaka and improve their trade with the Coromandel coast.[46]

According to Portuguese sources, pepper was available in plenty at Nagapattinam.[47] Thus there was no need to sail all the way to South-East Asia during this period. This in a way helped the Portuguese concentrate on procuring cloves from the Moluccas. The viceroy of Goa, with a view to keeping the Dutch away from Aceh, sent Francisco de Sousa de Castro on a peace mission to the sultan of Aceh, but he was murdered there by the sultan in 1638. This permanently sealed the fortunes of Portuguese trade in pepper with Aceh.[48]

Nutmeg from Banten

The port of Santhome of Mylapore had direct commercial contacts with Banten in Java during the rule of King Maulana Yusuf (1550-80). The Banten islands produced nutmeg (*sathikkai* in Tamil) which was exchanged for textiles from the Coromandel. The *shahbandar* of Banten was a Hindu who had originally migrated from Mylapore.[49] He had a Javanese title and his name was Kiayi Vijayamangala.[50] He owned several ships and became very rich through his cloth trade.[51] Another Chetti merchant, also a native of Mylapore, served as an interpreter in the court.[52]

From a reference dated 1604 we learn that there were Tamil merchants from the Coromandel coast serving as officials in Banten.[53] The *shahbandar* of Banten encouraged Tamil merchants as he held the monopoly for the purchase and sale of the cloth that came from the Coromandel. Besides, in 1608 a royal tax of 8 per cent called *ruba ruba* (anchorage duties) was collected by the shahbhandar on the ships that came to Banten from the Coromandel to load nutmeg.[54] English records indicate that some quantity of cloves was also bartered in exchange for Santhome textiles in Banten.[55] There was fierce competition between the Portuguese and the Dutch. The Portuguese seized 23 bales of painted cloth and 200 sacks of rice from a Dutch ship sailing from the Coromandel which was to be exchanged for nutmeg in Banten.[56]

The Dutch intensified their cloth purchases in the Coromandel coast to undermine the Portuguese textile business with Banten since nutmeg was available only there.[57] Sensing the impending threat, the Portuguese devised new plans to counter the Dutch onslaught. So fierce was the Portuguese competition that in 1614 the Dutch had to sell the Coromandel cloth at a much lower price than they had paid for it in the Coromandel, in order to purchase nutmeg in Banten.[58]

Cinnamon from Sri Lanka

Cinnamon was available in the kingdom of Kotte ruled by Bhuvaneka Bahu (1521-51). Kotte covered the area of Jaffna and Kandy in Sri Lanka. The Portuguese maintained strict vigilance over vessels sailing in the Bay of Bengal so as to ensure that no cinnamon was carried by native merchants. Portuguese merchants were permitted to trade in cinnamon but had to pay the necessary dues to the Portuguese Crown, failing which they were liable to pay a duty of 10 per cent. If any cinnamon was found in the native ships coming from Sri Lanka to the Coromandel, the entire stock of merchandise was seized by the Captain of the Coromandel coast. One-third of the value of the cargo was paid as reward to the informant or to the person who made the seizure.[59] When Dharmapala, Bhuvaneka Bahu's successor was converted to Christianity in 1557, he reserved the export of cinnamon from Sri Lanka as strictly a royal monopoly of the Portuguese Crown.

Even in the seventeenth century the Portuguese continued to trade in rice with Kandy in exchange for cinnamon.[60] Paddy cultivated in the Vellar riverine basin attracted private Portuguese traders who began to engage in rice trade from Porto Novo from where the rice was chiefly exported to areas where there was a shortage.[61] Textiles also were sent from the Coromandel coast in exchange for cinnamon. In 1602 traders in Bengal were prohibited to export rice or to procure cinnamon from Sri Lanka.[62] Ships caught trading in cinnamon illegally were ordered to be plundered at sea. The Portuguese Captains of Santhome and Nagapattinam were also ordered, in the meanwhile, to impede and prevent the natives of the region from carrying merchandise to Sri Lanka in exchange for cinnamon.[63] In a letter to the Portuguese viceroy in Goa, dated 26 February 1605, the king of Portugal said that the inhabitants of Sri Lanka were depending upon the supply of rice from Nagapattinam and he ordered that necessary instructions to be given to the Portuguese Captain in Nagapattinam to arrange to send the rice.[64] Rice, therefore, continued to be exported from Nagapattinam to Sri Lanka in 1618 in exchange for cinnamon.[65]

Portuguese traders were encouraged to sail in their own vessels from Nagapattinam and Santhome taking rice to Sri Lanka to obtain as much cinnamon as possible. In 1630, seven vessels of private Portuguese traders in the Coromandel exchanged rice for cinnamon.[66] The private traders of Nagapattinam who were engaged in rice trade during 1635 had brought such large quantities of cinnamon that its sales in Nagapattinam went up in one day alone (2 February 1635) to the tune of 50,000 *pagodas*.[67] It is noticed that at this time (in 1636), the daughters of Manuel Ledo and Cosmo Ledo, then living in Nagapattinam, loaned funds to one Francisco de Lima who was trading in cinnamon using his own ship.[68] The viceroy of India, in his letter dated 19 February 1636, reported to the king of Portugal that he had given instructions to the Captain of Nagapattinam to send the largest possible quantity of rice to Sri Lanka in order to purchase all the cinnamon available there.[69] The business in cinnamon was so profitable that even some Portuguese traders like Francisco de Brito de Almeida, a *casado* living in Sri Lanka, came forward to supply cinnamon to the Dutch who had promised him a higher price even though the Dutch were regarded as the enemies and competitors of the Portuguese. The Portuguese viceory of Goa ordered the Captain of Nagapattinam on 1 September 1637 to tighten surveillance because many ships were illegally trading in cinnamon.[70] Whatever the nature of trade, whether legal or illegal, abundant quantities of cinnamon were brought from Sri Lanka and was sold in Nagapattinam. The Portuguese, however, failed to stop the clandestine trade in cinnamon with the Coromandel.

Precious Stones from Burma and Sri Lanka

Rubies, topazes and emeralds formed the most important items of export from Pegu where they were available in abundance. These precious stones reached the port of Pulicat from Cosmin (Rangoon in modern Myanmar) in the early sixteenth century.[71] A letter written by António Dinis on 15 August 1516 highlights this flourishing trade and mentions that four or five ships carried textiles from Pulicat and returned with a cargo of rubies.[72] Khwaja Ali, the famous merchant who operated from Pulicat, made regular voyages to Pegu to buy emeralds, topazes and rubies.[73] The Portuguese, who established contacts with Pegu in 1519, were permitted by the king to settle there and carry on trade from the ports of his kingdom.[74] The Portuguese at this time also realized the importance of the port of Kunimedu on the Coromandel which received precious stones from the port of

Martaban on the Burmese coast.[75] António Dinis, who was appointed as the Portuguese Factor of Martaban made serious efforts to organize regular overseas commerce with the ports of the Coromandel coast.[76]

Since precious stones were brought to the port of Pulicat, Devikapuram in the hinterland of Pulicat emerged as a jewel-trading centre. Tirupati also became another famous trading mart in precious stones, where these gems were donated to the temple. Thiruvaiyaru in the hinterland of the port of Nagapattinam was also a jewel-trading centre in the southern stretch of the Coromandel coast.[77]

The rise of Pegu and its trade in precious stones coincided with the decline of the ports of Cosmin and Martaban. The people of Pegu did not know how to cut and polish the precious stones. These stones were therefore brought to Pulicat where there were excellent craftsmen to do the cutting.[78] The stones then finally found their way to the city of Vijayanagara where there was a capital market for jewels, gems and precious stones in the sixteenth century.[79] The jewel trade attracted many merchants and some Portuguese private traders like João Moreno who conducted overseas trade with Pegu from the port of Pulicat.[80] The Portuguese did not have their own trading factory at Pegu.[81] Those traders who desired to avoid the payment of heavy port duties were therefore encouraged to trade with Pegu from the Coromandel. Some Portuguese traders like Diogo de Almeida and Boas Varela illegally traded with Pegu after holding clandestine negotiations with the native merchants of the Coromandel from the port of Santhome.[82] The imposition of a tax called *bulibuliao* (special tax) at Melaka from the ships that came from Santhome, however, diverted the trade to Pegu.[83] The Portuguese Captain of Melaka therefore sent a fleet to watch the ports on the Pegu coast where the Coromandel ships traded by avoiding Melaka. This mission, entrusted to Manuel Falçao, did not, however, succeed in preventing the merchants from Pulicat from directly visiting the ports of Pegu.[84] The Viceroy of Goa had to issue orders forbidding certain private Portuguese traders, like Gabriel de Ataíde, to sail from Santhome to Pegu.[85] However, the Coromandel Pegu trade in precious stones continued to flourish owing to the heavy demand for jewels in the Vijayanagara city during the first half of the sixteenth century.

There is one repeated instance of a ship of Khwaja Marakayyar sailing illegally from the port of Nagapattinam to Pegu without obtaining a *cartaz* from the Portuguese Captain of Nagapattinam.[86] When this was brought to the notice of the Captain, he cancelled the permits granted to other Marakkayars. The Portuguese merchants continued to conduct regular voyages to Pegu from the port of Santhome. Many Santhome-based Portuguese traders felt emboldened to trade illegally because the viceroy of Goa had little effective control over Santhome. In another instance, in 1547 even a writer of the Portuguese factory at Santhome was accused of giving faked *cartazes* for illegal voyages to Pegu.[87]

The Italian traveller Cesare Federici even attests to annual sailings from Santhome to Pegu.[88] A ship is reported to have left for Pegu in September from Santhome. The merchants returned to Santhome from Pegu with rubies received in payment since precious stones were very cheap there.[89] The absence of heavy taxes and the availability of precious stones encouraged the merchants to participate in the Coromandel–Pegu trade during this period.

The Vijayanagara empire provided the perfect setting for the promotion of the jewel trade with Pegu. According to Gaspero Balbi and Cesare Federici, Coromandel merchants visited the port of Cosmin to procure rubies. Merchants from Santhome of

TABLE 32: RECORDED SHIPPING FROM THE COROMANDEL TO PEGU, 1541-57[90]

Period	Name of the port	No. of ships
1541	Pulicat	1
1543	Santhome	4
1545	Pulicat	1
1546	Santhome	1
1547	Santhome	6
1548	Santhome	1
1554	Santhome	1
1557	Santhome	5

Mylapore and Goa often stayed there for the whole season to complete their business transactions.[91] Buyers and sellers decided upon the price for rubies by touching their knuckles, with their hands held under a covered cloth.[92] This was chiefly done to maintain secrecy in their transactions. This system of bargaining was not rigid, because even after arriving at a price and paying it, the buyers were at liberty to change their mind and would receive a full refund without any deductions.[93] Absolute honesty in dealings was accepted as the very foundation of the jewel trade. There were several brokers called *tharagu* who were impeccably honest in arranging transactions between buyers and sellers.[94]

Towards the second half of the sixteenth century, there was a significant shift in the trade between Santhome and the port of Pegu as the Coromandel merchants were no longer interested in selling their textiles in exchange for rubies. Instead they demanded precious metals like silver or gold.[95] This change can be attributed to the destruction of Vijayanagara city in 1565. This great event signalled the decline of the jewel trade in south India.

Although voyages to Pegu from the Coromandel ports brought large profits, the merchants started to encounter difficulties towards the end of the sixteenth century. Prince Naresuan's (1590-1605) activities led to Siam becoming an independent kingdom, free from the suzerainty of Burma in 1591. The king of Portugal therefore prohibited Portuguese trade with Pegu from Santhome and Nagapattinam.[96] These orders were issued in the larger interest of maintaining a healthy relationship with the rulers of Siam. The war between Pegu and Arakan continued up to 1598, during which period the Portuguese viceroy in India maintained the status quo, preventing Portuguese trading with Pegu from the ports of the Coromandel.[97] Even the *cartazes* granted to individuals like Mathias Caravalho Ferreira to carry on official voyages from Santhome to Pegu were ineffective. But Ferreira's son João Ferreira da Costa requested the king of Portugal to permit him to undertake the voyage later.[98] The private Portuguese traders of Santhome and Nagapattinam, however, did not obey the royal orders very strictly but continued their trade in precious stones with Syriam in the Irawaddy delta.[99]

When the political conditions improved in the seventeenth century in the lower Burma region, trade in precious stones between Syriam in the kingdom of Arakan and Santhome began to flourish. All *navios* which came to buy Chinese goods from the Coromandel coast first visited Syriam and only then went on to Tennaserim. In 1608 the Portuguese Captain imposed a penalty on those ships that failed to visit Syriam in 1608. Therefore the ships of the Coromandel first touched the port of Syriam and then reached Tennaserim, where they paid the duty and unloaded their cargo in the port.[100] In 1613, the fleet of Mendonça continued to provide the necessary protection to the *navios* of Santhome and Nagapattinam sailing towards Syriam to trade in precious stones.[101] As trade began to flourish between Santhome and Syriam, the Bishop of Santhome, on 2 December 1613, expressed his opposition to the reopening of the Portuguese factory in Syriam. He stated that it was too early to take any decision as political disturbances might erupt once again. At this juncture Portuguese merchants of Santhome of Mylapore requested the king of Portugal in 1613 to permit them to start their trade in precious stones with Pegu.[102] The king therefore granted, in 1614, to the Portuguese traders a voyage each to Pegu, Mergui and Trang at very concessional rates. This is evident from the Table 33.

The aim of granting these voyages was to develop the trade in precious stones and to increase the royal income in the face of the Dutch competition in the Coromandel. Santhome of Mylapore's trade in jewels with Pegu faced problems after 1615 owing to the disturbed political conditions in Pegu.[103] Peter Floris, a traveller of that period (1614-15), lamented that the failure of ships to arrive from Arakan on the eastern coast of India had caused a rise in the price of rubies and diamonds.[104] The residents of

TABLE 33: SALE OF CONCESSIONAL VOYAGES, 1614[105]

Voyage	Purchaser	Amount in *xerafins*
Santhome–Pegu	Henrique de Sousa	366.66
Coromandel–Mergui	António Gonçalves	401.66
Coromandel–Trang	Martim Costa	573.33

Mylapore, who were anxious to trade with Pegu, wrote to the king of Portugal from Santhome on 29 December 1621 asking for permission to trade in precious stones with Pegu.[106] As permission was not forthcoming, they sent another petition on 2 July 1634 seeking sailing permits for voyages to Pegu in an attempt to revive the trade.[107] The next year (1635) only one voyage was undertaken between Pegu and Santhome.[108]

Precious stones such as sapphire, rubies, topazes and semi-precious stones from Sri Lanka also found their way to the Coromandel during the early sixteenth century.[109] Precious stones from Sri Lanka, with their sparkle and transparency, had a higher value than the stone from Pegu. Duarte Barbosa, the Portuguese traveller, mentions that high prices were quoted for the perfect rubies and precious stones. Those that were damaged or were of a dull colour were sold at a lower price.[110] The trade in precious stones between the Coromandel and Sri Lanka flourished up to the fall of Vijayanagara city in 1565. With a view to substitute the declining trade in precious stones with Sri Lanka, the Portuguese purchased quantities of cat's eye found in the *nayakdom* of Madurai. However these stones were not as good.[111]

Diamonds of South India

Three famous diamond merchants lived in Santhome, namely, Lucas Luís de Oliveira, Alvaro Cacela do Vale and António Ferreira. They went from Santhome to Golconda to purchase diamonds which came from the various mines of the kingdom of Golconda. The octroi collectors of the sultan of Golconda did not place any impediment in their way and these Portuguese traders travelled without fear and trouble.[112] The diamond trade at Santhome attracted even some German merchants like Hippe Escudo who left Goa to settle down in Santhome with his family in 1620. He travelled to Golconda and purchased diamonds and traded with Antwerp in Europe.[113]

Salvador Rodrigues was another important trader who invested large sums of money in procuring diamonds from the Golconda mines and exported them to England in a ship which left on 17 August 1683. Further, in 1684, many Portuguese traders like Bastião Rodrigues, Domingos de Costa, and Alvaro de Fonseca also left the ports of the west coast and settled in Santhome to engage in the diamond trade.[114] As the *Estado da Índia* levied heavy taxes on those Portuguese merchants who were engaged in the trade of diamonds, these traders moved over to settle in Madras.

The English port of Madras became a centre for Portuguese merchants after the capture of the town of Santhome by the Golconda forces in 1662. The Portuguese viceroy of Goa wrote a letter to the English governor of Madras on 29 April 1666 requesting protection for the Portuguese, and also to Fr. João Dias de Miranda.[115] Many rich Portuguese traders migrated from Santhome and were invited by the English to build houses in Madras. These rich traders of Santhome were happy to live under the protection of the English guns. The Portuguese population thus strengthened the English settlement of Madras between 1662 and 1678.[116]

Rich Portuguese merchants like João Perreira de Faria, Cosmo Lourenço de Madeira and Lucas Luís de Oliveira who migrated and lived in Madras were held in high esteem by the English Company and were presented with honours since they had brought prosperity to the English settlement. Many Portuguese private merchants traded in diamonds associated with their own family members. António Martins and his brother Diogo Martins were famous diamond traders and they received payment in cash from England in exchange for exporting diamonds. Another family of Portuguese diamond traders, Bartholomeu Rodrigues and his brother Diogo Rodrigues, migrated from Santhome in 1683 to reside at the port of Covelong (Kovalam) near Mahabalipuram. They travelled extensively in south India purchasing diamonds which they exported to England from the port of Madras.[117] Bartholomeu Rodrigues was also engaged in the coral trade in 1687.[118] João Perreira de Faria, a former merchant of Santhome, bought rubies and sold them to the English East India Company in Madras for export to England.[119] Samuel de Castro and David Lopez Fernandez were also engaged in the export of diamonds and corals to England from Madras.[120] The Portuguese merchants were therefore encouraged by the authorities of the English East India Company in Madras who provided them with financial assistance whenever they needed capital for their diamond business. João Perreira and Lourenço de Madeira were given 800 *pagodas* by the English Company in Madras for the purchase of diamonds. These Portuguese traders had to pawn their property or furnish other securities to obtain loans.[121] Further, the English in Madras also gave a concession on customs duties to traders like João Perreira for a period of ten years in Madras, until March 1681.[122]

Gold Import from Melaka

As early as 1506, the Portuguese had come to know that the Coromandel merchants brought considerable amounts of gold from Melaka.[123] Tomé Pires, the Portuguese traveller (1512-15), has mentioned the various kinds of gold which was available in Melaka which the Chettis bought there. These Chetti merchants, who purchased gold in *kattis* from Melaka, brought it to the Coromandel as it was an important item of import to the Coromandel. Tomé Pires further mentions that the purity of gold at that time was measured by the unit value of *mate* (*maathu* in Tamil).[124] The price of one *mate* of gold was valued at 3 *cruzados*. In 1540, each *katti* of gold was exchanged at Melaka for goods worth 200 *cruzados* and sold for 280 *cruzados* at Pulicat.[125]

Table 34 shows that the poorest quality of gold came from Brunei. The Chetti merchants of the Coromandel coast purchased gold mainly from Melaka. They preferred to buy only gold of purity of 9½ and 10½ (*patharai maathu* in Tamil) in *mates*. A separate duty of four *cruzados* on a gold *katti* was imposed.[126] The gold bazaar at Tirupati received gold from Melaka via the port of Pulicat.[127]

The gold mined from the Minangkabau region in Sumatra was brought to Melaka in large quantities, and, according to one report, the Portuguese Captain in charge of the Coromandel received 12,000 *cruzados* in freight which he took in gold. The *vedor da Fazenda*, in his letter dated 17 February 1547, complained about this to the king of Portugal explaining that the ship brought no revenue to the king.[128]

According to English sources, gold from Aceh also came to the Coromandel in 1603.[129] Huge imports of gold from South-East

TABLE 34: CENTRES OF GOLD IMPORTS FROM SOUTH-EAST ASIA AND THEIR STANDARD OF PURITY, 1512-15[130]

Gold imports from	Standard of purity ranged between (in *mates*)
Lawe	7-7½
Java	8-8½
Pahang	8-8½
Minangkabau	9
Cochin China	9½
Brunei	4½-6

Asia to Santhome necessitated the payment of increased duty at Santhome. Therefore, the people of Santhome wrote to the king on 2 March 1626 to reduce the duty as they also had to pay duty on gold purchased in Melaka.[131] The king ordered that a 2 per cent duty was to be levied on gold and other precious metals brought to Nagapattinam and other ports on the Coromandel Coast.[132]

Gold continued to be imported from Melaka inspite of the additional duty collected at the port of Santhome. José Pinto Ferreira, the *vedor da fazenda* and Diogo Rasquinho, the writer in Goa, obtained gold, which was available in plenty, from Santhome of Mylapore in the year 1629 for minting purposes at the *Casa da Moeda* (Mint) that functioned in Goa. Luís Mendez, the accountant of the Santhome factory, made the entries of transfer of gold from Mylapore to Goa and he issued the certificates and other documents prepared in connection with this transaction.[133]

In 1631 ships from Melaka which arrived at Nagapattinam brought gold in *kattia* worth 12,000 *pagodas*.[134] In 1635, 105 *marcs* of gold found their way to Santhome from Melaka, as recorded by Vicente Roiz Caravalho, the scribe of the Portuguese factory in Santhome of Mylapore. According to the account books of the customs house (dated 3 February 1635), 404 *xerafins*, 1 *tanga* and 3 *reis* were collected as duty on gold imports alone. The gold imported to Mylapore brought revenue to the Portuguese factory enabling it to pay the salaries of the officials.[135] Gold was always in great demand at this time in the

Tamil Coast since *pagodas,* which were in circulation, were minted from gold.

Import of Silver

Portuguese chroniclers have mentioned ports on the Siam coast where silver and tin were available in plenty. There were regular trade contacts as early as 1506 between the port of Mergui on the Siamese coast and the port of Pulicat on the Coromandel.[136] Great amounts of silver, lead and tin were sent to the ports of the Coromandel from the interior regions of Laos and Pegu.[137] Trading in these items was developed by the Chettis and Marakkayars in 1511 by concentrating their attention on the ports of the Bay of Bengal.[138]

Coromandel merchants, particularly the Chettis continued their trade with Siam in silver, tin and lead. They paid an export duty which was two-ninths of the value of these metals to the king of Siam.[139] Duarte Fernandes, the first Portuguese envoy, was received by the king of Siam, Ramathibadi II (1491-1524), in Ayuthia in October 1511. The Siamese ambassador carried to Goa jewels and other precious gifts to be sent by the Portuguese viceroy to the king of Portugal in Lisbon.[140] In 1518, the Portuguese were allowed to settle down in Siam and to trade at Ayuthia, Pattani, Mergui and Tennaserim. A treaty was signed between Duarte Coelho and the king of Siam in 1518.[141] Later, the king of Siam waived the payment of all duties by the Portuguese in the ports of Siam for a period of three years as in 1528 the Portuguese had helped him in his victory against Chiang Mai.[142]

Silver from China coming into Melaka in 1547, also found its way to the Coromandel.[143] Trade between the Coromandel and Siam was dominated by the native merchants in the first half of the sixteenth century. When Ayuthia, the capital of Siam, was captured by the Burmese in 1569, trade with Siam was much affected.

A new alignment took shape during 1576-7 and we find the Portuguese traders seeking the help of Tamil merchants to obtain silver from Tennaserim. Although Francisco de Aguilar owned ships, records dating to 1580 show that he always sailed to

Tennaserim in the company of Marakkayyar merchants.[144] Voyages were undertaken from the port of Nagapattinam by a union of Marakkayar merchants.[145] The privilege granted to António da Cova, a *fidalgo,* was avidly grabbed by the Marakkayars. The Captain of Nagapattinam was also able to increase his own private income from the profits made through these voyages as he was given a separate share.[146]

The Portuguese Captains at Nagapattinam therefore took care to personally supervise the loading operations of the Marakkayars vessels. However, between 1595 and 1599, the Portuguese residents at Nagapattinam protested against such interference by the Captain, leading to a breach of the peace in Nagapattinam.[147] Complaints were lodged with the king of Portugal against the supervision because it was not a part of the duties assigned to the Portuguese Captain. Later, when the system of granting privileges for sailings was abolished, the position of the Captain of Nagapattinam became less important.[148]

The Portuguese in the Tamil coast also tried to collect silver from Japan. Trade in silver was not successful owing to piracies. This prompted Jeronimo de Azevedo, the viceroy of India (1612-17), to order that the silver-laden ships of the Portuguese returning from the Far East were not to ply in the open seas without proper escort. On the other hand, the Viceroy feared that not sending ships to Japan could result in the trade in silver falling into the hands of the Dutch. It was therefore resolved that warships would be used to conduct trade to guard against piracy at sea.[149]

Permits for voyages to China and Japan were given, besides other assistance, to individuals in Mylapore in consultation with the local municipal council. This stipulation was enforced with effect from 31 March 1625.[150] The regulation further stipulated that a sum of 5,000 *taels* of silver should be given to Jeronimo Coutinho, the Portuguese resident in Mylapore, towards his share as he held the right through auction to collect customs duties. Dom Jeronimo Coutinho in the town of Mylapore obtained the privilege to undertake voyages to Japan and Manila in 1634. He had made a further agreement with Affonso de Morais, who was then living in Maçâo, to facilitate trade between Mylapore and Maçâo.[151] The Portuguese Captain of Maçâo therefore gave priority to voyages to China and Japan. The Portuguese officials of Mação also introduced a system under which 5,000 *taels* of silver were collected from each sailing towards the cost of the fortification of Mylapore.[152] Silver from as far away as Mexico and Peru reached the ports of the Coromandel coast via Manila because the Portuguese were so eager to trade in precious metals.[153]

Import of Copper and Other Metals

A few early seventeenth-century Portuguese records refer to the trade in copper which was chiefly used for making guns and cannons.[154] The king of Portugal, Filippe I (1580-98), instructed Mathias de Albuquerque, the Portuguese viceroy in India (1591-7), to ensure that all merchants and Portuguese Captains who sailed to China brought back as much copper as possible from there. In response to this, the viceroy of India stipulated that custom duties were not be collected in cash but in an equivalent amount of copper.[155] In view of the threats faced by the *Estado da Índia* from the Dutch, in 1608 the viceroy ordered the Coromandel armadas and seven warships to provide protection to the ship of Mação as it was bringing a rich cargo from China and Japan.[156] Considerable quantities of copper were brought from the ports of Japan and China to Mylapore. Ships brought as much as 100,000 *picos* (Chinese weight) of copper to Manila. The Spanish governor of Manila, however, was very concerned about the dangers faced by the ships, especially from pirates.[157]

Other metals imported to in Devanampattinam included lead, sulphur, alum and quicksilver from Sumatra and Borneo.[158] Between 1681 and 1686 the Portuguese in Nagapattinam were also engaged in the bullion trade with Manila.[159] The port of Manila in Philippines imported silk from Mação. Japan exported silver to Mação and Manila. Therefore, many Portuguese traders from the Coromandel were eager to trade with Manila. Tokugawa Shogu Iemitsu (1623-51) closed the country to foreign traders and the bullion trade with Japan came to an end. In 1656 all kinds of maritime trade with China was also prohibited. This policy was adopted to prevent anti-Manchu activities and to avoid Ch'eng-Kung raids in collaboration with foreign traders.

Maritime trade with China could be resumed only thirty years earlier, in 1690. But by this time the Dutch had settled at Deshima (1641-1853) and taken complete control of the bullion trade.

Establishment of the Mughal Mint in Santhome of Mylapore

A mint was established by the Mughals in 1702 in Mylapore.[160] As the English suspected (24 December 1706) that counterfeit *panams* were being minted there they carried out searches to detect the origin of the counterfeit *panams* at the toll collection centres but did not find any. Therefore they banned the circulation of Mughal coins minted in Mylapore for the purpose of trade in Madras. In 1708 Sunku Rama Chetti, the head of the Komati Chetti merchants was given the right by the Mughal *faujdar* of Santhome in 1708 to mint *panam* and *kasu*.[161]

The Council of Fort St. Geroge in Madras twice (in 1724 and 1727) prohibited the export of gold and silver from Madras to Mylapore.[162] This was done to prevent a fall in the mint revenue and to deny the Mughal mint from getting enough silver from Madras. The native merchants and *saraffs* of the region continued to evince interest in the bullion trade which seriously affected the English Company forcing it to lift the ban on the export of gold and silver from Madras to Santhome in 1729.[163]

As the Santhome mint functioned very well, it proved to be a constant threat, and also the main source of trouble in commerce, to the English Company in Madras. Imam Sahib, the Comptroller of Revenue of the nawab of Arcot, encouraged the Madras-based merchants to get their gold converted into *pagodas* of 81½ touch at the Santhome mint. To encourage wider circulation of money the nawab ordered the mint on 5 May 1744 to issue rupees of 12 diot. Those who were working in the mints bribed the *sarkar* officials and the *sarkar* minters in Santhome who persuaded the nawab to prohibit the coining of rupees in Madras by the English and in Pondicherry by the French.[164] Further, it is recorded that some men of Amin Beg, the *faujdar* of Santhome, stole some machinery from the mint of the English East India Company for melting gold and silver. The English official who discovered the theft, stopped these men from travelling from

Madras to Santhome.[165] The thieves were whipped and punished.[166] According to records, Dost Ali Khan, the nawab of Arcot, ordered the closure of the Santhome mint in 1744 owing to economic and political problems.[167]

The shift from 'bullion for goods' to the 'goods for goods' model and eventually to the 'goods for goods' and 'cash' model occurred when bullion came into wider circulation through the long-distance trade conducted by the Portuguese who imported bullion to the Tamil coast. There was a dramatic change in the situation in the early seventeenth century when the Portuguese and the VOC scrambled to acquire bullion and spices. The Portuguese were never able to monopolize the pepper trade. Moreover, the overland pepper trade conducted by the Arabs could not be stopped. The bullion for goods model introduced by the Portuguese and the Dutch did not work for very period owing to the non-availability of adequate quantities of gold and silver.

In the seventeenth century, the Portuguese Crown trade was on the decline as attention was diverted to fight the Dutch in the Bay of Bengal region. It can be said that the Portuguese had realized very early and very quickly the importance of gold imports from Melaka to the Tamil coast. Silver and copper imports to the Tamil coast happened much later. The trade in precious stones from Pegu and Sri Lanka was very brisk. However, with the opening of direct trade with China from the Coromandel, the Portuguese imported large quantities of silver and copper from China and Japan to the Coromandel. There must have been an equilibrium between the bulk goods that were exported from the Coromandel ports and the bullion that was imported from the East Asian countries. The Portuguese trade in bullion and precious stones was affected after the fall of the Portuguese settlements into the hands of the Dutch. Although the official Portuguese trade in bullion disappeared in the 1670s when the Dutch, the English and the French appeared on the Coromandel coast, some private Portuguese merchants continued to conduct trade in bullion and precious stones. The concept of portfolio capitalism had provided some scope for work in the seventeenth century[168] however, it cannot be applied to all major or rich merchants. With the development of the capitalist system big business magnets emerged and they tried to monopolize the market, but such features are absent in the case of Tamil merchants such as Khwaja Marakkayar trading with China and South-East Asia in the sixteenth century. These Marakayyars were not peddlers or insecure men but remained wealthy merchants. It was they who continued to bring more bullion along with the Portuguese who also became importers of bullion in the seventeenth century.

NOTES

1. Tomé Pires, *The Suma Oriental of Tomé Pires and the Book of Rodrigues*, vol. 2, Delhi, 1990, p. 272.
2. Raymundo António de Bulhão Pato, *Cartas de Affonso de Albuquerque*, vol. 7, Lisboã, 1888, p. 116.
3. Correia, *Lendas*, cap. X, tomo I, pt. I, p. 739; João de Barros, *Decades Asia*, doc. I, p. II.
4. *IANTT*, *CC*, I-76-112; I-82-1; Schurhammer, *St. Francis Xavier*, vol. 2, p. 81; vol. 3. pp. 341 and 604; Silva Rego, *Documentação*, vol. 4, no. 38, p. 200, *IANTT*, *Cartas dos Vice-Reis da India*, no. 154.
5. *IANTT*, *Coleção São Vicente*, XVII, fl. 24.
6. *IANTT*, Mss *Convento da Graça*, CX 6, tomo II, fls. 219-20.
7. *DRI*, vol. I, pp. xix, 165 (2 January 1608); *DRI*, vol. 3, p. 71 (4 February 1613).
8. M.A.P. Meilink Roelofsz, *Asian Trade and European Influence in the Indonesian Archipelago between 1500 and about 1630*, The Hague, 1964, p. 186.
9. *IANTT*, *DRI*, Livro 4, fl. 144.
10. *HAG*, *MDR*, Livro 12, fl. 218v.
11. *ACF*, vol. 1, pp. 40-1. The conquest of the free port of Banten by the Dutch took place in 1682.
12. *DRI*, vol. 3, p. 373 (6 February 1616).
13. *DRI*, vol. 1, p. 126 (2 April 1612); *DRI*, vol. 2, p. 229 (16 December 1614), *NA*, *Overgekoemen Brievien en papiern uit Batavia* (hereafter *OBPB*),VOC 1617, III, fl. 211 (22 October 1615).
14. *HAG*, *MDR*, Livro 22, fl. 63v. Large quantities of cloves were obtained by the Portuguese as mentioned in a correspondence dated 22 February 1625.
15. F.C. Danvers and William Foster, *Letters Received by the English East India Company, from its Servants in the East*, vol. 1, p. 72; Heert Terperstra, *De Nederlanders in Voor-Indie*, Amsterdam, 1947, p. 40; *HAG*, *Monções do Reino*, Liv.10, fl.286.
16. Heeres and Staple, *Corpus Diplomaticum Neerlando Indicum*, The

Hague, 4 vols, 1907-53. See, vol. 1, pp. 528-31, see the treaty of 1649 with Tiku Piraman and Indirapura.

17. Rofsolez, *Asian Trade and European Influence*, pp. 213-14.
18. Sebastião P. Gonçalves, *Primeira parte da historia dos religiosos da companhia de Jesus*, Atlantida-coimbra, 1962. That the importance of the Coromandel textiles was realized by the Dutch in the Moluccas during the seventeenth century is well known. See, Heert Terpstra, *De Nederlanders in Voor Indie*, Amsterdam, 1947, p. 40.
19. Letter of the king of Portugal to the viceroy written from Almeirim, dated 14 March 1565, in Hubert Jacob (ed.), *Documenta Malucensia*, 3 vols, Rome, 1974-84, vol. 1(1542-77), pp. 461-2.
20. *BNL*, *Fundo Geral*, Codice 8570, fl. 275v.
21. Danvers and Foster, *Letters Received by the English East India Company*, vol. 1, p. 70.
22. *BNL*, *Fundo Geral*, Caixa 207, no. 90, fls. 1-2v.
23. *GM*, vol. 1, p. 309 (6 January 1632).
24. Ibid., p. 614 (9 December 1637).
25. Tapan Raychaudhuri, *Jan Company in Coromandel*, p. 194.
26. Sousa, *Survival of the Empire: Portuguese Trade and Society in China and South China Sea, 1630-1754*, Cambridge, 1986, see Table 5.1.
27. *GM*, vol. 2, p. 498 (1 December 1651). The demand for cloves so outstripped the supply that the prices shot up from 300 to 400 *reals* per *bahar* of cloves.
28. António da Silva Rego, *Documentação*, vol. 4, pp. 90-1.
29. Godinho, *Os Descobrimentos e a Economia Mundial*, vol. 3, Lisbon, 1963-71, pp. 10-11, 73-5.
30. *HAG*, *MDR*, Livro 6B, fls. 13-14/5/3.
31. Letter of the Captain of Ternate António de Brito to the king of Portugal, dated 11 February 1523, *IANTT*, *Gavetas*, 18-6-9; Basilio de Sa, *Docurrentação*, vol. I, no. 20, p. 132.
32. *APO-CR*, Fas. III, pt. 2a, doc. 204, pp. 568-83.
33. *IANTT*, *CC*, Ia-11-50 (1512).
34. Mendez da Luz, 'Livros das Cidades', in *Boletim da Biblioteca*, vol. 21, 1953, pp. 90-1.
35. Basilio de Sa, *Documentação*, vol. 4, pp. 90-1 (March 1570).
36. Ibid., vol. 4, pp. 90-1.
37. The sultan of Aceh asked for permission to open a factory at Jeddah for the sale of pepper. In 1588 he also gave an oath in a mosque that he would not be friendly with Christians, B. Jorge de Lemos, *Historia de Cercos de Malaca* , Lisboã, 1982.
38. *BFUP*, vol. 2, p. 230; for details see *Bibliothéque Historique de la Marine* (hereafter *BHDM*), Paris, Codice Mss 109, no. 7, fls. 182-4.
39. *IANTT*, Mss *Convento da Graça*, CX 3, VI-L, p. 205 (18 January 1598).

40. C.R. Boxer, 'The Portuguese Reaction to the Revival of Red Sea Spice Trade and the Rise of Atjeh', 1540-1600, *Journal of South East Asian History*, vol. 10, no. 3, 1969, pp. 415-28.
41. A letter written from Goa dated 6 April 1604, *IANTT*, *Coleção São Vicente*, vol. 12, pp. 115-18.
42. Danvers and Foster, *Letters Received by the English*, vol. 4, p. 6.
43. Ibid., vol. 2, p. 334.
44. *IANTT*, Mss *Convento da Graça*, caixa 6, tomo II, p. 315.
45. *BNL*, Codice 1814, fl. 90.
46. Sanjay Subrahmanyam, *Portuguese in Asia*, p. 164.
47. António Boccaro, *Livro das Plantas* in *APO-BP*, pt. 2, pp. 1-2.
48. Denys Lombard, *Le Sultanate d' Atjeh au Temps d' Iskandar Muda, 1607-1636*, Paris, 1967, pp. 233-5.
49. Keuning, *De Tweede Schipvaart,* 7 vols, The Hague, 1938-47, vol. 1, p. 4; see Claude Guillot, Hasan and Jacques Dumarcay, *The Sultanates of Banten*, Jakarta, 1990, pp. 12-13.
50. Hoasein Djajadiningrat, *Critische Beschowing Van de Sejarah Banten Bijdrage ter Kenschetsing Van de Javaansche Geschiedschrijuing*, Haarlem, 1913, *Sejarah Banten*, 24, 2.
51. Ibid., *Sejarah Banten*, 27.
52. Ibid.
53. William Foster, *The Voyage of Sir Henry Middleton to the Moluccas, 1604-1606,* London, 1943, p. 124.
54. *NA*, VOC, no. 962.
55. W.Ph. Coolhas, *GM*, vol. I, p. 298; Danvers Foster, *Letters Received by the English*, 6 vols, London, 1896-1902, vol. 1, p. 72.
56. Lotika Varadarajan, *Memoirs,* p. 343.
57. *NA*, *Overgekomen Brieven en Papieren Uit Batavia* (*OBPB*), VOC 1616, III, fl. 3 (25 July 1615).
58. F.C. Danvers and W. Foster, *Letters Received by the English*, vol. 2, p. 269 (2 January 1614).
59. Tikri Abyesinghe, *A Study of Portuguese Regimentos on Sri Lanka at the Goa Archives*, Colombo, n.d., p. 8.
60. Lotika Varadarajan, *Memoirs*, p. 155.
61. *IANTT*, *DRI,* Livro 30, fls. 281v-282.
62. See the royal letter to the viceroy, 24 March 1605 in *HAG*, *MDR*, Livro 6B, 13-14/5/3.
63. See the letter dated 26 February 1605, in *HAG*, *MDR*, Livro 6B, 23/3-5.
64. Lotika Varadarajan, *Memoirs*, p. 1573.
65. *BNL*, *Fundo Geral*, Mss. 7150, doc. 4, fls. 97-8.
66. *HAG*, *MDR*, Livro 14, 54/1/3.
67. *HAG*, *MDR*, Livro 19A, 26/3-5.

68. *HAG*, *Livro de Segredo* (hereafter *LS*), Livro 1, 6/1, fl. 12v (16 April 1636).
69. *IANTT*, Mss, *DRI*, Livro 33, fl. 251v.
70. *HAG*, *LS*, 1, 7/4-5, fl. 17.
71. Duarte Barbosa, *The Book of Duarte Barbosa*, vol. 2, pp. 129-32.
72. L.F.F.R. Thomaz, *De Malaca a Pegu Viagens de um Feitor Portugues 1512-1515*, Lisbon, 1966, pp. 187-92.
73. *IANTT*, CC, I-77-18, fl. 2v.
74. Manuel Texeira, *The Portuguese Missions is Malacca and Singapore*, vol. 2, London, 1967, p. 71.
75. Barbosa, *The Book of Duarte Barbosa,* op. cit., vol. 2, pp. 157-8.
76. L.F.F.R. Thomaz, *De Malacca a Pesu*, pp. 187-92.
77. An unpublished inscription from the east Rajagopuram entrance at the left side of the Thiyaga Perumal temple at Tiruvaiyaru, records the sale of pearls and pavalam. The text runs as follows. *Sevappa nayakkar kattalai ittapadi ana- indu purva desathil pala raga muthu pavalam valayal mani vikkkuradukku* (line 3).
78. Barbosa, *The Book of Duarte Barbosa*, vol. 2, pp. 217-18.
79. Sanjay Subrahmanyam, *Improvising Empire*, p. 12.
80. *CAA*, vol. 7, pp. 5, 20 and 182.
81. *IANTT*, *CC*, I-76-102, fl.3v; *CC*, I-77-18, fl. 2v.
82. *CSL*, III, p. 456.
83. Silva Rego, *Documentação*, vol. 6, p. 186.
84. *IANTT*, CC, pt. II-117-123 (1530).
85. *CSL*, III, pp. 79-82.
86. *IANTT*, *Coleção São Vicente,* vol. X, fl. 120.
87. Armando Cortesão and Luís de Albuquerque, *Obras Completas de Dom João de Castro*, vol. 3, doc. 580, p. 1437.
88. Purchas, *His Pilgrims*, vol. 10, pp. 132-4.
89. Ibid.
90. Correia, *Lendas*, II, p. 717; *IANTT*, CC, IIa-120-17; I-77-18. fl.2v; *RCI*, no. 341. *As Fazendas Armadas Portugueses*, pp. 50, 52, 59, and 60-1; Cortesao and Alburgungue, *Obras Completas de Dom João de Castro*, vol. 3, pp. 195, 296 and 331-2; *APO-CR*. fasc. V, doc. 376.
91. For details see Ceaser Frederick and Gaspero Balbi, 'Voyages', in Richard Haklyut, *Voyages*, 8 vols, London, n.d.
92. Ibid.
93. Ibid.
94. Ibid., see also Purchas, *His Pilgrims*, vol. 10, p. 135.
95. Ibid.
96. Letter of Dom Filippe to Viceroy Mathias de Albuquerque, written from Lisbon, dated 12 January 1591, in *AHU*, Codice 281, fls. 113v.-114.

97. Order of Viceroy Francisco da Gama, 8 April 1598, in *APO-CR*, fasc. III, pt. 2a, pp. 897-8.
98. *BNL*, *Fundo Geral,* Codice 1816, fl. 187. Permission for voyages to Pegu from Santhome for meeting marriage expenses was given. There is a letter written by Joao Careano Barreto dated 1624 saying that concession voyages given on 20 November 1590 had not been undertaken. Hence permission was requested. See, *BNL*, Codice 1816, fl.183.
99. Ibid; see also, *HAG*, *MDR*, 1595-1601, Codice 22-23, fl. 400.
100. *HAG*, *MDR*, Livro. 9, 10, 11, 56/2/3, fl. 67 (17 September 1608).
101. *APO-CR*, vol. 6, doc. 248, p. 970.
102. J.F.J. Biker, *Colecao de Tratados*, vol. 2, Chap CLIX.
103. *Biblioteca Apostolica Vaticana* (hereafter *BAV*), Vatican City, *Fondo Confaloneri,* vol. 31, fls. 412-15, see fl. 413.
104. Danvers William, *Letters Received by the English East India Company*, vol. 2, p. 61.
105. *IANTT*, Mss *DRI*, Livro 38, fls. 334-5.
106. Silva Rego, *DRI*, vol. 9, doc. 50, pp. 3129-30.
107. *BFUP*, vol. 12, p. 410.
108. *BAV*, Fondo Confaloneri, vol. 31, fls. 412-15.
109. Tome Pires, *The Suma Oriental*, vol. 1, p. 86.
110. Barbosa, *The Book of Duarte Barbosa*, 2, p. 219.
111. *BNL*, Codice 11410, fl. 57.
112. *ACE*, vol. 4, p. 573.
113. Bulhao Pato, *Documentos Remetidos*, vol. 6, pp. 9-10.
114. *RFG*, *Despatches from England 1681-86,* p. 89.
115. *LRV*, Livro 2, 16/5, fl. 44v.
116. *DACB*, 1686, p. 14.
117. *RFG*, *Public Despatches from England,* vol. 5, see the entry dated 2 July 1684. See also, S. Jeyaseela Stephen, 'Emerging Trends of Diamond Mining Enterprise and Industrial Development in Pre-Modern Andhra, AD 1600-1800: A Study of Western Sources', in R. Soma Reddy et al., *Industries and Crafts in Andhra Desa: 17th and 18th Centuries,* Hyderabad, 1996, pp. 27-54.
118. *RFG*, *DACB*, 1687, p. 114.
119. Ibid., 1681, p. 3.
120. H. Dodwell, *A Calendar of the Madras Records, 1740-1744,* Madras 1917, p. 77.
121. *RFG*, *DACB*, 1681, p. 5.
122. *RFG*, *DACB*, 1681, p. 10.
123. *IANTT*, *Gavetas*, 20-4-15.
124. Pires, *The Suma Oriental*, vol. 2, pp. 275-6.
125. For Gold sales in 1517, see CC-I-22-62; for 1540 see CC-I-68-88.
126. Sadhu Subrahmanya Sastry, *Tirumali-Tirupati Deavasthanam*

Epigraphical Series (hereafter *TTDES*), 6 vols, Madras, 1931-8. See vol. 5, p. 66 (1544).

127. Pires, *The Suma Oriental*, vol. 2, pp. 275-6.
128. Letter of Vedor da fazenda to the king of Portugal dated 17 February 1547 cited in G. Schurhammer, *St. Frances Xavier*, vol. 3, p. 360.
129. Danvers and Foster, *Letters Received by the English East India Company*, vol. 1, p. 79.
130. Roelfosz, *Asian Trade and European Influence,* p. 166.
131. *BNL*, Codice 1814, fl.199.
132. *HAG*, *MDR*, Livro 57, fl. 109, *IANTT*, Mss DRI, Livro 56, fls. 221-4.
133. *HAG*, *MDR*, Livro 19A, fl. 50/2-3.
134. *NA*, *OBP*, VOC 1103, fl.145 & fls.147-149v (17 March 1643), doc. 147.
135. *HAG*, *MDR*, Livro 19A, fls. 50-51/4-2.
136. Barbosa, *The Book of Duarte Barbosa*, vol. 1, p. 199.
137. Joao de Barros, *Da Asia,* doc. III, pt. I, pp. 164-73.
138. Basilio de Sa, *Documentação*, vol. I, p. 104.
139. Pires, *The Suma Oriental*, vol. 1, pp. 103-10.
140. Correia, *Lendas*, vol. 2, p. 262.
141. Joao de Barros, *Da Asia*, II, pp. 151-2.
142. Manuel Faria e Sousa, *Asia Portuguesa,* 3 vols, Lisboa, 1666-74, 3, IV, p. 311.
143. Schurhammer, *St. Francis Xavier*, vol. 2, p. 360.
144. Correia, *Lendas*, Chap. II, p. 568; G. Schurhammer, 'Uma Relacao in edita de Padre Manuel Barradas, S.I. Sobre S. Francisco Xavier', *Studia*, vol. 11, Lisbon, pp. 60-1.
145. *IANTT*, *Chancelaria D. Filippe, Doações,* Liv. 24, fl. 72. Order issued from Lisbon dated 18 February 1591.
146. Ibid.
147. *BL*, *Additional Manuscripts,* no. 28432, fl. 10, Goa dated 18 December 1599.
148. *BNL*, Codice 581, fl. 170. These voyages were discontinued during 1607-8.
149. Cunha Rivara, *APO-CR*, vol. 3, p. 129.
150. *HAG*, *MDR*, Livro 21, fl. 105.
151. Ibid., Livro 19D/12-16 /1-5, fl. 1047.
152. Ibid., Livro 19D/12-16 /1-5, fl. 1046.
153. M.N. Pearson, 'The Flows and Effects of Precious Metals in India and China, 1500-1800', *Annales*, vol. 2, no. 2, 1993, pp. 51-69.
154. *DRI*, vol. 1, p. 95 (18 January 1607); see also p. 335 (17 February 1610).
155. *APO-CR*, Fasciculo III, p. 129. See the undated letter of February 1588.

156. AGS, *Secertarias Provinciales,* Codice 1479, fl. 258v.
157. *HAG*, *MDR*, Livro 19D, 12-16/1-5, fls. 1059-60.
158. William Methwold, *Relations of Goleonde.* See Schorer's account, footnotes 55 and 56 on the Moluccas trade. See also Cristof Glamann, *Dutch-Asiatic Trade, 1620-1740*, The Hague, 1981, p. 140; on Banten, see T.I. Poonen, *Dutch Beginnings*, pp. 33-4, on Sri Lanka see p. 55. See 'Schorer's account of the Coromandel Coast' in *Indian Historical Quarterly*, vol. 14, p. 827. See also William Foster, *English Factories*, vol. 1, pp. 25-6.
159. Sanjay Subrahmanyam, *Improvising Empire*, see Table 3.
160. R. Jawahar Babu and Hariahariah Oruganti, 'Copper Coins of Awrangzib from Mailapur Mint' in K.V. Raman (ed.), *Studies in South Indian Coins*, Madras, 1997, pp. 105-8. The copper coins from the Mailapur mint have the legends in the Persian and Nasthaleeq styles and belong to the period AD 1704-5 (AH 1115-16).
161. *RFG*, *PC*. See the entry dated 15 January 1707-8.
162. *OIOC*, *Madras Public Consultations*, vol. 73, pp. 160-9.
163. *OIOC*, *Madras Public Proceedings* (hereafter *MPP*), 22 February 1725, 8 March 1725, 6 April 1725 and 3 July 1725, fls. 51, 59, 86, 176, *OIOC*, *Letter Book*, vol. 21, fls. 398, 609. See also R.N. Banerjee, *Economic Progress of the East India Company on the Coromandel Coast, 1702-1746*, Nagpur, 1974.
164. *PC*, vol. 74, pp. 169-80.
165. COCO, vol. 1, pp. 1-17.
166. COCO, vol. 1, pp. 46-7.
167. *PC*, vol. LXXIII, 20 June 1743.
168. Sanjay Subrahmanyam, 'Portfolio Capitalists and the Political Economy of Early Modern India', in Sanjay Subrahmanyam (ed.), *Merchants, Markets and the State in Early Modern India*, Delhi, 1990.

8

Gauging the Impact, Implications and Effectiveness of Portuguese Trade: The Urbanization of Tamil Ports

The evolution of human settlements on the Tamil coast into urban centres has not received much scholarly attention so far and this includes the Portuguese trading ports as well. This may probably be due to the inaccessibility of Portuguese source materials of the period. From the conceptual point of view, the first twelve centuries of the Christian era may be said to have consisted of three broad phases so far as urbanization is concerned. The first phase covered the first four centuries of the Christian era when urbanization was marked purely by the growth of trade and commerce. The second phase covering the next four centuries was a period of urban decay with very little trade and commercial activity in and around the coastal settlements. The next four centuries, however, were marked by the revival of the old coastal settlements and the formation of towns in the hinterland. The emergence of the Chola kingdom in AD 893 marked the beginning of a new phase of development accompanied by considerable administrative and military activity attracting a sizeable number of administrative and military functionaries to the settlements on the coast and the *nagarams* in the hinterland, although the names of inland towns did not always carry the suffix *nagar*. Most of these towns flourished in the hinterland where mercantile settlements came up. The administration of these inland settlements often remained with merchants and merchant guilds.[1] A region-wise survey of both the pearl fishery coast and the Coromandel coast, along with a chronological survey of the emergence of ports during the medieval Pandya, Sambuvaraya and Vijayanagara rule, seems imperative before any inferences can be drawn on the changes that took place in the pattern of urbanization after the advent of the Portuguese on the Tamil coast.

There has been a growing realization among scholars in recent years that the study of urbanization, should be linked with the socio-economic history. Urbanism attempts to unfold the various stages in the evolution of human agglomerations from an agrarian background into a non-agrarian orientation. This chapter endeavours to identify the geophysical as well as socio-economic factors that determined the growth of settlements after the advent of the Portuguese in the Tamil coastal region.

Most of these port towns grew up close to the estuaries endowed with backwaters and lagoons, as otherwise the sailing vessels would have neither safe landing ground nor anchorages. The *nayaka* rulers realized the advantages accruing from these new settlements and therefore did not impose restrictions. Further, it has to be seen as to why places like Porto Novo and Tranquebar did not emerge as anything more than *parangi* settlements while other settlements such as Mylapore, Devanampattinam and Nagapattinam developed into ports on the coast.

Scholars have either emphasized the functional aspects of port towns or highlighted the geophysical aspects of urbanism. It is necessary to link both these aspects so as to arrive at a balanced view which would be acceptable to social anthropologists, urban geographers and economic historians. Urban areas are defined as agglomerations with a majority of its inhabitants engaged in various nonagricultural pursuits. How did the *nagarams*, or marketing centres, which functioned autonomously, react to the arrival of the Portuguese? Did the inhabitants, who were economically independent, support or oppose the Portuguese penetration? How did the trade in the hinterland contribute to the rise of Portuguese colonial towns? Did the Portuguese, after gaining control over the overseas trade, come into conflict with the local kingdoms? Was manufacturing allowed to be carried on by the Portuguese inside their urban settlements? Did the Portuguese towns function as federations of villages adjoining the fort and grow by accretion or extension? Did the natives prefer to settle in the villages near the town or live within the

Portuguese colony? All these questions call for answers while studying the urban history of the Portuguese settlements. It would be interesting also to examine whether the Portuguese pattern was superimposed on a pre-existing indigenous pattern in the Tamil coast, and if so, how? Scholars interested in the study of the urban history of the Portuguese settlements on the Tamil coast cannot also ignore the study of its socio-economic and cultural impacts.

In 1506, the king of Portugal instructed his countrymen to build their fortresses solely for the protection of their own lives and the merchandise and not with any warlike intent.[2] In the year 1507, the Portuguese establishment in India conveyed to the king of Portugal a suggestion that there was no need to appoint a Captain or to open a factory anywhere on the Coromandel coast as there were only fugitives from the royal fleets and fortresses there.[3] However, thirteen years later, in 1520, the king of Portugal issued an order to establish a factory on the Coromandel coast and appointed a Captain to be in charge of it. Because of the intimidative Portuguese presence on the west coast of India, most of the Persian and Arab merchants who came to India went straight to the eastern coast.[4] In due course of time, the Portuguese settlers on the east coast also felt the need for fortresses to be set up at places like Vedalai, Punnaikayal, Devanampattinam, Santhome of Mylapore and Nagapattinam in the Bay of Bengal region.[5] It is to be seen how far the Portuguese were at first struck by the idea of opening a factory and later were propelled to erect a fort on the Tamil coast.

The prospects for trade in bulk goods and luxuries was the chief reason Portuguese soldiers on the western coast moved into the Coromandel region on the eastern coast of India. Those who felt stifled under the Crown's service preferred to move towards the flourishing Coromandel ports. As many as 300 Portuguese army deserters and other disgruntled royal servicemen were found trading in the Coromandel region in the 1520s.[6] According to a report of Francisco Rodrigues de Silveira in 1524, many Portuguese soldiers who were subjected to maltreatment in Goa migrated to the Coromandel coast. These soldiers turned to maritime trade particularly in rice and textiles with South Asia and South-East Asia.[7] They had moved to the Coromandel coast even before the official-sponsored Portuguese trading activity made its appearance there. Gaspar Correia, the Portuguese chronicler, also confirms that the Portuguese official trade commenced in the Tamil coast only after the Portuguese private traders had already come to the Coromandel.[8] In fact, Pulicat became the first port asylum for many of the Portuguese who abandoned the west coast to participate in the country trade on the Coromandel coast. They sailed in the *naus* (ships) of Pulicat and in the junks of Melaka which carried textiles and rice.[9]

These early Portuguese settlers in the Coromandel coast were even accused of ignoring the dictates of their conscience and leading a life unbecoming of a Christian. They had come from Portugal many years ago and did not even remember that they were married, and stayed on in the Coromandel and pearl fishery coast without providing for or writing to their wives in Portugal. Whenever they felt threatened by the mandates issued either by the king of Portugal or by the missionaries, or else by any other legal measures of censure, they took asylum in the Coromandel and subsisted by carrying on trade on their own. The Portuguese community in India, composed of nobles, soldiers, etc., had a sneaking desire to engage in other lucrative pursuits. Moreover, the Portuguese settlers in the Coromandel were practically free from any political control. Neither the Portuguese governor of Goa nor any other authority exercised any kind of check over them or their activities.[10] Altogether it was a period which saw the emergence of a new class of bourgeoisie on the Tamil coast.

As coastal settlements such as Mylapore, Devanampattinam and Nagapattinam were under the political control of the *nayaka* rulers, the Portuguese traders were encouraged to settle down and carry on trading activities in these port settlements as this enhanced the *nayak's* revenue from maritime trade. In 1559 and 1577 the Portuguese settlements of Santhome and Nagapattinam were raided by the rulers as the activities of the Portuguese came to be regarded as undesirable by the Hindu merchants.[11]

DEVANAMPATTINAM

Missionary records of the period provide information about the Portuguese settlement of Devanampattinam in 1543. The Portuguese invited the *parava* converts who had been serving them to come and live in this settlement. This was done with the intent to populate and develop the port.[12] According to the official records the Portuguese factory in Devanampattinam was officially established only in 1585 with the prior permission of Vaiyappa Krishnappa Nayak (1580-93) of Gingee. Eventually a mud fort was built there in 1589 with the approval of the *nayak*. The ruler had also agreed to provide protection to the Portuguese. Thus Devanampattinam, which started as a settlement, grew into a port and eventually into a fort town. The Portuguese fortified it by raising the mud walls in close to the mouth of Gadilam, a tributary of the South Pennar River (then Pennaiyar). As commerce began to flourish, they felt the need to fortify the settlement. Thus Devanampattinam emerged somewhere midway between Santhome of Mylapore in the north and Nagapattinam in the south, the two principal centres of Portuguese trade on the Tamil coast.

A perusal of the Portuguese fort plan of Devanampattinam shows the existence of churches, factory and godowns. The fortress was square-shaped with walls on four sides for the protection of the Portuguese and their merchandise. The Portuguese Captain of Devanampattinam resided there. The Portuguese residents built their houses alongside the northern wall of the fort at Devanampattinam so that the residential area could be encircled by walls to serve as a bulwark on three sides. Seven big buildings meant to serve as saltpetre godowns were located separately, a little away from the residential area. After the development of the port, the Portuguese acquired Manjakuppam, Thirupathiripuliyur, Thiruvendhipuram, Vandipalayam, Varakalpattu, Surappanchavadi and Singarathoppu—the seven villages around Devanampattinam. They had paid 1500 *pardaus* and a reference dating to 1608 mentions that the Portuguese in Devanampattinam continued to possess these villages.[13] Thus the port developed slowly by absorbing its immediate neighbourhood area.

The Portuguese fort and the settlement of Devanampattinam were given to the Dutch by the *nayak* of Gingee in 1608 when they approached the ruler with their plan to develop trade in the port.[14] The location of the port proved to be ideal because there were many villages in the hinterland which produced good quality textiles. Even rice and paddy was available in plenty. As the Dutch and a local merchant, Achyutappa Chetti had a good understanding, the port of Devanampattinam remained under the former till the death of Achyutappa Chetti (in 1634).

As the fort of Devanampattinam was considered important by the Portuguese, the *ouvidor* (judge) and aldermen of Nagapattinam were asked on 29 January 1630 by Miguel de Noronha, the Viceroy of Goa (1629-35), to seek the help of the *nayak* of Thanjavur in expelling Dutch from Devanampattinam.[15] On 28 January 1634 a report was sent by the Captain of Nagapattinam to the viceroy of Goa about the attempts made with the help of the *nayak* of Gingee to drive the Dutch away.[16] Further, orders were issued on 15 March 1634 by the viceroy of Goa, transferring Simão de Mello, the then resident Captain of Nagapattinam, where he had proved his skill in confronting the Dutch, to Devanampattinam so as to take steps to recover the fort from the Dutch.[17] A letter sent by the Bishop of Mylapore to the viceroy in Goa on 27 September 1634 described the situation at Devanampattinam.[18] The Portuguese also planned to approach the king of Vijayanagara in 1634 to regain the fort. On 11 October 1634, the Portuguese sent Fr. Pero Mexia with presents to meet the *nayak* of Gingee.[19] At the same time, the Jesuit missionaries in Santhome also requested the king of Vijayanagara to expel the Dutch from Devanampattinam. Chinnana Chetti, the brother of the leading merchant, Achyutappa Chetti, however, did not act according to the orders of the *nayak* of Gingee.[20] This was because the native merchant had strong trade links with the Dutch and did not favour the entry of the Portuguese into the port. In fact, in 1635 Simão de Mello Ferreira was ordered by the viceroy of Goa to present to the *nayak* of Gingee two elephants and two horses to obtain the port of Devanampattinam. The Portuguese, in the meanwhile, even planned to destroy Devanampattinam in the event they failed to recover the fort from the Dutch.[21] It is reported that the king of Vijayanagara was in favour of the Portuguese and agreed to give them the fortress of Devanampattinam which had been rebuilt by Achyutappa, alias Malaya Chetti.[22]

The urbanization of the port of Devanampattinam owes much to the efforts of the Portuguese. The Dutch lived at

Thirupathiripuliyur, a little towards the interior, where their warehouses were located. They, in fact, used the fort originally built by the Portuguese. The trading activities of the port with Banten, its population, the geographical advantages of the Gadilam River and the political climate of the times favoured the Dutch. Hence the Portuguese were unsuccessful in rescuing the fort of Devanampattinam which had been taken over the Dutch in 1608, although the Portuguese made attempts to recover the port even as late as the 1630s. The Portuguese traders eventually migrated to Porto Novo, a neighbouring port town.

NAGAPATTINAM

The Portuguese settlement of Nagapattinam in the *nayakdom* of Thanjavur was well established necessitating the posting of a Captain there in 1542 when Sevvappa Nayaka was the ruler (1532-76). Nagapattinam under the Portuguese saw a meteoric rise and was very prosperous handling considerable international trade. That the port settlement had acquired some of urban features during this period can be gleaned from the writings of travellers who visited Nagapattinam during this time. According to Cesare Federici, in 1567, the Portuguese settlement, which was very close to the sea, was very large.[23] Nagapattinam was situated between two outlets of the Kaveri River, namely, Uppanar in the south and Kudavaiyar in the north. A marketplace had taken shape within a distance of just about one league attracting a large number of merchants. The Portuguese lived separately in a settlement.[24] The Captain, who was appointed for a three-year term, was made responsible for the trade and administering the settlement taking care of the Portuguese and the native Christians.[25] The Tamil-speaking Muslims, called Marakkayars lived in their own settlement, Nagore, located nearby. They were, however, free to enter Nagapattinam for purposes of trade. According to Gaspero Balbi, the Italian traveller, the Portuguese had erected a mud fortification in 1582 around their settlement to defend themselves against possible attacks from their rivals and enemies.[26] By 1594 the earlier temporary structures were replaced by stone structures. The Portuguese Captain of Nagapattinam was given the right to collect a revenue of 1,400 *xerafins* by the *nayak*.[27] William Finch, the English traveller who visited Nagapattinam in 1608, however, says that there was only a factory but no fort.[28] Conde de Linhares, the Portuguese viceroy (1629-35), persuaded the Portuguese settlers at Nagapattinam to fortify their settlement against possible attacks from the Dutch.[29]

A local body of leading citizens, chosen to be members of the *Os Eleitos de Negapatão* (the Elect of Nagapattinam), was an institution that was formed during this time to maintain cordial relations with the royal court at Thanjavur. This unofficial council consisting of five members was formed by the *casados* of Nagapattinam to administer the affairs of the growing town. Its members were powerful traders who sat together and settled disputes among the local residents.

Although Nagapattinam originated as a sea port, it slowly grew to establish contacts with many interior market centres and thus it came to be connected to faraway Goa through a land route.[30] Another route connected Nagapattinam to Thanjavur via Thiruvarur.[31] There was also a route from Kochi to Nagapattinam and Tuticorin.[32]

The Portuguese quarters came up west of the northern bend of the river. The river flowed in a northerly direction on three sides of the settlement. The native quarters of the Brahmins and others grew up around the Soundararaja Perumal and Nilayadakshi Amman temples. Manuel Barradas alludes to the existence of a Buddhist vihara as well.[33]

Although Conde de Linhares, the Portuguese viceroy of Goa, had persuaded the Portuguese settlers in Nagapattinam to fortify their settlement against Dutch attacks, the notables of Nagapattinam (*Os Eleitos de Negapatão*) refused and resisted the proposal because they wanted to avoid problems with the *nayak* of Thanjavur.[34] They also feared that once Goa acquired a foothold at Nagapattinam, the king of Portugal would set up a customs house in the name of the Iberian Crown, which would hurt on their private trade as it would be subjected to multiple taxes. However, on 15 December 1635, the Portuguese residents, fearing Dutch occupation, themselves approached the *nayak* of Thanjavur, to permit them to erect fortifications around the settlement.[35] The *nayak* refused. At this time, when the sultan of Bijapur attacked Thanjavur, the *nayak* took shelter at

Nagapattinam and the Portuguese came to his aid. Later, on 31 March 1637, when the Portuguese once again requested the *nayak* for permission to improve the fortifications, he himself came forward to carry out minor improvements to the fortifications at Nagapattinam.[36] However the fortifications were not adequate. The Dutch attacked the prosperous settlement on 12 April 1642, demanding 50,000 *pardaus*.[37] As the Portuguese were unable to pay the Dutch took some hostages. The *nayak* of Thanjavur came with a large army and drove the Dutch away from Nagapattinam. On 2 May 1642, thirty people from Nagapattinam wrote to Dom João IV, the king of Portugal (1640-56), asking for protection.[38] The Dutch suspected that the *Eleitos de Negapatão* may have sought the help of the *nayak* and refused to release the Portuguese hostages.[39] The *nayak* of Thanjavur himself wanted to free his territory from the clutches of foreign traders. The Dutch once again approached him to evict the Portuguese from Nagapattinam. On his refusal, the Dutch returned to Pulicat.[40] The citizens of Nagapattinam in the meanwhile requested the Portuguese viceroy in Goa to provide the town with walls and towers for its defence.[41] The Portuguese also came forward to pay the customs duties to the king of Portugal.[42] The Portuguese viceroy discussed the issue of fortifying Nagapattinam with the State Council in Goa and decided in favour of it on 28 July 1642. Thus the Portuguese settlement of Nagapattinam came under the protection of the king of Portugal, and on 31 December 1642, it was officially incorporated into the *Estado da Índia*.[43]

However, when the Portuguese started fortifying the port of Nagapattinam (1642), Vijayaraghava Nayak of Thanjavur (1634-73) sent a force of cavalry and infantry and laid siege to the town since permission had not been sought for fortifying the town.[44] Later, the Portuguese requested the *nayak* of Thanjavur for permission to fortify the settlement and with his approval the work resumed. A strong fort with major fortification in a way helped the *nayak* because he took shelter at Nagapattinam when his capital city was attacked for the second time (on 8 March 1649) by the army of the Bijapur sultan.[45]

The *povação* (settlement) turned into a large fortified town (*cidade*) after it came under the protection of the king of Portugal on 31 December 1642.[46] The fort was of a rectangular shape. The residents of Nagapattinam were ordered to pay tax to His Majesty the King of Portugal. The *veradores* (aldermen) and the officers of the municipality of Nagapattinam were also asked to carry out the fortification of the town.[47] The salt merchants of Nagapattinam were also ordered to contribute towards, expresses of the fortification. Orders were also issued to ensure the safety of the customs house and the fort. On 2 January 1645 three security men were ordered to be posted as guards at all three directions facing the land. The *vedor da fazenda* was given charge of the three keys for the three gates and of supervising the guards every day. Lourenço Correia de Silva was confirmed as the accountant by the regulation of 20 March 1645, while Manuel de Barros became the writer of the fort.[48] One Gaspar Ferreira was made the procurator of the municipality while João Velho was made the accountant of the municipality. Baltazer da Faria was appointed the judge in Nagapattinam to render justice. António Amaral de Menezes was made the Captain to maintain law and order and Augustinho Simões Francisco de Cunha was made the accountant of the factory in Nagapattinam. All of this appointments point to the growing importance of the town as an administrative centre. In the meanwhile, on 13 March 1645, the residents of Nagapattinam requested the king of Portugal to grant the town all those privileges that had already been given to Kochi.[49] On 29 August 1645, Dom Filipe de Mascarenhas, the Portuguese viceroy (1641-51), dedicated the city to Mary, the Mother of Jesus and declared that henceforth it would be called the City of Our Lady of Immaculate Conception. The citizen of Nagapattinam requested the king of Portugal once again on 29 November 1645 to exempt the port from the payment of customs duties on commodities such as wood, coir, and areca nut.[50] The customs duty to be paid by the merchants of Nagapattinam was fixed at 6 per cent, out of which 5 per cent was to be remitted to the king of Portugal and the remaining 1 per cent were to be retained to strengthen the fortifications of the town. The accounts of the tax amount to be paid to the king of Portugal were maintained in the books of accounts of the customs house of Nagapattinam. The details of the money spent for the fortification of the town were also recorded there.[51]

When and how the Portuguese got ten villages around the port of Nagapattinam and their revenue is not known. However, it is clear that Vijayaraghava Nayak of Thanjavur granted them these ten villages. The villages were Pudur, Nagore, Anthanapettai, Karuvelankadai, Puravacheri, Anaimangalam, Sengamangalam, Nangudi, Manjakollai and Nirthinamangalam.[52] The right to collect an annual revenue of 1,400 *xerafins* from these villages was also given to the Portuguese Captain.[53] The *nayak* gave 200 *xerafins* from his share of customs duties to the Portuguese Captain for his services.[54]

The Portuguese, in turn, were asked to pay to the *nayak* in Thanjavur an annual tribute (the exact amount is not known) out of the revenue collected by them. Cloth and food grains exported from Nagapattinam and commodities imported were free from import and export duties. All wrecked ships that washed up on the shores of Nagapattinam were declared the property of the Portuguese as they were the masters of the sea. Regarding the extradition of fugitives merchants and other individuals belonging to the Portuguese Company who misappropriated cash and other properties of the company and who took shelter in the villages of the *nayak*, were handed over to the Portuguese together with their properties.[55]

As trade flourished in Nagapattinam between 1577 and 1630, the Portuguese population also increased. Many Portuguese came from different places to settle there and carry on trade. The settlement had 60 *casados*, 200 Eurasians and 300 Indian Christians in 1577.[56] According to Bocarro's report (in 1630), there were 140 white *casados* and 360 *topasses* (artillery men) in Nagapattinam. By 1642, the number had risen to 700 Christians. During this period Nagapattinam town had the largest population compared to any other Portuguese settlement on the Tamil coast.[57]

When the Portuguese fort and settlement of Nagapattinam was captured by the Dutch on 23 July 1658, many of its residents fled. Later (1661), about sixty Portuguese settlers migrated from Nagapattinam to Santhome.[58] The Portuguese viceroy subsequently, in a letter dated 22 March 1663, addressed to the Danish governor of Tranquebar, requested him to give shelter to the Portuguese who had migrated from Nagapattinam.[59] This goes to show that the Portuguese had a great stake in the town even after Dutch occupation. The rectangular-shaped fort was converted into an octagonal-shaped one, as is evident from the Dutch map of Nagapattinam, when the Dutch East India Company shifted its commercial headquarters from Pulicat to Nagapattinam in 1690.

Santhome of Mylapore

Mylapore, located near the city of Madras (now Chennai), was a famous trading centre even under the medieval Cholas.[60] It became famous after the advent of the Portuguese to the Coromandel coast as the Portuguese came to believe that the tomb of St.Thomas, one of the Apostles of Jesus, existed there. The Portuguese who had settled around the sepulchre believed it to be that of St. Thomas and called the place São Thomé de Meliapor. The origins of trade at Santhome can be traced to the Armenians who had settled at Mylapore. After the arrival of the Portuguese, the cult that centred around the name of Saint Thomas developed even further.[61]

Many Portuguese war veterans, who in the meanwhile came to Santhome to seek their fortune, free from the shakles of Crown-imposed restrictions, built their magnificent dwellings there. They were attracted to Mylapore by the prosperous trade, in the region around Pulicat and, above all, by their devotion to the Apostle St. Thomas. According to João de Barros, the sixteenth-century Portuguese chronicler, three Portuguese stragglers went in the year 1519 to reside there for the first time.[62] Diogo Fernandez, one of the early settlers in Mylapore, reported that when the Portuguese went to Mylapore, the people there felt relieved because they would now get protection against the pirates who had been harassing the native ships.[63] Many *casados* who had initially begun to trade in bulk goods from the west coast started moving over to settle at Santhome of Mylapore as early as 1520.[64]

Gaspar Correia, another Portuguese chronicler, passed through Santhome on two occasions, in 1531 and 1534. When he visited Santhome for the second time he was amazed to find how much of the settlement had expanded. The earlier vacant spaces in the settlement were now transformed into streets along which the nobles had built rows of houses.[65]

The Portuguese settlers here wrote a lengthy letter in the year 1537 to the king of Portugal giving a detailed description of the conditions that prevailed in Mylapore.[66] They reported that Santhome had as many as fifty Portuguese households at that time. The number of inhabitants increased to 60 *casados* in 1538. The letter tacitly conveyed the apprehension of the Portuguese that they might be disturbed from Mylapore and recalled to Goa under the orders of the Portuguese governor in Goa.[67] The residents further made a plea in the letter to the king of that in future only a resident of the settlement should be given the post of Captain.[68] The very same year Garcia de Noronha, the viceroy of Goa (1538-40), ordered the deportation of the residents of Mylapore to the west coast of India and he sent Manuel da Gama with powers to deport them and raze the settlement.[69] Manuel da Gama managed to bring some of the residents to Kochi.[70] The viceroy was keen to develop the Portuguese settlements on the west coast as the number of Portuguese in India was too small at that time. Therefore, he did not want the Portuguese to scatter everywhere. In 1539 he tried to recall the recalcitrant Portuguese in the Coromandel to Goa by planning to destroy the settlement of Santhome. Dom Constantino Bragança, the next viceroy, also followed the same policy of bringing the Portuguese back to the west coast and he too was determined to prevent the Portuguese stragglers from selling down in Santhome, but the Portuguese at Santhome refused to return to the west coast.[71]

The people in the Coromandel coast, during this period (1540), had to face immense suffering due to a famine. The people from the surrounding areas migrated in large numbers to the town to escape the rigours of the famine.[72] The Portuguese in Santhome rendered immense service to the local people and King Achyutadevaraya thanked them and sent a letter of appreciation to the Captain of Santhome.[73] Conditions later improved and the Portuguese population increased as more people from the west coast migrated then. A letter by the Portuguese viceroy on 30 November 1550 to the king of Portugal mentions that the total number of Portuguese citizens living in India was 6,007. There were 600 permanent residents in the various ports along the Coromandel coast.[74]

POPULATION OF SANTHOME

The Portuguese population in Santhome increased steadily from 60 families in 1538 to 100 in 1543. The Portuguese population in 1545 was around 500.[75] Francis Xavier, the great missionary, in one of his letters dated 10 November 1545 mentions that there were more than 100 married Christians in Santhome.[76] By 1546 there were 500 Portuguese in Santhome with their slaves.[77] By 1559 the population of Santhome had risen to 2,000 including the Portuguese and natives.[78] In 1563 as many as 4,000 Christians lived there besides 60 war veterans with their families.[79] It is noteworthy that in 1565 more than 2,000 Portuguese men left the service of the king of Portugal because the viceroy of Goa had not paid them either their salary dues or their food allowances. Most of them went to Santhome and some to other places in the Coromandel coast. The number of Portuguese families in Santhome which stood at around 80 in 1563, increased to 200 families in 1575 due to the influx of large number Portuguese attracted by Santhome's flourishing trade with Melaka and Pegu.[80]

Gaspero Balbi, the Italian traveller who visited Santhome on 29 May 1582, tells that the Portuguese settlement of Santhome was different from the native quarters. The port of Santhome on the landward side faced the sea on the west. Many blocks of houses were also located facing the sea.[81] The gateway facing the sea was so low that elephants could not enter but horses could without any difficulty. He says that Santhome was surrounded by mud walls. The native quarter was called Mylapore, which was inhabited by the Hindus, where an officer of the king of Vijayanagara was stationed.[82] This local official looked after the affairs of the Hindus, administered justice and leased out the right to collect port taxes. The resident Portuguese Captain of Santhome, appointed by the king of Portugal, issued *cartazes* to the merchants who conducted long-distance trade with various ports. According to Jesuit sources, Santhome's defences and fortifications were not very strong.[83]

A letter written by the *vedor da fazenda* to the king of Portugal in 1535 describes some of the Portuguese residing in the Coromandel—such as Diogo Rebello, former Factor of the Coromandel and the fishery coasts, Miguel Ferreira, another former Captain of the Coromandel, and Aires de Figureido, the then Captain of the Coromandel—as being so rich that the king of Portugal could even raise a loan from them.[84] Another letter written in 1538 by the *vedor da fazenda* in Kochi to the king of Portugal says that João Caeyro, Nuno Preto, Cristôvão Mendes de Vasconcelos, and Vicente Nuniz, residing in the *povacão* (settlement) of St. Thomas the Apostle in Mylapore, could be approached for a loan since they were the richest *casados* in the Coromandel, trading mainly in bulk goods.[85] The early Portuguese settlers were so rich that in due course many magnificent mansions with beautiful gardens came up in Santhome of Mylapore. The settlement was well protected by mud fortifications on all sides.

Jesuit letters written between 1559 and 1563, however, reveal that the Portuguese merchants at Santhome were engaged in unlawful trading practices driven by the sole motivation of making money. The letters point out that they were corrupt and their moral standards very low[86] and many of those who had settled at Santhome were either criminals or deserters. There was rampant lawlessness in the settlement and the king of Portugal was forced to appoint a resident *ouvidor* in 1585 to keep a watch over the activities of the Portuguese residents there. This judge appointed by the viceroy held trials and disposed of the cases. He was paid 50,000 *reis* per annum, although the post was worth only 500 *cruzados* per annum due to the meagre income of the factory and lack of work.[87] The judge here became more powerful when the post of Resident Captain fell vacant in 1604.[88]

THE MUNICIPALITY OF SANTHOME

Taking into account the laudable services rendered by the Portuguese Captain and the residents who married local women, brought up their children well and built houses at their own expense, Santhome of Mylapore was raised to the status of a *cidade* (town) in 1609 through a royal order of the king of Portugal notified subsequently by the viceroy of Goa. A *Câmara Municipal* (Municipal Council) invested with the power to frame rules to regulate the civic life in Santhome was established. From then on Santhome came to be referred as *cidade* in the official records of the *Estado da Índia* and were brought on a par with the Portuguese city of Evora in Portugal and two other Indo-Portuguese cities of Goa and Kochi in India. It was conferred all the privileges and rights enjoyed by these Portuguese cities.[89] The autonomy of Santhome was acknowledged by the governor of Goa whenever the Portuguese Captain of Santhome attempted to encroach upon the authority of the municipality. An inspector was appointed to look after the cleanliness of Santhome. The Portuguese Captain in Santhome had his own beautiful official residence which he had to vacate on relinquishing office.[90] The *Senado da Câmara* (Senate House) of Santhome was modelled after the one at Evora in Portugal. It was also ordered by the king of Portugal that only local laws, regulations, customs and conventions should be observed with regard to matters relating to the indigenous people in the port of Santhome. The natives were permitted to live in Santhome without any distinction. As for others, it was stipulated that there should be a civil registry in Santhome so that none could pretend to be a subject of any other ruler even though he may be a friend or a foe of the Portuguese. Enumeration of families and individuals was undertaken for the first time in 1614 in Santhome.[91] A prison was also built there for which a warden was posted on 26 December 1617 with full authority over the prison in the town of Mylapore.[92] The *Alcaide-mor* (commander of the fortress) performed the functions of the principal police officer in the customs house.[93]

FORTIFICATIONS AT SANTHOME

In view of the threat faced by the Portuguese from the Dutch in Pulicat, the process of fortification of Santhome engaged their attention for a considerable period of time. The main constraint was lack of funds. The money required for carrying out the fortification of Santhome was not provided by the Portuguese viceroy of Goa or by the king of Portugal. Hence the ultimate responsibility of mobilizing funds came to rest on the shoulders of the traders and the local authorities in Santhome. The lands were obtained by the grant of the privilege for undertaking commercial voyages from the Coromandel coast to those who could venture into such profitable sailings. Such privileges continued to be granted up to 1625.

The need for fortification of the settlement of Santhome was felt by the residents because of its flourishing commerce and the Dutch threat of attack. The king of Portugal informed the viceroy of Goa in 1609 that the profits from three voyages to Melaka and three voyages to Pegu should be given to the municipal council of the town of Mylapore to be used for its fortification.[94]

The *Câmara Municipal* of Santhome was given the task of undertaking the fortification work in 1611 with the income derived from the grant of the privilege for two commercial voyages from the Coromandel to Melaka.[95] The inhabitants of Mylapore, in a letter dated of March 1613 to Filippe II, the king of Portugal (1598-1621), demanded additional financial help for the fortification.[96] They further suggested that a customs house on the model of the one functioning under the jurisdiction of the king of Vijayanagara could be established there. A customs duty of 4 per cent could be collected on all commodities and used for the fortification of Mylapore. It is further learnt from the Annual Jesuit Letter (1610) that one Pillai of Kanchipuram appointed by the *nayak* functioned as *adhikari* (officer) in Santhome, collected the revenue from the port and paid it to the *nayaka* treasury in Chandragiri.[97]

After mobilizing some funds, the Portuguese attempted to fortify Santhome. As the work commenced. Venkata II, the Vijayanagara ruler, in the year 1613 attacked the settlement since permission had not been obtained for erecting a fort there. Manuel de Frias, the Portuguese Captain of Santhome, therefore, stopped the fortification work.[98] The Portuguese could continue only after Venkata II, the king of Vijayanagara, died in October 1614.[99] The king of Portugal was keen to know about the progress of the work on the fortifications of Santhome and whether the construction of the *fortaleza* (fort) had commenced in Mylapore and the funds sanctioned by him utilized.[100]

Fernão de Albuquerque, the viceroy of Goa, authorized the Portuguese Captain of Mylapore for the second time in January 1612 to use the profits from the voyage the Melaka for the fortification of Santhome of Mylapore.[101] A third order was issued in March 1613[102] to make all necessary provisions to begin the work through profits made from the voyage to Melaka. Once again, on 30 January 1614, orders were issued permitting the use of the profits from voyages to Melaka[103] and Tennaserim,[104] especially to meet the cost of the fortifications.

In 1615 two more voyages from Santhome to Tennaserim were granted with the special stipulation that the profits earned through these voyages should be spent towards the acquisition of ammunition necessary for the defence of the Portuguese settlement at Santhome.[105] In 1616, profits from two voyages from the Coromandel to Pegu were alloted by the king of Portugal[106] and the viceroy of Goa proceeded as per the royal instruction. On 21 March 1619, the viceroy in Goa sent a letter to the Portuguese Captain of Santhome asking him to speed up the work on the fortifications.[107]

Funds from the treasury were also sanctioned for the fortification, as ordered on 2 May 1620.[108] The Captain was advised on 12 September 1620 to seek the assistance of an expert engineer to execute the work with the help of local workers in Mylapore.[109] Additional funds of 4,000 *pagodas* were also sanctioned by the king of Portugal.[110] Another commercial voyage was permitted on 20 February 1621 from the Coromandel the profits of which were added towards the fortification of the town of Mylapore.[111] Profit from two more voyages to Tennaserim were also alloted on 20 March 1625.[112] This process of extending Portuguese sovereignty over the land was perhaps possible only because there was no effective local ruler at that time in the region.

In 1628, the *Câmara Municipal* of Maçāo in China transferred its accruals from the sale of voyages to Japan to the *Câmara Municipal* of Santhome.[113] On 28 February 1630, the municipality of Goa contributed some money for the fortification work at Santhome.[114] The contributions were given to a bursar appointed for the purpose. He kept the money in the treasury, the keys of which were held in his custody.[115] This new arrangement was made to ensure full utilization of funds for the fortification without diversion. One António Simoes, a member of the clergy in Goa in 1630, desired that some portion of the profits from the pepper trade also be spent towards fortification of the town of Mylapore.[116]

Santhome Fort

A plan for the development of the fort and the town of Santhome, as drawn by Júlio Simão, the chief engineer of the Portuguese State of India (who succeeded João Baptista Cairato), was completed on 18 February 1621.[117] A provision was made for a public square in the town of Mylapore on 19 March 1623, and it was incorporated in the project.[118] Bastions necessary for the town were also ordered to be built immediately and the work was undertaken quickly as the Portuguese suspected that the Dutch were making preparations to dislodge them from Santhome.[119] There was such widespread fear that a letter dated 12 December 1625, written by the residents pleaded for fortifying the town in all the directions.[120] Further, they demanded sufficient artillery to protect them against Dutch attacks, as is evident from another letter dated 22 March 1627.[121] The artillery of the town of Santhome could not be strengthened as quickly as required. After the Dutch attacked and plundered the town in 1632, a batch of fifty soldiers was maintained in Santhome. As late as 24 July 1634, new taxes were collected as protection fees and used to meet the expenditure incurred in connection with the security men employed in Santhome.[122]

By 1635 Santhome had walls around it with four gates including the *porta de terra* (land gate) and the *porta de mar* (sea gate) to protect the town. The gate on the western side was located near the Franciscan Church and was named after St. Francis of Assisi. By 1639 the town of Santhome was fully protected on all sides.[123]

On the eastern side of the town, facing the sea, there were nine bastions. Six of the bastions were named after various saints and three after some notables. The bastion of St. Dominic was located on the north side with a bulwark in the middle protected by artillery. The bastion of St. Paul was situated on the south. One of the four gates of the city, with a watchtower on top in the form of a bulwark, was located in front of St. Dominic's bastion, on which two guns were mounted. Further on was St. Santiago bastion with a postern. The bastion of St. Antony was near the coast and the bastion of St. Augustine followed next.[124] Facing the landward north-western side of the town there was a gate (one of the four) with a new bulwark, and close to it came another stretch of wall with a large bastion named after Francisco de Almeida, the first Portuguese viceroy of India. Beyond that stood the bastion of Salvador de Resende and a little further was that of João de Sousa. Behind these was the bastion of Madre de Deus which was in line with the bastion of St. Paul. All the bastions facing the seashore were built at fifty metres distance and those facing the land were built at a distance of thirty metres.[125]

In view of the looming Dutch threat it was felt necessary to have one artillery unit in Mylapore for the purpose of defence. The artillery of the town in the 1640s consisted of three iron guns with three, six and nine pounders, besides one made of brass. There was also a swivel gun of forty iron hoops with twelve falcons and four wall pieces.

The circumference of the town of Santhome (in 1646) was 2,600 paces on the land. The wall was about 5 metres high including its parapets which were ten bricks thick at the top of it.[126] Only the Portuguese lived within the walls of their fort in Mylapore. Most of the houses within the fort of Santhome were built of brick and stone. As the native hamlets of the low castes were located very close to the wall of Santhome, they were all destroyed because the enemies could sneak right up to the base of the wall.[127] There was a settlement of artisans and blacksmiths on the north-western side of Santhome.[128]

By a royal order dated 20 June 1654, a tablet bearing the inscription of the Immaculate Conception of Mary, the Mother of Jesus Christ, was ordered to be placed at the entrance of all cities in Portugal. Two years later the same order was made applicable to Goa and Kochi on the west coast and Mylapore on the Coromandel coast.[129]

SANTHOME'S ROADS

The port of Santhome was well connected with various distant marketplaces in the hinterland. Mylapore was connected with the Vijayanagara city via Penugonda, Udayagiri, Chandragiri, Tirupati and Pulicat.[130] There was a trade route between Santhome and Chandragiri via Tiruvallur.[131] Santhome was also connected with Goa through a overland trade route.[132] Further, Mylapore was connected with Kochi via Athur (near Salem) and Palghat.[133] There was another route which connected Mylapore with Kochi via Gingee, Chidambaram, Nagapattinam, Talaimannar, Punnaikayal, Tuticorin and Kanyakumari.[134]

MARKET AT SANTHOME

Evidence suggests that a place for a market was selected in Santhome outside the western gate and the natives were encouraged to bring supplies to the town.[135] There was a bazaar within the fort of Santhome.[136] Several commodities were brought there for sale and resale by merchants, both women and men.[137] Peasants too brought cartloads of their produce to the market for sale.[138] Butter was brought in hollow bamboo pole containers.[139] Trees were cut from the nearby forests and the timber was brought to the market.[140] Sacks of husked rice were brought by men as headloads.[141] In fact, merchants were encouraged to bring chiefly rice and other provisions to meet the requirements of the town population. However, commodities all were checked before they were unloaded.[142] There was a small check point where tolls and other duties were collected on commodities brought into Santhome from other places.[143]

On 4 January 1686, the English in Madras had introduced a multi-point duty on tobacco which was brought from many places for sale. For this reason many merchants preferred to carry tobacco to Santhome where only-single-point duty was imposed.[144] Traders from Kodambakkam were sometimes prevented by the English from taking provisions to Santhome since these commodities were not brought to Madras.[145] Coins such as *panams* which were minted in Santhome were in wide circulation in the market.[146] Some of the merchants borrowed money for the purpose of trade in Santhome. A monthly interest of 3 per cent was charged on loans.[147]

Revenue from several nearby villages came under the control of the Portuguese Crown.[148] Aurangzeb, the Mughal emperor, reconfirmed in a *farman* on 15 January 1702, the continued possession of Santhome by the Portuguese along with gardens. Revenue from three villages Mambalam, Alandur and Adambakkam, continued to be allowed to be collected by the Portuguese.[149] This shows that the Portuguese derived revenue not only from the neighbourhood of Santhome but also from the seashore.[150] Revenue from a *pettai* (manufacturing-cum-market zone), which existed in Santhome, was also derived by the Portuguese Crown.[151] Manufacturers in and around Santhome too contributed towards the wealth and prosperity of the part.[152]

Regarding the population of Santhome at different intervals of time, we find that in 1635 it had 120 Portuguese families and 200 Tamil Christian families.[153] Nine years later (1644), Andre Lopez, the Jesuit Provincial of Malabar, mentioned in his Annual Report sent to the Superior General in Rome that there were 1,700 Christians in Santhome.[154] On 23 July 1658, when Nagapattinam was captured by the Dutch, many more Portuguese came and settled in Mylapore. The white population of Santhome increased by a further 180. Further, forty-three more citizens returned to Santhome. Along with them sixty came from Nagapattinam, and seventeen from Jaffna and Mannar. In 1661, 60 priests and 200 *topasses* lived in Santhome.[155] When the town was occupied by the sultan of Golconda in 1662, many Portuguese fled and the population decreased. According to contemporary sources, there were only 600 Portuguese *mestiços* (mixed population) who continued to live there in 1669. There were some Armenians but the Portuguese population was very insignificant.[156]

Vicissitudes of Santhome 1662-1749

There was a lack of a strong political power in the region and the Muslims were trying to extend their influence. The sultan of Golconda wanted to extend his control over the Portuguese settlement of Santhome rather than allow the port fall into the hands of the Dutch. Therefore he besieged the town in January

1662.[157] Santhome was defended stoutly by the Portuguese forcing the commander of Golconda (name not mentioned in the document) to leave the town without plundering. As a kind gesture, the Portuguese gave a gift of two guns to the Sultan's Commander.[158] In April 1662, Nekham Khan, the commander of Golconda, laid seige to Santhome. The Dutch, in response to the sultan of Golconda's request, sent three ships to help him capture the port of Santhome. The Portuguese finally surrendered on 1 May 1662 as they could not put up sufficient resistance against the army of the sultan of Golconda. Santhome was occupied by the Golconda forces on 2 May 1662.[159] Even after the seige of Santhome by the Golconda forces and its fall on 1 May 1662, the wall of the fort on the seaward side was in sound condition.[160] John Nieuhoff, the Dutch traveller who visited Santhome in 1662, says that the fort was made of stone and strengthened by bastions.[161] John Fryer, the English traveller who also visited Santhome, says that the wall of the fort which faced the seashore looked like marble.[162]

The port came under the jurisdiction of the sultan of Golconda and it was held by him for a period of eleven years. The Portuguese missionaries in Mylapore were expelled by the sultan in February 1663, as he did not want them to live in Santhome.[163] Several of the Portuguese traders who lived on the outskirts of Santhome were permitted to retain their property and houses in Santhome so that they could continue their trade and bring prosperity to the town.[164] The Portuguese, however, faced difficulties in paying tax to the *havildar* (revenue collector) as their trade had suffered greatly. The additional taxes imposed by the *havildar* could also not be paid. In 1644, however, the Portuguese managed to ward off the threat by paying a lump sum of 500 *pagodas* as demanded by the *havildar*.[165] From time to time the Muslim revenue collector also sent his peon to the Portuguese asking for more money but they refused to pay him.[166]

Dom Affonso VI, the king of Portugal (1656-67), keen to recover the settlement wrote to the sultan of Golconda in 1633 requesting him to return Santhome.[167] On 20 May 1664, the viceroy of Goa wrote once again to the sultan requesting the return of Santhome to the Portuguese.[168] This dispute continued for some years and in the meanwhile, hostilities continued. On

8 January 1667, the Portuguese captured the goods from a ship which belonged to the sultan to force him to return Santhome.[169] The viceroy of Goa, who got the news of the impending destruction of Santhome, wrote immediately, on 22 March 1667, to the sultan and to Nekham Khan, the commander-in-chief of Golconda who was to march towards Santhome and execute the orders of sultan requesting them to avoid destroying the buildings in Santhome.[170]

On 23 March 1667, the viceroy of Goa sent Fr. João dos Reis to the sultan of Golconda to negotiate terms but nothing materialized.[171] Further, on 13 September 1672, Luís de Mendonça Furtado Albuquerque, the governor of Goa (1671-7), sent a letter to the sultan of Golconda desiring to establish a cordial relationship and requesting the return of Santhome to the Portuguese.[172] Santhome continued to remain under the control of the sultan of Golconda in 1673. Langhorn, the agent of the English East India Company, requested the sultan of Golconda in October 1674 to demolish Santhome because it posed a constant threat to the flourishing commerce of the English in the neighbouring port of Madras. As late as 28 March 1676, the sultan still planned to destroy Santhome because the Portuguese continued to attack his ships.[173]

The sultan of Golconda asked Abdul Hassan, the Muslim general to demolish the town. However, giving due some consideration to the representation of the resident Muslim revenue collector in Santhome to the sultan that the demolition of such a fine town would cause damage to the royal commercial interests, the sultan sent a message to the Muslim general to spare the buildings in the town. Subsequently, modified instructions were issued from the court to the general of Santhome that the Portuguese fort and its walls in the town were not to be demolished.

The French, who in the meanwhile had made their appearance on the scene, desired to possess Santhome and approached Abdul Hassan, the Muslim general, to cede the town to them for which they agreed to pay a sum of 10,000 French crowns.[174] As this did not materialize, they attacked Santhome and captured it on 14 July 1672. As a first step, all the dead bodies found there were immediately buried near the seashore.[175] When the French entered the town of Santhome they found twenty-one guns fixed on the walls of the town. They took possession of the magazine which contained 18,000 pounds of gunpowder.[176] They also found 25,000 cannon balls, 100 ingots of lead, 10,000 pounds of musket shot, and sulphur.[177] There were also many horses left, behind by the Golconda forces in the town of Santhome.

The French found the walls of the fort on the landward side in a bad shape at several places. Soon after its capture in 1672, De la Haye, the French naval commander, immediately issued orders that necessary repairs should be carried out.[178] The northern section where there was a marshy land below the bastion was considered to be the most vulnerable part of the fort as that part of the wall did not have any parapet.[179]

The Portuguese from other places were invited by the French to come back to Santhome.[180] Ribeiro, the former Portuguese Captain of Santhome who helped the French to bring the Portuguese back to Santhome died at this time and was buried in the cathedral with full military honours by the French.[181] A High Mass was said in the cathedral and prayers were offered for the repose of his soul.[182]

A commissioner was appointed by the French naval commander and he was asked to make a list of all that had been found in Santhome town. He was requested to carry out an enumeration of the houses and prepare a detailed report on the extent of Portuguese territory, its dependencies and such other matters related to the town.[183]

On hearing of the arrival of the French in Santhome, many Portuguese returned as several houses, which had been seized by the Muslims were still in their possession.[184] The Portuguese refugees who returned to Santhome were asked to register themselves with the commissioner and submit their names, details of their status along with any claims which they wished to put forward.[185]

French records describe that Santhome at that time had well laid out straight streets intersecting each other at right angles. A sketch plan of Santhome preserved in the National Archives of France in Paris shows the development of the town.[186] It can be seen that after the Portuguese surrender in 1662, the town developed into the shape of a semicircle with four bastions projecting towards the south, south-west, north-west and north. It is reported in the French records that the once-resplendent houses were found in ruins. Most of the houses were in a very bad condition at that time as the Muslims who had occupied them neglected to maintain them.[187]

When the French captured Santhome on 15 July 1672, they found that the fortifications on the landward side were strong. On the seaward side the only defence was a small but unflanked wall eight to ten feet in height in the same condition as it had been when the Portuguese had first constructed it.[188] The main gate of the town (*La Porte Royale*) in the west was located in the middle of the fort. There was also another gate facing south. The French, so elated by their success, lost no time in renaming all the bastions in Santhome.[189]

Between 13 December and 16 December 1673 there was heavy rain in Santhome inundating many parts of the town. The rains were so heavy that the walls on the western side were completely washed away by the flood waters. These walls had been constructed of a mixture of mud and bricks sometime earlier. Orders were issued to repair the walls on the western side. Workmen were engaged to carry out the repair work.[190] All these precautionary measures did not, however, help the French in any way because they had to surrender the town to the Dutch[191] on 6 September 1674 when they were defeated. The French handed over the fortifications to the Dutch in the same condition in which they had found them at the time of the port's capture. Thus Santhome was under the French for a brief interval of about two years from 15 July 1672 to 6 September 1674. Under the French all the inhabitants of Santhome including the Portuguese had been allowed to go wherever they wanted within fifteen days.[192]

Although the Dutch had assisted the Golconda forces in recapturing Santhome from the hands of the French, their possession of Santhome town under them did not last long. The proximity of Santhome to Madras encouraged the English to annex it.[193] The English prohibited all ships and other small seagoing vessels from loading and unloading cargo at Santhome as they wanted to develop the port of Madras instead of Santhome.

The Portuguese sent a delegation under the leadership of Fr. Luís de Piedade, an Augustinian monk, to the court of Golconda in 1686 to request the sultan to return the town of Santhome to them. The sultan of Golconda issued a *farman* on 18 December 1686 granting permission to the Portuguese to reestablish themselves at Santhome.[194] The Portuguese were, however required to pay 7,000 *xerafins* annually as revenue to the sultan. Many Portuguese returned to Mylapore between July and September 1687. They rebuilt the town of Santhome and erected minor fortifications without receiving financial assistance from the royal treasury of the sultan of Golconda. Dom Rodrigo da Costa, the Portuguese viceroy of Goa (1686-91), felt it was necessary to resettle at Santhome all the Portuguese private traders who had settled elsewhere in various ports all over the Tamil coast. He therefore appealed to them to come back and settle at Santhome under the protection of the Mughals.[195] This order was read out from the pulpit of the Catholic church at Porto Novo in 1687. Express messengers were sent to the Portuguese living in Nagapattinam, Tranquebar and Madras, where a large number of them had taken up trading with the Dutch, the Danes and the English companies.[196] In 1687 the English in Madras prevented the Portuguese traders from migrating to Santhome through an order which proclaimed that no Portuguese resident should be absent from Madras for more than six days. Those Portuguese traders who continuously overstayed elsewhere were not allowed to enter the English settlement of Madras, their houses were confiscated and the property passed into the hands of the English East India Company.[197]

The English, in the meanwhile, obtained Santhome from the *diwan* on annual lease. However, they did not find the renting of Santhome very convenient. Hence on 26 July 1687, Chinna Venkatadri, one of the native merchants of the English East India Company, was conferred the power to rent Santhome by the President and Council of Madras. Chinna Venkatadri took the lease of Santhome town for a period of three years at 4,100 *pagodas* per annum. The revenue of the town included its customs duties and agricultural revenue derived from the paddy fields in the adjacent villages. The Portuguese traders and residents in

Santhome were given a tax remission amounting to 500 *pagodas* due to be paid by them to Chinna Venkatadri.[198] When Chinna Venkatadri died in 1687, Santhome was leased out to Kasi Veeranna, the chief of the native merchants in Madras, for 3,800 *pagodas* per annum which was lower than the amount paid by his predecessor Chinna Venkatadri. This was because the trade of Santhome was affected due to political disturbances in the region.[199] An agreement was reached in this connection in 1688 between Kasi Veeranna and the English East India Company.[200] At this time the Portuguese soldiers living in Madras were encouraged to settle in Santhome to develop the trade of the English.[201]

In 1693, Aurangzeb, the Mughal emperor, extended his empire in the south and appointed Daud Khan as governor of the Carnatic. The Mughal ruler also appointed Hajee Mohammed Ali in 1694 as the *havildar* of Santhome.[202] In 1720, Arcot became the capital of a *subah* and Sadat Ullah Khan became the *subedar* of the Mughal ruler there. The port of Santhome was annexed and retained as *khalisa* (Crown possession) land. It was later farmed out to a *faujdar* (military chief of a district).[203]

There were some Portuguese ship owners and traders who continued to live in Santhome in 1696. Manuel Pacheco arrived at Madras from Santhome on 21 May 1696 in his ship the *Nossa Senhora de Remedo*.[204] There was also another ship in Santhome called the *Nossa Senhora de Rosario* in which José de Sousa, a private merchant was carrying on his trading operations.[205] In order to develop the trade in Santhome, Matheus Caravalho de Silva was appointed Captain by the viceroy of Goa in 1701. One of his duties was also to look after the welfare of the Portuguese residents of Santhome. Whenever there were disputes among the Portuguese in Santhome, the Captain settled the matter. In 1703, two more ships called *The Good Hope* and *St. Caetano* were engaged in country trade between Santhome and Madras. There were some signs of prosperity at this time as the Feast of Christ the king was celebrated in Santhome on a grand scale by the Portuguese on 24 November 1703 to thank the Lord for his mercy and all the blessings showered upon them.[206]

Nuno Sodre Frade was appointed as the Portuguese Captain of

Santhome in 1706.[207] The only privilege that the Portuguese Captain enjoyed was the right to display the flag of the king of Portugal on Sundays and feast days.[208] On hearing about the cordial relations that existed between the Mughals and the Portuguese, João V, the king of Portugal (1706-50), wrote to the Portuguese viceroy of Goa in 1707 to take steps to enable the Portuguese and other natives who had earlier fled from Santhome to return to the town. On 24 November 1708, the Portuguese viceroy gave an assurance that all Portuguese and natives who returned to Santhome would receive the best of treatment including security and protection of their life and property. The natives would also be allowed to practice their own religion without any imposition of taxes. The viceroy was authorized to negotiate the terms in connection with this order with the Mughal resident officer of Santhome.[209] As the relations between the Mughals and the Portuguese developed, the Portuguese viceroy appointed a police official (in 1712) in Santhome to maintain law and order among the Portuguese.[210]

Trade activities, in the meanwhile, were revived with the help of the native merchants. Santhome flourished so well under the Mughals that the English and the French became eager to extend their control over it. They understood the importance of Santhome and wanted control over the town. However, in September 1749, Santhome was given as a *jagir* by Chanda Sahib to Fr. António de Purificação on the strength of an illegal *farman* granted by Muzzafar Jung without Nazir Jung's consent.[211] The English in Madras at this time successfully negotiated terms with the ruler of Arcot and the town of Santhome was given to them in 1749.[212] At last Boscawn, the English military chief, hoisted the English flag in Santhome on 17 October 1749.[213] The Portuguese flag stopped flying there from 15 August 1751.[214]

Portuguese records contain considerable topographical details of Santhome which may be mentioned here. The port of Santhome was half a league away from the sea when the Portuguese first arrived in Mylapore in 1507. The seashore was located about 100 paces (about 50 metres) away from the Church of St. Thomas.[215] The coastline of Santhome, however, eroded due to seawater intrusion in 1646.[216] There was a lagoon to the south of Santhome. Rainwater from the hilly terrain to the west of Santhome flowed into a lagoon within gunshot distance from its walls before emptying into the sea. Towards the north of Santhome there was another lagoon even closer to the sea than the other one. These two lagoons could be easily connected so that the whole town was surroundered by a moat. A topographical plan of Santhome entitled 'Plan and perspective of the city of St. Thome de Meliapore and its domains taken by the English in October 1749 from the Crown of Portugal' preserved at the Public Library and District Archives of Evora in Portugal carries details of the environs of Santhome before it went into the hands of the English.[217] The river Adyar and the island that had formed in the south of Santhome can be seen on the plan. The villages around Santhome, such as Kottur, Theynampettai, Little Mount and St. Thomas Mount, are mentioned, from where the Portuguese derived revenue. Further, the town of Santhome at this time, excluding the fort area, was 300 *toises* in extent according to a Jesuit letter.[218] As mentioned earlier, Santhome officially ceased to be the possession of the king of Portugal when it was taken away by the English on 17 October 1749.

Importance of Urban Centres

The Portuguese settled along the Tamil coast only where they could anchor their ships and these places slowly grew into ports and over a period of time acquired urban characteristics in the sixteenth century. These urban centres were not 'established' by the *Estado da Índia*. However, the *Estado da Índia* took care to fortify them after the Dutch appeared on the scene in the seventeenth century. These ports served as viable centres in maritime Asia since they essentially comprised a chain of coastal strongholds of forts (*fortalezas*) and unfortified trading factories (*feitorias*). While many ports on the western coast including Goa, the capital of Portugal's eastern empire, had reached their apogee towards the close of the sixteenth century, the ports of the Tamil coast, like Santhome of Mylapore, Nagapattinam and Devanampattinam were beginning to emerge as prominent Portuguese trading settlements.

These Portuguese settlements on the Tamil coast played a significant role in the political, military, economic, social and cultural history of the region. Evaluating the importance of these urban centres in history in the early modern period is necessary, for they are the earliest examples of the globalization of trade in the preindustrial era and the earliest repositories of Western culture in the orient. Here emerged an urban community with a distinctive style and character depending upon its amenability to Western cultural influences.

Most of the Portuguese port settlements came into existence in the proximity of already existing native ports. These coastal towns did not have the usual pattern, of native men of the fishing community alone on the coast. Neither did they retain the traditional pattern of housing set on various caste lines; they had distinct Luso-Indic features. Wherever Portuguese settlements developed on the Tamil coast, in all such places churches, convents, monastries and other institutions appeared.

These towns were not treated as corporate units of the *Estado da Índia*. The Portuguese kings and viceroys alloted funds to develop them. They took serious steps to fortify their trading settlements only after the arrival of the Dutch. The expenses for the fortifications on the Tamil coast were derived from various sources which included profits from voyages, customs duties, etc. Thus much of the money was earmarked for the defences of port towns on the Coromandel coast.

The experience that the Portuguese had gained in Goa and Kochi on the west coast enabled them to plan the development of port towns on the Tamil coast. Divisions of port towns with specialized functional quarters, development of sites for markets, construction of churches, convents and other civic buildings like municipality and the erection of fortifications and walls were the hallmarks of urban planning in Portuguese towns. Thus the orderly arrangement of residential, commercial, administrative and religious divisions marked the urban features of port towns for the first time on the Tamil coast. Roads connecting the different parts of the country to the port towns were an important feature of this planning in the Tamil coast and hinterland.

While studying the origin and development of Portuguese

colonies an important aspect to be noted is that these urban centres, which at one point of time were non-productive under the administration of the medieval Pandyas, Sambuvarayas and the Vijayanagara rulers who depended heavily on the hinterland for their survival, gradually became productive centres under the Portuguese on the Tamil coast. Boundaries between the town and the countryside were marked by boundary walls. The king of Portugal raised Santhome and Nagapattinam from the status of *povaçãos* to a *cidades*. The growth of Santhome and Nagapattinam was dependent upon their economic importance and these towns grew and expanded because of their contacts with the foreland or with areas overseas and in the hinterland.

NOTES

1. See Om Prakash Prasad, *Decay and Revival of Urban Centres in Medieval South India,* AD *600-1200,* Delhi, 1989.
2. Letter of the king of Portugal written in April 1506, in Artur Basilio de Sa, *Documentação Para a Historia das Missões do Padroado Portuguese do Oriente,* 5 vols, Lisboã, 1954-8, vol. 1, pp. 3-13.
3. *IANTT*, *Gavetas*, XV-19-11.
4. Ibid.
5. Zella Nutall, 'Royal Ordinances Concerning the Laying Out of New Towns', *The Hispanic American Historical Review*, 4, 1921, pp. 743-53. Coastal settlements were planned in accordance with the instructions of the king of Portugal issued in the year 1573 in his, *Ordenanzas para descubrimientos, nuevas poblaciones y pacificaciones* (Ordinances for the newly discovered possessions in pacific).
6. *IANTT*, *CC*, III-9-94, *CC*, I-107-86. This manuscript is dated 12 December 1565. It mentions that two other Portuguese had left the Crown service for not having been paid their salary and food allowances.
7. Cunha Rivara, APO-CR, Fasc. 6, p. 113; Silva Rego, *Documentação*, III, 252.
8. Correia, *Lendas*, II, pp. 721-2.
9. *IANTT*, *CC*, I-9-92; *CC*, I-16-106.
10. Silva Rego, *Documentação*, II, p. 147(f); *IANTT*, *Gavetas*, XV-12-2 (1533-5).
11. Diogo do Couto, *Decada,* XVII, pp. 55-6; Paulo da Trinidade, *Conquista Espiritual do Oriente*, Lisboã, 1967. See also, T.R.

Chintamani (ed.), *Sahitya Ratnakara*, Madras, 1932, Canto X, Sloka 68, III, 68, 972.

12. *ARSI*, Mss Goa, no. 12, fls. 209, 216-17.
13. *NA*, *OBP*, VOC 1055; see J.K.J. de Jonge, *De Opkomst Van het Nederlansche Gezag in Oost-India*, 1595-1844, 17 vols., The Hague, Amsterdam, 1862-1909, 3, pp. 345ff; António Mariz Carneiro, *Descrição da fortaleza da Sofala e das mais da India*, Fundção Oriente, Lisboã, 1990. See the plan of Devanampattinam.
14. *MPJA*, *Litterae Annuae*, 1609. The Bishop of Mylapore asked Fr. Levanto to obtain a letter from the *nayak* of Gingee ordering the expulsion of the Dutch from Devanampattinam. See also, Tapan Raychaudhuri, *Jan Company in Coromandel*, The Hague, 1962, p. 92.
15. *HAG*, *MDR*, Livro 19A, 2-9/3-1, letter no. 7.
16. Pissurlencar, *Assentos do Conselho do Estado* (hereafter *ACE*), 6 Fasciculos in 10 vols, Nova Goa, 1857-77. See *ACE*, vol. 2, p. 503; see on Chinnana Chetti in *BFUP*, p. 418, doc. 49; *ACE*, vol. 2, p. 503.
17. *MDR*, Livro 19A, 14-2.
18. Pissurlencar, *ACE*, vol. 2, p. 516; ibid., doc. 10, p. 516. See also the letter of the Portuguese viceroy to the Bishop of Mylapore on matters related to Devanampattinam dated 23 October 1634 in doc. 13, p. 552.
19. *HAG*, *MDR*, Livro 41-2, 4/1, ibid., Livro 19-D, 42/3/5, 11 October 1634.
20. *ARSI*, Mss *Litterae Annuae*, letter of Fr. Pero Mexia written from Vellore dated 13 July 1634.
21. *IANTT*, Mss *DRI*, Livro 36, fl. 43.
22. Ibid.
23. Caeser de Federici, 'The Travels of Caeser Federici', in Samuel Purchas, *His Pilgrims*, vol. 10, Glasgow, 1905.
24. Mendez da Luz, 'Livro da Cidades Fortalezas que o Coroa de Portugal tem nas Partes da India e das Capitanias Mais cargos que nelas ha, e da Importancia deles', *Studia* , no. 6, July 1960, pp. 352-3.
25. Josef Franz Schutle, *Valignano's Mission Principle for Japans* (tr.), John J. Coyne, St. Louis, Missouri, 1985, pp. 75-6.
26. Gaspero Balbi, 'The Voyage of Gaspero Balbi', in Purchas, *His Pilgrims*, vol. 10, Glasgow, 1905.
27. António Bocarro, *Livro das Plantas*, in *APO-CR*, decada 1.
28. William Foster, *Early Travels in India*, London, 1820.
29. Sanjay Subrahmanyam, *The Portuguese Empire in Asia: A Political and Economic History*, London, 1993, p. 165. The Portuguese Viceroy's plan to acquire the Danish fort at Tranquebar, however, did not succeed.

30. *BA*, Mss *Jesuitas na Asia*, Codice, 51-VIII-51, fl. 322.
31. V. Gopala Krishna and Keladi Gunda Jois, *Tanjavur to Vijayagiri Durga: A Travelogue in Kannada Printed from a Palm-leaf Manuscript*, Chennai, 1997, p. 26; Bernado Gomes de Britto (ed.), *Descrição du Cidade de Colombo: Historia Tragico-Maritima*, vol. 1, Lisbon, 1735, pp. 253-307.
32. Purchas, *His Pilgrims*, vol. 10, pp. 217-19; S. Jeyaseela Stephen, *The Coromandel Coast*, p. 98.
33. Sanjay Subrahmanyam, *Improvising Empire*, p. 82.
34. Bocarro, *Livro das Plantas*, vol. 2, pp. 252-3.
35. *IANTT*, Mss *DRI*, Livro 35, fl.5v.
36. Ibid., Livro 29, fl. 29 ; *MDR*, Livro 19A, 2-9/3-1, Letter no. 7; *IANTT*, Mss *DRI*, Livro 39, fl. 29; *MDR*, Livro 40, fl. 29.
37. *HAG*, Mss *MDR*, Livro, 51, fl. 12; J. Castests, 'How Negapatam in 1642 became the First Possession on the Coromandel Coast', *Journal of the Bombay Historical Society*, vol. 5, no. 2, 1939, pp. 129-34. See also, *MDR*, Livro 51, fl.12 (20 December 1642).
38. *IANTT*, Mss *DRI*, Livro 51, fl. 118v; *AHU*, Caixa 20, doc. 4; Pissurlencar, *ACE*, vol. 3, pp. 656-7; see also *IANTT*, Mss *DRI*, Livro 49, fl. 214.
39. *IANTT*, Mss *DRI*, Livro 51, fls. 119-21.
40. Ibid., Livro 48, fl. 266.
41. Pissurlencar, *ACE*, vol. 3, doc. 128, p. 361.
42. Ibid., p. 655. See also Pissurlencar, *ACE*, vol. 3, doc. 22. The Portuguese had added in their letter that to fortify Nagapattinam they could use the leftover out stones found scattered in and around the premises of the mosques and temples.
43. Ibid., vol. 3, doc. 139, p. 383.
44. *AHU*, Mss *CDI*, Livro 20, doc. 4, fls. 1v-2v.
45. Pissurlencar, *ACE*, vol. 3, doc. 83; see also *ACE*, vol. 2, doc. 83, p. 124.
46. Portuguese documents of this period refer to Nagapattinam as a city since there was a fortress which was located on high ground to protect the place. Nagapattinam in this chapter is described as a large town only to distinguish it from the connotation of a city as we understand it today.
47. *IANTT*, Mss *DRI*, Livro 56, doc. 39, fl. 225. For the fortifications of the customs house in Nagapattinam, the names of the following individuals are recorded in the document: António de Mendonça de Brito, Cosmos Ledo de Lima, Francisco Tibao Maracote, Simão de Almedia, António Pessanha, Jassinto de Moraes Monteiro, Baltazer de Sousa de Meneses, António Pais Pachecho, Manoel de Almeida, Domingo de Almedia, Gonçalvo Caravalho, Vicente Pires, Domingos

Pires, Francisco Frayao, João Vierao, Gaspar Pereira Avanha, Gonçalvo de Sequeira, Theotonio de Jesus, Manuel Lima Francisco, Francisco Dias de Silva, Francisco de Lima, Manuel Garcia de Almeida, Manuel Madeira Francisco, João Perreira de Faria, Jacome Cardoso Barreto, Gaspar de Caravalho, Nicolao de Lourenco, Jeronimo Moniz Correia, Andre de Morais de Sousa, Francisco Borges de Mesquita and João Proel de Barbado.

48. *IANTT*, Mss *DRI*, Livro 56, doc. 39, fl. 223. The book of regulations of the customs house was signed by the Captain, the Factor, merchants and others on 26 October 1645. Francisco de Cunha was the writer of the factory at that time.
49. *MDR*, Livro 56, fl. 83.
50. *IANTT*, Mss, *DRI*, Livro 56, doc. 39, fl. 202.
51. See, *Regimentio de Alfândega de Negapatão* (orders of the customs house of Nagapattinam) in *IANTT*, Mss *DRI*, Livro 56, fl. 221.
52. K.A. Nilakanta Sastri, 'Two Negapatam Grants from the Batavia Museum', in *South India and South East Asia: Studies in their History and Culture*, Mysore, 1978, pp. 200-2. The following names are found in the inscription: Puttur, Muttam, Antonipet, Karuveppangadu, Poruvalacheri, Alingili Mangalam, Sanga Mangalam, Nariyangudi, Manjakolle and Niruthina Mangalam. The last two places have not been identified. Nagore was then known as Muttam. See *Alphabetical List of Villages in the Taluks and Districts of Madras Presidency*, Madras, 1924, p. 546.
53. *DR*, 1678, p. 149.
54. Bocarro, *Livro das Plantas*, in *APO-CR*, pt. 2, p. 2.
55. K.A. Nilakanta Sastri, '*Two Negapatanam Grants*', see the translation on pp. 202-3.
56. George Davison Winius, 'The Shadow Empire of Goa in the Bay of Bengal', in *Itinerario*, vol. 7, no. 2, 1983, p. 92.
57. Bocarro, *Livro das Plantas*, in *APO-CR*, pt. II, p. 8. Santhome of Mylapore had a population of 120 whites and 200 blacks.
58. *DR*, 1661, p. 42.
59. *BFUP*, vol. 11, pp. 176 and 179.
60. Ptolemy, the Greek writer, mentions the port of Mylapore as Maillarpha in AD 120. The fact that 770 punch-marked coins were found along with a single denarius of Augustus (27 BC-AD 14) in a pot in Saidapet located in the hinterland of the port of Mylapore suggests that an active trade was conducted with the Roman world. See *Madras Museum Annual Report* (hereafter *MMAR*), 1919-30, p. 6. See also the report of 1931-2, p. 2. The port and the hinterland of Mylapore were located in Kottur *nadu* in Puliyur *kottam*. See *Chennai Managara Kalvettugal* (hereafter *CMK*), Madras, 1980, no. 115 of 1967. That an

official came and plundered the place of Mylapore (*surai kondu pogave*) is mentioned during the rule of the Kulottunga period in AD 1178. For details see, *CMK*, 104 of 1967. The place was called Thiru Mylapore as found in *CMK* 113 of 1967. The *uravar* (members of the village) of Thiru Mylapore (sacred peacock centre) is mentioned in the thirteenth century inscription. See *CMK* 63 of 1967. The Nandi Kalambagam mentions Nandi varman as *Mayilai kavalan* (Protector of Mylapore). The Saivite saint Sundarar who sang in praise of Mylapore (*Andu Thuraikond Sempavalam irrul agatrrum jothi thon Mayilai*) mentions it as a harbour. Arunagiri Nathar who came to Mylapore in AD 1456 sang on Singara Velan mentions that the then temple was located on the seashore in his Thirupugzhal. He describes it as *kadal karai thriai arugay sul Mayilai padithanil uraivanae.* We find that the merchant community of Mylapore and Tiruvottiyur had cooperated to acquire a new village and made it as a *devadana* gift to the temple of Tiruppasur during the period of Rajendra Chola I.

61. Lotika Varadarajan, *Memoirs*, p. 60.
62. Barros, *Da Asia*, 1, 9, 7, p. 303; see also pp. 3, 7, 11 and 2226-7.
63. Ibid.
64. Correia, *Lendas*, III, p. 424.
65. Silva Rego, *Historia das Missões*, vol. 1, p. 53.
66. Silva Rego, *Documentação*, vol. 2, pp. 249-55 (1 September 1537).
67. Ibid., pp. 357 and 147; see also *DI*, vol. 1, p. 81.
68. Ibid., vol. 2, pp. 249-55.
69. Correia, *Lendas*, 4, p. 112.
70. Ibid., p. 157.
71. *DI*, vol. 4, 70; vol. 5, 180; Biblioteca Vaticana, Vat. Lat. Mss no. 7746, Capitulo, LXII.
72. Correia, *Lendas*, vol. 4, pp. 131-2.
73. Ibid., p. 131.
74. *IANTT*, Mss *Casa Forte*, no. 48; see *CSL*, vol. 5, fls. 101-101v.
75. Silva Rego, *Documentação*, 2, 252-4; 3, 165: see for the statistics of Portuguese residents in Coromandel, *IANTT*, *CC*, III, 9-94 (1521); Elaine Sanceau, *CSL*, 3, pp. 64-5.
76. *DI*, 2, 16; Silva Rego, *Documentação*, 3, p. 165; *Monumenta Xaveriana*, 2 vols, Matriti, 1899-1912. See, vol. 1, p. 387.
77. Schurhammer, *St. Francis Xavier*, vol. 2, p. 549.
78. *DI*, vol. 5, 181.
79. *IANTT*, *Gavetas*, II, 8-19-7; see also *DI*, vol. 5, 743.
80. *IANTT*, *CC*, I-107-86 (12 December 1565) ; *DI*, vol. 10, pp. 486-7; *DI*, vol. 13, p. 187; Silva Rego, *Documentação*, vol. 12, p. 512.
81. Purchas, *His Pilgrims*, vol. 10, pp. 146-8.
82. Ibid.

83. *ARSI*, *Litterae Annuae*, Codice Goa, 38, fls. 352-75 (AD 1568).
84. *IANTT*, *Gavetas*, XV, 12-2 (1533-5).
85. Ibid. (1533-5 and 1538). The list contains the names of forty-eight individuals who were wealthy in this period.
86. *DI*, vol. 4, pp. 89-93.
87. Mendes da Luz, '*Livro das Cidades*', pp. 1-144.
88. *ARSI*, *Litterae Annuae*, 1604-6; Gurreiro, vol. 2, p. 321.
89. *BA*, codice 51-VII-14; K.S. Mathew and Afzal Ahmad, *Emergence of Cochin in the Pre-Industrial Era: A Study of Portuguese Cochin*, Pondicherry, 1991.
90. Varadarajan *Memoirs*, p. 88.
91. *IANTT*, Mss, *DRI*, Livro 7, fls. 117-18.
92. *MDR*, Livro 12, 29/2-5.
93. *IANTT*, Mss *DRI*, Livro 38, fls. 198-291.
94. Letter of the king of Portugal to viceroy Rui Lourenço de Tavora, dated 17 March 1609, in *MDR*, Livro 9-10-11, 49-50/4/14, fls. 36-8.
95. Bulhão Pato, *DRI*, vol. 4, doc. 929, pp. 252-3.
96. *IANTT*, Mss *DRI*, Livro 6, fl. 45.
97. *ARSI*, Mss, Litterae Annuae Provinciae Malabarensis, 1604-6, no. XXVI.
98. Manuel de Faria Y Sousa, *Asia Portuguesa*, 3 vols, Lisboã, 1666-75, see tomo III, pt. III, Chap. IV, p. 257.
99. Henry Heras, *The Aravidu Dynasty of Vijayanagara*, Madras, 1927, p. 450.
100. *MDR*, Livro 12, 48/1/3, fls. 143-4.
101. *MDR*, Livro 18, fl. 94; Bulhão Pato, *DRI*, vol. 7, pp. 149 and 390.
102. *IANTT*, Mss *DRI*, Livro 6, fl. 223.
103. Ibid., Livro 7, fls. 258-9; *HAG*, *Registo do Cartas*, no. 109, fls. 217-18.
104. *MDR*, Livro 19, fl. 14v.
105. Silva Rego, *Documentos Remetidos da India ou Livros da Monções*, Lisboã, 1982, vol. 10, doc. 40, p. 37.
106. *MDR*, Livro 12, fl. 218v.
107. *HAG*, *Livro dos Reis Vizinhos* (hereafter *LRV*), Livro 1, 3/1, fl. 3.
108. Ibid., 44/5, fl. 108v.
109. Ibid., Letter of the governor dated 12 September 1620 in Livro 52/9, fl. 130.
110. *BNL*, Mss Microfilm, F.2525, fl. 91.
111. *MDR*, Livro 15, fl. 21.
112. *IANTT*, Mss *DRI*, Livro 21, fl. 93.
113. *HAG*, *Provisões, Alvares e Regimentos*, 1183, fl. 123. *Assentos Conselho da Fazenda*, 1159, fls. 7-7v; 1161, fls. 28-28v, fl.100; 1162, fls. 42v-43, fl. 90v. See also Bulhão Pato, *DRI*, vol. 1, pp. 92, 126, 180, 182, 239, 338; vol. 2, pp. 8, 189; vol. 6, pp. 373-4.

114. *MDR*, Livro 27, fl. 307.
115. Ibid., fl. 52.
116. *BNL*, Codice *Fundo Geral*, 7150, doc 4, fls. 97-8.
117. *MDR*, Livro 15, fl. 72v; Bulhão Pato, *DRI*, vol. 7, pp. 105-9, 245.
118. Ibid., Livro 18, fl. 133.
119. Ibid., Livro 13, fl. 87.
120. Ibid., Livro 22, fl. 81.
121. *MDR*, Livro 24, fl. 426.
122. Ibid., Livro 19D, 31/3/4.
123. Bocarro, *Livro das Plantas*, pt. 2, p. 4. One hundred paces (about 50 metres) away from the cathedral in Santhome was a temple in the west. This is the Shiva temple in Mylapore.
124. *BL*, London, Pero Barreto Rezende, *Livro do Estado da Índia Oriental*, dated 1646, in the Sloane collection. A similar manuscript copy is available in *BNL*, Lisboã, entitled *Descrição das Fortalezas da India Mss Iluminado*, no. 140, fl. 242B. A plan of Santhome entitled Survey of S. Thome de Meliapor at the time of its conquest (1687) by the English (copy after an English map from the 17th century), is kept at Sociedade da Geografia, Lisboã (hereafter *SGL*), *Livros das Plantas as Fortalezas Cidades e Pracas e do Estado da India Oriental*. The dimension of the is map is 140 x 162 cm. See *Cota gavetas* H. 57, published by António de Mariz Carneiro. The map of Santhome is included under no. 49.
125. *BNL*, Mss Iluminado, no. 140, p. 242B.
126. *BNL, Pero Barreto Rezende, Descricao das Fortalezas da India*, Mss Iluminado, no. 140, fl. 242B.
127. Lotika Varadarajan, *Memoirs*, p. 126.
128. *BNL*, Mss Iluminado, no. 140, fl. 242B.
129. It may be pointed out here that this stone was unearthed in Mylapore during the archaeological excavations conducted by Fr. Henry Hosten with the permission of the Archaeological Survey of India in 1916. In this the inscription in Portuguese reads, *Lowada seia a purissima conceicao*. In the centre of the stone, around the decorative carvings there, an oval medallion with the bust of a bearded man wearing a cap is found. This is well preserved now in the diocesan museum at Mylapore.
130. *DI*, vol. 13, pp. 46-8.
131. R.H. Major, *India in the 15th Century*, p. 7.
132. Schurhammer, *St. Francis Xavier*, 2, p. 57; 3, p. 204 (321 fn).
133. Ibid.
134. Purchas, *His Pilgrims*, vol. 10, pp. 217-19.
135. Varadarajan, *Memoirs*, p. 120.
136. Henry Davidson Love, *Vestiges of Old Madras, 1640-1800: Traced*

from the East India Company's Records Preserved at Fort St. George and the India Office and from Other Sources, 3 vols, London, 1913 (rpt.), Delhi, 1988, vol. 1, p. 315.
137. Varadarajan, *Memoirs*, pp. 119-20.
138. Ibid., p. 370.
139. Ibid., p. 394.
140. Ibid., p. 419.
141. Ibid., p. 257.
142. Ibid., pp. 257 and 267.
143. Ibid., pp. 119 and 144.
145. Love, *Vestiges of Old Madras*, p. 321.
146. Varadarajan, *Memoirs*, p. 119.
147. Ibid., pp. 312.
148. Ibid., pp. 213, 224 and 474.
149. HAG, *LVR*, no. 8, fl. 93v.
150. *BFUP*, p. 738.
151. Bulhão Pato, *DRI*, 1619-22, vol. 7, pp. 413-15.
152. Lotika Varadarajan, *Memoirs*, p. 85.
153. António Bocarro, *Livro das Plantas*, p. 8.
154. *ARSI*, *Litterae Annuae Provinciae Malabarensis*, 1644.
155. *DR*, 1661, p. 42.
156. John Davis, *Voyages and Travels of John Albert de Mandelso into the East Indies*, 1669, London, 1910, p. 941.
157. Mir Jumlah, the first nawab of Carnatic, attacked Santhome of Mylapore in 1646. See *OIOC*, Mss, *Original Correspondence* (hereafter *OC*), no. 20009 (26 November 1646).
158. *ACE*, vol. 4, doc. 25, p. 79.
159. Manucci, *Storia do Mogor*, vol. 3, p. 276.
160. Varadarajan, *Memoirs*, pp. 62-3.
161. John Nieuhoff, *Zee en Lant Reize Door Verscheide Gewesten Van Ost-Indien*, Amsterdam, 1682.
162. John Fryer, *A New Account of the East Indies and Persia: Being Nine Years Travels*, 1672-1681, ed. W.C. Crooke, London, 1698, p. 12.
163. *LRV*, Livro 2, 4/7, fl. 10.
164. Varadarajan, *Memoirs*, p. 1444.
165. Ibid., p. 1442.
166. Ibid., p. 1444.
167. HAG, *RV*, Livro 2, 4/1, fl. 10.
168. *DR*, 1664, p. 447.
169. *ACE*, vol. 4, doc. 68, p. 176.
170. *LRV*, 2, 20/4/5, fls. 54v-55. The major part of the document is illegible.
171. *LRV*, Livro 21/1, fl. 55v.

172. *ACE*, vol. 4, p. 565.
173. *DR*, 1676, p. 56.
174. Bibliothéque Nationale, Paris (hereafter BNP), Mss *Nouvelle Acquisitions* (hereafter *NOA*), no. 9352 fl.58.
175. Lotika Varadarajan, *Memoirs*, p. 381.
176. Ibid., pp. 300 and 301.
177. Ibid., p. 88.
178. Ibid., p. 256.
179. Ibid., pp. 56 and 441.
180. Ibid., pp. 380, 394 and 418. Archives Nationales (AN), Paris, Mss *Correspondance Generale 1666-76*, Colonies Serie C2, Inde 62.
181. Varadarajan, *Memoirs*, pp. 293-4.
182. Ibid., p. 381.
183. Ibid., p. 120.
184. Ibid.
185. Ibid.
186. The area of the town extended in the north up to the modern school for the blind in the Santhome High Road, in the south up to the present-day Leith Castle Street and in the west up to the end of Rosary Church Road.
187. Varadarajan, *Memoirs*, p. 119.
188. Ibid., p. 60.
189. Centre des Archives d' Outre-Mer, Aix-en-Provence, Depot des Fortifications. Portefeuille 31.B, no. 327. One bastion was named after Colbert, the famous finance minister of France in the Court of the king of France, was on the south-western side. Bastion Dauphin was situated on the north-eastern corner. Bastion Bourbon, which was at the middle of the east, faced the defence wall. The next bastion was called Le Marin followed by Bastion L'amiral at the southern corner of the fort in the east. Bastion St. Louis was located at the north-western corner. Young, armed soldiers were placed on guard duty at *la gueritte* located in between the Royal Gate and the Bastion of St. Louis. Between the port de la Haye and the bastion of Colbert two more bastions called Bastion Caron and Bastion Maior, were located on the southern side. Similarly, between Bastion St. Louis and Bastion Dauphin were three bastions called Bastion Redere, Bastion Reabre and Bastion le Soleil Royal in the northern direction in addition to L'escalade.
190. Varadarajan, *Memoirs,* p. 295.
191. Wheeler, *Madras in the Olden Times,* Madras, 1861, p. 65.
192. Bibliotheque Nationale, Paris, Mss. *Nouvelle Acquisitions,* nos. 9348-51, entry dated 6 September 1674, 180, *DR*, XXII, p. 300.
193. Dodwell, *A Calendar of Madras Records*, p. 169.

194. *ACE*, vol. 4, p. 573.
195. Varadarajan, *Memoirs,* p. 1071.
196. Ibid.
197. Ibid.
198. Records of Fort St. George (hereafter *RFG*), *DACB*, 1687, p. 115.
199. Varadarajan, *Memoirs,* p. 215.
200. *RFG*, *Public Consultations,* vol. 14. See the entry dated 16 July 1688, p. 253; 1706, p. 108.
201. *RFG*, *DACB*, 1687, pp. 102-3.
202. Ibid., 1696, vol. CXXI. See the entry dated 19 October 1694.
203. Ibid., 1693, Madras, 1917, p. 9.
204. Ibid., 1696, p. 73.
205. Ibid., 1696, p. 73.
206. Ibid., 1703, p. 86.
207. *BFUP*, vols. 38-40, pp. 231, 261-2.
208. Love, *Vestiges of Old Madras*, pp. 576-7.
209. Letter of the king of Portugal to the viceroy of Goa, dated 9 August 1710, in *APO-BP*, tomo I, vol. 3, pt. 2, p. 35.
210. Letter of the viceroy of Goa, dated 16 May 1718 in *APO-BP*, tomo I, vol. 3, pt. 2, p. 346.
211. Casimiro de Nazareth, *Mitras Lusitanas no Orinte*, vol. 2, Bombay, 1888, vol. 2, p. 201. H. Dodwell, *Calendar of the Madras Despatches*, pp. 8-10. See also, *Public Despatches to England*, vol. 17, pp. 61-97.
212. *Fort St. David Consultations* (hereafter *FSDC*), vol. 17, 7 October 1749.
213. *Despatches to England,* vol. 27, 2 November 1749.
214. Ibid., vol. 19, pp. 8-21.
215. Barros, *Decada* 5, 11, p. 107; 6, p. 230; John Davis (ed.), *Voyage and Travels of J. Albert de Mandelso 1669,* p. 941.
216. *BNL*, Pero Barre to Rezende, *Descricao das Fortalezas da India* , Mss *lluminado,* no. 140, fl. 242B.
217. *BPADE*, *Sistema Marcial Asiatico,* Codice 408. See also, *SGL*, *Mapa Topografica de cidade S. Thome de Meliapore os Dominios Tornado Pelo Inglezes em Outobro de 1749 a Coroa de Portugal,* pasta no. 8. The dimensions of it were 887 × 578 mm. See also, Walter Rossa, *Cidades Indo-Portuguesas: Contribuicoes para o estudo do urbanismo Portugues no Hindustao ocidental,* Lisboa, 1997, p. 25. The author examines six Indo-Portuguese only cities, namely, Cochin, Goa, Chaul, Bassein, Diu and Daman.
218. *Lettres Edifiantes et Curieuses Ecrites des Missions Etrangers par Quelques Missionaires de la Compagnie de Jesus,* Paris, 1717-1810, 1829-32, 40 vols. See Tome Quinizieme, p. 312. One *toise* was equated with 6 feet or approximately 2 metres in that period.

9

Conclusion

The global economic system has a history of at least 5,000 years according to some scholars like Andre Gunder Frank and B.K. Gills.[1] Similarly, C. Chase-Dunn and Thomas Hall opine that there have been world economic systems since long before the rise of capitalism. They say that there were state-based world systems which could be termed as a core which accumulated resources by exploiting the peripheries.[2] The study of Samir Amin also stressed the fact that there were connected regional economic systems in history, that is, the tributary system both in China and in India before the rise of merchant capital in Europe. In fact, this merchant capital paved the way for industrialization, qualitatively a new phenomenon in world history which took shape along with the outbreak of the industrial revolution.

Three types of 'world economy' have been identified by Fernand Braudel.[3] The first one is at the horizontal level structured through a geographic centre and periphery (i.e. metropolis and satellite). The second is at the vertical level structured through individuals, groups and market relations, besides ownership and control of the economy. The third is at the chronological level where the organization of the world economy is classified into identifiable periods made up of long cycles of events.

Following the lines of Fernand Braudel, K.N. Chaudhuri approached the analysis of world economy by attempting to identify both spatial contours (the traditional areas of Asia) and institutional features (structural composition of various civilizational entities) during specific epochs.[4] It was an approach to present a static vision of Asian economy before AD 1750.

Like K.N. Chaudhuri, Frank Perlin also adopted an integrative analysis to world trade relations.[5] He traced the growth of independent, indigenous merchant capital which operated from the sixteenth century onwards at the international level.

Further, Andre Wink examined the space that he defined as the 'Indo-Islamic World', which included a good part of South, South-East, and West Asia. The growth of trade is portrayed as the sole factor of change in the system and the rise of Islam, according to him, played a key role in this world system.[6] Janet Abu-Lughod used the concepts of 'world economy' and 'international trade economy' as having an interchangeable (integration and co-hesion) meaning. According to her, the heartland of the world economy in the medieval period was West Asia. This world economic system took shape in the fourteenth century and it integrated all the five regions of world trade, namely, South, West, South-East and East Asia, in addition to the Mediterranean. In her opinion there was co-existence and mutual tolerance and exchange within the larger world economic system. None of these systems were dominant and there was no single hegemony of power.[7] While these are prevalent theoretical formulations, this chapter shall examine the regional character of the economy of the Tamil coast based on the various empirical studies conducted so far, to help understand better how these various theories propounded by the scholars either converge or diverge in the context of maritime trade in this part of the world.

The Tamil country in the medieval period had a very dynamic economy supported by a thriving agronomy and plentiful natural resources with commercial contacts and trade networks having links with the whole of South-East Asia. The revenue derived by the medieval Chola rulers consisted of a variety of taxes and duties. Some rulers of the Tamil country, like Kulottunga Chola (1070-1120), were called the *sungam thavirtha cholan* as they encouraged overland trade and overseas commerce by abolishing customs duties.[8] Meera Abraham's study has shown that the two well-known medieval merchant guilds, *ayyavole* and *manigramattar* in the twelfth century had the greatest amount of trading activities in the mainland of south India and extended their operations to the island of Sri Lanka. The overseas trading activities of these two famous guilds during the thirteenth century appear to have been impressive even when the Chola empire was on the decline, since there are inscriptions which speak of the presence of these merchant guilds at Pagan and Quanzhou even during this period of decline. Development of ports by the Cholas is discussed at length by many scholars. They also examine the long-term interests of the Cholas in trade. But George W. Spencer has highlighted the short-term policy of plunder.[9]

Medieval rulers of the Tamil country like the Pandyas, the Kadavarayas, the Sambuvarayas and the Vijayanagara empire were chiefly concerned with enriching their royal treasury by attracting foreign traders from the Islamic world. Along with foreign trade, the domestic trade in the Tamil hinterland also flourished. The presence of godowns at Chinnamanur (Pandya period) belonging to private traders attests to the prominence of private trade in the Tamil country. After the Muslim invasions, resettlement of merchants was encouraged by the temples at *anjinan pugalidams*, which in turn led to the revival of commerce and handicrafts in these temple towns. Manufacture of cloth was patronized in many centres in the hinterland through the settlement of weavers at *thirumadaivalagams* of temples which also brought revenue to the temple and the ruler.

Ports on the Tamil coast which had been the terminals under the Cholas became mere stopping points for ships destined for Kozhikodu, Kochi and Kollam on the west coast of peninsular India during the Pandya period. Spices to China were directly exported from Malabar and not sent through the ports of the Tamil coast. Another feature of the new development was the migration and settlement of Tamil-speaking Chettis and Marakkayars from the ports of the Tamil coast to Malabar. In these circumstances, the ports in the Tamil country had little opportunity for direct overseas trade transactions on the eve of the arrival of the Portuguese. Further, an interlocking system of intra-regional trade developed in the Bay of Bengal region when ports served mainly as intra-regional redistribution points for goods of the region. Pulicat, a little north of Madras, and Kayal in the south revived as active ports during this period on the east coast.

Also during this period, pearls were exported to China in large quantities as there was heavy demand for them even before the advent of the Portuguese to the pearl fishery coast. The demand was so great that merchants sailing from the Tamil coast are known to have smuggled pearls by hiding them in the linings of their clothes and in their umbrella handles to evade the heavy customs duty in China. In the late-medieval period pearls were taken to Vijayanagara which had by then emerged as a famous market for gold and precious stones.

The drain of gold for pearls was so heavy that there was a ban on the export of gold from China to the Tamil coast. The craze for gold in the Tamil country was met through imports from South-East Asia. Commercial transactions in the Tamil country took place to a large extent through the medium of gold. The abundance of gold was the main reason the Delhi sultanates invaded, annexed and ruled the Tamil country in the fourteenth century. In fact, Malik Kafur looted and plundered the wealth of the Tamil country, sending to Delhi 96,000 bars of gold which were carried from Madurai on 312 elephants along with the many boxes of pearls and precious stones. This marked the beginning of the loss of wealth from the Tamil-speaking region, long before the English East India Company could drain its wealth. Medieval overseas trade in China was state-sponsored, while it was left to private initiative on the Tamil coast, although it flourished because of the protection extended by the Tamil rulers.

The medieval states in the Tamil country grew into vigorous mercantile entities under their rulers. The medieval Pandya state in the Tamil country depended on revenue particularly from the overseas trade, while merchant guilds developed on liquid capital under the protection of the rulers. The thirteenth century also saw the highest watermark of the *ayyavole* guild in the Pandya kingdom. As the Pandyas declined, this merchant guild also started declining in the later half of the fourteenth century.[10] Trade relations with China developed transforming the barter economy into a monetary one prompting the inflow of gold into the Tamil country fuelled by overseas trade originating on the Tamil coast. The ports on the Pandya coast slowly grew into urban settlements which were different from those located in the interior, and the differences between them could be explained by the distinct economic roles performed by those settlements. The ports served as points of exit for manufactured products such as cotton textiles, and also for agricultural products such as rice to foreign markets across the seas. The ports of Kayal, Kilakkarai and Periyapattinam on the pearl fishery coast served also as entry points to interior places like Madurai, the capital of the medieval Pandyas. These ports may be said to have achieved their optimum growth during the rule of the Pandyas. Neither the Arabs nor the Chinese enjoyed any kind of monopoly over the trade in commodities brought to the ports of the Pandya coast.

The Arabs and the Chinese were thus the originators of multilateral trade, sowing the seeds of globalization of commerce in medieval times. In the initial stages of the globalization of trade, the Hindus also participated in the trading of agricultural commodities and natural resources like pearls. During this period, the Chettis (especially the *Kudirai* Chettis) were the most influential merchants and took part in the horse trade in a big way although the Arabs dominated the horse trade as these horses were mostly brought from Persia and Arabia. However, with the arrival of the Portuguese, the domination of the Arabs and the Chettis in the horse trade declined. The rise of the port of Melaka at the end of the fourteenth century was also responsible for the expansion of international trade from the Tamil coast which was conducted by the Chettis and the Marakkayars.

The Pandya rulers appreciated the importance of the oceans and their royal emblem was the fish. They extended the boundary of their maritime empire up to Kollam and also sent ambassadorial missions to China to develop trade. Similarly, the Kakatiya rulers, who had extended their sway over the riverine region of Palar, introduced a new maritime policy in AD 1224-45 which assured that foreign trading vessels which got wrecked on the coast would not have to forfeit their whole cargo to the state.[11] The Vijayanagara rulers extended the boundary of their overseas trade to Sri Lanka and the ruler of Sri Lanka sent his envoy to the court of Vijayanagara in 1378 to pay tribute, as attested to by Ferishta, the Persian chronicler.

In south India, the establishment of the Vijayanagara kingdom in 1336 was an important turning point in its history. In the Bay of Bengal region, the Tamil coast, with its many sea ports, formed a distinct commercial zone. There were some dominant ports both on the pearl fishery coast and on the Coromandel coast. A number of other coastal villages also emerged as minor trading ports close to the weaving centres in the Coromandel, and met the requirements of ports on the Tamil coast. They were gradually drawn into the orbit of the growing regional Tamil economy with the participation of Arab and Chinese merchants, besides the Hindu Chettis under the Vijayanagara empire. The trading ports of the pre-Portuguese period, that is, under the Vijayanagara empire on the Tamil coast, were not merely passive recipients of goods but were also active agents in the seaborne trade. The commodities involved, such as pearls, rice and textiles, were all surplus products of the region. The revenue farming system introduced in the Tamil country by the Vijayanagara rulers served as a great stimulus for the growth of agriculture, which, besides creating a surplus, was also an incentive for developing crafts such as weaving of fabrics, dyeing, etc. The agricultural surplus found a ready market on the west coast. However, the trade contacts of the Tamil coast were confined to West Asia and South-East Asia at a sub regional level.

Immanuel Wallerstein's study emphasized the need to move beyond the national economies to broader economic regions in which national economies were embedded. According to him a world system was a network of economic activities which encompassed the multiplicity of ethnic and other cultural groups having a wider, though not necessarily global reach. The writings of Immanuel Wallerstein are not based on the traditional historian's tool of original archival research. His focus was on the struggle for hegemony among the European powers in the emergence of a global capitalist economy in the seventeenth century. He, like Karl Marx and Max Weber, provided an interesting account of the development of merchant capitalism in the period after AD 1500.[12]

Ravi Arvind Palat sketched the growth of trade and accumulation of capital in the Coromandel and Gujarat regions in India. According to him, the world economy had a regional base in India.[13] In his opinion the core seems to be an economic empire with political, economic, social and perhaps to some extent cultural ramifications. He concluded that the whole range of cores, peripheries and semi-peripheries existed all through the period of political fragmentation between the foundation of the

Vijayanagara empire in AD 1336 up to its fall in the battle of Talikota in AD 1565.

Wallerstein and his followers have further opined that AD 1500 marked the beginning of the process of capital accumulation with the expansion of Portuguese commercial activities in the Indian Ocean. The study of M.P. Prabhakaran deals with the chronological stages leading to the incorporation of India into the newly emerging capitalist world system.[14] He points out the portuguese attempts to peripheralize India via the west coast.[15] He further adds that by the turn of the seventeenth century, rivalry within the system resulted in Portuguese decline and the rise of Dutch control over the spice trade conducted from South-East Asia.[16] In the light of the above theoretical formulations, let us examine their applicability or relevance during the Portuguese presence on the Tamil coast.

When a couple of Muslims in Calicut wanted to know the reason for the arrival of the Portuguese in India, one of the companions of Vasco da Gama replied that they had come in search of Christians and spices. During this first voyage to India in 1498, Vasco da Gama had heard about the availability of pearls in the pearl fishery coast. The Portuguese, however, did not buy pearls even during the subsequent voyages for they were interested in procuring only pepper and other spices. Later they learnt about the availability of rice in the Tamil coast which they wanted to exchange for pepper on the Malabar coast. They were thus prompted by circumstances to participate in the rice trade from the Tamil coast. Francisco de Almeida, the first Portuguese viceroy, sent a team of four persons in 1507 to assess the possibility of the rice trade and also to obtain all possible information about the tomb of Apostle St. Thomas in Mylapore. Even at this time, the Portuguese were not quite aware of the flourishing textile trade that existed between Melaka and the Tamil coast in which the Arabs were engaged at that time. They understood its importance only in the year 1511, after they captured the port of Melaka and drove the Muslim sultan out of there.

The rice trade from the Tamil coast to Malabar was slowly developed by the Portuguese as they needed the rice to exchange of pepper in Malabar. Further, it was also needed as payment of salary for the soldiers in Goa and Kochi. In the meanwhile, the early Portuguese traders began to organize their trade in textiles with the help of the Chettis and Mudaliars and participated in the Coromandel trade with Melaka. The mutual rivalry and conflicts between the native Hindu chief of Kayal and the Muslim chief of Kilakkarai paved the way, initially, for the Portuguese to intrude into the region. The Portuguese agreed in the meanwhile to supply horses to Tumbichi Nayaka of Paramakudi in return for pearls. The conflicts between the paravas and the Muslims led to the large-scale conversion of the paravas to Christianity from 1536 onwards, which enabled the Portuguese to gain control over the region. Eventually the Portuguese established their control over the pearl fishery operations, from which they derived considerable revenue and proclaimed themselves masters of the seas. The horse trade continued till the fall of the Vijayanagara empire in 1565 for there was a great demand for it as the Hindu rulers showed no inclination to master the new military technology that was first introduced by Babur, the Mughal ruler, in the First Battle of Panipat.

The growing Portuguese commercial influence brought about through large-scale conversions of paravas in Kayal slowly eroded the Muslim influence in the area. Arab and Tamil Muslims, who found themselves insecure, left Kayal and migrated to nearby Kayalpattinam to continue their trading activities. The Portuguese who had by then established themselves in Punnaikayal came to enjoy monopoly in pearl fishery and extracted revenue from it. They collected *thithe* from pearl divers for providing them protection with their armed vessels against piracy. Whenever the Vijayanagara rulers demanded tax from the paravas they were prompted by the Portuguese not to pay it because their contention was that since the open seas belonged only to them the revenue derived from the seas could not be shared with others. This posture of defiance by the Portuguese was prompted by the right conferred on them by successive Popes through their various Papal Bulls. The Vijayanagara rulers attacked the Portuguese collectors to extract the revenue by force. The kings of Vijayanagara, the local *nayaks* and the Pandyas attacked separately, at different times the settlements of

Punnaikayal and Tuticorin when the levies on pearl fishery were not paid by the paravas.

The seasonality of pearl fishery operations led the Portuguese to divert their attention to trade in other commodities such as rice and cotton textiles for which the hinterland of the Coromandel was geographically suited. The cultivation of paddy in the river valleys of the Kaveri, Vellar, Pennar and Palar rivers helped to create an agricultural surplus which catered to the foreign markets. The extensive cultivation of cotton in the black soil areas of the Coromandel provided an impetus for the natural growth of textile-weaving in the Tamil hinterland. Production of many varieties of cotton textiles also contributed to the growth of overseas trade. The quantity available was so great that it led to its export to Melaka and other South-East Asian markets, which, in turn, gave rise to the export of goods in bulk quantities, necessitating the pooling of resources for procurement, export and other connected operations.

Subsequently, that is, from 1560, the Portuguese, having learnt of the availability of saltpetre on the Tamil coast, attempted to diversify their trading activities to the Tamil coast. They purchased saltpetre for cash initially. As the demand for war animals continued, the Portuguese began to supply horses and elephants to the *nayak* of Thanjavur in exchange for cash. When the Portuguese were pressed for ready money and also could not meet the specifications (the height of elephants or the length of the tusks) of the *nayak* of Madurai, they sold him a variety of luxury commodities. Saltpetre purchased by the Portuguese from the coastal region was exported to Lisbon where it was urgently needed owing to the demand for the manufacture of gunpowder. Competition for saltpetre with the Dutch and the Danes from the Madurai *nayakdom* led to an increase in its price in the Tamil country. The purchase price of one *bahar* of saltpetre fixed by the *nayak* of Madurai during the period between 1633 and 1635 ranged from 25 *xerafins* to 27½ *xerafins*.

Although there were many ups and downs in the relations between the Portuguese and the *nayaks* of Madurai, Gingee and Thanjavur, they were very often tempered by practical necessity till the arrival of the Dutch in Pulicat in 1606 and the English in

Madras in 1639. The Portuguese, who came as traders, seem to have found the political climate in these parts conducive for expanding and enforcing their political power in the region. The native rulers sometimes felt threatened by them and so summoned up their forces to meet the challenges. They were very often successful in overpowering the Portuguese, even though they could not match the superior gun power of their European opponents. Nevertheless, official and private Portuguese enterprises on the Tamil coast constantly evolved in response to changing local conditions and were remarkably successful in blending with the indigenous commercial networks and also with the native merchants of the Tamil country.

The *nayak* of Thanjavur maintained his identity as a ruler zealously protecting his territory against political intrusions. He was much like the rulers elsewhere in India encountering a new type of aggression, that is, conquest through maritime trade and proselytization. The Portuguese, although familiar with the new political strategy, through a new fuel mix of overseas trade and gunpowder diplomacy put into operation for the capture of Goa and Melaka, did not attempt to use it in establishing their authority on the Tamil coast.

Articulation of commercial power and practice, Vijayanagara governance, commercial vision and market practices tell us that the Vijayanagara state's notion of economy was not anti-commerce. State practices in different contexts of the Portuguese trade by the *nayaks* are well-known. The Vijayanagara state exercised not only political power but also control over routes, commodities, markets and infrastructure in the Tamil hinterland. Trade in strategic commodities conducted by the Portuguese passed through different phases. The *nayak* rulers at first followed an open-door policy in trade by inviting the Portuguese merchants to supply the horses required by them. In the first phase, Portuguese merchants were engaged in supplying horses for the purpose of profit. In the second phase, the Portuguese having learnt about the availability of saltpetre on the coast, changed the pattern of their trade and began to supply elephants to the *nayaks* in exchange for saltpetre to be exported to Europe for making gunpowder. This trade led to many diplomatic contacts with the courts of the *nayak* rulers. During the third phase, the Portuguese adopted a different trade policy after the arrival of the Dutch in the Coromandel in the early Seventeenth Century, sending missionaries to negotiate terms with the *nayaks*. However, the Hindu Vijayanagara rulers treated both the Portuguese and the Dutch equally without distinction. The good offices of the missionaries, notably the Jesuits who maintained cordial relations with the native rulers mostly as healers, were used in a large measure by the Portuguese to cope up with the Dutch who entered the Tamil coast in the early seventeenth century. The Jesuits played an influential role in the courts of the *nayaks* of Gingee, Thanjavur and Madurai. Thus the Portuguese on the Tamil coast made use of spiritual powers to facilitate trade and commerce. The *nayaka* rulers encouraged moneymaking occupations such as textile manufacture and trade. The policy of the government was to maximize the import of bullion. Kannada and Telugu-speaking people migrated to the fertile lands of the Tamil country. These two underdeveloped regions in south India could not be the frontiers of a world economy in the sixteenth century. Slowly, the Coromandel, the Tamil coast in the later period, was caught in economic instability in the markets and so Bengal emerged at the end of the seventeenth century.

Contemporary Portuguese intellectuals developed their own theories regarding the political and economic supremacy of Portuguese royalty. João de Barros, the sixteenth-century Portuguese official chronicler, justified the assumption of the title of *Senhor da navegação, conquista e comercio da Ethiopia, Arabia, Persia e India* (Lord of navigation, conquest and commerce with Ethiopia, Arabia, Persia and India) by Dom Manuel, the king of Portugal, in 1501 on the strength of the sanction granted by the Papal Bulls that gave him right to appropriate the lands that the Portuguese discovered or would discover.[17] It was stated that the lands inhabited by the Muslims and Hindus were to be taken out of their hands since they were unlawful possessors who did not acknowledge Jesus Christ and were therefore condemned to eternal damnation, even though Portuguese overlordship of the seas continued to be a contentious issue.[18] Portuguese penetration into the Tamil coast has to be examined only in the light of these ideas, which held sway over the minds of the intellectuals in Europe during that period.

An important feature of medieval trade on the Tamil coast prior to the arrival of the Portuguese was the freedom enjoyed by the merchant community to deal in all commodities without any kind of restriction imposed by the rulers. Moreover, the seas were open to all and traders from Arabia and China could visit the Tamil ports without any hindrance. It may, in other words, be described as a period of free trade.

However, after the arrival of the Portuguese, restrictive trade practices were introduced while a monopolistic system of trade also made its emergence. The monopoly was originally enjoyed only by the Portuguese Crown. However, in due course, this monopoly was granted to the *fidalgos* who belonged to the nobility more as a form of granting privileges for meritorious service or for a consideration. Yet another feature to be noted was that the Crown lacked the necessary experience and expertise to deal directly with overseas trade on a massive scale. Even the efforts of the Portuguese rulers to form a company to carry on the Crown monopoly trade were not very successful as the first company, started in, the 1580s, did not last for more than a few years. Moreover, Portugal with a population of less than one million until the 1498 was not a powerful political entity in Europe in terms of population. But the discovery of the Cape route alone catapulted it to a position of dominance over the seas and Christendom, for which the country, its people and the ruler were not adequately prepared in terms of both human and material resources.

Prior to the advent of the Portuguese, many ports had developed in the Tamil littoral, but afterwards the few Portuguese settlements like Santhome of Mylapore, Nagapattinam and Devanampattinam alone dominated the maritime trade from the Tamil coast, which testifies to the important role played by the Portuguese in the overseas trade of the Tamil coast. The Chettis and the Mudaliars gave loans to the Portuguese against interest, as they needed finance for conducting trade.

Large-scale overseas trade could be promoted by mobilizing capital from different sources through a pattern of partnership. In this venture, the Tamil merchants came to rely increasingly on a system under which one co-venturer, who may not necessarily be a vaishya, donated capital or goods and remained resident in the port of the Tamil coast while the other, who was most probably a vaishya, contributed his time and energy to transporting and selling the commodities overseas. In some cases the agents of a vaishya would undertake trade on behalf of the vaishya, and this is what happened in the case of the voyage undertaken by the Crown of Portugal with Nayinar Chetti who owned a ship. However, the trade contract lasted only for the duration of one particular voyage and the liability of the person was also limited to the amount invested.

After the arrival of the Portuguese, the Muslims on the Tamil coast gradually lost their hold over the trade in bulk goods. As the long-distance trade of the Marakkayars with South-East Asia in bulk goods declined they were forced to divert their trade from the Coromandel to the Malabar via overland routes. In these circumstances, some of those in the employ of these Marakkayars turned to the Portuguese whose ships were trading with the Coromandel to become pilots, sailors and navigators. The mercantile activities of the private Portuguese were founded upon intimate collaboration with the Hindu merchants, which helped both trading groups.

Many of the bulk goods and products of the Coromandel were in great demand in all South Asian and South-East Asian markets and they formed a substantial part of the goods involved in the long-distance trade. The Portuguese participated in the distribution of agricultural surplus such as rice. Regular textile trade was organized from the Coromandel Coast with South-East Asia in exchange for spices. The Portuguese bought pepper from Aceh, cloves from Makassar, the Moluccas and Amboina and nutmeg from Banten, which were then exported to Lisbon via India. Thus the trade in textiles and rice developed and this commerce in bulk goods continued for a long time.

There was stiff competition between the Dutch and the Portuguese in the cloth trade. The Dutch East-India Company was successful in the organization and production of textiles in many weaving centres of the Coromandel Coast as they advanced money directly to the weavers. Forming joint-stock companies of suppliers at Pulicat was another significant move that developed the Dutch cloth trade.[19] The main factor that helped the Dutch trade of the period was the production-oriented advances given to textile artisans who manufactured cloth according to the desired specifications and requirements of the Dutch in the hinterland villages of the Tamil coast during the seventeenth century. Portuguese private traders on the other hand were not equipped to compete with the Dutch, as they continued to buy cloth only through brokers. Although it was the Portuguese who sowed the seeds of the textile industry and its impressive trade from the Tamil coast with South-East Asia, the Dutch and the English were more successful in exporting the cloth to Europe by and it was they who reaped the benefits that flowed from the pioneering efforts of the Portuguese.

The export of bulk commodities from the Coromandel on behalf of the Portuguese Crown was carried out in partnership with the Chettis till AD 1535. This arrangement was replaced by the grant of trading privileges to *fidalgos* who had moved to the Coromandel. Later, after 1560, the system of offering concessions to private Portuguese traders was introduced and this lasted up to the 1570s. The Spanish occupation of Portugal in 1580 brought about the decline of the Portuguese Crown trade which was followed by a concurrent decline in their power and influence in the Eastern hemisphere.

Ships being the most useful instrument for both the transhipment of commodities and travel for merchants across the oceans, the size and carrying capacity of these vessels made tremendous progress. Ships built in the time of Ibn Battuta in the fourteenth century were larger than those built during the period of Marco Polo in the thirteenth century. Further, in the period of expansion of the Portuguese, ships of 600 to 800 tonnage were used for their trade on the Tamil coast. Although the regional trade of the Tamil coast with Sri Lanka and Malabar and the interregional trade with China and South-East Asia were always strong between AD 1300-1500, the interregional trade came to be replaced with intercontinental trade, more specially through the export of pepper and spices to Europe and the import of silver from America via Manila to the Tamil coast through the efforts of the Portuguese.

The Portuguese imported gold from Melaka in large quantities as it was always in great demand in the Tamil country. They also imported various other metals such as copper, tin, lead and silver which were needed by the Tamils. The development of the export trade on the Coromandel Coast enabled the growth of an equally extensive import trade. All of these imports were not meant for local consumption. The abundant export potential of the Coromandel Coast resulted in the import of a variety of goods from different parts of Asia. The extensive commerce of the Portuguese led to the import and flow of economic surpluses from South, South-East and East Asian countries to the Tamil coast. Portuguese imports like precious stones and spices were re-exported to upcountry markets in India and Europe. The import of precious metals opened up the whole of the Tamil Coast to rapid monetization of the economy. It was altogether a mutually advantageous economic relationship between the Tamils and the Portuguese.

The Portuguese traders on the Coromandel coast were to a large extent instrumental in the modernization of the economy in which they were partners with the local merchants. This trade was to be beneficial to both the Portuguese as well as the indigenous merchant community; it turned out to be beneficial to the economy of the Tamil coast. Domestic production of precious metals such as gold, silver and copper had always been very marginal in the Tamil country. The internal needs of the Tamil economy for coinage, consumption and other purposes was to be met only through imports. The Portuguese realized early the importance of gold import from Melaka to the Tamil coast. Silver and copper came to the Tamil coast from Manila and Maçāo via Mexico and Peru. However, with the opening of direct trade with China from the Coromandel, the Portuguese started importing large quantities of silver and copper from China and Japan to the Coromandel. The minting of gold coins of *pagodas* and silver coins of *panams* necessitated the flow of gold from Melaka, Minagkabu, Pahang and Brunei and silver from Siam to the ports of the Tamil coast. Copper which had been imported was used in making vessels, guns and cannons. Other metals like tin, lead, sulphur and quicksilver were also brought by the Portuguese to the Tamil coast where there was a ready market them for making *panchaloga* idols.

The social life of the Tamil people during this period attained a high cultural level imparting a degree of sophistication to the economy. A number of imports were luxuries as well as essentials. In this connection it may be said that cosmetics, astringents, aromatics and perfumes also formed a major component of imports as there was a demand for these items among the prosperous sections of the Tamils and royalty. Further, commodities like lac and dye roots were imported to be used in the textile industry. Benzoine was imported to be used in confectionery while camphor was used for medicinal purposes. The Portuguese traded in luxuries such as silk, china ware and porcelain which were also used by the well-to-do and the most prosperous sections of the Tamil society. Precious stones such as rubies, emeralds, topaz and cat's eye were brought to Burma and Sri Lanka and trade in these articles was very active until the fall of the Vijaynagara empire after the Battle of Talikota. The Portuguese trade in bullion, precious stones and luxuries, continued but it was much affected after the fall of the Portuguese settlements into the hands of the Dutch. Although the official Portuguese trade in bullion disappeared in the 1670s when the Dutch, the English and the French appeared on the Coromandel coast, some private Portuguese merchants continued trading in bullion and precious stones.

The Arabs who had been the traditional enemies of the Portuguese since the days of the Crusades became their commercial rivals after the fall of Constantinople in 1453. Portuguese relations with the native Hindus and Hindu rulers were much more cordial than with the Muslim chieftains and rulers. They had to fight the Arabs and Muslim rulers, but tried to establish diplomatic contacts with the native Hindu rulers, especially because the latter were more tolerant towards all foreigners. India, a Hindu country ruled by Hindu rulers, first had to contend with Muslim invaders who eventually became, at least politically, assimilated into the Indian polity. The Hindus, or the Hindu rulers did not start a war of liberation with the invaders. Even the foreign Muslim rulers adapted themselves to the local conditions, and to a large extent, respected Hindu customs and conventions, such as those adumbrated in the *Arthashastra*. But with the arrival of the Portuguese, there was a political metamorphosis in peninsular India as there were now three leading actors in the drama that came to be enacted on the stage of subcontinental politics. The Hindus were the original inhabitants of the land, very often tolerant even towards the invaders. Now, after the advent of the Portuguese, it was a triangular contest. But the situation took a turn for the worse after the arrival of the Dutch and then the English and the French, giving rise to more conflicts of interests, diplomatic activities and military adventures.

With the arrival of the Dutch in India, another Christian power from Europe, the theory propounded by João de Barros was called into question in the early seventeenth century. Hugo Grotius refuted the arguments of João de Barros saying that India was well known and its trade had been famous for centuries and so the Portuguese claim that they discovered it was unacceptable.[20] Even granted that the Portuguese had 'discovered' India, they did not have the right to appropriate the newly discovered land for themselves and deprive the Hindus who had occupied it for ages. Grotius declared that the Pope, who was the spiritual head, did not have any temporal authority over India or the Indians; he had nothing to do with the Hindus since the Hindus did not belong to the Church and did not come under his jurisdiction at all.[21]

The objections raised by Hugo Grotius in favour of Dutch right of freedom over the seas in the East were subsequently countered by Portuguese scholars. Frei Serafim de Freitas upheld the right of the Portuguese to the East Indies, especially on the basis of the right to freedom to propagate Christianity. He admitted that Portugal did not have direct jurisdiction over the non-Christians in India but affirmed its indirect jurisdiction. The Pope, being the Universal Pastor, had the right and duty to assign the mission of converting the unbelievers and he had delegated this power to the king of Portugal. He added that the Pope also held the power to assign monopoly of trade to the Portuguese since the missionaries needed money for their survival.[22] The king of Portugal could not claim the monopoly of trade if he did not send missionaries to India.[23] It is against this background that Portuguese activities in the seventeenth century have to be considered. It may be pointed out here that the Portuguese arguments in favour of *mare clausum* (closed seas) were weak. Frei Serafim de Freitas in the seventeenth century had considerably deviated from the views expressed by João de Barros in the sixteenth century. The Dutch vigorously assaulted the Portuguese monopoly of Eastern trade both as a concept and in its application. The Portuguese could achieve little success in their closed-sea policy in the Tamil waters.[24]

Some of the very enterprising Portuguese who had earlier served the Portuguese *Estado da Índia* finding the Coromandel Coast very conducive for commerce, moved along the Coast, initially to Kanyakumari, which was a kind of meeting point between the east and west coasts of India. As during the gold rush, there was a scramble for pearls among the early stragglers who came to the pearl fishery coast. The king of Portugal appointed sea Captains to enforce Portuguese authority over the seas as their trading activities gradually increased and expanded. When the trading activities and their involvement in the pearl fishery increased, factories, which were something like warehouses-cum-lodging houses, were established for the convenience of these mobile traders and stragglers. Hence the Portuguese Crown found it necessary to appoint a separate Factor to be in charge of the land where there was a trading factory.

The authority wielded by the *Estado da Índia* showed signs of being too weak to exercise control over the Portuguese settlements on the Tamil coast, which led to maladministration in these settlements. The Portuguese Captains also felt free to act in a manner which was inclined, more towards seeking personal profit than protecting the interests of the Crown. The absence of effective local authority in the Portuguese settlements resulted in the frequent eruption of disputes and conflicts among the settlers leading to anarchy. Even the ecclesiastical authorities could not exercise sufficient control while temporal authority was minimal. With the defeat of the Portuguese and the passing of their settlements into the hands of the Dutch between 1658 and 1662, only private Portuguese traders continued to participate in the coastal trade.

In the absence of a Portuguese company to match the powers of similar companies launched by the Dutch, the English and the French, the Portuguese shippers, financiers and traders both big and small were almost at liberty to trade in an atmosphere of *laissez faire* but lacked the strength of joint-stock-companies, and therefore found it advantageous to collaborate with the Dutch, French and English East India Companies. In these circumstances the English East India Company at Madras attracted a considerable number of stranded Portuguese traders. These traders mainly used the developing English settlement of Madras and traded in partnership with the English. Some Portuguese traders in Madras served as frontmen for the English. The Portuguese did not altogether vanish under the Anglo-Dutch onslaught but instead found new niches and established alternative commercial networks. Trade continued to register steady growth in the Bay of Bengal region without any major change in its pattern and direction. South-East Asian and East Asian trade control was stronger and in the Bay of Bengal, it was less controlled by the Portuguese. The native merchants had always practised free trade and the Portuguese trade did not affect the traditional commercial linkages.

Some Portuguese private traders, over a period of time, developed their trade to such an extent that they came to own their indigenously built ships. These Portuguese shipowners lived chiefly at Porto Novo. Private Portuguese trade from the Tamil coast was very prosperous and formed a substantial part of the trade of Asia, even though Portuguese influence and power were on the decline. It was almost invariably conducted in some form of partnership with indigenous merchants.

The accumulation of surplus capital in the hands of Portuguese traders slowly led even some of their household members into the diamond trade. Portuguese diamond merchants, through their family members, established links with the English East India Company which was interested in exporting diamonds to London. Some Portuguese also traded in rubies and corals with the English.

Another class of Portuguese traders in some ports like Nagapattinam also had sufficient capital to engage in the bulk trade of textiles. These textile traders went as far as Aceh, Makassar, Tennaserim, Mergui, Melaka and Mação. With the decline of the Portuguese since 1662, the *Estado da Índia* was no longer in a position to provide effective protection to the textile traders operating from the Tamil coast. There traders, therefore, faced greater onslaught by the Dutch and lost a major part of their accumulated capital.

Under the Portuguese, Punnaikayal and Vedalai developed as important trading centres, but the most important feature was pearl fishing. The small beginnings made by the Portuguese in Kayal and Kilakkarai led to the growth of commercial enterprises in Punnaikayal and Vedalai. Most of these Portuguese port settlements came into existence in the proximity of already existing native ports to draw on the available facilities for quick growth. The importance of these ports came to rest on their commercial and pearl fishing activities. When the pearl fishing operations shifted to the island of Mannar in Sri Lanka, the importance of Punnaikayal and Vedalai dwindled.

The Portuguese initially established themselves adjacent to ports where the native Coromandel merchants traded. They erected mud fortifications to defend themselves and their trading establishments. They could build only mud fortifications as the local rulers had banned foreigners from erecting buildings made of lime and stone. As the Portuguese gained sway over the seas, they moved on to seaports to establish land-based factories. Stone structures developed in the ports only when they became full-fledged administrative centres of the king of Portugal. All the Portuguese settlements developed an overwhelmingly Lusitanian character resulting in an extremely hybrid culture, with the Portuguese population remaining under the administrative control of the Captain while natives lived in their own quarters under an *adhikari* who was appointed by the native ruler. The Indo-Portuguese towns of Santhome of Mylapore and Nagapattinam being multicultural towns did not allow themselves to be easily absorbed into the system of single ownership by either the *nayaks* or the Portuguese.

The judiciary, that is, the appointment of *ouvidors* besides the administrative structure with the post of Captain was another phase of urban development. There were security men and soldiers appointed in the Portuguese settlements for the purpose of defence. The local rulers did not object to this for the Portuguese were not their subjects.

In the seventeenth century the Portuguese settlements along

the Tamil coast slowly acquired urban characteristics over a period of time. These urban centres were not 'established' by the *Estado da Índia*. However, the *Estado da Índia* took care to fortify them after the Dutch appeared on the scene in the seventeenth century. These ports served as viable centres since they essentially comprised a line of unfortified trading factories and forts. Santhome of Mylapore, Nagapattinam and Devanampattinam which functioned only as settlements in the sixteenth century emerged as urban centre in the seventeenth century.

These Portuguese settlements played a significant role in the political, military, economic, social and cultural history of the Tamil region during the sixteenth and seventeenth centuries. They were the earliest arenas of globalization of trade on the Tamil coast in the pre-industrial era and served as gateways for the penetration of Western influence into the Tamil country. The growth of Santhome and Nagapattinam was dependent on their economic importance and these towns grew and expanded because of their contacts with the overseas markets and the immediate hinterland. In due course of time, the towns of Mylapore and Nagapattinam came to be administered by a municipality and a council elected from amongst the elder citizens of the port settlements.

These Indo-Portuguese port towns were not exclusively populated in the usual pattern by native fishermen but comprised Portuguese traders and missionaries. The towns did not retain the traditional pattern of housing set on various caste lines but developed distinct Luso-Indic features. The Portuguese quarters developed with churches, convents, monastries and other institutions. Two other major representative bodies of the Portuguese were the Municipal Council and the Holy House of Mercy in these urban centres. The Portuguese kings and viceroys even allotted funds to develop them. They took serious steps to fortify their settlements. The money required for the fortifications on the Tamil coast was generated from local sources which included profits derived from voyages, customs duties on commodities, etc. Thus a lot of money was earmarked for the defences of the port towns on the Coromandel Coast as even the local merchants converged to these new towns for security more than anything else.

Since medieval times, there had been several traditional elements of planning in respect of temple towns in the Tamil country, but there seem to have been none for port towns. There were, however, many elements of town planning, especially in the Portuguese port settlements on the Tamil coast. Some of the port towns, such as Santhome and Nagapattinam, had specialized functional quarters, specified sites for markets, churches, convents and other civic buildings like the municipality, and even fortifications. Thus the orderly arrangement of residential, commercial, administrative and religious divisions marked the urban features of the port towns for the first time on the Tamil coast. Roads connecting the port towns with different parts of the country were an important feature of this planning on the Tamil coast and the hinterland.

The Portuguese Captains were permitted by the *nayaks* to collect revenue in the surrounding areas of the ports particularly from seven villages near Devanampattinam, ten villages near Nagapatttinam and five villages near Santhome of Mylapore. This shows that the Portuguese were powerful and their urban presence in the ports extended to the immediate suburban areas as well. The Portuguese urban centres, which at one point of time were non-productive under the administration of the medieval Pandya, Samburvaraya and Vijayanagara rulers, depending heavily on the hinterland for their survival, gradually became productive centres under the Portuguese. The boundaries between the town and the countryside were, however, marked by gateways. The Tamil coast was the centre of the Bay of Bengal world system with the Coromandel as its eccentric centre, and the busiest concourse of ships and shipping lines operated from different ports of East Asia and South-East Asia. The Portuguese played a key role in this trend of transformation using the existing indigenous commercial network.

After losing most of their accumulated capital many of the Portuguese began to slowly move out of the Tamil coast slowly to Goa to live under the protection of their own ruler, while the rest got assimilated with either other European settlers or the locals. It can be asserted that the Portuguese did not indulge in either draining or plundering the wealth of the Tamil country but only contributed towards the growth of trade and economy by carrying surplus products from the Tamil country to Europe and South-East Asia and opening new marts, although they did also export textiles and pearls to Lisbon. The idea of colonization had not gained ground even when Portuguese power had declined on the Tamil coast by the middle of the seventeenth century. It would be historically improper to brand the Portuguese as colonialists along with the British and others.

The nature of the Portuguese trade as the *cartaz*-armada-*cafila* system served the double purpose of controlling and directing trade.[25] Portuguese trade can be classified according to the nature of involvement. The first type relates to the royal trade on behalf of the Crown, by the Crown officials. The second type is presented as controlled local participation in trade by issuing *cartazes*. The third category deals with the intra-Asian trading networks, where the crown initially made claims to certain routes and later underwent privatization. The fourth type is the private-level trade conducted by both officials and non-officials.[26] The fifth category includes the priests and the missionaries who indulged in trade.[27] The emergence of the *cartaz* system and the *alfandegas* or customs houses has given credence to the hypothesis that private trade was a recognized perspective of the Portuguese presence.[28]

Several general conclusions drawn by various scholars are not applicable to the Tamil coast trade. Some writers have opined that the contribution of the Portuguese was in several ways more favourable for the Atlantic trading world than the Indian Ocean.[29] C.R. Boxer says that the Portuguese seaborne empire was primarily dependent on trade across the oceans, and to ensure their goals of monopoly on the trade of certain products of Asia, the Portuguese brought in elements of violence.[30] This is also not true in the case of the Tamil coast. Some works on the Portuguese enterprise have concentrated on the nature of the enterprise, seen overwhelmingly as a royal monopoly in order to control and direct the trade in certain products of Asia to Europe.[31] The Portuguese on the Tamil coast exported pearls, diamonds and saltpetre to Portugal via Goa and they did not have a monopoly. According to M.N. Pearson, the basic nature of the trade did not change as there was no change in the basic commodity structure.[32] The fact that pearls, diamonds and saltpetre were exported proves that there was definitely a change in the commodity composition of Indo-European trade moving away from the earlier policy of exporting of pepper and spices.

NOTES

1. Andre Gunder Frank, *Capitalism and Under Development in Latin America,* New York, 1969; A.G. Frank and B.K. Gills, *The World System: Five Hundred Years or Five Thousand,* London, 1993, pp. 292-3.
2. C. Chase-Dunn, *Global Formations*, Cambridge, 1989.
3. Fernand Braudel, *Capitalism and Civilization: 15th and 18th Centuries,* 3 vols, London, 1981-4.
4. K.N. Chaudhuri, *Asia Before Europe: Economy and Civilisation of the Indian Ocean from the Rise of Islam to 1750,* Cambridge, 1990.
5. Frank Perlin, 'Proto-industrialization and Pre-colonial South Asia', *Past and Present,* XCVIII, 1983, pp. 30-95.
6. Andre Wink, *Al-Hind: The Making of the Indo-Islamic World,* vol. 1, Leiden, 1990.
7. Janet Abu-Lughod, *Before European Hegemony: The World System AD 1250-1350,* New York, 1989.
8. *South Indian Inscriptions,* vol. 2, no. 58, line 50.
9. See, George W. Spencer. *The Politics of Expansion: The Chola Conquests of Sri Lanka and Srivijaya*, Madras, 1983.
10. Meera Abraham, *Two Medieval Merchant Guilds of South India,* Delhi, 1988, p. 67.
11. *Epigraphia Indica,* vol. 12, pp. 196-7. The Kakatiya rulers earlier took away by force the whole cargo that was carried by ships and vessels after they were wrecked and washed up on the Shore.
12. Immanuel Wallerstein, *The Modern World System I: Capitalist Agriculture and the Origins of the European World Economy in the Sixteenth Century,* New York, 1974, p. 46. See also his works, *The Capitalist World Economy,* Cambridge, 1979; *The Modern World System II: Mercantalism and the Consolidation of the European World Economy, 1600-1750,* New York, 1980; *The Modern World System III: The Second Era of Greater Expansion of the Capitalism and World Economy, 1730-1750,* New York, 1989. See also, M.N. Pearson, *Before Colonialism: Theories on Asia-Europe Relations, 1500-1750,* Delhi, 1988.
13. Ravi Arvind Palat, 'From World-Empire to World-Economy: South Eastern India and the Emergence of the Indian Ocean World Economy, 1350-1650', Ph.D. thesis, Binhampton, 1988.

14. M.P. Prabhakaran, *The Historical Origins of India's Under Development: A World System Perspective,* New York, 1990. See also, Sugata Bose (ed.), *South Asia and World Capitalism,* 1990; T.R. Shannon, *An Introduction to the World System Perspective,* San Francisco, 1989.
15. Prabhakaran, *The Historical Origins*, p. 51. According to him, Portuguese rule in India never extended beyond the distance of a day's march from their ships and the Indian rulers successfully resisted all Portuguese attempts to expand their power. He says that India was not yet on the periphery also because the overall impact of Portugal's India trade and commerce was minimal.
16. Ibid., p. 74.
17. João de Barros, *Da Asia,* decada I, pt. II, pp.11-12.
18. Ibid., pp. 16-17.
19. Tapan Raychaudhuri, *Jan Company in Coromandel, 1605-1690,* The Hague, 1962.
20. Hugo Grotius, *Mare liberum Sive de jure quod Batavis competit ad Indicana commercia Dissertatio*, translated by Ralph Van Deman Magoffin and James Brown Scott, *The Freedom of the Seas or the Right which Belongs to the Dutch to take part in the East Indian Trade,* New York, 1916, p. 13.
21. Ibid., p. 16.
22. Frei Serafim de Freitas, *De Justo Imperio Asiatico dos Portugueses,* Lisboa, vol. 2, p. 93.
23. Ibid., p. 94.
24. S. Arasaratnam, 'Mare Clausum, the Dutch and Regional Trade in the Indian Ocean, 1650-1740', *Journal of Indian History,* LXI, pts. 1-3, April-December 1983, pp. 73-91.
25. Pearson, *Merchants and Rulers*, p. 40.
26. Ibid., pp. 33-9.
27. C.R. Boxer, *The Portuguese Seaborne Empire*, p. 77.
28. James C. Boyajian, *Portuguese Trade in Asia Under the Habsburgs, 1580-1640,* Baltimore, 1993, p. 4.
29. Felipe Fernandez-Armesto, 'The Indian Ocean in World History', in Anthony Disney and Emily Booth (eds.), *Vasco da Gama and the Linking of Europe and Asia*, Delhi, 2000, pp. 11-30.
30. C.R. Boxer, *The Portuguese Seaborne Empire, 1415-1805*, London, 1969. See also, A.J.R Russel-Wood, *A World on the Move: The Portuguese in Africa, Asia and America, 1415-1808*, New York, 1993.
31. R.S. Whiteway, *The Rise of Portuguese Power in India, 1497-1550*, Westminster, p. 899; B.W. Diffie and G.D Winius, *Foundations of Portuguese Empire, 1415-1580*, Minneapolis, 1977.
32. M.N. Pearson, *Portuguese in India: The New Cambridge History of India*, 1.1, New Delhi, pp. 61-80.

Glossary

adhikari	Native nomenclature for an officer.
alcaide-mor	Commander of a fortress, steward of a castle.
alcalde	Mayor, judge.
alfândega	Customs house.
aljofar	Seed pearl, imperfect pearls.
almoxarife	Administrative post concerned with civil supplies.
alvara	Decree of the Portuguese king or viceroy valid for a limited period.
amaldar	Officer in-charge of a district.
armazem	warehouse.
arratel	Portuguese weight equivalent to a pound, known as *rattal* in the vernacular;1/32 of an *arroba*.
arroba	Portuguese weight of 32 *arrateis* equivalent to a quarter of a heavy quintal (15 kg).
ashrafis	*Xerafin* or *ashrafi* was the silver currency of Goa.
bahar	A measure of weight commonly used in South Asia and South-East Asia which varied according to commodity and region. Fifteen *naali* was one *bahar*. The word *bahar* originally derived from the Sanskrit word *bhara*.
bairro	Quarter of a town
bakshi	Paymaster.
beatilha	Derived from the Portuguese. Muslin sometimes dyed sometimes striped or embroidered.
bendhara	A magistrate dealing with all civil and criminal affairs who also had charge of the king's revenue.

bizalho	A small container or a wooden lac box used to transport pearls and precious stones.
bulibuliao	Special tax
cabotagem	Coastal trade.
cafila	Naval convoy.
caldeirao	Municipal tax.
câmara de comptos	Revenue office or chamber of accounts.
câmara municipal	Municipal council.
candy, candil	A measure of weight equivalent to 480 *arrateis*. It is equal to 16 *arrobas*.
capitão-mor	Captain-major.
carreira da India	The voyage from Portugal to India and India to Portugal via the Cape of Good Hope.
carta de quitação	A certificate of acquittance.
carta regia	Royal letter.
cartaz	Pass issued by the Portuguese to a merchant ship.
casa da moeda	Mint.
casa da pólvora	The gunpowder factory.
casado	A married Portuguese settler.
casticola	Person of good heritage. Usually used to describe persons from Portugal as opposed to those from a mixed marriage.
cavaleiro	Knight.
chackram	Fanam of base gold. It was equal to 25 *reis*. In Kollam it was equal to 40 *reis*.
chank	Mother of pearl.
chintz	Derived from Malay. Cotton or silk worked in colours.
colecta	Tax on food.
conhecimento	Receipt, voucher or bill of lading.
conselho do estado	State Council
conselho da fazenda	Financial Council.
corja	Four *corjas* made a packet. One *corja* contained 20 pieces of cloth.
covado	Equal to 30 inches, or to 3 *palmo* or 65 cm.
cowle	Permit.

cruzado	A coin which had a cross of the Order of Christ on the obverse. It was Portuguese coin usually of silver with a fixed value of 400 *reis*.
degredado	Condemned by common law, exile.
desembargadores	Judges.
diziam de pescado	Tithe on fishing.
diwan	Chief minister.
estado da Índia	State of India, the Portuguese empire east of the Cape of Good Hope to the region of Japan.
fanam	A tiny gold or silver coin used in the Coromandel of different and fluctuating values called *panam* in Tamil, equal to 25 *reis*. It was also known as *fanão* and its value varied from 10 *reis* in Sri Lanka to 29 in Nagapattinam. In Pulicat 10 *fanams* were equivalent to 1 *pardão de fanões*.
faraçola	One-twentieth of a *bahar*.
fardo	A bale or a pack containing 25 *corjas*.
farman	Royal order or decree.
faujdar	Army commander; military governor of a province.
feitor	Factor, the person in-charge of a trading factory; a commercial agent, the executive head of a factory.
feitoria	Crown trading post or an agency in an Asian port.
fidalgo	Petty nobleman or a Portuguese gentleman, literally 'son of a somebody'.
florins	Guilder, the Dutch monetary unit. It was subdivided into *stuiveres* and *penningens*.
fusta	Single-masted oared boat with about 40 oarsmen and of about 40 tonnes. In English it was called a foist.
ganta	Equal to 3 kilograms.
idangai	Left hand division of caste in south India.
inam	Grant of rent-free land.
jagir	An assignment of land under the Mughals

	made in return for service usually military. A temporary revenue assignment for three years.
juiz	Judge or magistrate.
juiz da fazenda	A treasury inspector.
juiz de alfândega	Customs appraiser.
killedar	Commander of a fort
kottai	A unit generally used for measuring rice and paddy in the Coromandel.
liberdade	Privilege, immunity, the perks given to an official of the Estado.
mandado	Warrant.
marakkal	A unit of measurement.
marc	Equal to 0.5 *arratel*, 8 *oncas*, 1,152 *carats*, 64 *oitvas*, 4,608 *graos*. One marc was equal to 245 grams.
mate	Derived from the Tamil word *maathu*. One mate was equal to 9 or 10 fineness of gold.
maund	Equal to 8 *viss* or 40 *sers*.
mercador de loja	Petty retailers.
merinho	Overseer
mestiço	Eurasian, of mixed blood from Portuguese merchants and local women.
morin	Plain cloth generally of blue colour.
nakhoda	Captain of an Indian vessel.
naali	Equal to 16 *gantas*.
nau or *não*	Ship used for trade with three decks and three masts.
navio	Larger ship.
nayaka	Chief or leader in the Vijayanagara period; it usually meant a chief of a territory.
nayinar	A petty police official.
ola	Literally a palmyra leaf, hence the leaf on which a deed or document is written.
ordinaria	An allowance paid to the Catholic clergy.
ouvidor	Judge with appellate jurisdiction.
ovuidor geral	Senior crown judge or superior crown magistrate in a high court.

padroado real	The Portuguese royal patronage to religious missions.
pagodas	*Varahan* or *hun* known as *pardão d'ouro*. It was equal to 370 *reis*. Gold coin with the image of Vishnu.
poarau	Small galley with 20 or 30 rows of oarsmen.
pardão, pardau	Used to denote an Indo-Portuguese coin equivalent in value to 360 *reis*.
pecha	Tax or duty.
pico	Chinese weight of 100 *kattis* (61 kg).
pipa	Equal to 26 *almudes* or 430 litres.
povação	Village or settlement.
provedor	Hospital administrator.
provedor dos defunctos	Purveyor of the estates of the deceased.
quintal	Equal to 4 *arrobas*.
regateiros	Street vendors.
regimento	A sort of order which denoted an act of law. General instructions and regulations.
reis	Real Portuguese monetary unit of the smallest denomination.
reinol/ reinois	Portuguese from the kingdom of Portugal.
relação	High court, the tribunal of justice at second instance.
roteiros	Navigational guide or sailing manuals.
ruba-ruba	Anchorage duties.
sanad	Royal decree.
santa Casa da misericórdia	Holy House of Mercy, a charitable institution run by a brotherhood.
senado da câmara	Senate House.
shahbandar	The head of a group of foreign merchants in a port, generally a port official. Harbour master.
sikka	A die for coining.
sisas	Excise.
subah	Province.
tael	Derived from the Malay *tahil*; 1 *tael* of silver was equal to 48 grams. A Chinese weight.

taforea	A kind of ship equipped for carrying horses.
tanga	Silver coin valued at 60 *reis*. It was used in Goa. Derived from a south Indian coin. Sometimes it meant a copper coin in the pre-Portuguese period.
topasses	Artillerymen.
treslado	Contract.
valangai	Right hand division of caste in south India.
varahan	Gold coin synonymous with the *pagoda*.
vedor da fazenda	Comptroller of revenue. Chief financial official.
vendeiros	Grocers.
vereador	Alderman or municipal councillor.
xerafin	Standard silver coin of Portuguese India valued at 300 *reis*. The word *xerafin* is derived from the Persian *ashrafi*, which meant gold coin weighing 150 grains.

Bibliography

PRIMARY SOURCES

I. Archival Sources

PORTUGAL

A. Instituto Arquivo Nacionais / Torre Do Tombo, Lisboã

Corpo Cronológico
Followed by Maço and Document Numbers

Part I
6-82; 7-62; 9-92; 13-113; 14-49; 16-106; 22-62; 22-80; 25-68; 30-36; 37-84; 38-1; 38-50; 49-24; 57-76; 59-98; 60-17; 68-86; 68-88; 76-102; 77-18; 77-26; 76-112; 82-1; 100-122; 107-86.

Part IA
11-50; 13-74; 83-90.

Part II
41-144; 46-98; 49-24; 53-93; 101-44; 102-19; 103-74; 103-150; 114-21; 115-67; 117-22; 117-23; 118-32; 118-38; 118-40; 118-41; 118-69; 118-172; 119-103; 120-47; 128-40; 128-41.

Part IIA
7-84; 30-196; 109-104; 112-10; 112-104; 112-105; 114-4; 115-40; 115-95; 117-154; 117-156; 117-170; 117-194; 117-195; 118-31; 118-45; 118-48; 118-49; 118-52; 118-69; 118-112; 118-172; 119-103; 119-104; 119-109; 119-112; 120-17; 120-25; 120-103; 121-41; 121-44; 123-83; 123-154; 124-98; 125-2; 126-87; 126-102; 130-2; 130-212; 132-8; 132-19; 132-20; 132-109.

Part III
7-115; 9-94.

Carta Orientais
No. 59.

Casa Forte
Mss no. 48.

Chancelarias Reais

D. João III, Livros 1, 15, 18, 21, 35, 64, 67.
D. Sebastião, Livros 15, 19, 71.
D. Sebastião e Henrique, Livros, 2, 6, 15, 19, 22, 40, 45.
D. Filippe I, Livros 15, 17, 24, 25.
D. Filippe II, Livros 3, 7, 20, 35.
D. João IV, Livro 17.

Fragmentos

Caixa 3, maço 3, doc. 17.
Cartas dos Vice-Reis da India
No. 15.

Coleção São Lourenço

Vol. V.

Coleção São Vicente

Vols. X, XII, XVII.
Manuscritos do Convento da Graça
Caixa 6, tomo II; Caixa 3, tomos VI-L.

Manuscritos da Livraria

No. 805.

Núcleo Antigo

Nos. 609, 808, 873.

Gavetas

XI-8-18; XI-8-19; XV-12-2; XV-19-11; XV-19-37; XVIII-6-9; XX-4-15.

Documentos Remetidos da India

Livros 1-62, AD 1605-60.

B. Arquivo Histórico Ultramarino, Lisboã

Caixas da India

Caixa 01, doc. 22; Caixa 2, doc. 44; Caixa 6, doc. 47; Caixa 11, doc. 15; Caixa 11, doc. 44; Caixa 14, doc. 116; Caixa 20, doc. 4.
Codice 281, 282.
Mss, Documentos Avulos, Maço 8.

C. Biblioteca Da Ajuda, Lisboã

Jesuitas na Asia

Codice 49-IV-50; 49-VI-12; 50-VI-21; 51-VII-14; 51-VIII-46; 51-VIII-51; 52-VH-63.

D. Biblioteca Nacional, Lisboã

FundoGeral: Codice 7638, 7640, 7150.
Mss, Iluminado, no. 140.
Mss, Codice 581, 1540, 1783, 1814, 1816, 1975, 1976, 1983, 2702, 8358, 8570, 11410.
Mss. Microfilm, F. 2525.
Reservados, Codice 638.

E. Biblioteca Pública E Arquivo Distrital, Évora

Codice 408.
Codice CIII/2-17, CV/2-7, CXV/2/1, CXVI/1-37.
Reservados 752.

F: Biblioteca Universidade De Coimbra, Coimbra

Mss 459.

SPAIN

G. Archivo General De Simancas, Valladolid

Secretarias Provinciales: Consultas Decretos Originales y Outros Papeies de Fiicio y Partes, 1606-68, Libro 1479, 1490, 1494, 1550, 1551.

H. Biblioteca Nacional, Madrid

Mss, Codice no. 2352.

UNITED KINGDOM

I. The British Library, London

Sloane Collection, Mss. 197.
Additional Manuscripts, 9853, 20892, 26110, 28432.

Oriental and India Office Collections

G/14 Cuddalore and Porto Novo, 1681-7.
G/19 Fort. St. George, 1655-1750.
G/21/4 Factory Records Java, 1675-6.
Original Correspondence No. 20009.
Public Despatches to England, vol. 13.
Letter Book, vol. 21.
Madras Public Consultations, vol. 73.

ITALY

J. Biblioteca Apostolica Vaticana, Vatican City.

Fondo Confaloneri, vol. 31.
Ottobon, Lat. 467.
Vat. Lat, 6424, 7746.
Mss. Section, Ind. 24.

K. Archivum Romanum Societatis Jesu, Rome

Catalogi Trien Cochin et Malabar, Goa, vol. 29.
Malabarica, 53, 55, 56.
Litterae Annuae: Provinciae Malabarensis, 1603, 1604, 1606, 1607, 1608, 1609.
Litterae Annuae Missionis Madurensis, 1607-1632. Goa, vol. 51, vol. 53.

THE NETHERLANDS

L. Nationaal Archief, The Hague

Loose papers: VOC 548, 666, 671.
Overgekomen Brieven en Papieren: VOC 1047, VOC 1055, VOC 1056, VOC 1066, VOC 1070, VOC 1103, VOC 1136, VOC 1158, VOC 1163, VOC 1231, VOC 1634, VOC 1635, VOC 1642.
Bataviaasch Uitgaand Briefboek: VOC 856, VOC 857, VOC 861, VOC 866, VOC 867, VOC 879, VOC 882, VOC 962.
Overgekomen Brieven en Papieren uit Batavia: VOC 1616, VOC 1617.

FRANCE

M. Archives Nationales, Paris

Mss Serie, T. 1169.
Microfilms, Correspondance Generale 1666-1676, Colonies, Serie C^2, Inde, 62.

N. Bibliotheque Nationale, Paris

Mss Nouvelle Acquisitions: no. 9348, 9349, 9350, 9351, 9352, 9354.

O. Centre Des Archives D' Outer-mer, Aix-en-provence

Dépôt des fortifications des colonies, Indes orintales, Portefeuille 31B, no. 327.

INDIA

P. Historical Archives, Panaji, Goa

Mss Monções do Reino, Codice 1-28B (AD 1565-1663)
Mss, Codex nos. 1419, 1420, 3027.
Privileges, Alvaras e Regimentos, Liv. 2.
Conselho da Fazenda: Codice 1161, 1162, 1163, 1164, 1166, 1168.
Reis Vizinhos: no. l (Mss no. 969).
Segredos: nos. l, and 2 (Mss nos. 1416 and 1417).

Q. Madurai Province Jesuit Archives, Shembaganur

Litterae Annuae Provinciae Malbarensis, 1585 to 1609, vols. I-VI
Litterae Annuae Missionis Madurensis, 1609, 1610, 1627, 1630, 1642, 1644, 1648, 1656, 1666, vols. I-XXI.

R. Tamil Nadu State Archives, Chennai

Public Department: Sundries 1687-8.
Public Consultations, Fort St. George, 1731-41.

S. Vidya Jyothi, Delhi

Hosten Henry, *Jesuit Missionaries from Lisbon to the East, 1541-1724*, unpublished papers in the work of Fr. Hosten, vol. 21, *Jesuit Annual Letter* of 1597.

II. Printed Sources

IN PORTUGUESE

Albuquerue, Affonso de, *Cartas de Affonso de Albuquerque*, 7 vols., Lisboã, 1884-1935, ed. Raymundo Antonio de Bulhão Pato.

Almeida Calado, Adelino de, 'Livro que trata das Coisas da India e do Japão', in *Boletim da Bibilioteca da Universidade de Coimbra*, vol. 24, 1960.

Baiao, António, *Historia quninhista in edito do segundo cerco do Dio, llustrado com a correspondence original Tambem, in edita de D. João de Castro, D. João de Mascarenhas e outras,* Coimbra, 1925.

Barros, João de, *Decades Asia,* vols. 1-4, 8 vols. (1777-8), rpt. Lisboã, 1973.

Basilio de Sa, Artur, *Documentação para a Historia das Missões do Padroado Portugues do Oriente: Insul India,* 5 vols., Lisboã, 1954-8.

Biker, J.F.J., *Coleçãao de Tratados e Concertos do Pazes que o Estado da India Portuguesa Fez com os Reis e Senhores em que teve Relações nas Partes da Asia e Africa Oriental desde o Principio da Conquista ate ao fim do Seculo XVIII,* vols. 1-14, Lisboã, 1881-7.

Bocarro, Antonio, *Decada 13, da Historia da India,* Lisboã, 2 vols., 1876

Boxer, C.R, *Asia Sinica e Japonica,* Macao, 1988.

Braganca Pereira, *Arquivo Portugues Oriental,* 11 vols., Bastora, Goa, 1936-40.

Castanheda, Fernão Lopes de *Historia do Descobrimentose Conquista da India Pelos Portugueses,* 9 books in 2 vols. (rpt.), Porto, 1975.

Coelho, Ramos, *Alguns documentos da Torre do tombo a cerca das navegaçõoes e Conquistas Portuguesa,* Lisboã, 1892.

Correia, Gaspar, *Lendas da India,* 4 vols., rpt., Porto, 1975.

Cortesão, Armando and Luis de Albuquerque (eds.), *Obras Completas de Dom João de Castro,* vol. 3, Coimbra, 1976.

Couto, Diogo do, *Decadas da Asia,* 4 to 12, Lisboã, rpt., 1973.

Cunha Rivara, J.H. de, *Archivo Portuguez-Oriental,* 6 Fasciculos in 9 vols., Goa, 1857-76.

Diario da Viagem de Vasco da Gama, 2 vols., Porto, 1945.

Documentos Remetidos da India ou Livros das Monções , vols. 1-5, ed. R.A. de Bulhão Pato, Lisboã, 1880-1935, vols. 6 to 10, ed. Antonio da Silva Rego, Lisboã, 1974-82.

Documentos Sobre os Portugueses em Moçambique e na Africa Central, 1498-1840, 9 vols., Lisbon, 1962-80.

Figueira, Christovão Suarez de, *Historia y Anaal Relacion de las Cosas que Hizieron los Padres de la Companhia de Jesus por las Padres de Orienter y Outras en la Propagation del Santo Evangelico los Anos Passados de 607 y 608,* Madrid, 1614; rpt. 1913.

Guerreiro Fernão, *Relaçam Anual das Coisas que Fezeram Os Padres daCompanhia de Jesus Nas Suas Missões,* 2 vols., Coimbra, 1931.

Goncalves, Sebastião P, *Primeira Parte da Historia dos Religiosos da Companhia de Jesus,* Atlantida-Coimbra, 1962.

Jacob, Hubert (ed.), *Documenta Malucensia,* 1542-77, vol. 1, Rome, 1974.

Lemos, B. Jorge de, *Hiystoria dos cercos que os Achens e Laos pu serao a fortaleza de Malaca,* Lisboã, 1982.

Lima Felner and Rodrigo Jose de (ed.), *Subsidios para a Historia da India Portugueza,* Lisboã, 1868.

Luz, Mendez da, 'Livro das Cidades e fortalezas que o Coroa de Portugal tem nas partes da India, e das capitanias e mais Cargos que nelas ha, e da importancia deles', in *Boletim da Biblioteca da Universidade de Coimbra,* vol. 21, 1953, pp. 1-144 (rpt. in *Studia,* no. 6, July 1960).

Orta, Garcia de, *Colloquies on the Simple Drugs of India,* Dehradun, 1979.

Pissurlencar, Panduranga S.S., *Regimentos das Fortalezas da India,* Bastora, Goa, 1951.

———, *Assentos do Conselho do Estado (1618-1750),* 5 vols., Goa, 1953-83.

Queyroz, Fernao de, *The Temporal and Spiritual Conquest of Ceylon,* S.G. Pereira, Colombo, 1930.

Ribandeneira, Marcelo de, *Historia de las islas del archipelgo y reyno de la grand China tartaria Cochin China, Malaca, Siam, Camboxa y Iappon,* Barcelona, 1601.

Ribeiro, Luciano, *Registo da Casa da India,* 2 vols., Lisboã, 1954-5.

Sanceau, Elaine, *Cartas de D. João de Castro,* Lisboã, 1954.

———, *Colecão de São Lourenco,* 3 vols., Lisboã, 1973-83.

Schurhammer, Georg and E.A. Voretzsch, *Ceylon Zurr Zeit des Konigs Bhuvaneka Bahu und Franz Xaviers, 1539-1552,* 2 vols., Leipzig, 1928.

———, *Epistolae S. Francisci Xaverii alia que eius scripta,* Rome, 1944.

———, Uma Relação in Edita de Padre Manuel Barradas, S.I. Sobre S. Francisco Xavier, *Studia* II, Lisboã, 1958, pp. 43-90.

Silva Rego, Antonioda, *Documentaçãro Para a Historia das Missoes do Padroado Portugues do Oriente,* vols. 1-12, Lisboã, 1947-58.

——— (ed.), *As Gavetas da Torre do Tombo,* vols. 1-12, Lisboã, 1960-77.

——— (ed.), *Documentação Ultramarina Portuguesa,* 5 vols., Lisboã, 1960-7.

Trinidade, Paulo da, *Conquisto Espiritual do Oriente,* 2 vols, Lisboã, 1962-7.

Wicki, Jose and J. Gomes, *Documenta Indica,* vols. 1-18, Roma, 1948-88.

———, 'Duas relações sobre a situação da India Portuguesa nos annos 1568 e 1569', *Studia,* vol. 8, 1961, pp. 133-220.

IN DUTCH

Colenbrander, H.T and W.Ph. Coolhas (eds.), *Jan Piertsz, Coen, Beschedien Omtrent Zijn Bedrijf in Indie,* 8 vols., The Hague, 1919-53.

Coolhas, W.Ph. (ed.), *Generale Missiven van de Gouverneurs-Generaal en*

Raden Aan de Heren XVII der Verenigde Oost-Indische Compagnie, 1610-1725, vols. 1-7, The Hague, 1960-79.

Dagh-Register Gehouden int Casteel Batavia van het Passerende doer leer Plaetse als over geheel Nederlandts Indie (*1624-1682*), 31 vols., The Hague and Batavia, 1887-1931, various editors.

Heeres, J.E. and F.W. Stapel, *Corpus Dipolomaticum Neerlando-Indicum,* 6 vols., The Hague, 1907-53.

Jonge, J.K.J. de, *De Opkomst van het Nederlandsch Gezag in Oost Indie', 1595-1844,* 17 vols., The Hague, 1862-1909.

Prakash, Om. (ed.), *The Dutch Factories in India 1617-1623: A Collection of Dutch East India Company Documents Pertaining to India,* Delhi, 1984.

IN ENGLISH

Danvers, F.C. and W. Foster, *Letters Received by the English East India Company from its Servants in the East (1602-1617),* 6 vols., London, 1896-1902.

Dodwell, H., A *Calendar of the Madras Records, 1740-1744,* Madras, 1917.

———, *Calendar of the Madras Despataches, 1744-1755,* Madras, 1920.

Fawcett, C., *The English Factories in India* (new series), *1670-84*, 4 vols., Oxford, 1936-45.

Foster, William, *English Factories in India: A Calendar of Documents in the India Office, British Museum and Public Relations Office, 1618-1619,* vols. 1-13, Oxford, 1906-21.

Records of Fort St. Greoge

Country Correspondence, Military Department, vols. 1-6, 1753-58, Madras 1908-10.

Diary and Consultation Book, 1672-81, 1686-94, 1696-1746, 1749-56, Madras, 1910-50.

Despatches from England, vols. 1-54 (1670-7, 1680-92, 1696-1751), Madras, 1914-31.

Despatches to England, vols. 1-18 (1694-6, 1701-51), Madras, 1916-29.

Factory Records: Fort St. David Consultations, vol. 17, Madras, 1936.

Letters to Fort St. George, vols. 1-45 (1681-2, 1684-7, 1693-4, 1699-1700, 1703-4, 1707, 1711-12, 1718-19, 1723, 1729, 1731-3, 1735, 1738-82, 1744-6, 1750), Madras, 1916-29.

Public Consultations, vols. 73, 74, Madras, 1936.

IN FRENCH

Lombard, Denys, *Memoires d' un Voyage aus Indes Orientales: Un Marchand Normand a Sumatra,* Paris, 1996.

Martineau, Alfred, *Memoirs de François Martin,* 3 vols., Paris, 1932-4.

Varadarajan, Lotika, *India in the Seventeenth Century: Memoirs of François Martin,* Delhi, 1980.

IN TAMIL

Price, Frederick, K. Rangachari and H., Dodwell, *The Private Diary of Ananda Ranga Pillai, 1736-1761,* 12 vols. (rpt.), Delhi, 1985.

III. Epigraphical Sources

Aiyar, K.R. Srinivasa, *Inscriptions in the Pudukottai State,* Pudukottai, 1929.

Annual Report on Epigraphy (including Indian and South Indian Epigraphy) from 1881 to 1990.

Butterworth, Alan and Venugopal Chetty, *A Collection of the Inscriptions on Copper Plates and Stones in the Nellore District,* 3 vols., Madras, 1905.

Deivanayagam. K., *Dharumai Adheena Seppedugal,* Dharmapuram, 1988.

Epigraphia Indica, vols. 1-12, Mysore, 1900-78.

Kasinathan, N.S., Raja Gopal and N. Vedachalam, *Thirumalai Nayakkar Seppedugal* (Copper Plate Inscriptions of Thirumalai Nayakkar), Madras, 1994.

Nagaswamy, R., *Chennimanagar Kalvettugal* (Inscriptions of Madras), Madras, 1979.

Raju, S., *Sethupathi Seppedugal,* Thanjavur, 1990.

Sastry, Sadhu Subramanya, *Tirumalai-Tirupati Devasthanam Epigraphical Series,* 6 vols., Madras, 1931-8.

South Indian Inscriptions, texts (publication of the Archaeological Survey of India), vols. 1-16, Madras and Delhi, 1890-1990.

Srinivasan, P.R. and Marie Louise Reiniche, *Tiruvannamalai: A Saiva Sacred Complex of South India,* vol. 2 (inscriptions), Pondicherry, 1990.

Subramaniam, T.N. *South Indian Temple Inscriptions* (Madras Government Oriental Series), 3 vols., Madras, 1954-7.

IV. Travelogues

Balbi, Gaspero, 'The Voyage of Gasparo Balbi', in Samuel Purchas, *His Pilgrims,* vol. 10, Glasgow, 1905.

Baldeaus, Philip, A *True and Exact Description of the Most Celebrated East India Coasts of Malabar and Coromandel as well as of the Isle of Ceylon,* 1672 (trs.), London, 1703.

Barbosa, Duarte, *The Book of Duarte Barbosa: An Account of the Countries Bordering the Indian Ocean and their Inhabitants*, 2 vols., Delhi, rpt., 1989.

Battuta, Ibn, Shans-al-din[e] Abdullah bin Muhamed, *Travels in Asia or Africa, 1325-1354*, ed. and tr. H.A.R. Gibbs, Delhi, rpt., 1986.

Couttre, Jacques de Teensma et al. (eds.), *Jacques de Couttre,* Madrid, 1990.

Federici, Caesar de, 'The Travels of Caesar de Federici', in Sammual Purchas, *His Pilgrims,* vol. 10, Glasgow, 1905.

Fitch, Robert, 'The Voyage of Robert Fitch', in Samuel Purchas, *His Pilgrims,* vol. 10, Glasgow, 1905.

Foster, William, *Early Travels in India,* London, 1820.

———, *The Voyage of Sir Henry Middleton to the Moluccas, 1604-1606,* London, 1943.

Fryer, John, *A New Account of the East Indies and Persia: Being Nine Years Travels (1672-1681*) (ed. W.C. Crooke), London, 1698, rpt., Nedeln, 1967.

Gibb, H.A.R, *Ibn Battuta*: *The Travels in Asia and Africa, 1325-1354*, rpt., Delhi, 1986.

Krishna V. Gopala and Keladi Gunda Jois, *Tanjavur to Vijayagiri Durga: A Travelogue in Kannada Printed from a Palm-leaf Manuscript,* Chennai, 1997.

Lanchaster, James, *The Voyage of Sir James Lanchaster to Bengal and the Coast of Indonesia,* London, 1940.

Linschoten, John Huyghen Van, *The Voyages of John Van Linschoten to the East Indies,* 2 vols., London, 1885.

Ma-Huan, *Mahuans's Ying-yai Sheng-lan: The Overall Survey of the Oceans Shore* (1433), ed. and tr. J.V.G. Mills, Cambridge, 1970.

Major, R.H. (ed.), *India in the 15th Century: Being a Collection of Narratives of Voyages to India in the Century Preceding the Portuguese Discovery of the Cape of Good Hope from Latin, Persian, Russian and Italian Sources,* London, 1857; rpt., Delhi, 1974.

Mandelso, John Albert, edited by John Ravis, *The Voyage and Travels of John Albert Mandelso 1669,* London, 1910.

Manucci, Nicolao (ed.), William Irvine, *Storia do Mogor, 1653-1708,* 4 vols., Delhi, 1981.

Methwold, William, *Relations of Golconda in the Early Seventeenth Century,* London, 1931.

Moule, A.C. and P. Pelliot, *Marco Polo: The Description of the World,* London, 1938.

Nieuhoff, John, *Zee en Lant Reize Door Verscheide Gewesten Van Ost-Indien,* Amsterdam, 1682.

Pires, Tome, *The Suma Oriental of Tome Pires and the Book of Rodrigues,* 2 vols., Delhi, 1990.

Purchas, Samuel, *His Pilgrims,* vol. 10, Glasgow, 1905.

Temple Richard (ed.), *The Life of the Icelander Jon Olaffson, Traveller to India,* 2 vols., London, 1932.

Texeira, Pedro, *The Travels of Pedro Texeira,* tr. W.F. Sinclair, London, 1902.

Travels of the Jesuits into Various Parts of the World, 2 vols., London, 1762.

Valentijn, Francois, *Description of Ceylon,* ed. S. Arasaratnam, London, 1978.

Varthema, Ludovico di, *The Travels of Ludovico di Varthema in Egypt, Syria, Arabia desert and Arabia Felix in Persia, India and Ethiopia,* AD *1503-1508,* London, 1928, ed. G.P. Badger, tr. J.W. Jong.

V. THESES AND DISSERTATIONS

Flores, Jorge. 'Os Portugueses e o Mar de Ceilao', 1498-1543: Trato, Diplomatica e Guerra', Dissertacao Mestrado, Universidade Nova de Lisboã, 1991.

Palat, Ravi Arvind, 'From World Empire to World Economy: South Eastern India and the Emergence of the Indian Ocean World Economy, 1350-1650', Ph.D. dissertation, Binhampton, 1988.

Teles e Cunha, João Manuel de Almeida, 'Economia de um Imperio: Economia, Politica do Golfo Persico, Elementos Conjuntaria, 1595, 1635', Dissertação Mestrado, Universidade Nova de Lisboa, 1995.

Thomaz, L.F.F.R, 'Os Portugueses em Malacca 1511-1580', Baccalaureate thesis, University of Lisbon, 1964.

SECONDARY WORKS

Abeysinghe, Tikiri, *Portuguese Rule in Ceylon, 1594-1612,* Colombo, 1966.

———, *A Study of the Portuguese Regimentos on Sri Lanka at the Goa Archives,* Colombo, n.d.

Abraham, Meera, *Two Medieval Merchant Guilds of South India,* Delhi, 1988.

Ahmad, Afzal, *Indo-Portuguese Trade in Seventeenth Century, 1600-1663,* Delhi, 1993.

Aiyar, R. Sathiyanatha, *History of the Nayaks of Madura,* Oxford, 1924.

Arasaratnam, S., *The Dutch Power in Ceylon,* Amsterdam, 1958.

———, *Merchants, Companies and Commerce on the Coromandel Coast, 1650-1740,* Delhi, 1986.

———, 'Slave Trade in the Indian Ocean in the Seventeenth Century', in K.S. Mathew (ed.), *Mariners, Merchants and Oceans,* Delhi, 1995.

Arunachalam, S., *The History of the Pearl Fishery of the Tamil Coast,* Annamalai Nagar, 1952.

Babu, Jawahar and Hariahariah Oruganti, 'Copper Coins of Awrangzib from Mailapur Mint', in K.V. Raman (ed.), *Studies in South Indian Coins,* vol. 7, Madras, 1997.

Bagchi, 'Chinese Coins from Tanjore', *Sino-Indian Studies,* vol. 1, October 1994.

Bailey, W. Diffie and G. Winius, *Foundation of the Portuguese Empire, 1415-1580,* Minneapolis, 1977.

Banerjee, R.N., *Economic Progress of the East India Company on the Coromandel Coast, 1702-1746,* Nagpur, 1974.

Basset, D.K., 'The Amboyna Massacre of 1623', *The Journal of South East Asian History,* vol. I, no. 2, 1960, pp. 1-11.

Bastin, John, *The Changing Balance of the Early South East Asian Pepper Trade*, Kuala Lumpur, 1960.

Bayly, Susan, *Saints, Gods and Kings: Muslims and Christians in South Indian Society, 1700-1900,* Cambridge, 1989.

Boxer, C.R., *Francisco Viera de Figureido: A Portuguese Merchant Adventurer in South East Asia, 1624-1667*, The Hague, 1967.

———, 'The Portuguese Reaction to the Revival of Red Sea Spice Trade and the Rise of Atjeh, 1540-1600', *Journal of South-East Asian History,* vol. 10, no. 3, 1969, pp. 415-28.

———, *The Portuguese Seaborne Empire, 1415-1825,* London, 1923.

———, 'Macao as a Religious and Commercial Entrepot in the 16th and 7th Centurie', *Acta Asiatica,* 26, Tokyo, 1974, pp. 64-90.

———, *Portuguese India in the Mid-Seventeenth Century,* Bombay, 1980.

———, *Portuguese Conquest and Commerce in Southern Asia 1500-1750,* London, 1990.

Boyajian, James C., *Portuguese Bankers at the Court of Spain, 1620-1650,* New Jersey, 1983.

———, *Portuguese Trade in Asia Under the Habsburgs, 1580-1640,* Baltimore, 1993.

Braudel, Fernand, *Capitalism and Civilization: 15th-18th Centuries: Perspedines of the World,* Sian Reynolds (tr.), 3 vols., London, 1981-4.

Broeze, Frank, *Brides of the Sea: Port Cities of Asia from the 16th-20th Centuries,* London, 1989.

Bruijn, J., F.S. Gaastra and I. Schoffer, *Dutch Asiatic Shipping in the 17th and 18th Centuries,* The Hague, 1987.

Bruijn, J. and Femmer S. Gaastra (eds.), *Ships, Sailors and Spices: East India Companies and their Ships in the 16th and 17th Century,* Amsterdam, 1994.

Caldwell, R., *A History of Tinnevelly,* Madras, 1881; rpt., Delhi, 1982.

Castests, J., 'How Negapatam in 1642 became the First Possession on the

Coromandel Coast', *Journal of the Bombay Historical Society,* vol. 5, no. 2, 1939, pp. 129-34.

Champakalakshmi, R., *Trade, Ideology and Urbanisation: South India, 300 BC to AD 1300,* Delhi, 1996.

Chang, P., 'The Evolution of Chinese Thought on Maritime Foreign Trade from the Sixteenth to the Eighteenth Century', in *International Journal of Maritime History,* vol. 1, no. 1, June 1989, pp. 51-64.

Chang T'en-Tse, *Sino-Portuguese Trade from 1514 to 1644,* Leiden, 1934.

Chaudhuri, K.N., *Trade and Civilization in the Indian Ocean: Economic History from the Rise of Islam to 1750,* Cambridge, 1985.

Curtin, Philip D., *Cross-Cultural Trade in World History,* Cambridge, 1984.

Danvers F.C., *The Portuguese in India,* London, 1894.

de Silva, Chandra Richard, 'Portuguese Policy towards the Muslims in Ceylon', *The Ceylon Historical and Social Studies,* vol. 9, 1966, p. 114.

———, *The Portuguese in Ceylon, 1617-1638,* Colombo, 1972.

———, 'The Portuguese and Pearl Fishing off South India and Sri Lanka', *South Asia,* vol. 1, no. 1, 1979, pp. 14-28.

Disney, Anthony, *Twilight of the Pepper Empire: Portuguese Trade in South West India in the Early Seventeenth Century,* Cambridge, 1978.

Disney, Anthony and Emily Booth (eds.), *Vasco da Gama and the Linking of Europe and Asia*, Delhi, 2000.

Flores, Jorge Manuel, 'The Straits of Ceylon and the Maritime Trade in the Early Sixteenth Century India: Commodities, Merchants and Trading Net Works', *Moyen Orient et Ocean Indien,* vol. 7, 1990, pp. 27-58.

———, 'Cael Velho, Caelpatnao and Punicale: The Portuguese and the Tambraparni Ports in the Sixteenth Century, *Bulletin de Ecole Francaise d' Extreme-Orient,* vol. 82, no. 2, 1995, pp. 9-25.

Furber, Holden, *Rival Empires of Trade in the Orient, 1600-1800,* Minneapolis, 1976.

Glamann, Cristof, *Dutch-Asiatic Trade, 1620-1740,* The Hague, 1981.

Godinho, Vitorino Maghales, *Os Descobrimentos e a Economia Mundial* Lisboã, 1965.

———, *Les Finances de etat Portugais des Indes Orientales (1517-1635),* Paris, 1982.

Heras, Henry, 'Venkatapatidevaraya I and the Portuguese', *Quarterly Journal of the Mythic Society,* vol. 14, 1923-4, pp. 312-17.

———, 'Jesuit Influence in the Court of Vijayanagara', *Quarterly Journal of the Mythic Society,* vol. 14, pp. 135-40.

———, 'Early Relations Between Vijayanagara and Portugal', *Quarterly Journal of the Mythic Society,* vol. 26, 1925-6, pp. 63-74.

———, *The Aravidu Dynasty of Vijayanagara,* Madras, 1927.

Hirth, F. and W.W Rockhill, *Chau-Ju-ka: His Work on the Chinese and*

Arab Trade in the Twelfth and Thirteenth Centuries Entitled Chu-fan-chi, St. Petersburg, 1911.

Hosten, Henry, *Antiquities from Santhome and Mylapore*, Calcutta, 1936.

Kaeppelin, Paul, *La Compagnie des Indes Orientales et François Martin, 1664-1719*, Paris, 1908.

Karashima, Noborou, 'Trade Relations between South India and China during the 13th and 14th Centuries', *Journal of East-West Relations*, vol. 1, 1989, no. 2, pp. 9-81.

Krishnaswami, A., *Tamil Country under Vijayanagara*, Annamalai Nagar, 1964.

Lombard, Denys, *Le Sultanate d' Atjeh au Temps d' IskandarMuda, 1607-1636*, Paris, 1967.

Love, Henry Davidson, *Vestiges of Old Madras, 1640-1800: Traced from the East India Company's Records Preserved at Fort St. George and the India Office and from other Sources*, 3 vols., London, 1913; rpt., Delhi, 1988.

Malekandathil, Pius, *Portuguese Cochin and the Maritime Trade of India, 1500-1663*, Delhi, 2001.

Mathew, K.S., *Portuguese Trade with India in the Sixteenth Century*, Delhi, 1983.

———, 'Trade in the Indian Ocean and the Portuguese System of Cartazes', in Malyn Newitt (ed.), *The First Portuguese Colonial Empire*, Exeter, 1986, pp. 69-94.

———, *Indo-Portuguese Trade and the Fuggers of Germany*, Delhi, 1997.

Mathew, K.S. and Afzal Ahmad, *Emergence of Cochin in the Pre-Industrial Era: A Study of Portuguese Cochin*, Pondicherry, 1991.

Matos, Artur Teodoro de, *O Estado da India nos anos de 1581-88 Estructura, Administrativa, e Economia, Alguns Elementos, para o seu Estudo*, Ponta Delagada, 1982.

McPherson, Kenneth, 'Anglo-Portuguese Commercial Relations in the Eastern Indian Ocean from the Seventeenth and Eighteenth Centuries', *South Asia*, vol. 19, 1996 (special issue), pp. 41-57.

Meersman, Achilles, *The Franciscans in Tamilnad*, Schoneck Beckenried, 1962.

Panikkar, K.M., *Asia and the Western Dominance: A Survey of the Vasco da Gama Epoch of Asian History, 1498-1945*, London, 1953.

Pearson, M.N., *Merchants and Rulers in Gujarat: The Response to the Portuguese in the Sixteenth Century*, Delhi, 1980.

———, *The Portuguese in India*, The New Cambridge History of India, Cambridge, 1987,

———, *Before Colonialism: Theories on Asian-European Relations, 1500-1750*, Delhi, 1988.

———, 'The Flows and Effects of Precious Metals in India and China, 1500-1800', *Annales*, vol. 2, no. 2, 1993, pp. 51-69.

Pieris, P.E., *Ceylon and the Portuguese,* Teliapalai', 1920.
———, *The Kingdom of Jaffnapatnam,* Colombo, 1944.
Poonen, T.I., 'Dutch Beginnings in India Proper', *Journal of the Madras University,* 1933, pp. 1-70.
Prakash, Om, 'Long Distance Maritime Trade in Asia: Decline and Revival', in K.S. Mathew (ed.), *Studies in Maritime History,* Pondicherry, 1991, pp. 29-37.
———, *Precious Metals and Commerce: The Dutch East India Company in Indian Ocean Trade*, Variorum, 1994.
———, *Bullion for Goods: European and Indian Merchants in the Indian Ocean Trade, 1500-1800*, Delhi, 2004.
Ptak, Roderich (ed.), *Portuguese Asia: Aspects in History and Economic History, 16th-17th Centuries,* Wiesbaden, 1987.
———, 'Yuan and Early Ming Notices on the Kayal Area in South India', *Bulletin de Ecole Francaise de Extreme-Orient,* vol. 80, no. 1, 1993. pp. 137-56.
Ptak, Roderich and Dietmar Rothermund (eds.), *Emporia, Commodities, and Entreprenurs in Asian Maritime Trade c. 1400-1750,* Stuttgart, 1991.
Quiason, S.D., *English Country Trade with the Philippines, 1664-1765,* Quezon City, 1966.
Rangachari, V., 'The History of the Naik Kingdom of Madura', in *Indian Antiquary,* vol. XLIII, 1914, pp. 1-48.
Rao, Velacheru Narayana, David Shulman and Sanjay Subhramanyam, (ed.), *Symbols of Substance: Court and State in Nayaka Period Tamilnadu,* Delhi, 1992.
Raychaudhuri, Tapan, *Jan Company in Coromandel,* The Hague, 1962.
Ray, Hara Prasad, *Trade and Diplomacy Between India and China: A Study of Bengal during the Fifteenth Century,* Delhi, 1991.
Reid, Anthony, 'Sixteenth Century Turkish Influence in Western Indonesia', *Journal of South East Asian History,* vol. 10, no. 3, 1969, pp. 400-1.
———, 'The Rise of Makassar', *Review of Indonesian and Malaysian Affairs,* vol. 17, 1983, pp. 117-60.
Roelofsz, M.A.P. Meilink, *Asian Trade and European Influence in the Indonesian Archipelago between 1500 and about 1630,* The Hague, 1964.
Rossa, Walter, *Cidades Indo-Portuguesas,* Lisboã, 1997.
Russel-Wood, A.J.R., *A World on the Move: The Portuguese in Africa, Asia and America, 1415-1808*, New York, 1993.
Sastri, K.A. Nilakanta, 'Shivaji's Charter to the Dutch on the Coromandel Coast', *Proceedings of the Indian History Congress,* Calcutta, 1939, pp. 1156-65.
———, 'Tirumalai Naik, The Portuguese and the Dutch', *Proceedings of*

the Indian Historical Records Commission, vol. 16, Calcutta, 1939, pp. 32-40.

———, *Sources of South Indian History with Special Reference to South India* (Heras Memorial Lectures), Bombay, 1964.

———, 'Two Negapatam Grants from the Batavia Museum', in *South India and South East Asia: Studies in their History and Culture,* Mysore, 1978, pp. 200-2.

Sauliere, A., 'Extracts from Some Jesuit Annual Letters: Malabar and the Fishery Coast Translated from Latin', in *The Indian Athenaeum,* Calcutta, vol. 1, no. 2, August 1923, pp. 55-8.

———, 'The Annual Letter of 1582', in *The Indian Athenaeum*, vol. 1, no. 3, September 1923, pp. 11-16.

Schurhammer, Georg, 'Iniqitembrane and Bete Perumal: Chera and Pandya Kings in South India', *Journal of the Bombay Historical Society,* vol. 3, 1930, pp. 1-40.

———, *St. Francis Xavier: His Life, His Times,* Rome, 1977.

Sethuraman, N., *The Imperial Pandyas,* Kumbakonam, 1978.

Sewell, Robert, A *Forgotten Empire,* Delhi, 1962.

Shokoohy, Sharad, 'Architecture of the Muslim Port of Qail on the Coromandel Coast, South India', *South Asian Studies,* vol. 9, 1993, pp. 137-66.

Sousa, George Bryan, *The Survival of Empire: Portuguese Trade and Society in China and South China Sea, 1630-1754*, Cambridge, 1986.

Spencer, George W., *The Politics of Expansion: The Chola Conquest of Srilanka and Srivijaya,* Madras, 1983.

Srinivasachari, C.S., *A History of Gingee and its Rulers,* Annamalai Nagar, 1943.

Steensgard, Niels, *Carracks, Caravans, and Companies: The Structural Crisis in the European and Asian Trade in the Early Seventeeenth Century,* Copenhagen, 1973.

Stephen, S. Jeyaseela, 'Port Administration and Maritime Trade of Porto Novo on the Coromandel Coast of India', *Proceedings of the Indian History Congress,* 51st Session, Calcutta, 1990, pp. 517-23.

———, 'Pulicat Based Shipping and Trade (AD 1500-1530)', *Purabhilekh-Puratatva,* vol. 9, no. 2, July-December 1991, pp. 1-11.

———, 'Portuguese Sources and the Coastal Trade Economy of Tamilnadu in the Sixteenth Century: Some Reflections', *Indian Archives*, vol. LXI, no. 2, July-December 1992, pp. 15-27.

———, 'The State, Decentralization and Revenue Farming: Some Aspects of Vijayanagara Rule in the Coromandel Region in the Sixteenth Century', *Journal of the Institute of Asian Studies*, Madras, vol. 11, no. 1, September 1993, pp. 1-15.

———, 'Diamond Mining Industry, Vijayanagara State Policy and the Regional Economy of Late Medieval South India', *Quarterly Journal of the Mythic Society*, vol. LXXXVI, no. 2, April-June 1995, pp. 81-112.

———, 'The Role of the Tamil Muslim Mercantile Community of the Marakkkayars in the Late Medieval Maritime Trade on the Coromandel Coast: A Study Chiefly based on Portuguese Sources, AD 1506-1537', *Islamic Culture,* vol. LXIX, no. 4, October 1995, pp. 59-71.

———, 'O Livro de Receita e despesa do Feitor do Coromandel, Manuel da Gama: A Portuguese Source on the Port Economy of Tamil Coast in 1526-1527', *Proceedings of the Tamilnadu History Congress*, Madras, vol. 2, 1996, pp. 15-24.

———, 'Markets, Towns and Overland Trade in the Coromandel Region of South India, 1500-1600', *Journal of the Institute of Asian Studies,* Madras, vol. 13, no. 2, March 1996, pp. 103-28.

———, 'Maritime Trade between the Tamil Coast in South India and Thailand: An Analysis of New Archival Data in Europe and India, 1624-1740', *Proceedings of the Sixth International Conference on Thai Studies*, vol. 7, Chiang Mai University, Thailand, 1996, pp. 209-18.

———, 'Transactions of Trade at the Port of Thirumalairayan Pattinam in the Cauvery Delta and the Portuguese', *Proceedings of the Indian History Congress*, Calcutta, 1996, vol. 57, pp. 245-52.

———, 'Portuguese Nau: A Study of the Cargo Ship in the Indian Ocean Region During the Sixteenth Century', in K.S. Mathew (ed.), *Shipbuilding and Navigation in the Indian Ocean,* AD *1400-1800,* Delhi, 1997, pp. 62-81.

———, 'Seasons, Sea-Currents, Tides and Trade-winds along the Shores of Coastal India: Evidences from Portuguese Sources', ed. S.R. Rao, *An Integrated Approach to Marine Archaeology,* Goa, 1997, pp. 53-8.

———, *The Coromandel Coast and its Hinterland: Economy Society and Political System, 1500-1600*, Delhi, 1997.

———, *Portuguese in the Tamil Coast: Historical Explorations in Commerce and Culture*, Pondicherry, 1998.

———, 'The Trade Economy of Melaka Port in the Sixteenth Century', in K.S. Jomo (ed.), *Rethinking Malaysia,* Malaysian Social Science Association, Kuala Lumpur, 1999, pp. 185-202.

———, 'Medieval Trade of the Tamil Coast and its Hinterland, AD 1280-1500', *The Indian Historical Review*, vol. 25, no. 2, January 1999, pp. 1-37.

———, 'The Nayaks of Tamil Country and the Portuguese Trade in War Animals', in Pius Malekandathil and T. Jamal Mohammed (eds.), *The Portuguese, the Indian Ocean and European Bridgeheads, 1500-1800,* Tellicherry, 2001, pp. 212-22.

———, 'Rise and Decline of Pulicat under the Dutch East India Company

AD 1612-1690', *The Historical Review,* vol. 10, new series, January-December 2002, pp. 1-26.

——— (ed.), *Trade and Globalisation: Europeans, Americans and Indians in the Bay of Bengal (1511-1819),* Jaipur/Delhi, 2003.

———, 'Cowles, Farmans, Nishans, Parwanas and Sunnads: Aspects of State Policy Towards Commerce in the Bay of Bengal, 1603-1732', *Bharta Vidya*, vol. 3, 2004, pp. 27-49.

Subrahmanyam, Sanjay, *The Political Economy of Commerce: Southern India 1500-1650,* Cambridge, 1990a.

———, *Improvising Empire: Portuguese Trade and Settlements in the Bay of Bengal, 1500-1700,* Delhi, 1990b.

———, *The Portuguese Empire in Asia: A Political and Economic History,* London, 1993.

———, 'Noble Harvest from the Sea: Managing the Pearlfishery of Mannar, 1500-1925', in Burton Stein and Sanjay Subrahmanyam, *Institutions and Economic Change in South Asia,* Delhi, 1996, pp. 134-72.

———, *The Career and Legend of Vasco da Gama,* Cambridge, 1997.

Texeira, Manuel, *The Portuguese Missons in Malacca and Singapore, 1511-1598*, Lisboã, 1967.

Thinakaran, *The Second Pandyan Empire, 1190-1312,* Madurai, 1987.

Thomaz, L.F.F.R, *De Malaca a Pegu Viagens de um feitor Portugues 1512-1515,* Lisbon, 1966.

———, 'Nina Chatu e o Commercio Portugues em Malaca', in *Memorias do Centro de Estudos de Marinharia,* vol. 5, Lisboã, 1976, pp. 3-27.

———, 'Les Portugais dans les mers de l'Archipel au XVIe Siecle', *Archipel,* vol. 18, 1979, pp. 105-25. Available in translation in *Trade and Shipping in the Southern Seas: Selected Readings from Archipel*, Paris, 1984, pp 75-91.

Tracy, James D. (ed.), *The Rise of Merchant Empires: Long Distance Trade in the Early Modern World, 1350-1750,* Cambridge, 1991.

Vriddhagirisan, *The Nayaks of Tanjore,* Annamalai Nagar, 1942.

Whiteway, R.S., *The Rise of Portuguese Power in India,* London, 1899.

Wicki, Jose, 'Duas Relações sobre a Situação da India Portuguesa nos annos 1568-1569', *Studia,* vol. 18, 1961, pp. 151-3.

Winius, George Davison, *The Fatal History of Portuguese Ceylon: Transition to Dutch Rule, 1638-1658*, Cambridge, 1971.

———, 'The Shadow Empire of Goa in the Bay of Bengal', in *Itinerario,* vol. 7, no. 2, 1983, p. 92.

———, The Portuguese Asia 'Decadencia' Revisited, in Alfred Honer and Richard A. Preto-Rodas (eds.), *Empire in Transition: The Portuguese World in the Time of Cameos*, Gainesville, 1985.

Index